INVENTORY 98

INVENTORY 1985

BARTÓK

JÓZSEF UJFALUSSY

BÉLA BARTÓK

CRESCENDO PUBLISHING COMPANY

Boston

Translated by Ruth Pataki
Translation revised by Elisabeth West
Binding by Edit Zigány

ISBN 87597-077-X

Printed in Hungary
for
Crescendo Publishing Company, Boston
by arrangement with Kultura Trading Co., Budapest

First U.S. edition, 1972

PREFACE

The original Hungarian version of my book was published in 1965. Even then, I did not consider the disclosure of new data and findings to be its primary aim, but rather the compilation of as many factors as possible from the gratifyingly increasing number of publications referring to Béla Bartók's life and art. Since then of course, the literature has been enriched by many new and valuable publications, I have endeavoured to supplement the earlier version of my book by including new data in order to correct some mistakes and make up for certain inadequacies.

I am fully aware that the time has not yet come, and most probably will not come for quite a long time, for a detailed, definitive, scientific study, reliable in all respects. However, it is still my conviction that there is a need for this kind of transitional analysis, even if certain gaps have to be bridged by assumptions. It can aid in forming an adequate picture of Bartók as far as the general public is concerned, and though indirectly, it can also be useful for detailed analytical and philological research.

Although our biographical knowledge of Bartók's works is by no means complete, our present concept of his life, personality, creativity, ideals and compositions is not in need of basic correction. For this we can be grateful to the disclosure of an increasing amount of data from documents referring to his life, to the thorough analytical studies made of his compositions, and also to earlier biographies.

This book owes its existence to such predecessors, and in the new aspects discussed, it endeavours to go further than previous volumes by giving a more detailed picture of the social conditions pertaining to Bartók's life and creativity. From these observations, an attempt is made to follow the development of the composer's personal and creative ideals, and to discover the signs of these forms of inspiration in his music, thus finding a key to its meaning.

Before the preparation of the foreign-language version, I had to consider whether non-Hungarian readers would be interested in such a detailed presentation of Hungarian and Central-European conditions of the time. Finally, however, I had to stay with my conviction, that an insight into pertinent conditions can give a more valid explanation of many significant characteristics of Bartók's life and music than an endeavour to understand his life solely through details of personal events or a structural analysis of his compositions. That is why I believe I can best serve both my non-Hungarian readers, and the cause of Bartók research, by probing links less familiar in the international literature.

The English text of quotations from Béla Bartók's writings was taken either from the original English, or from the English versions and translations already published. Corvina Press, Budapest and Faber and Faber, London obligingly allowed me to use the translations of those letters not written in English from the English-language collection of his letters published jointly.

Budapest, February 13, 1970

József Ujfalussy

ACKNOWLEDGEMENT

It is my pleasant duty to acknowledge the kindness of all those who have assisted me in the production of my book on Béla Bartók.

I owe a particular debt of gratitude to the members of the Bartók family living in Hungary: Mrs. Béla Bartók, Ditta Pásztory, pianist; Mrs. Éva Voit-Oláh-Tóth, staff member of the Musicological Institute of the Hungarian Academy of Sciences and the Institute's Bartók Archives; and Béla Bartók jr., Chief Counsellor of the Hungarian State Railways. They provided me with information and placed at my disposal documents which were used in the preparation of the first version of my book in Hungarian.

I owe a particular debt of gratitude to violinist József Szigeti for his profound attention and valuable assistance. He provided details in his possession previously unpublished and thus rounded out our inadequate knowledge on the origin of *Contrasts*.

Academician Bence Szabolcsi and Professor András Szőllősy, the readers of the Hungarian version of my book, contributed many valuable suggestions at all stages of its preparation. I should like to take the opportunity here to thank them for their work. My special thanks are due to András Szőllősy, because he made it possible to use the most complete and accurate list of Béla Bartók's writings known so far, which he compiled. This added a great deal of value to the book.

The constant help of the staff members of the Musicological Institute of the Hungarian Academy of Sciences and the Institute's Bartók Archives was indispensable in my work. I should also like to thank the internationally recognized Bartók researcher, Denijs Dille, Department Head of the Bartók Archives, for the information and documents he put at my disposal. I am especially grateful for his kindness in allowing me to publish his list of Bartók's early works, the most complete on record. Ferenc Bónis, Dr. Zoltán Falvy and László Somfai, scientific co-workers, assisted me with advice, information, criticism and documentation. The discography of Bartók's compositions is the result of László Somfai's careful work. I am greatly indebted to him for his kind co-operation.

This book could not have been written without the self-sacrificing work of János Demény, candidate in musicology. We owe our minute knowledge of Bartók's correspondence and documents pertaining to Bartók's life to his tireless activity. I also owe a personal debt to János Demény for keeping me in touch with his latest results in the course of my work.

CONTENTS

9

the 'folklorist' and the 'avant-gardist'. Strongholds of international musical life

Chapter XI. Oppressive Political Atmosphere. Nationalist Attacks at Home and Abroad. Retreat. Collecting Tour in Turkey. Folk-Music Studies and Great Musical Compositions. 1931–1936

Chapter XII. Last Years and Works in Europe. 1937–1940

CHAPTER I

CHILDHOOD AND STUDENT YEARS. 1881–1898

1 CHILDHOOD. MUSICAL EXPERIENCE WITHIN THE FAMILY

'*I was born on 25th March, 1881 in Nagyszentmiklós, Torontál County.*' With these words Béla Bartók begins his autobiography, published in *Hármas Könyv*, the annual supplement of the newspaper *Az Est*.

It is a statement which must appear obscure to contemporary readers unfamiliar with the recent history of Central and Eastern Europe. This is not the place for a comprehensive account of the history of Hungary such as that to be found in the opening chapters of Halsey Stevens' *The Life and Music of Béla Bartók* (New York, Oxford University Press, second edition, 1964). But to enable the reader to understand what follows, we must make clear the terms of the peace treaties of 1920 which divested Hungary of a considerable part of her territory on ethnic grounds. The area near the western border was ceded to Austria, the northern part of pre-war Hungary to Czechoslovakia, Transylvania and the Banat to Romania and the semi-autonomous regions such as Croatia, Slavonia and Bácska to Yugoslavia. The north-eastern Carpathians were ceded to Czechoslovakia between the two world wars and have been part of the Ukranian Soviet Socialist Republic since the end of the Second World War. These areas are now bilingual or multilingual.

Thus Bartók's birthplace, Nagyszentmiklós (now Sînnicolaul Mare), became part of Romania.

The Bartók family did not originate in Eastern Hungary. Denijs Dille, one of the first of Bartók's biographers to undertake research in this field, traced the family tree and discovered that Bartók's forbears came from Borsodszirák in the far north of Hungary. The family later moved south, probably during the lifetime of Bartók's great-grandfather who, according to Dille, died in Nagybecskerek (now Zrenjanin, Yugoslavia). Bartók's grandfather, János, was at the time of his death in 1877 the headmaster of the agricultural school at Nagyszentmiklós. The composer's father, Béla, succeeded to the post and in 1880, at the age of twenty-five, married Paula Voit of Turócszentmárton (now Martin, Czechoslovakia). A year later, in 1881, their first child, Béla, was born.

Very little is known about the short life of Béla Bartók, the young headmaster of the agricultural school. But from the few facts which are available it is clear that Zoltán Kodály's description of the composer is equally applicable to the composer's father: a man who was *novarum rerum cupidus*, a man, that is, of a restless nature, endowed with an enquiring mind. For Bartók's father made an original contribution to the teaching of agriculture in Torontál County. He founded a journal, wrote numerous articles, and drew up schemes for the development of intensive farming and for the organization of instruction in agricultural subjects. He was also very interested in cultural developments, and kept a record of his life and thoughts in a diary written in a consciously literary style. He was particularly interested in music. He played the piano, composed minor dance pieces, founded the Nagyszentmiklós Music League and later learnt to play the 'cello so that he could take his place in the orchestra of the League.

Nagyszentmiklós was at that time a community with a population of ten thousand. As in other places in those regions it was a mixed community including Hungarians, Romanians, Germans and Yugoslavs. Socially and intellectually the influence of the Hungarians was naturally decisive, and it is not unlikely that there were frequent expressions of hostility between the various national groupings. In such circumstances it was a noble and difficult enterprise for Béla Bartók to undertake the organization of a Nagyszentmiklós Music League. There was already in existence a local amateur orchestra which had given some public performances, usually at dances. It was Béla Bartók's ambition to raise the standard of this orchestra to meet the needs of a more demanding musical public and so gain the support of the local intelligentsia. When the League was founded at a meeting held on 16th January 1887, Béla Bartók was unanimously elected president.

Music was also a familiar feature of the Bartók household. Mrs. Béla Bartók (Paula Voit) was herself an accomplished pianist. She wrote for her grandchild an account of the composer's childhood which is of inestimable value and which reveals in every line the musical atmosphere in which the family lived. The parents watched with loving attention for the first signs of their son's interest in music. They did not have to wait long: the young Béla reacted to certain favourite pieces of music even before he began to speak at the age of two and a half. 'We noticed that he liked music and singing very much at a very early age. His nurse used to sing to him a great deal, and he listened with great delight. The following happened when he was one and a half years old: I was playing a dance piece, to which he listened attentively, and the very next day he pointed to the piano as if signalling for me to play (he could not yet speak at the time); I played various dance pieces but he kept shaking his head. Then I played that particular piece and he smilingly nodded. On the third day, I tested him to see whether it was a coincidence, but he behaved in the same way as the day before until I played the piece he wanted . . .'

These notes by the composer's mother provide us with a record of the successive stages of the child's involvement in the musical life of the family. At the age of three, when his mother played the piano, he was able to accompany her on the drum and very soon he could follow the changes of rhythm (a further testimony to the care with which his parents planned his musical education). 'When he was four years old, he could beat out with one finger on the piano the melodies of all the folk-songs he knew; he knew forty in all, and began playing them immediately on hearing merely the first line. Even then, he had a remarkable memory . . .'

But the child was not satisfied for very long with these one-finger piano performances. The orchestra of the Music League provided him with a whole new range of experience that further stimulated his interest in music. 'They held their first concert in the Nagyszentmiklós restaurant —with the tables all round them of course—and we took him with us to hear the performance. That was the first time he heard orchestral music. I clearly remember that the first item was the Semiramis overture. The other guests went on eating and drinking but he put down his knife and fork at once and listened with complete absorption. He was delighted, but annoyed that the other people could go on eating while such beautiful music was being played.'

János Demény, to whom we are indebted for the publication of a considerable number of documents relating to Bartók's life and work, corrects minor errors in the mother's memoirs and informs us that this was not the first concert given by the Music League. Their *début* was on February 6, 1887, and Rossini's Semiramis overture was the seventh item on the programme of their second concert given on March 26. According to Mrs. Bartók's memoirs this was also the time when the child was first given piano lessons: 'He had become impatient by that time and begged me to give him piano lessons . . . We began the lessons on his fifth birthday, March 25, and on April 23, his nameday, he surprised his father with a little piece for four hands.'

If the piano lessons were indeed begun as a result of the effect of the Music League concert or the rehearsals for the concert, then the date is that of Bartók's sixth birthday, not his fifth. There would seem to be further support for this view in the succeeding paragraph of the memoirs: 'His instruction was interrupted many times, because of either his or his father's illness.' This is a reference to the year 1887 when the father's health deteriorated and he spent the holidays with his son at Radegund (Austria).

It is of course possible that the child did in fact begin his piano lessons at the age of five, in 1886, one year before the concert given by the Music League. But these are uncertainties which are of concern to the biographer and do not alter the fact that the child was very talented and that, in the musical atmosphere fostered by the whole family, he eagerly and quickly absorbed every available experience of music. When he was seven years old, his parents were delighted to discover that he had absolute pitch. 'He could identify notes and even some chords immediately upon hearing them in another room,' wrote his mother.

Unhappily, the father's death brought to a halt the gradual and measured progress of the child's musical studies and altered the way of life of the whole family. When in the autumn of 1887 a crisis occurred in the affairs of the Music League and complaints appeared in the local press about the general lethargy of the community, it was no longer possible to draw on the admirable organizing ability of Béla Bartók to save the situation. He resigned from his post at the end of the year because of illness and died on August 4, 1888, in the thirty-first year of his life.

After the death of the head of the family, wrote Mrs. Bartók, 'sad days followed, all music ceased'. These sad days lengthened into long and difficult years during which the mother had to maintain the family. The loss of the father served to strengthen the already close ties between mother and son.

As a child Béla was often ill. He suffered from frequently recurring attacks of bronchitis and his misery was increased by a skin complaint from which he was not completely cured until he was five years old. In her book on Bartók, Agatha Fassett quotes a description given by Bartók's second wife, Ditta Pásztory, of the child's solitary life, his lack of companionship, his avoidance of people generally, and the endless patience of his mother as she nursed him during his illness. Various passages in the mother's memoirs add to our understanding of this period of the composer's life: 'Poor child, he hid away from people because it upset him to hear them say "Poor little Béla!" ... Since he could not play with the other children (because of the eruptions on his skin), it is no wonder that he became a quiet, serious child. Whenever he was ill and had to lie in bed, he always wanted me to sing or tell him stories ...' The early memories they shared strengthened the emotional bond and there developed between them an intimacy that deepened and matured in the difficult years that followed.

The family now consisted of Mrs. Bartók, her son Béla, and her two-year-old daughter Erzsébet, or Elza, as she was called at home. Soon they were joined by Mrs. Bartók's older sister, Irma Voit (the aunt so often mentioned in later correspondence). She gave much-needed household help, for the widow had to devote most of her time to earning a living. For one year she continued to give piano lessons in Nagyszentmiklós, and she also began to give her son more regular instruction than previously. Then, in 1889, she accepted a post as a teacher in a school at Nagyszőllős in the Carpatho-Ukraine.

The Bartók family stayed in Nagyszőllős until 1892, a period of three years which marked a significant stage in Bartók's musical career. It was there that he began to compose, at the age of nine, 'various dance pieces, and other pieces too'. And it was there that Keresztély Altdörfer, a visiting organist and composer from Sopron, recognized his talent. 'He was the first to predict a great future for him. He said that Béla's talent was extraordinary and that he would be called upon to do great things in music.' One year later, Altdörfer's opinion was endorsed by the distinguished composer and pianist, Károly Aggházy of Budapest, and it was only thanks to Mrs. Bartók's common sense and foresight that the ten-year-old Béla did not go immediately to Budapest to continue his studies there.

Mrs. Bartók, however, did not harbour the illusions so often fostered by parents of child prodigies and she was determined to help her son to develop all his potentialities, not merely as a musician, but as a human being. Béla therefore completed the first four grades of the elementary school in Nagyszentmiklós at the age of eight. He repeated the fourth grade in Nagyszőllős, and then completed the first grade of the higher elementary school. In addition, he was given private lessons in Latin, and in the autumn of 1891 he enrolled in the second form at Nagyvárad (now Oradea, Romania), where Michael Haydn had once been active. There he lived with his aunt, Emma Voit.

The year he spent in Nagyvárad did not bring the success he had expected. The child who had always done well at school was now in danger of failing in two subjects. 'The teachers were very strange. They only cared for the children of wealthy parents and were most unjust to the others,' wrote his mother. She could barely manage, by giving private lessons, to scrape together the money to send him to school, and so the unfortunate child became one of 'the others'. Finally, to spare him the humiliation of failure, she took her son from the school in Nagyvárad. The following year, in April 1892, Béla returned to Nagyszőllős and on May 1st he played at a concert. Among other pieces he played the first movement of the Beethoven op. 53, the 'Waldstein' Sonata and his own composition *The Flow of the Danube*.

His performance brought immediate success. There was enthusiastic applause, there were favourable reviews in the press and all this resulted in an important change in the life of the Bartók family. 'Thanks to his performance at the concert, I had the good fortune to secure the goodwill of the local school inspector who helped me to obtain a year's leave of absence. I took advantage of this by packing up all our things and going to Pozsony [now Bratislava in Czechoslovakia] where I hoped to get a post. There at last his musical education was in good hands. His teacher was László Erkel. [The son of Ferenc Erkel, the opera composer.] Béla began to make rapid progress though he was at the same time attending the second grade of the higher elementary school which he completed with high honours . . .'

But though Béla made good use of the year at Pozsony, it did not put an end to their wanderings. Mrs. Bartók failed to get the post she had hoped for, and when her leave expired, she was forced to move back to Eastern Hungary with her family. In the following autumn, in 1893, she was transferred to Beszterce (now Bistriţa in Romania) where, in contrast to the encouraging interlude at Pozsony, the Bartók family had to spend eight months in a small town that was almost completely devoid of musical culture. At last, in the spring of 1894, Mrs. Bartók was appointed to the staff of the State College for Teacher Training at Pozsony. In April of that year the family moved back to Pozsony and the five difficult years of uprootedness came to an end. During his adolescence Bartók found a home for the second time in Pozsony; there he was able to study in peace.

3 SYSTEMATIC MUSIC STUDIES IN POZSONY. INFLUENCE OF BRAHMS AND DOHNÁNYI

At first there was no time for music, for the family arrived in Pozsony only six weeks before the end of the school term. The immediate concern of the Bartók family was to ensure that Béla finished the third form studies begun at Beszterce. He had missed a great deal during the first months of his year in the third form, partly because of his difficulties with the German language used in the Saxon higher elementary school at Beszterce and partly because of his own frequent illness. During the first six weeks in Pozsony he had to revise the entire syllabus of the third form if he was to pass the examination. By leading a harshly self-disciplined life he succeeded, and even gained a special commendation from his teachers. In her diary his mother described the effort he made: 'He got up at six o'clock every morning and studied before going to school. After lunch he went back to his studies again—prepared his drawings, wrote his essays, and studied and studied. He did not touch the piano (this was the greatest sacrifice of all) and did not even go to see the Danube although he loved it so much. He spent all his time studying.'

It was only at the beginning of the next term that he was able to begin once again his music lessons with László Erkel. The boy's studies had suffered from constant interruptions in the past, and he had never been able to study for long under one teacher; it was therefore important for him to settle down now and pursue a regular and continuous course of study.

His earliest experience of music was when he listened to the pieces played in his own home, and those played by the Nagyszentmiklós Music League. We have no means of knowing for certain just what these pieces were, but it is possible to select the pieces likely to have had an appeal for the average bourgeois music lover of that period from popular items to opera transcriptions. It is very probable that his mother often played classical pieces by nineteenth-century composers; these pieces, together with the étude literature so inseparable from the study of the piano, constituted the musical phraseology to which his mind, ear and hand became accustomed. In Nagyszőllős, his first composition was a waltz, and this was followed by other small dance pieces. The opus numbering of the piece composed in his youth *The Flow of the Danube* (op. 18) is proof that he had a number of other compositions to his credit in addition to the Waltz, Mazurka and Polka which have long been a matter of public record. *The Flow of the Danube* bears the stamp of the programmatic genre-music of that period, the turns are stereotyped, and the piece merits attention only because there are in it definite indications of the boy's talent. In itself the idea, of transposing the melody into a minor key to show that the Danube is sad when it leaves Hungary, might be dismissed as naive, but this idea, together with some others reveals the ten-year-old boy's ability to sense, and even to achieve in his own work, the traditional character of sound, together with its meaning, inherent in the musical turns he had so often practised. He was making a conscious effort to apply, in however elementary a manner, the knowledge he had absorbed.

Mrs. Bartók reproached Ferenc Kersch, Béla's piano teacher in Nagyvárad, for 'teaching him too many pieces in a rather superficial way, and giving him pieces that were too difficult for him. He liked to show the boy off and was happy when Béla could learn a difficult piece in a week. Of course it goes without saying that this could not be perfect.' Undoubtedly, Ferenc Kersch erred in overburdening his pupil with tasks beyond his strength. But this was not entirely the fault of the teacher. The boy's own eagerness no doubt encouraged the permissive teacher to acquaint him with as many musical scores as possible. This was probably where Béla Bartók first apprehended the existence of the great mass of classical music. It seems reasonable to suppose that his choice of Beethoven's 'Waldstein' Sonata for his recital in Nagyszőllős indicates that it was there that he first became familiar with the composer's major works. It was a familiarity he maintained throughout his life.

The year spent at Beszterce brought no improvement in his technical ability because, as his mother wrote, he was the best pianist the town had to offer. But he did find a fellow-musician, a forester called Schönherr, who could play the violin quite well and for whom the 'son of the new schoolmistress' proved to be an excellent sonata partner. They met weekly at Bartók's home where, as Mrs. Bartók wrote, they often 'played, among other pieces, Beethoven's violin sonatas, including the ... "Kreutzer", then Mendelssohn's Violin Concerto.'

In his fourteenth year, after the interruption of the months spent in Beszterce, Béla Bartók resumed his musical studies in Pozsony, first under Erkel, later under Hyrtl. There he embarked upon a wider course of study: he continued to learn piano technique but he also studied harmony and piano literature. When Erkel died on December 3, 1896, 'Hyrtl took over his music studies'.

László Erkel was a man fully capable of guiding the talented boy entrusted to his care. Bartók has acknowledged in words as well as in his achievements Erkel's remarkable gifts as a teacher. It is true that the atmosphere of the town fostered the spirit of music and influenced Bartók's development, but this fact in no way diminishes the part played by his teachers: their activities contributed to the favourable local conditions.

Pozsony played an important role in the history of Hungary. For centuries it was the coronation town of the Hungarian kings and until 1848 the seat of the Hungarian Parliament. Because it was so near to

Vienna and had close links with the imperial capital it became the centre of the extravagant social life pursued by those members of the aristocracy who had settled near the western borders and who were loyal to the Habsburg dynasty. Vienna, however, was not only the capital of the Habsburg monarchy, the seat of absolute power and the Holy Alliance, the home of Metternich and the secret police, it was also an active centre of the arts and the meeting place of all those interested in the finest achievements of bourgeois culture. It was also a centre for the expression of revolutionary bourgeois ideals, especially in respect of Hungary. Some of the writers who first advocated the movement for the enlightenment and enfranchisement of the Hungarian people were once members of the guard of Hungarian noblemen who attended Maria Theresa and her successors at the court of Vienna; and it was in Vienna that they first came into contact with the ideals and literature of the French Revolution. Vienna was also a centre of music and fostered the genius of Haydn, Beethoven and Mozart.

The influence of Vienna may be traced through the cultural traditions of Pozsony. Already in the eighteenth century the town was inhabited by a cultured bourgeoisie who made it one of the first centres of Hungarian musical theatre. Haydn's opera ensemble visited the town, Mozart played there as a child, and it was the birthplace of Johann Nepomuk Hummel, Mozart's famous disciple. The great musical personalities of Europe were frequent guests in the town. Here was the living centre of the cultural heritage of Western Hungary through whose inspiration Hungarian patriots of German descent—Erkel, Liszt, Mosonyi—became the greatest figures of the Hungarian Reform Age and of nineteenth-century progressive culture. It was the same spirit which some generations later inspired the great composers: Ernő Dohnányi, born in Pozsony, Béla Bartók, born in Eastern Hungary and educated in Pozsony, and Zoltán Kodály of Kecskemét who was educated at Galánta and Nagyszombat (now Galanta and Trnava in Czechoslovakia). László Erkel, Bartók's teacher, who came back to his ancestral home, is a truly representative figure in the continuity of Hungarian musical heritage.

Music was no mere holiday activity in Pozsony but rather an integral part of everyday life. Some of the references in Mrs. Bartók's diary indicate how general the custom of playing chamber music at home was.

24

Róth, the school inspector, heard the young Bartók practising through an open window. He made enquiries in the local shops and introduced himself to the Bartók family. He himself was an accomplished 'cello player and he invited Bartók to become a member of his own domestic chamber group. They met weekly and this regular absorption in chamber music became Bartók's most important source of musical nourishment. 'Many of the pieces he became acquainted with there contributed to his musical education. He liked going there because he enjoyed encountering unfamiliar compositions.'

But the Róth chamber-music group was not the only one in Pozsony. 'He frequented the Rigele home where he also played chamber music.' And there were doubtless many other families similarly engaged in music-making. A third family must be mentioned here, that of the teacher Frigyes Dohnányi, in which his brilliant son, Ernő, was the centre of interest. We can also be certain that the dominant influence on the character of these chamber-music soirées was the music of the great masters of the Viennese school: Haydn, Mozart and Beethoven. For the works of the great masters were popular not only in Pozsony, they were also played by chamber-music groups initiated by members of the intelligentsia in the principal towns throughout the country. In this way Bartók maintained his familiarity with the works of Beethoven, from his early childhood a determining factor in his development as a composer. His mother had good reason for noting that among the scores bought by her son was that of Beethoven's *Missa Solemnis*.

The close proximity of Vienna is also reflected in the attitude of Pozsony musicians during the controversy about the development of German music after Beethoven. During the years when Bartók was a schoolboy debates were still continuing between the followers of Schubert, Schumann and Brahms on the one hand, and the enthusiasts for the musical trend represented by Liszt and Wagner on the other. Vienna was the centre of the most resolute support for the cause of Brahms. It was Eduard Hanslick, the fearsome Viennese critic, who organized the attack on Liszt and Wagner in the name of the true spirit and heritage of German music. The influence of Schumann and Brahms was very strong in Pozsony. The tone and style of musical expression of these masters is basic to Bartók's compositions of this period. He was directly influenced by his own knowledge of the work of the masters and also indirectly through the compositions of Dohnányi whose musical style always faithfully reflected his most intense musical experiences as a youth. 'At that time, after I had heard Dohnányi's early works, notably his first opus, it was Brahms and Dohnányi, four years my senior, who exerted the greatest influence on me,' wrote Bartók in his autobiography.

Our present knowledge of this influence still comes to us indirectly rather than from any familiarity with Bartók's early works. From various sources we have been provided with recordings of compositions dating from the Pozsony period: piano pieces, three songs with German lyrics, two violin sonatas, a piano sonata, a piano quartet and a violin quartet. In the later years of his maturity as a composer Bartók did not, however, include these works in his œuvre and he preserved them apart from the compositions that were published. The family archives have only recently become available to research workers and Bartók's compositions as a schoolboy are now being studied carefully for the first time.

But Pozsony after all was not Vienna and Hanslick's judgement did not have the same authority there as in Vienna. As in Sopron, there were those in Pozsony who cherished the memory of personal contact with Liszt; they did not apply the label of heresy to the work of Liszt and Wagner as was the case in Vienna. And although the character and quality of Bartók's works at that time reveal chiefly the influence of Brahms, yet Bartók was also familiar with the art of Liszt and Wagner. He included some of their pieces in his piano recitals. (His mother recalls in her memoirs that in 1897 he played Liszt's *Spanish Rhapsody* and in 1898 Wagner's *Tannhäuser* overture.)

The effect of the years in Pozsony may be best summarized by saying that it was there that Bartók acquired a sound knowledge of the whole field of European musical culture; in his own words, 'By the age of eighteen, I was quite well acquainted with musical literature from Bach to Brahms. In Wagner, however, I only got as far as Tannhäuser.'

After leaving the secondary school the next step for Bartók was naturally to embark upon a career in music, and in Pozsony it seemed only reasonable to assume that he would continue his studies at the Conservatoire in Vienna. Mrs. Bartók recorded in her memoirs the exact day on which he set out for the great capital. 'On December 8, 1898, we left for

Vienna, where a teacher at the Conservatoire heard him play the piano and listened to his compositions. He played one of his piano sonatas. The teacher was highly delighted and said that although he was Hungarian-born, he would be admitted to the Conservatoire tuition-free and would be given a scholarship from the Emperor's private funds.'

But this project did not materialize. Bartók's plans were changed, presumably during the Christmas holidays, as a result of a meeting with Dohnányi, who advised him to go to the Academy of Music in Budapest. Dohnányi's own success proved to be a most convincing argument in favour of such a course.

In January 1899, the Bartóks travelled to Budapest to meet István Thomán, Dohnányi's teacher. Mrs. Bartók described their reception: 'He was immediately pleased with his playing and said that he would be admitted to the Academy without taking an entrance examination, and he wrote to Professor Koessler, recommending him highly and suggesting that he might take a look at some of Béla's compositions. Wherever we went we met with a marvellous response.'

In February, Bartók suddenly became ill. This was the first appearance of a lung condition which was to interrupt his studies at the Academy several times. Although he was able to matriculate, he had to abandon the piano for a long time. He spent the summer with his mother in Carinthia, and in September reported for admission to the Academy in much better health. On this occasion, Ödön Mihalovich, the distinguished director of the Academy, unexpectedly required him to take the entrance examination which, however, he passed with flying colours in spite of the preceding months of illness when he had not been well enough to practise the piano. Mihalovich himself congratulated him. It remained for the Bartóks to find lodgings in Budapest, and then Béla embarked upon his years of study at the Academy.

CHAPTER II

STUDENT YEARS AT THE BUDAPEST ACADEMY OF MUSIC
1898–1903

1 GUIDANCE FROM ISTVÁN THOMÁN. ACQUAINTANCE WITH THE WORKS
OF WAGNER

By the turn of the century Budapest had become one of the great capital cities of the world. The city was becoming rapidly industrialized and the appearance of the city was being transformed with equal celebrity: an eclectic style of architecture was being superimposed on the neo-Classicism of the Hungarian Reform Age. The cultural life of the city was very different from that to which Bartók had been accustomed in Pozsony. There he had been brought up to have a conventional respect for tradition. In Budapest there was a mixture of national pride and allegiance to more recently acquired cultural standards based on international capitalism. Pozsony was still influenced by Vienna; in Budapest the forces of both nationalism and capitalism were expressed in a feverish desire to be independent of Vienna. Because of the conservative foundations of its political and social life, Endre Ady, the greatest Hungarian poet of the first decades of the twentieth century, had written of Budapest as 'a suburb of Vienna'; but now the younger generation was learning to emulate Parisian trends. In the streets of Budapest at that time there was just as much of the flavour of Paris as of Vienna. There were still casinos to be seen, evidence of the manner of life preserved by wealthy members of the aristocracy and the ruling parliamentary party, but there was also a Parisian atmosphere in the busy streets, in the coffee-houses, and in the theatres; and the influence of Paris was especially noticeable in literary circles and among the young poets of Pest.

In the same way the musical atmosphere of Budapest differed from that of Pozsony. When Bartók decided to take Dohnányi's advice and approached István Thomán for admittance to the Academy, he had no idea of the decisive nature of his action. At Pozsony he had learnt to have the greatest respect for Brahms, but he was now to find in István

Thomán a staunch supporter of the Liszt tradition. The building in which Bartók lived during his years at the Academy from 1899 to 1903, at the corner of Andrássy út (formerly Sugár út) and Vörösmarty út, was the very same in which Ferenc Liszt had taught during his last years.

The spirit of Liszt was reflected in István Thomán's attitude to his pupils and Bartók was surprised to find himself the object of much thoughtfulness in small ways.

> Professor Thomán was most considerate today. After the lesson, at a quarter to eleven, he asked me to go with him, and wanted to know why I had put on low shoes when it was so cool this morning ... I thanked him for his advice ... it was really very nice of him,

he wrote to his mother on September 22. On another occasion Thomán gave some music to his favourite but impoverished pupil.

The extent of his thoughtfulness is most clearly shown in the guidance he gave to Bartók in his development as an artist and in the way in which he later helped to launch his pupil into his career. There had been a similar informality in the personal contact cultivated by Ferenc Liszt towards the permanent circle of his most gifted pupils; he had always tried to involve them in his own artistic experiences, drawn their attention to major musical events throughout the world, introduced them to his most distinguished guests and used the weight of his authority to help them along the road to success.

From the time when he first heard Bartók play in January 1899, István Thomán never relaxed the close attention with which he followed the young man's development as a musician. Later, in 1927, on the occasion of István Thomán's fortieth anniversary as a teacher, Bartók recalled some of his memories of those early years:

> In my last year at Pozsony, something happened that made me sense that in studying with Thomán I should acquire more than a mastery of piano technique, that the education offered by Thomán would be directed not only towards the hands of a pianist and the ear of a musician, but towards the human soul. It was two months after my audition and I certainly did not expect that Thomán will remember me. But quite unexpectedly I received a letter from him. It was an invitation to come to Budapest for the performance of Beethoven's Ninth Symphony at which our philharmonic orchestra was to be conducted by the famous János Richter. Thomán had decided that this

promised to be a musical experience that could be very important for the development of a young musician and he asked me to be his guest for the evening.

This kindly gesture was the first impulse of a lasting solicitude on the part of Thomán, the 'Auftakt', as Bartók put it, of the relationship between teacher and pupil which developed into a bond of friendship.

The details of piano technique as taught by Thomán, for example the position of the hands on the keyboard and economy of movement generally, were derived from Liszt whose methods, Bartók wrote,

> were instinctive, though they have since been incorporated into modern educational methods. Thomán, a former pupil of Liszt, had acquired his knowledge direct from the master.

The basic feature of Liszt's method, now employed by Thomán, was the performance of a given piece for the benefit of the pupil. It was not that either Thomán or Liszt considered their own renderings as definitive but rather a desire to impress upon the pupil the effect of the work as a whole. This enabled the student to study the technical details in a more interesting way, for these became incidental to his attempt to master the whole piece.

Thomán also required his pupils to listen conscientiously to the great guest artists who appeared in the concert halls of Budapest; he encouraged them to form their own opinions and to learn everything they could from the performances. Bartók's letters written during his years at the Academy show that he assiduously followed these instructions; there are references to concerts with Emil Sauer, Eugen d'Albert, Teresa Carreño and others, together with criticism and comparisons. His letters to his mother describe other musical experiences—performances by Jan Kubelik, chamber concerts including those of the Hubay–Popper string quartet, orchestral concerts and opera performances.

But the experience which affected him most profoundly during this period was his introduction to the later works of Wagner. Visits to the opera were not always easy to arrange. When the popular singer, Madame Ábrányi, left the company, the students demonstrated their loyalty to her in such a manner that their free passes were confiscated. Nor was this the only occasion when they were punished in this way. However, in February, 'Mihalovich took steps to retrieve their box', and though he was not immediately successful, the matter was settled. János Demény's account of the affair, which is largely based on Bartók's letters, shows that Bartók was greatly upset by the ban; immediately after the passes were returned, during the three weeks between May 17 and June 9, 1900, he made no fewer than twelve visits to the opera. The season included four works by Wagner, *Siegfried, Tannhäuser, Lohengrin* and *Die Walküre*. In a letter dated June 3, Bartók underlined the title of the opera *Die Walküre*, which was billed for the final performance of the season and added in brackets 'at all costs', an indication of the intensity of his desire to hear it.

There is constant reference in the letters to his study of Wagner. *Das Rheingold* and *Die Walküre* are mentioned several times and he has even scribbled out parts of the score for the family. In his autobiography other works by Wagner are mentioned:

> Soon after my arrival, I plunged into an enthusiastic study of the works by Wagner which were still unknown to me *(Tetralogie, Tristan, Die Meistersinger)*, also the orchestral works of Liszt.

It is clear from the list of operas planned for the season that Budapest was one of the strongholds of Wagnerian opera. As a young man the director of the Academy of Music, Ödön Mihalovich, had met both Liszt and Wagner. He had initiated the Wagner cult in Hungary and from the eighteen-sixties onwards had been responsible for its promotion. In his own compositions he remained faithful to the Wagnerian style; he was also a personal friend of the family. Liszt too had greatly esteemed Mihalovich whose works he had tried hard to popularize. Mihalovich, for his part, gave Liszt considerable assistance in organizing the Academy of Music. After the death of Liszt he became the director of the Academy, a position he retained from 1887 until 1919. Assisted by close personal connections with leading politicians, Mihalovich showed great foresight in his administration of the Academy which, during the period of his directorship, became one of the most important centres of music in Europe; he was largely responsible for the increased respect in which Hungarian music began to be held throughout the world.

Mihalovich also played a part in raising the standard of the performances in the Budapest Opera. He arranged for Gustav Mahler to be invited to become the director of music. This eminent Viennese conductor and composer was a Wagner enthusiast and could not hope for such an opportunity in Vienna where Hanslick was still influential. Mahler accepted the invitation and held the post of director of music from 1888 to 1891 when he was compelled to leave as a result of internal intrigues. But even during this short period he raised the musical standard of the Opera, particularly in the performance of works by Wagner.

Mahler's efforts during his brief stay in Budapest were not wasted, for they were continued by his successor, Géza Zichy, himself a pupil of Liszt and just as devoted to Wagner as Mihalovich. The idolatry of Wagner which was gaining ground throughout Europe was yet another encouragement to Wagner lovers in Budapest. János Richter, who was Hungarian by birth and a frequent guest conductor in Budapest, was also a Wagner enthusiast; and a continuous musical tradition was also demonstrated at about this period by notable performances of the works of Mozart, Beethoven and Wagner by István Kerner, a pupil of Sándor Erkel. While still a young student at the Academy, Bartók thus had the experience of hearing some impressive performances of the works of Wagner. This enabled him to judge for himself the characteristic differences between Budapest and Vienna, and especially between Pozsony and Budapest, as centres of music.

2 UNCERTAINTY AS A COMPOSER. ILLNESS

The effect on Bartók of this sudden impact of Wagner was not, however, immediately apparent for he was at that time studying composition with János Koessler. It was many years later that the influence of both Wagner and Liszt became discernible as a significant element of the new kind of unity found in Bartók's music.

For the time being, he was silent. In his autobiography he comments briefly on this fact:

> During this period my creative activities were at a standstill. I had abandoned the style of Brahms but even my newly acquired knowledge of Wagner and Liszt could not help me to find the new path for which I yearned. (At that time I still did not understand the musical significance of Liszt, and saw only

the outward forms of his art.) The result was that I accomplished virtually nothing for about two years and I was known at the Academy only as a pianist.

Bartók's teacher of composition, János Koessler, was also to some considerable extent responsible for his silence during these two years. Koessler's attitude to music was very different from that of Mihalovich and Thomán; he was an orthodox representative of the Brahms tradition. Thus his teaching was based on a formal academic interpretation of Beethoven, a method which Bartók had already outgrown while still in Pozsony. (It is of course important not to fall into the error of equating Brahms's works with the scholastic dogmatism of some of his followers who did not understand his work.) While István Thomán, a man of striking personality, and with all Liszt's healthy disregard for petty detail, was able to help Bartók to discover new aspects of music, János Koessler could offer him no new horizons. He looked upon the young man's search for self-expression with suspicion and lack of understanding, and even discouraged Bartók by some of his remarks. Bartók later learnt to ignore his teacher's misgivings, but in his first year he felt bitterly this lack of guidance.

This was confirmed by Kodály when he wrote, 'We can find that the cause of this long period of inactivity lies not so much in the fact that he was busy practising the piano but rather in the fact that János Koessler was his teacher. He was actually advised by Koessler to stop composing for a time ... he came to a deadlock and Koessler could not help him.' Some of the letters are very revealing of the relationship that existed between Koessler and Bartók: for instance Bartók wrote to his mother on January 5, 1900:

> Yesterday I took along the quintet. Professor Koessler said that none of it was any good at all, that I should not even continue it but should attempt simpler things, songs for example. I have no idea what was bad in it, because he spoke only in generalities: that I should make a better selection of subjects and so on. Accordingly, none of the subjects are worth anything. But if these are not worth anything, then I don't know if I shall be able to write anything better a year from now. And why did he not say last January that those pieces were not worth anything either. In my opinion, this quintet is better in every respect than last year's quartet. At that time I thought that my compositions were good in general and they only needed one or two modifications, mostly in

form. But if they are so bad that they cannot be improved at all, well then, that's pretty serious.

So for the time being, his development as a composer was halted. But during the second half of the term there were two notable dates in his career as a pianist. On March 31, at a students' concert, he played the first movement of Beethoven's Piano Concerto in C Minor when he was accompanied by his piano teacher, István Thomán; and on May 8, he accompanied David Popper at a concert in the Park Club arranged by the Committee of the Sanatorium for impoverished consumptives as a means of raising money for a new sanatorium. The audience was made up exclusively of aristocrats and other socially prominent personalities. It was typical of such occasions that the dressing room was 'an elegant W.C.' and that the artists could not be paid because 'not enough money was taken in at the box-office'.

'Fortunately, the school year of 1899–1900 came to an end. His report was excellent and his health also seemed to have improved,' wrote his mother in her diary. For even in October, at the very beginning of that particular school year, Bartók had been in bed suffering from an acute attack of bronchitis and had been obliged to return to Pozsony for a long convalescence. It was then that one of his doctors advised him to abandon his musical career and 'perhaps to take up law'. By December, however, towards the end of that year, he was again in Pest, this time in the care of Aunt Irma, and was able to finish the school year without interruption.

During his second year at the Academy he was not so fortunate. Full of health and high spirits, he spent the summer holidays with his mother in St. Johann bei Herberstein in Styria. They visited Radegund, a place of which both had happy memories, for it was there that Mrs. Bartók had first met her husband and Béla had spent some time there with his father in the summer of 1887. But on the day before they were due to leave for home he developed a temperature. For almost a month he was confined to bed suffering from pneumonia and pleurisy, and when at last he was able to return home, the doctor took a very grave view of his condition and feared that he might not survive. The lung specialist was, however, more reassuring and held out some hope of recovery—but only if he could be sent to Meran. This was arranged and from the middle of November, when he started the cure, he began to make a rapid recovery;

34

indeed his progress was so satisfactory that from January 1, 1901, he was allowed to practise the piano. At the end of March, he returned to the Academy of Music, heavier by ten kilogrammes and completely cured.

3 SUCCESSES AS A PIANIST. PATRONS, FRIENDS, MRS. EMMA GRUBER SÁNDOR

It was only after his recovery, in the autumn of 1901, that he was able to embark upon a course of uninterrupted study at the Academy. Originally he had enrolled in the second-year classes to study both piano and composition. At the end of his first year he had taken a combined examination in composition covering both the second and third-year courses. During his second year he had therefore begun the fourth-year class in composition and the third-year class in piano. But he had scarcely benefited at all from this year because of his illness and so, during the year 1901–2, he repeated these courses.

After his long rest he began to work with renewed energy. He had been occupied for some time with Liszt's Sonata in B Minor, a work which he found it difficult to accept whole-heartedly. Ten years later, in *Liszt zenéje és a mai közönség* (Liszt's Music and Today's Public), he described how he attempted to master the sonata, first playing it himself then listening to Dohnányi's rendering. But still he had reservations. 'Of course,' he added, 'this was at a time when I did not understand Beethoven's last sonatas either.' He began to study the work again during his convalescence in 1901, primarily in order to master the technical difficulties.

> As I studied it, I gradually, if not unconditionally, came to like it. Later I spoke to Dohnányi about the Sonata and to my amazement, he told me that he had had exactly the same experience. From this it seems that it is necessary to get used to certain kinds of music.

Whatever the doubts he may have still harboured concerning this work, he at any rate performed it in public at an Academy concert on October 21, that is, at the beginning of the school year. The concert was arranged to celebrate the ninetieth anniversary of the birth of Liszt. Bartók's performance was given considerable publicity in the press, it was praised unanimously by the reviewers and Bartók was named for the first time as Dohnányi's successor.

Bartók followed up this success by performing at other concerts given during the school year. On December 14, he played at the Lipótvárosi Kaszinó, and on December 20, he was favoured with an invitation to play at a private gathering of the staff of the Academy of Music. On this occasion Jenő Hubay played his latest composition, the Second Violin Concerto, and Bartók accompanied him on the piano.

These two December concerts were typical of the musical events which were a feature of social life in Budapest at that time. A not inconsiderable number of the wealthier members of the bourgeoisie believed that they had a special responsibility to patronize the arts and to encourage new talent. This was their intention when they arranged musical evenings such as those which took place in the highly respectable and lavish surroundings of the Lipótvárosi Kaszinó when young artists were given an opportunity to perform in public. Nor was this the only occasion when Bartók's work was heard in the Kaszinó: ten years later, in 1911, his entry for a competition organized by the Kaszinó was his first work for the stage, a one-act opera, *Bluebeard's Castle*.

The patronage extended by the upper ranks of the bourgeoisie was for the most part superficial, a gesture made for the sake of appearance only. But there was also some genuine understanding of the arts; and an atmosphere in which the arts were socially acceptable also encouraged the development of progressive literature, art and music in Hungary during the first years of the twentieth century.

The musical life of Budapest society was not at that time confined to the Opera and the concert hall. Music was an integral part of home life in many middle-class families who often numbered well-known musicians among their friends or relatives. The Arányi family, for instance, with whom Bartók later became friendly, was related to the eminent violinist Josef Joachim. Jelly, one of Arányi's two daughters, studied with Jenő Hubay and made a name for herself as a violinist in London. The second daughter, Adila, also played the violin. In such families in Budapest it was customary to speak German, but, as we learn from a letter written in the autumn of 1902, French was the language used in the Arányi household. It was in their home too that Bartók met Jenő Kerpely who later became a famous 'cellist.

The staff of the Academy maintained social relations with a number of the bourgeois patrons of art in Budapest, and the fact that Bartók was accepted in both circles clearly signified that he was recognized as István Thomán's brilliant pupil, 'the second Dohnányi'.

The home of Mrs. Gruber (Emma Sándor before her marriage) was a meeting place for those with a more serious interest in music than that of the guests at most social gatherings. The hostess was herself an excellent musician; she was an accomplished pianist whose compositions were almost professional in their competence. Bartók mentions her as a collector of Hungarian folk music in his book *A magyar népdal* (The Hungarian Folk-Song) (1924). She was closely acquainted with the director of the Academy of Music and various gifted members of the staff but her guests also included some of the more outstanding students. From the autumn of 1902 onwards Bartók was a frequent visitor at her home. There he renewed acquaintance with a number of old friends including Dohnányi who was by then acknowledged as a virtuoso throughout Europe. There too, in 1905, he was introduced to Zoltán Kodály. In this friendly atmosphere a number of significant works were first performed. It was here that the most talented masters of the twentieth century, all still young men, first heard and discussed each other's compositions. With her profound knowledge of music and acute judgement, the hostess was also able to take an active part in the discussions. Emma Sándor became the wife of Zoltán Kodály in 1910. She died in 1958.

4 RICHARD STRAUSS'S 'ZARATHUSTRA'. 'EIN HELDENLEBEN'. NEW COMPOSING ORIENTATION. THE 'FOUR PIANO PIECES' AND THE 'SYMPHONY'

In the course of this particular school year Bartók was moved to start composing once more. On February 2, 1902, the philharmonic orchestra performed Richard Strauss's symphonic poem, *Thus Spake Zarathustra* and, as Bartók says, the work

> pulled me like lightning out of my stagnation ... The composition which most of the Pest musicians listened to with abhorrence, filled me with delight. At last, I saw a way forward that contained the promise of something new. I plunged into a study of Strauss's scores and started to compose again.

His absorption in the works of Strauss is best illustrated by the fact that he learnt to play the symphonic poem *Ein Heldenleben* without a score. And he played with such artistry that his performance was talked about even in Vienna. His rendering amazed Emma Gruber, and István Thomán became so enthusiastic that he included it in the programme of a private concert given for the professors of the Academy on December 22, 1904. Only four days previously, on December 18, Bartók had performed the Schumann Sonata in F-Sharp Minor at a public concert given at the Academy. His mother recorded his success in her diary: 'The director [Mihalovich] went up to him, embraced him and invited him to stay for the private dinner given for the professors. During the dinner, Jenő Hubay toasted Bartók, the youngest artist of them all . . .'

In the middle of January 1903, Koessler asked Bartók to play the Strauss score for him.

> He was astonished at my knowing it by heart; on the other hand, he spoke disparagingly of *Heldenleben* itself.

Afterwards, on the tram, the music critic Aurél Kern congratulated Bartók: 'I am told that you play this divinely.'

On January 26, Bartók was invited to play the *Heldenleben* by the Viennese Tonkünstlerverein. It was an event which received widespread notice in the press. The performance was acclaimed in true Viennese style though the critics did not miss the opportunity of denouncing Strauss's music. Yet when the recital was being discussed at a private gathering, even Hanslick, now an old man, was moved to comment: 'He must be a genius, but it is a pity that he spends his time on Strauss.' Bartók described these reactions in a letter to his mother. It is clear that there was a remarkable unanimity of opinion between Hanslick, Koessler and the public audiences of Vienna.

It is probable that the music of Strauss first stimulated Bartók's imagination and moved him to creative activity as early as during the summer of 1902. He may have begun work on his first symphony when he was still in Pozsony; it is certain that during the autumn of that year he could already play two of the movements for István Thomán, who was particularly pleased with the Scherzo. Bartók played the Adagio for Koessler whose response was less than enthusiastic. This was to be expected, however, for Koessler was of the opinion that modern composers were unable to produce good adagio movements; how then could he expect more of Bartók? He thought that even Dohnányi's adagios were not without their flaws. 'If you have done all you can with it,' he told Bartók, 'then you had better leave it and go on with the other movements.'

The tone of the first movement of the symphony reflects the influence of Bartók's study of Wagner. But during the succeeding years of prolific activity the chamber works, piano pieces, songs and also the *Kossuth Symphony* were unmistakably composed under the impact of his first encounter with the works of Strauss. The extent of Strauss's influence on the works themselves is still an open question; there was no direct use of the musical elements found in the works of Strauss. Even in these early compositions it is possible to detect the characteristic feature of Bartók's creative imagination that was to remain one of its most striking traits. The influence of contemporary music did not merely manifest itself in easily recognizable outward similarities; the music was rather a source of inspiration in the formation of his own creative work, a means to the release of his own genius so that he could make his unique contribution to music. In a letter dated March, 1903, Bartók himself raises this intriguing question as to the extent to which his work was influenced by Strauss. He described an occasion when Ernő Dohnányi unexpectedly entered the room where Mrs. Gruber was playing Bartók's *Phantasy No. 1* which was composed on February 8 and dedicated to Mrs. Gruber. Dohnányi did not know the piece and after some deliberation declared that it must have been written 'either by Strauss or Bartók'. Later, however, he described it as 'modernized Tchaikovsky'. Thomán felt that it was Brahmsian and Herzfeld likened it to Liszt. Others found Wagnerian elements in the work.

It is undoubtedly true that the influence of Strauss is recognizable, even at a first hearing, in the *Phantasy* and other works composed at that time. If we study the work without looking for any direct adaptation of musical turns but rather concentrating on the similarity of working methods, then we certainly find some reflection of the school of Strauss in the rhythmic and tonal loosening of the melodic lines, the free, sharp collisions of chromatic changes and transitional notes—early indications of the major–minor chords which later became a typical feature of

Bartók's work. Bartók was particularly stimulated by the orchestral sound achieved by Strauss and also by his orchestration, for he responded not only by writing a symphony but also by basing his handling of the orchestra for a long time on Strauss's orchestration.

But we must look beyond these superficial similarities if we are to find the most essential element of Strauss's influence on Bartók as a composer; this was the quality to which the critics responded with so much reserve in *Zarathustra*—Strauss's use of all the means of composition which were then thought of as new and astounding for the free symphonic expression of a spiritual experience and message. It was essentially a quality that came within the tradition of Wagner, and especially of Liszt. In fact the impression made on Bartók earlier by these two masters, which he had not clearly understood at the time, was now renewed and strengthened by the astonishing brilliance of Strauss's music. This is the view taken by Bence Szabolcsi in his introduction to *Béla Bartók—His Life in Pictures* (Boosey and Hawkes, London and Corvina Press, Budapest, 1964).

Thus we must respect the musical judgement of those of Bartók's contemporaries who recognized in *Phantasy No. 1* the voices of Liszt and Wagner as well as those of Strauss and Brahms. They sensed something that even Bartók himself only realized later, that his experience of Strauss brought his understanding of Wagner and especially of Liszt to an earlier maturity.

It is true that in his autobiography Bartók does not claim to have fully recognized the power of Liszt until a much later date. And it is undoubtedly true that at a later stage of his career as a composer he deliberately applied himself to a further study of Liszt's works. Since 1904, in letters to Lajos Dietl, the piano teacher of the Vienna Conservatoire, he had been expressing his unreserved admiration for the Strauss songs as and when he became familiar with them. In works written during this period, however, there are more indications of the increasing influence of Liszt than of the temporary and merely evocative stimulus of Strauss.

The conspicuously large number of Scherzos written by Bartók as a young man cannot pass unremarked. The Scherzo movement of his first symphony written in 1902 was the most successful part of the entire work, it was the only movement that he orchestrated and it was played at the philharmonic concert given by graduate composers on February 29, 1904. The last of the *Four Piano Pieces*, written in 1903, is also a Scherzo; and there is another *Scherzo* for piano and orchestra dating from 1904. We must also take into account the innumerable different types of Scherzo movements to be found in his later works and the fugato in the *B Minor Sonata*; and if we read what he says about the irony in Liszt's music in his book *Liszt's Music and Today's Public* (1911), and recall the character of Mephistopheles, we realize the significance of his use of the scherzo form.

It is even more rewarding to study the Scherzos in their context and not merely in isolation. In the descriptions of the symphony the Scherzo is always discussed together with the apparently unresolved Adagio movement. Reference to the dates on the manuscripts of the various movements shows that it is very probable that these two movements were the first part of the symphony to be completed. One year later, in the *Kossuth Symphony*, we find a similar pairing of two movements: the final tragic *Marche Funèbre* follows a satirical parody of the 'Gott erhalte'. And again, in the *Four Piano Pieces*, the Scherzo follows the slow Phantasies, while the Rhapsody (1904) is rounded out into slow–fast form. These paired movements with their contradictory content and atmosphere are an expression of the problem with which Bartók struggled throughout the period of his creative development, a problem not so much of outward form but rather of inner content—the conception of the world as the continuous process of contradiction.

The origin of these paired movements may be traced through the music of Liszt, Berlioz, Schumann and Schubert, and finally as far back as Beethoven, thus encompassing the musical heritage of the nineteenth century. It is clear that the 'lightning' of Strauss's music illuminated for Bartók a whole complex of problems of content which was the legacy of Beethoven but which he had previously encountered only piecemeal through the works of Liszt and Wagner on the one hand and, in respect of the more academic aspects, through the cult of Brahms in Pozsony. After his period of stagnation in the atmosphere of academic formalism, his creative genius was revived by this new attitude in which content was the guiding principle.

CHAPTER III

THE FIRST GREAT WORKS. 1903–1905

1 PATRIOTIC FAITH AND ZEAL

Bartók became fully aware of the ideological significance of music when contemporary events began to arouse in him a concern for social and political questions. It was thus that his musical aspirations were resolved and that the contribution he personally wished to make to music became clear to him.

> The spirit of nationalism was stirring in Hungary at that time and making itself felt in art too. The idea arose that it might be possible to create a specifically Hungarian type of music. This idea took root in my mind and I found myself turning to Hungarian folk music in those days.

In these few sentences Bartók has weighed every word; the significance of his statement cannot be overestimated.

The emotional atmosphere of this period of national fervour is evoked even more vividly in the memoirs of Zoltán Kodály: 'For our generation, 1849 [the defeat of the Hungarians in the War of Independence] was still a grim and living memory. Old men who had taken part in the uprising and who still wore their beards in the style of Kossuth, were still to be seen frequently in the streets. Bartók may even have met some of them. And in the newspapers, when they died, one read the invariable refrain of the obituaries: "they witnessed great times". The house in which I myself lived, had been hit by a cannon. When I was a school-child, it was decreed that instead of observing March 15 [the day on which the Hungarian revolution and War of Independence broke out], we had to celebrate April 11, the date when the April Laws were passed. Young people defied the decree and secretly organized a procession to the Patriot's statue, to take place at night,' said Kodály in 1946, remembering Bartók. 'This nation-wide longing for independence reached its climax just after the turn of the century. People demanded that everything be strictly Hungarian, the coat of arms, the language used in the army; and they demanded that the Hungarian anthem be sung instead of the

Gott erhalte [of the Austrian Empire]. Kuruc songs reviling the Germans reverberated throughout the land,' he added in an article written in 1950: 'Bartók the Folklorist.'

This tremendous outburst of national feeling had its origins in the preceding period of Hungarian history when, economically and politically, the country was moving towards imperialism. After the Compromise with Austria in 1867 Hungary entered a period of industrial growth which was initially rapid but was later slowed down by two impending factors—the feudal system of landed estates and political leadership of the landed aristocracy on the one hand, and on the other, the country's economic and political dependence on Austria. The development of large estates benefiting from large-scale farming led to the mass prole-tarianization of the peasantry. The new factories could absorb only a limited number of former agricultural labourers and soon large numbers of impoverished peasants were emigrating to the United States. Those who remained were increasingly influenced by the working-class movements of the eighteen-nineties and began to demonstrate for their rights more openly than hitherto.

The internal crisis and the growing contradictions of capitalist develop-ment combined to make the economic and political structure of the Compromise more and more untenable and strengthened the resentment felt by the Hungarian ruling classes because they were still economically and politically dependent on Austria. But the Hungarian rulers could only secure a more advantageous agreement with Austria by oppressing even more mercilessly both the Hungarian people and the national minorities who were organizing their own struggle against double oppres-sion and also by using the slogan of national independence to break up the unity between Hungarian and non-Hungarian industrial and agrarian proletarians alike on the basis of their common class interests.

The millennium parade was held in the spirit of this national chauvinism and the slogans were intended to encourage members of the petit-bourgeoisie to support the Hungarian ruling classes. The situation became even more grave with the strengthening of Hungarian finance capital and of the bourgeoisie who were feeling an urgent need for more inde-pendence in their development of Hungarian capitalism.

This tense situation reached a point of open crisis during Bartók's last year at the Academy in 1902–3. Towards the end of 1902, the Defence Minister, Géza Fejérváry, submitted to Parliament a bill proposing a substantial increase of Hungary's contribution to the Imperial army. Parliamentary opposition centred round such issues as national sovereignty, the independence of the Hungarian army, the use of the Hungarian language, coat of arms and badges by the army, and its oath to the Hungarian constitution. The longing for independence reached fever-pitch throughout the country. The singing of the 'Gott erhalte' was a constant incitement to unrest and there were almost daily clashes with the police when people refused to sing the Imperial Austrian anthem.

Bartók supported these aspirations with the ardent faith of a radical. He wrote to his mother describing in detail the political situation that arose as a result of parliamentary obstructionism. He inveighed with violence against the foreign monarch, and he took to wearing national costume. 'Only a Hungarian can be the king of Hungary,' he wrote in June 1903, and later in the same letter he used the Hungarian version of his younger sister's name, Elza:

> I suggest (and fully expect you will accept my suggestion immediately and with general approval) that my younger sister be called Böske from now on.

He spent part of the summer with his mother at Passail in Styria, but at the end of August he went for a month to Gmunden where he took piano lessons from Dohnányi. It is clear that the political events of the day were still a constant subject of conversation, and Bartók was able to discover Dohnányi's attitude to the question of nationalism. It seems that Bartók's mother did not have a very favourable opinion of Dohnányi in general for in a letter dated September 23 we find Bartók defending him.

> You are quite wrong about Dohnányi. I think very highly of him both as a man and an artist. There is not a trace of malice in him. As an artist, he is too severe on his fellow artists; but that's not such a very great fault. His much worse and unforgivable sin is his lack of patriotism. This excludes the possibility that there might ever be a 'better relationship' between us.

This letter was written barely a week after Franz Joseph's notorious Chlopy command of September 17 in which he made harsh use of his prerogative as a monarch to bring to an end the bitter disagreement over the language to be used in the army. He refused to accede to the nation-wide demand for the use of the Hungarian language in the army. By this action the Emperor rejected even the pretence of Hungarian statehood as laid down by the Compromise of 1867. Bartók responded with a passionate outburst against Habsburg rule. When he wrote to István Thomán in August he used writing paper headed with the Hungarian coat of arms and the first line of the Hungarian national anthem. On a letter dated September 23, he himself sketched the Hungarian coat of arms and encircled it with the words 'Down with the Habsburgs!' In this letter he mentions a concert planned to take place in Pozsony:

> If you happen to meet Rigele, please tell him on no account to invite the Archduke's family to my recital. I do not want to play to such a corrupt, predatory, murderous lot!

In the preceding letter dated September 8, he appeals to his family to use the Hungarian language and to advocate its use generally; in the same letter he formulates his aim in life conceived as a result of his experiences during the previous months:

> Everyone, on reaching maturity, has to set himself a goal and must direct all his work and actions towards this. For my own part, all my life, in every sphere, always and in every way, I shall have one objective: the good of Hungary and the Hungarian nation. I think I have already given some proof of this intention in the minor ways which have so far been possible to me.

2 A season in Berlin. Concerts abroad

The 'minor ways' in which he proved his intention included his participation in various musical events during his last year at the Academy and at the beginning of his career as a professional musician. The biographical data listed by János Demény include nine public appearances, some of which we have already mentioned, during the school year of 1902–3. Included among them is a solo recital at Nagyszentmiklós on April 13. He played some of his own compositions, including *Phantasy No. 1* and *Study for the Left Hand*—two of the *Four Piano Pieces* already completed. He ended the programme with Liszt's *Spanish Rhapsody*, a piece he also performed at his last examination concert at the Academy of Music on May 26. His rendering of this piece was mentioned in the press as the highlight of the evening and the young pianist was again compared with Dohnányi.

His professors found it unnecessary for him to take any formal examinations. His name may be seen among the list of performers at a second charity concert given on June 8 and organized by the reading circle of the Academy of Music. He played two of his piano pieces and the third movement of his *Sonata for Violin* then in preparation, the latter with one of his fellow-students, Sándor Kőszegi. Again the press was enthusiastic, and Bartók was especially commended by Pongrác Kacsóh, a pioneer of musical education in Hungary, and the author of a number of popular musical dramas that were national in character. In *Zenevilág*, July 2, Kacsóh devoted the leading article to an account of Bartók's career to date and also expressed his admiration for Bartók as a composer. It was after this concert that Bartók took leave of his professors and left the Academy of Music.

After his holiday in Passail and the period of study at Gmunden, Bartók spent the season of 1903–4 in Berlin. Thomán had paved the way for this experience by giving Bartók an introduction to Leopold Godowsky, the noted pianist who looked after the young man while he was in Berlin. On December 14, Bartók gave a solo recital as a result of which he became acquainted with Busoni.

During the course of the year Bartók travelled abroad on a number of occasions to give recitals. On November 4, at a concert given by the Vienna Konzertverein, he played Beethoven's Piano Concerto in E-flat Major. On November 25, he appeared in Budapest together with Ferenc Vecsey, the child prodigy, who was already on the path to world fame. On January 22, 1904, Bartók repeated in Pozsony the programme of his recital in Berlin and on January 25, he again played in Budapest at a concert held by the Hubay–Popper string quartet when he introduced his *Sonata for Violin* with Hubay as soloist. He played the same sonata in Vienna with Rudolf Fitzner on February 3, and on February 7 he again performed at a chamber-music concert in Budapest.

The most notable event of this active year was the composition and first performance at home and abroad of the *Kossuth Symphony*. This large symphonic work had been finished towards the end of his time at the Academy, during the spring and summer of 1903. At the end of the school year he had played it for Koessler who expressed approval and encouraged Bartók to orchestrate it.

The fate of this work was decided when Richter visited Pozsony at the end of June. Bartók played the *Kossuth* for him and Richter praised it highly, adding that it was by no means out of the question that he would perform it in Manchester the following year (Richter at that time played a leading role in the musical life of Britain). Bartók worked feverishly through the summer orchestrating the piece and in August he was able to tell Thomán that the date of the Manchester performance of the *Kossuth Symphony* was fixed for February 18, 1904. On that occasion, he wrote to Thomán, he would also be required to play Liszt's *Spanish Rhapsody* (with Busoni's orchestral accompaniment) and Volkmann's *Handel-variations*.

The British performance of the *Kossuth Symphony* was, however, preceded by the première in Budapest on January 13, 1904, with István Kerner conducting the orchestra of the Philharmonic Society.

Two sources of inspiration, Strauss's programmatic symphonic poems and Bartók's own patriotism, are clearly discernible in the conception of the *Kossuth*. Bartók himself worked out the programmatic content, basing it on events in the life of Lajos Kossuth. 'The work comprises 10 closely related parts, with an explanatory inscription at the head of each,' he wrote in the introductory notes. In developing the train of thought and musical structure Bartók certainly took as his model Strauss's symphonic poems. The characterization of the protagonist at the beginning and the way in which he is presented in various situations reminds us of the method used in the *Zarathustra* and the *Heldenleben*. However, there is one radical difference in that the basic idea of Bartók's work is not developed through the individual fate of the central character but through the tragic history of the nation as a whole; this is the essential theme which becomes more and more dominant with each movement. The seventh section relates the story of the gathering of the Hungarians and here Bartók puts into the mouth of Kossuth lines from János Arany's Hungarian epic, *Toldi*, 'Come, come, noble Hungarian soldiers, noble champions of Hungary'. In the eighth section, the enemy forces are lined up to the sound of a parody of the 'Gott erhalte', and in the ninth and tenth sections, the funeral march with the words 'all is lost' and 'all is still', is reminiscent of Mihály Vörösmarty's lines in his ode, 'A Summons',

'Around the graves where we shall lie
A weeping world will come.'

We have already mentioned Bartók's use of the scherzo; the closing funeral march is another characteristic feature of Bartók's work, an artistic form he was to employ again and again in his music throughout his life. This was the only movement which, in its most polished and definitive version, appeared in print.

Thus, in the construction of the work, in the method of realizing the musical content and in the orchestration, there are traces of the influence of Richard Strauss. But the content derives from Bartók's own personal experience and has less in common with Strauss than with the later works of Liszt such as his *Csárdás Macabre, Csárdás Obstine* and the *Hungarian Historical Portraits*. The mournful tone and dramatic contradictions of the last sections, even the intonation, reveal an unconscious debt to Liszt.

Some of the non-Hungarian members of the orchestra refused to play the *Kossuth Symphony* because of the parody of the 'Gott erhalte', but the press notices were without exception patriotically enthusiastic. In Dohnányi's earlier Symphony in D Minor the public had already begun to look for a new Hungarian symphonic art. In the *Kossuth Symphony* they thought they had at last discovered it and the general feeling of satisfaction was reflected in the reviews. Pongrác Kacsóh wrote in the *Zenevilág*, 'When the name of Bartók appears once again on our front page we are stirred to the depth of our souls by a pleasant blend of lofty sentiments—satisfaction, pride and patriotism.' In the columns of the *Budapesti Hirlap*, Aurél Kern hailed the emergence of a 'new musical genius'. Géza Molnár, famous aesthete and critic, also known by the pseudonym Mr. Emgé, headed his article in *Nyugat* 'Musica Militans', while in the *Ország Világ*, Zsigmond Falk announced a 'new Hungarian musical genius'.

But even in the first sentences of Aurél Kern's review there is a sharp hint of the divergent origins of nationalist feeling which we have already mentioned. 'Something very strange has happened,' he wrote. 'A spirit of uncompromising Hungarian chauvinism has pitched its tent on the Philharmonic stage.' Aurél Kern was here voicing a reactionary and conservative nationalism. Even as early as the end of 1902 Bartók had already mentioned that Aurél Kern would have preferred to close down the Academy of Music rather than allow it to spread 'poison and fatal disease' through the organs of musical life in Hungary.

Behind the slogans of nationalism there were two contradictory trends and attitudes in Hungarian political life which divided the nation. True, the contradictions inherent in the development of Hungarian capitalism and its need to be self-sufficient and independent, made the progressive members of the intelligentsia realize the inevitability of a bourgeois democratic revolution. It is also a fact that this small group of clear-sighted intellectuals recognized that the cause of their nation and their people, of land reform and the agrarian proletariat, of Hungarian national independence and the liberation of national minorities, were inseparable parts of the one struggle; and for the cultural content of their political programme they looked, not to Vienna or Berlin, but to Paris. One year in Paris had taught Ady not to regard bourgeois democracy as the *non plus ultra* of social progress. But opposed to the intellectuals there was a group of reactionary chauvinists, heirs of the right-wing gentry of 1848, who interpreted independence in their own feudal manner. And at that time, these reactionary chauvinists were in the majority.

In musical circles there was none of the progressive thought found amongst the more advanced writers and journalists. In his biography of Bartók, Bence Szabolcsi gives a very clear summary of the lessons to be learnt from the history of the period outlined in his works on nineteenth-century romantic music in Hungary and those on the last years of Liszt. At that time, the urban middle classes almost without exception favoured German music, that is to say, the music of Brahms and Wagner; meantime the nationalist trend, deprived of its roots and cut off from the main stream of European development, sank into provincialism. 'Town and country became separated and even opposed to each other. The great musical institutions in Budapest, the Opera, the Philharmonic Society and the Academy of Music, were disseminating almost exclusively Viennese and German musical culture, while Hungarian provincial towns were drowned in the flood of gypsy music, songs of literary sentimentality and *csárdás* music. "European culture" and "national tradition" were separated from each other in an unhealthy fashion and even appeared at times to be antagonistic ... Cosmopolitanism without roots on the one hand, dilettantism, pseudo-culture and sheer backwardness on the other —this was the situation in Hungary as far as music was concerned around 1900, the period marked by the emergence of Béla Bartók and Zoltán Kodály,' wrote Szabolcsi.

The wave of nationalist feeling was responsible at one and the same time for the revival of a rustic provincialism in music and a chauvinistic, narrow and false patriotism in politics. At the time of the Compromise and throughout the following years the Budapest press was critical of Ferenc Erkel for his failure to emulate Wagner; now in its nationalistic fervour the same press sought to find in the Wagnerite Mihalovich, director of the Academy of Music, another Erkel, now considered to have been misunderstood in the past, or, even worse, they hoped to hear in his work the very tone of the popular nationalist songs. Since the music critics could scarcely expect the successors of the Liszt–Erkel–Mosonyi generation to bring about a sudden revival of national music, they were all the more ready to find in Bartók's *Kossuth Symphony* a new musical expression of patriotism which was to their own taste. Nor did Bartók's music of that period refute this fallacy for he had not yet begun to move resolutely and unambiguously in the direction taken by Ady and his associates. With no knowledge of the career that lay ahead of Bartók, a contemporary would have required an exceptionally gifted and unbiassed ear to discern in the *Kossuth Symphony* the composers' individual brand of patriotism which was so different from their own. Contemporary critics did not recognize that the ideals of 1848 were being revived in the truly radical spirit of Kossuth and they were unable to realize that this symphonic formulation had to achieve in the spirit of Liszt a fusion of national and European developments in music far transcending the reach of his Hungarian imitators. They could not recognize the *Kossuth Symphony* for what it really was and though they acclaimed it in their own fashion, they did so for the wrong reasons. Within the next few years they were to feel bitterly disappointed by the young composer in national costume.

The reviews of the first performance in Manchester on February 18 were decidedly more objective and restrained than the extravagantly patriotic notices that had appeared in Budapest. Bartók, as usual, lost no time in writing to Thomán about the concert. On a postcard dated February 19 he wrote:

> I had quite a success last night, mainly as a pianist. They did not like *Kossuth* so much, although they received it favourably enough.

Soon after this experience Bartók was again searching for new ways of expressing through music human problems, while at the same time solving technical difficulties. Struggling with problems of both form and content he advanced far beyond his achievements in the *Kossuth Symphony*.

This period of varied experience as an active concert pianist was followed by long months of absorption in work. Even in March, when he was staying in Berlin after the concerts in England, he was writing to Lajos Dietl of his 'complete retirement, studying all five branches of Art,' and he mentioned that he was particularly engrossed in composition. Probably it was at this time that he wrote the *Piano Quintet* which was given its first performance by the Prill Quintet on November 21 of that year.

In the same letter he told Dietl that after leaving Berlin he planned to spend two days in Pozsony and then go to the Plains for a summer holiday 'where I may live in even greater retirement than I do here . . .' The Plain in question was that of Gerlicepuszta and we learn from the letters that it was in those regions, in the village of Ratkó in Gömör County, that Bartók stayed from March onwards for a period of more than six months. He left for home only one week before he was due to give a recital in Pozsony on November 10.

His retreat at Gerlicepuszta was interrupted only once for any considerable period of time. This was during the month of August when a Wagner scholarship enabled him to make a pilgrimage to Bayreuth, the Mecca of all Wagnerites. In a letter dated August 21, and written from Regensburg during the journey to Bayreuth, Bartók mentions for the first time the name of Kálmán Harsányi who was at that time about thirty years old. It is clear that Bartók was already familiar with the poet's work, though he may not previously have met him, for he had composed two different settings for the poem 'Evening' sometime during the spring of 1903 when he was working on the *Kossuth Symphony* (one version was for voice with piano accompaniment and the other was for male chorus); and Bartók wrote the first line of the poem, 'All is lost, all is still', above the final section of the symphony.

Harsányi's poems written at that time show close spiritual kinship with Bartók's work of that period. The history of their native land was for both of them a saga of heroism and romance. This similarity of outlook explains why, when they met at Gerlicepuszta in 1904, they very soon became friends, though only for a brief period. It is to this friendship that we owe the existence of a letter written from Regensburg in which the young composer makes an interesting confession about his first reaction to Wagner's *Parsifal*. He found the work disappointing: he told Harsányi that he did not find it as impressive as *Tristan* and that he found the constant praying on the stage particularly disturbing.

On September 18, in yet another letter from Gerlicepuszta, this time to István Thomán, he mentions the people he was meeting at Bayreuth, and in particular a further meeting with Richter who was a regular guest conductor at the festival performances. Now Bartók was able to show a new work, a *Scherzo*, to the man who had sponsored the *Kossuth Symphony*. One can assume, from the data available, that this work was the *Scherzo* for piano and orchestra, possibly a version of the *Burlesque* enumerated as op. 2 in the list compiled by Denijs Dille (1939). The work was to have been performed on March 15 at a concert of the Budapest Philharmonic Society but the Scherzo movement of the 1902 symphony was performed instead. The manuscript score has only recently been found amongst Bartók's papers.

The opus number indicates that the *Scherzo-Burlesque* is a later work than *Rhapsody* which is listed as op. 1 and which was first composed for piano and later transcribed for piano and orchestra. The *Rhapsody* merits attention insofar as it is the only work from that period which the composer continued to include in his recitals even as late as 1936.

It was first intended as a piece for the piano but even this first form is known in two versions, one consisting of a slow 'adagio mesto' while the other has an additional fast dance rhapsody in *csárdás* rhythm and a passage in a major key, somewhat in the manner of a hymn, recalling a few bars of the slow movement. On the title-page of the longer version is written 'Gerlicepuszta–Pozsony, October–December 1904'. But it is possible that this is where both versions were composed, for both are dedicated to 'Emma Gruber, November 1904'.

The original composition for piano was later published as the 'first version' of *Rhapsody*. This first version, in a more complete form, would appear to have been the work which Bartók later adapted for orchestra and entered in the Rubinstein competition in Paris in the summer of 1905. He refers to it in his letters as 'Concertstück'. Still later he added an introduction of thirty-nine bars, thus completing the 'second version' which he played for the first time in 1909.

The history of the *Rhapsody* and its successive rearrangements illustrate in the clearest possible way the composer's working methods during the creative period between 1902 and 1905, especially if we consider the progress of this work together with Bartók's development as a concert pianist. The period of solitary retreat at Gerlicepuszta ended with Bartók's solo recital at Pozsony. The programme was dominated by the works of Liszt, the first item being the *Weinen-Klagen Variations* and the sixth the *Funérailles*. A programme note beside the latter title reads 'On the death of Lajos Batthyány' (president of the Hungarian revolutionary government of 1848, who was executed in 1849). The eighth and final item on the programme was the *Mephisto Waltz*. In a study specially written for the concert by János Batka, a Pozsony archivist who was devoted to music, we find the remark, 'Bartók seems to have dedicated himself to the task of becoming a virtuoso performer of Liszt's piano pieces.' The *Weinen-Klagen Variations* and the *Funérailles* were included in the programme of Bartók's solo recital given in Vienna on February 18, 1905, and the composer played the *Funérailles* again on March 15 at a Philharmonic Society concert in Budapest.

The sensitive ear of the music critic of the *Daily Dispatch* did not deceive him when, after hearing the Manchester première of the *Kossuth Symphony*, he noted a connection between Liszt and the heroic and funeral themes. As a composer Bartók was fully aware of the impossibility of evading the problems raised by Liszt. As a responsible Hungarian artist of the twentieth century it was inevitable that any attempt to penetrate to the reality of the form and content of a national music should lead him direct to Liszt. But this confrontation with Liszt was also a logical stage in the development of European music: it was an essential step for Bartók if he was to advance further along the path chosen by Wagner and Richard Strauss and pursue it to its end.

The very title, *Rhapsody*, indicated that in pairing slow and fast movements the composer had deliberately chosen Liszt as his master. The later additions to and transcriptions of this work trace the stages of Bartók's development to maturity as the dramaturge of his own compositions. The increasing frequency with which he chose Liszt's works for inclusion in his recital programmes leaves us in no doubt of the close connection between his problems as a concert pianist and as a composer.

The *Suite No. 1*, composed in Vienna in the spring of 1905, brought to an end this particular phase of the composer's activity. It followed the *Scherzo* to become op. 3. One part only was given a first performance on November 29 of that year by the Vienna Philharmonic Orchestra conducted by Ferdinand Loewe. The first performance in Hungary was given at the inauguration of the new building for the Academy of Music on May 15, 1907. This too was only a partial performance of the work; the first, second and fifth movements were performed. The first complete performance was given by the Academy Orchestra conducted by Jenő Hubay on March 1, 1909. Even at the time, Bartók's contemporaries were impressed by the freedom and gaiety of the work, its brimming self-confidence and expert orchestration. Béla Reinitz, the composer, who set to music the poems of Endre Ady and who was in charge of music policy in the 1919 Hungarian Republic of Councils, recalled in 1917 that when he first heard the work it aroused in him feelings of 'shock and horror'. Writing in the *Népszava* after the premiere of *The Wooden Prince* he confessed to the readers that 'at that time I gained the impression that I was listening to the work of a young dare-devil, emotionally immature and revelling in a narcissistic enjoyment of his own cleverness as a musician...' There is no doubt that Bartók, who had already acquired a fund of knowledge about folk-like art-songs, as well as having absorbed the musical heritage of the nineteenth century, including the

54

orchestration techniques of Strauss, was at that time supremely confident of his ability to solve any technical problem with which he might be confronted. But the problems contained within the works following the *Scherzo* he had put aside—in the *Kossuth Symphony*, in the transcriptions of the *Rhapsody* and the pieces which followed—could not be solved on this level; they were to remain continually in Bartók's mind, and in his later periods he sought always for a deeper solution.

These years of creative effort from 1902 to 1905 had a more lasting effect on Bartók's development than he himself could have imagined; nor has the importance of these years been fully appreciated by students of Bartók. Yet what happened during these years was nothing less than that the most important problems of form and content in nineteenth-century music became part of his own personal experience. With sure insight of genius he found the point of convergence between these problems and those peculiar to Hungarian music in Liszt's works.

During the process of reformulating these problems Bartók summarized the contradictions inherent in his own vision of the world, devising for this purpose three main structural forms through which he could deal with the most important problems of content and form in nineteenth-century music and which at the same time proved to be significant and enduring formulations which he was able to use for many years, and even, in some instances, throughout his life.

The first composition based essentially on the structural principle of pairing fast and slow movements was the *Rhapsody*. Here Bartók was directly following Liszt from whom he took over the work of adapting to musical expression the old forms in which could be felt the particular tone of patriotism and nationalism associated with the 1848 War of Independence. The inspiration he received is evident throughout the following decades in his later rhapsodies and in the first version of *Contrasts*. In his later works consisting of several movements, it was indeed the decisive driving force in the dynamic quality of their form.

The precursors of the *Kossuth Symphony* are to be found in the stage and symphonic music of the nineteenth century which mourns the defeat of the great revolutions and pays its tribute in tragic finales and funeral marches to the heroic past. Obvious examples of this kind of music are Wagner's *Tetralogie*, Siegfried's funeral march in the *Götterdämmerung* and Brahms's Symphony No. 4. Works which may be said to have grown out of the *Kossuth Symphony* signify a period of Bartók's own compositions dating from *Bluebeard's Castle* to *The Miraculous Mandarin*, including the intermediary works, *Four Orchestral Pieces*, the *Suite* for piano and the *String Quartet No. 2*.

The most firmly developed and finished use of the slow–fast basic unit is to be found in *Suite No. 1* with its five-part symmetrical arrangement of contrasting movements and a Scherzo between the two slow central movements. Earlier examples of this structure which Bartók could have used as models may be found in, to mention only the most important sources, Beethoven's Symphony No. 6 and the late string quartets, and in the *Symphonie Fantastique* by Berlioz. In *Suite No. 1* Bartók further developed the internal thematic kinship which he had merely indicated in the *Kossuth Symphony*, thus intensifying the solidity of this form. This principle too may be said to have evolved as a result of the creative work of Berlioz and Liszt. Through similar arrangements and variations of the five-part symmetrical form with a central Scherzo placed between two slow movements, Bartók was to find a means of expressing and synthesizing, in many different ways, his own vision of the world; examples of his use of this form may be readily found in the œuvre.

The *Kossuth Symphony* and the *Suite No. 1* exemplify for the first time that outward and inward kinship between two great works to which Kodály pointed after the performance of *Bluebeard's Castle* and *The Wooden Prince* in one programme.

CHAPTER IV

EXPERIENCE OF FOLK MUSIC. 1905–1907

1 LISZT'S TWOFOLD EXAMPLE: SEARCH FOR A NEW AND HUNGARIAN MUSICAL STYLE

Bartók's years at the Academy did not constitute one distinct phase of his creative development. He was halfway through his academic studies when, inspired by the music of Strauss, he entered upon a period of creative activity which did not cease until two years after he had left the Academy. It was during this period that he produced his first mature works. There followed two years of silence, an interval of inactivity similar to that which followed the years in Pozsony. Bartók abandoned the *Suite No. 2* which he had begun in Vienna in 1905, and did not resume work on it until 1907 when he wrote the fourth movement.

This interval of inactivity was again a period during which the composer arrived at a new vision of the world and a new means of expressing that vision, but this time there was a more profound transformation of his whole outlook. During the earlier period of creative inactivity the composer's changing attitude to life and the direction of his interests indicated a slowly developing philosophy: at the close of the second period he had arrived at a complete and mature evaluation of his beliefs. Events in Europe, of which Hungary was a part, compelled every responsible artist at that time to take up a definite position in regard to world movements. And in the final analysis it was the crystallization of Bartók's beliefs that enabled him to work out those artistic forms which he himself could later recognize and acknowledge as his own unique contribution to music.

In creative art, the content, however profound, can only grow and finally emerge during the technical process of composition, through the practical application of the means of expression. Bartók's human and moral development during his years at the Academy now confronted him with a twofold demand: his music must be Hungarian in character, and it must be new in tone. To achieve this double aim, he could only make use of the musical heritage which was available at the time. All that was Hungarian in this heritage consisted of nineteenth-century romantic music, the pseudo-folk songs and *verbunkos* music, while the modern means of expression consisted of the music of Strauss and the developments of nineteenth-century German music. He could not, however, avoid the crisis resulting from the contradictory and incongruous nature of two elements. Bartók himself could not escape the experience of Liszt, and it soon became apparent that the shallow sentimental lyricism of the popular folk art-songs was even more unsuitable as a medium through which to express the spirit of the age than it had been in Liszt's time, twenty or thirty years earlier.

The third of the four songs from texts by Lajos Pósa, 'There is no such sorrow', composed in 1902, is already burdened with a more significant content than that of the average example of this genre at the time. This inherent contradiction becomes even more apparent in the dense, taut tone of the *Phantasies*, the *Kossuth Symphony* and the *Rhapsody*, while the brilliant *Suite No. 1* proved that works based on larger structural elements could be neither built up nor maintained by means of musical material that was *csárdás*-like in character. With all the youthful vigour of this first outburst of creative energy the composer constantly enriched the elements of his music with melodic, metric asymmetries, endeavouring in this way to reinforce its inherent weakness and prevent its collapse beneath the too ponderous structure.

When Liszt encountered similar contradictions in the course of his work he was compelled to extract the main features of the musical idiom common to the various social strata of his age, that is to say the popular music that was everywhere in evidence, though in an increasingly weakened version, and to inject into it a concentrated national music worthy of his own conceptions. At the same time he began to take an interest in the historical body of modal music and in the legacy of East-European folk music with words in Russian dialect. In different historical circumstances Bartók was similarly compelled towards the oldest and deepest levels of the folk music of his own country.

Bartók's quest for folk music was both difficult and prolonged. He first began to look for a Hungarian musical idiom when he was composing the *Kossuth Symphony* at a time when he still did not question the

58

generally accepted idea that folk-art songs were in fact a form of genuine folk music. In a letter dated April 1, 1903, he wrote to his younger sister, Böske, asking her 'as an eminent student of folk-song: what are the words of these 2 folk tunes . . .' and he wrote out for her the notes of the first lines of two well-known and popular folk-art songs, one of them being 'Az egri ménes mind sárga'. And we know from Kodály that 'several attempts at arrangements are extant in manuscript, experimenting primarily with the canon possibilities of the melody'. These attempts are reminiscent of the 'Hungarian fugue' written by Sándor Bertha, a Hungarian composer who earlier had emigrated to Paris.

Bartók's own musical taste, however, soon led him to suspect that there was a difference between the popular folk-art songs and genuine folk music.

> I recognized further that the Hungarian tunes mistakenly known as folk-songs are in reality more or less trivial popular folk-art songs and afford little of interest,

he concluded in his autobiography. Kodály has recorded that 'it was part of a tune sung by Lidi Dósa, a Székely woman who worked for him,' that made Bartók aware of the peculiar quality of Székely music.' One of Lidi Dósa's songs, 'From the withered branch no rose blooms', has become widely known as the seventh piece in a collection of folk-songs published in 1906. For some time to come, however, popular folk-art songs and genuine folk-songs were still not clearly differentiated in Bartók's mind. For the time being, when deciding on the quality and origin of a work he relied on his own musical instinct rather than the infallible knowledge and judgement which he acquired later. 'He heard the same woman singing a fragmentary melody known throughout the country,' continued Kodály. This he published as *A Székely Folk-Song* (*Magyar Lant*, 1905). This song appears as No. 313 in Bartók's comprehensive book *The Hungarian Folk-Song*. He names Kibéd in Maros-Torda County as the place of origin because Lidi Dósa was born there. To her also may be traced the song enumerated as 234/a (1904). In an earlier edition of the 1906 collection of folk-songs, however, Bartók also included a melody by Szentirmay beginning with the words, 'Ucca, ucca . . .' In the stubbornly repeated minor thirds which occur in so many of Bartók's later works Kodály thinks he can recognize the influence of this particular Szentirmay melody.

Hearing the melodies sung by Lidi Dósa, it became clear to Bartók that in the recognition of genuine folk music he could find no adequate guidance from his family, however musically gifted, nor from the musically initiated members of the urban bourgeoisie with whom he was acquainted. He must explore further afield. The first hint of his project for collecting folk-songs occurs in a letter written to his younger sister and dated December 26, 1904:

> I have a new plan now, to collect the finest examples of Hungarian folk-songs, and to raise them to the level of works of art with the best possible piano accompaniment. Such a collection would serve the purpose of acquainting the outside world with Hungarian folk music. Our own good Hungarians of course find this beneath them. They abhor anything serious. They are much more satisfied with the usual gypsy slop that makes any cultured foreigner take to his heels . . .

At first sight these words seem merely a resuscitation of Liszt's romantic dreams. But towards the end of the quotation our attention is caught by a new and significant theme, a concern for the prestige of our music in the eyes of the world as realized by a young and not unobservant artist who had travelled abroad. It was in similar fashion that Ady, in his Paris sketches, had singled out, as if through the eyes of a West European, the reverse side of those characteristics of our society cherished not only in the provinces but by the nation as a whole. An immediate consequence of Bartók's projected plan was the first attempt to differentiate between 'the finest Hungarian folk-songs' and the degenerate music of the cafés, 'the usual gypsy slop'; inherent in all this was Bartók's own criticism of society.

In this scheme we can trace one of the most important peculiarities of Bartók's methods. Here we see illustrated the twofold dialectical principle of his work of regenerating the world: the inseparable unity between a critical destruction of the past and the construction of a new world outlook and system of values. At a time when there was a universal desire to establish new spiritual values in the world, Bartók, in common with all the greatest and most truly creative of the intellectuals, was motivated by clearly defined ideals: unlike those numerous anarchists who merely wished to criticize the past and by so doing destroy it, he had the ardent hope of gradually building a new world which would be primarily based on elements of the old but newly evaluated and built into a new system. By recognizing the decay of the old, Bartók was urged towards the new. And new ideals accelerated the destruction of the old.

2 PARIS EXPERIENCES. FAILURE AT THE MUSICAL COMPETITION. KODÁLY'S STIMULUS, THE FIRST FOLK-MUSIC COLLECTING TOURS

Bartók was so powerfully influenced by this new understanding that in 1905 he took the decisive step in folk-music research which Liszt had not been able to make in the course of his own lifetime. The strength of Bartók's determination is made clear in a letter to Thomán written on April 21, 1905, when he was working on the *Suite No. 1,* in which he enquired about the fate of his application 'with regard to folk-song collecting.' The musicologist, Dezső Legány, has explained that this is a reference to Bartók's appeal for state aid for his plan to collect folk-songs in the Székely region. This was forwarded to the Ministry on April 30, 1905, by Ödön Mihalovich, together with a long and very warm letter. We know from Kodály that Bartók was granted this aid. Although it was not until 1907 that Bartók spent some time collecting folk-songs in the Székely region, it is certain that he left Vienna for a period of rest in Sziladpuszta, near Vésztő, just as he had retreated from Berlin to Gerlicepuszta the previous summer. Emil Oláh Tóth, the husband of Bartók's younger sister, Elza, was working there as steward on the Wenckheim estate. Bartók probably stayed with him from early or mid-June until he had to leave for the international Rubinstein competition to be held in Paris at the beginning of August. Bartók's mother stayed behind in Sziladpuszta with her daughter and son-in-law.

Much of this peaceful country vacation was taken up with preparation for the competition, but Bartók also noted down some folk-songs. It is true that he did not do this with any regularity, and, according to Kodály, he confined his activity to songs known by the household servants. But this experience in Sziladpuszta and Kertmegpuszta contributed to his later interest in folk music. In a letter dated August 15, he wrote enthusiastically to Irmy Jurkovics, a childhood acquaintance in Nagyszent-miklós, about the wealth and variety of Hungarian folk music, and he enclosed notes of folk-songs which, unfortunately for us, have since disappeared.

It was in that year that the international Rubinstein competition was held in Paris and Bartók entered both as a composer and as a pianist. He submitted two of his own works, a variation of the *Rhapsody No. 1* with orchestral accompaniment and the *Piano Quintet*. Only one prize was awarded in the piano class and this was given to Wilhelm Backhaus.

> I don't say that I admit that Backhaus can play better than I do,

opines Bartók in a letter home on August 15,

> but he is at least a worthy opponent and it's a matter of taste whose performance you prefer.

And earlier he had written to his mother,

> I'm not in the least surprised that I didn't win a prize as a pianist, and there's no need to feel disappointed on that score. But the way in which the prizes for composers were distributed—or rather not distributed—that was quite outrageous.

From the very beginning it was a depressing experience.

> And how they bated me! I was within an ace of being compelled to withdraw. They began by saying that the parts of the Concertstück were faulty, the piece was too difficult and could not be played because time was too short for rehearsals. I corrected the parts (there were 10 to 15 mistakes all told), and, after much wangling, it was finally played rather well, after all.

The *Piano Quintet* was not performed, and Bartók played the *Sonata for Violin* instead with Lev Zeitlin, a pupil of Leopold Auer, as violinist. Zeitlin could be numbered among those who understood Bartók's art. In later references to the violinist, it is always as an enthusiastic advocate of new music. Debussy met him during a concert tour of Russia and in a letter to his wife, he referred to Zeitlin as an unwavering disciple. In the mid-twenties, he was the leader of an excellent ensemble which played without a conductor, the Moscow Persimfans, which was in existence from 1922 to 1932.

Bartók had his supporters among the audience and among the musicians but the jury remained totally uncomprehending. A further indication of the attitude of the jury is the fact that they passed over Bartók in favour of the Italian composer, Attilio Brugnoli, whose works Bartók had described as 'absolutely worthless conglomerations'; yet for Brugnoli the jury recommended a certificate of honour and placed him above Bartók.

> I wouldn't say a word if a composer of any worth at all had beaten me for the prize. But the fact that those dunderheads declared my works unworthy of the prize shows how extraordinarily stupid they were,

wrote Bartók. János Demény has quoted from contemporary accounts, confirmed by the unofficial remarks of Lajos Dietl, a member of the jury, indicating that the judges had not acted in an entirely irreproachable manner, a fact which only increased Bartók's wrath. It appeared that the jury had decided in advance that they would make no awards because the interest from the foundation's capital funds was not sufficient to cover the prize money.

> If that is so,

fumed Bartók in his letter home,

> it was a monstrous piece of impudence and deception to allow the composer competitors to flock to the place on a wild-goose chase.
> Well, so much for that,

he concluded philosophically. But in fact his failure in Paris made a deeper and more lasting impression than even he himself would have thought possible at the time. This, at any rate, is what one is led to believe when one reads the verses he wrote in Paris about the members of the jury. These events in Paris probably induced him to rearrange the *Rhapsody* and may account for the fact that he continued throughout his life to include this work in his concert programmes as if to prove over and over again that it had been unjustly rejected. (It is interesting to note that the more complete piano version of the *Rhapsody* also met with cool reception when it was first performed in Pozsony on November 4, 1906.) But his failure in Paris also led to the crisis in his development as a composer: in the struggle between obsolete tradition and new ideals, this failure acted as a spur, urging him on towards the folk music which was to provide him with a new musical model.

In his first experience of peasant folk music he gained an intimation of the scope and variety of the material and realized that to make it known in all its richness, systematic scientific research was necessary. In his initial explorations he was guided only by his own musical instincts, but later on, the scientific pioneering work of Zoltán Kodály gave him a clearer sense of direction. It was Kodály who, by personal example, advice, and through his writing, launched Bartók into his life-work—the systematic, scientific collection of folk music.

> It was my great good fortune to meet Zoltán Kodály who was outstanding as a musician and as a teacher. He had a sharpness of perception and a critical judgement which was of inestimable help to me: he guided and advised me in my study of every kind of music,

Bartók freely acknowledged in his autobiography. And Kodály has added to our information: 'He studied with great interest my first collection published in the *Ethnographia* in 1905 and my essay "The Stanza Structure of the Hungarian Folk-Song", published in 1906, and he put searching questions about the methods of collecting and the contacts made with the peasants. He made himself familiar with the phonograph.'

The phonograph had already become an indispensable piece of equipment for the collector of folk-songs. The first scientist in Hungary to collect folk-songs with the aid of a phonograph was the ethnographer Béla Vikár, who did so in 1896. With the help of this instrument it was naturally possible to check the notes, and to process and store the material. The introduction of the phonograph and its use in research brought the period of semi or completely amateur collecting to an end, and replaced the erroneous conclusions and misinterpretations made, with accurately recorded material that could be used for scientific purposes.

But these technical facilities merely created the conditions necessary for scientific processing. The main task could only be accomplished by highly qualified research workers gifted with perfect pitch and thoroughly familiar with scientific methods like Kodály and Bartók. Kodály acquired a scientific training in the philological faculty of the Eötvös College from which generations of Hungary's finest teachers had graduated, while Bartók, with incredible diligence, trained himself through practice in the field. Throughout his life he searched for the truth, endeavouring to reproduce what he heard as faithfully and accurately as possible. His notes, constantly rewritten, every detail checked and minutely analysed, provide us with a fascinating record of his self-discipline as a scientist.

If we look at the map of his collecting tour of 1906, it is noticeable in how many different places he found his material. It would seem that his first intention was to gain a comprehensive picture of folk music in widely differing regions of the country. Naturally enough, he found that this would be impossible without the aid and support of his friends and acquaintances, and a letter written by his mother tells us that he visited mainly those places where he could count upon help and guidance. Most of the collection he made during the summer of 1906 originates from Békés County, in the neighbourhood of Vésztő, Dobos and Gyula. It is probable that the hospitality of Mrs. Gyula Baranyai, a friend of his mother, made it possible for him to gather information and note down some folk-songs in the nearby districts of Csanád and Csongrád. In the 1906 collection, there are songs from Pest County, Tura and Tápiószele, but there occur also place names from Fejér County as well as songs collected in Vas County and even from places as far away as Hajdú-sámson. Of the places mentioned in the Balaton region and in the counties of Zala and Somogy, that which occurs most frequently is Felsőireg (now Ireg-Szemcse) in Tolna County. Here Bartók made a rich find. A large proportion of the songs in the 1906 collection originate from this village, to which he returned in 1907. Kibéd in Maros-Torda County, birthplace of Lidi Dósa, has been appended beside the name, Anna Dósa, with the date 1906; it would seem that she was visiting Lidi in Budapest when Bartók heard her singing and took down her song.

His long-cherished plan to collect material in Transylvania was not realized until the following year, 1907. 'Transylvania gave him no rest,' wrote Kodály. 'He applied for and was granted a scholarship (worth sixteen hundred crowns) to "study Székely folk music," and in the summer of 1907 he set out for Csík County.' Tirelessly diligent, he wandered for weeks, not only in Csík County but also in the counties of

Gyergyó and Kolozs until finally his boundless exertion was rewarded with treasures such as he himself could not have imagined. He described his work on a postcard, dated August 17, written to one of his pupils, Etelka Freund:

> I have made a rather strange discovery while collecting folk-songs. I have found examples of Székely tunes which I had previously believed to be lost.

His intuitive attraction to Transylvanian folk art was fully justified by what he discovered: he had penetrated to the most ancient body of Hungarian folk music, to the world of pentatonic melodies. In addition to his own account of his work we have that of Kodály who wrote: 'He returned with so many pentatonic melodies that after collating them with my own simultaneous findings in the north, we suddenly realized the fundamental significance of this scale which had hitherto been ignored.'

Two years of systematic collecting provided enough evidence to show that a wealth of material still awaited discovery. In the preface to his *The Hungarian Folk-Song* Bartók himself states that the collection in 1906–7 yielded from Felsőireg alone three hundred and seven melodies, quite apart from those found in other regions, of which Transylvania was the richest. From that time onwards, he spent some time every year in collecting folk-songs. Transylvania proved to be a continuous and inexhaustible treasure-house, but Bartók extended his tours to other parts of the country as well.

> I began my research work from a purely musical standpoint and exclusively in a Hungarian-speaking area, later I extended my work to the Slav and Romanian regions,

he wrote in his autobiography.

In fact his research work extended far beyond the frontiers of his own country and gradually evolved into a vast scientific project encompassing the whole of Eastern Europe, a field of study which Bartók cherished throughout his life.

3 CONTACT WITH EUROPEAN CITIES AND HUNGARIAN VILLAGES. THE FIRST PUBLICATION OF FOLK MUSIC

The question inevitably arises as to why the young composer repeatedly abandoned his life in the capital cities of Europe and set out for the most remote villages, walked through the mud and breathed in the dust of the country roads, sacrificing the comforts of home for the sole purpose of collecting folk-songs in their thousands. We can only wonder at the urgency with which he seemed to be driven to note down with such painstaking care the folk-songs recorded on the wax cylinders, and to persist in his work of checking and rearranging them until the very last days of his life.

For the work of collecting requires not only expert knowledge but also unbelievable perseverance and patience. Even in 1906, during the hot summer days of his fruitless searches near Vésztő, Bartók had already had a foretaste of the difficulties inherent in the work. And this depressing experience was repeated many times during his tour of Transylvania in 1907. There he had to endure the additional discomforts of social backwardness.

> In the streets of Bánffy-Hunyad the filth and litter is quite Moroccan without any of the amenities imported there for the sake of the Europeans,

he wrote his mother on July 5. Also, the peasants were suspicious of anyone wearing city clothes. Only by exercising a very special tact could the village folk be induced to sing. In a letter to Stefi Geyer dated August 16, Bartók described his ordeals, writing out, in dialogue form, a fruitless conversation between himself and a peasant woman. Almost he lost patience. 'I can't bear it any longer,' he burst out at the end of his letter from Kilyénfalva.

> Impossible! Endurance, perseverance, patience . . . to hell with you all . . . I am going home . . . I shan't wear high boots nor see preserves till Christmas.

Such disappointments, however, did not discourage him from going on with his task; on the contrary, his interest and pleasure in collecting folk music was thereby increased. His creative interest in music fostered in him such an overmastering urge to collect folk-songs, that, in Kodály's words, 'if his interest had been turned towards money, he would long since have become a billionnaire'. We know from his mother's biographical notes and from the memoirs of his older son that during his secondary-school years Bartók had collected plants and insects which he arranged with meticulous care, a hobby which he never abandoned. From 1905 onwards, this predilection for collecting and systematizing embraced also his discoveries in folk music and was also a basic feature of his scientific activities.

A passion for collecting is of course only a superficial explanation of his unflagging enthusiasm for an endless programme of scientific activity. It was only a single manifestation of his insatiable desire to know the universe. The objects he collected were not chosen aimlessly or as the result of a passing whim; his choice was governed by his own development towards an ordered vision of the world. Through his interest in folk-songs it is possible to trace the crystallization of his philosophy.

When Kodály questioned what it was that Bartók valued above all else in the villages he visited, he found a ready answer: 'First and foremost, he found a constant stimulus. He found an unknown world of Hungarians believed to be long extinct but which was actually flourishing. This was enough to revive his faith in the Hungarian people.'

> Shortly after I had won a scholarship in 1905, being then at the restless age of
> twenty-four, I was seized with Wanderlust,

Bartók told the correspondent of an American newspaper in 1928. The way in which he gratified this 'Wanderlust' and also his thirst for knowledge, was effectively canalized by his need to create a Hungarian music that was at one and the same time Magyar and modern European in character. This quest had been the guiding thread running through his life up to this point, influencing him in his early development as a man and as a composer. Now, with the same objective always in view, he began to travel further afield and to search out new sources of information. He was spurred on to explore the large European capital cities as well as the remotest corners of his native land. In 1904 he left Berlin for Gerlice-puszta, returning there after only a brief interval in Bayreuth. In 1905 he deserted Vienna for the villages near Vésztő, but when he had gone as far as Sziladpuszta he went straight from there to Paris. In the spring of

1906 he accompanied Ferenc Vecsey on a tour of Spain and Portugal, made an excursion to the African coast and came home by way of Milan and Venice. He devoted the entire summer to the folk music of his own country. In the autumn it was with reluctance that he began to practise for the recitals he was to give. He would have preferred to continue collecting folk music. He spent the summer of 1907 collecting music in Transylvania, while letters written during 1908 record the places he visited in Switzerland and France. Kodály has commented on his later travels: 'He spent one summer near the North Pole, another in Africa. Had he not lived between the two world wars, he would surely have encircled the globe.'

In an earlier letter written from Berlin there is an account of how he studied the great masterpieces of European culture. The letters from Paris in which he describes the art treasures of the city are particularly engaging. It caused him great pleasure to

> recognize, one after the other, the masterpieces with which we are so familiar in reproduction . . .

and he also commented that

> few paintings have ever had such a profound effect on me as Murillo's larger works in the Louvre.

He said that these works had the same effect on him as *Tristan, Zarathustra,* and other great musical masterpieces. He saw the Impressionist collection in the Luxembourg Museum and paid tribute to the great figures of French culture, visiting the memorials to them in the Parc Monceau. But towards the end of the same letter to Irmy Jurkovics, after mentioning Bach, Beethoven, Schubert, Wagner and Liszt, he went on to describe the variety and powerfully expressive quality of Hungarian folk music and the inborn talent of the peasants. The fact that he wrote of these subjects when he was so far from home is an indication of how constantly he made comparisons between Paris and Sziladpuszta; it is clear that when he compared the peasants' songs with the greatest examples of man's creative achievements they fared better in the comparison than 'the usual gypsy slop' which he had spoken of with such anger on a previous occasion.

Almost from the first moment, Bartók and Kodály recognized the immense importance for the development of Hungarian musical culture, of their joint discovery of the wide dissemination of the pentatonic scale. They realized its significance nationally in the field of music education and this in turn led to the idea of publishing a book to popularize folk music. It was typical of the cultural conditions in Hungary at the time that they should have to organize a prolonged campaign to recruit subscribers to subsidize the projected publication. Letters written by both Bartók and by his mother in 1906 are very illuminating on this subject. The book, entitled *Magyar Népdalok* (Hungarian Folk-Songs), for voice with piano accompaniment, was ready towards the end of that year and was published by Károly Rozsnyai. It contained twenty folk-songs, some of them having been collected by Vikár, others by Bartók and Kodály. Bartók wrote the piano accompaniment for the first ten songs and Kodály composed the other ten.

> For 3 days I have been conferring with Kodály about the proposed book of songs . . . We are writing a preface in which we have some harsh things to say about Hungarian audiences,

Bartók informed his mother in Pozsony on a postcard dated September 10, 1906.

This preface was written by Kodály and contains a declaration of his intention to make himself responsible for the popularization of folk music. His ambition, he wrote, was 'to make the general public acquainted with, and appreciative of, folk music'. To achieve this it was necessary to exercise great care in the choice of songs; to pick out only the best examples and to arrange them so that they would be acceptable to the general taste. The two men made every effort to select those songs which gave some idea of the richness of Hungarian folk music and yet were not so alien that they might repel the people whose ears were attuned to the popular folk-art songs. In composing the arrangements for these songs the guiding principle was not only the necessity to meet the public taste but also a desire to adapt the score to suit a new environment: 'Allowing for home circumstances, we put the melody in the accompaniment as well.'

The preface concludes with a final statement of the author's intention:

'May these manifestations, some of them very old indeed, of the spirit of our people, meet with even half the love they deserve. It will be long before they take their rightful place in our musical life, either in public or in private. The majority of people in Hungary today cannot respond to these songs because they do not feel strongly Hungarian, and they have neither the naiveté nor yet the education necessary for the appreciation of folk music. They think it strange that Hungarian folk-songs should be sung in a concert hall and ranked equally with the internationally known masterpieces of music; they even hesitate to put them in the same class as the folk-songs of other countries. But the time will come when Hungarian folk music will be readily accepted. When Hungarian families making music in their own homes will not be content to play either cheap foreign couplets or the products of our own music-mongers. One day there will be Hungarian singers. And the connoisseurs will not be alone in their recognition of the difference between Hungarian folk music and "Ritka búza" and "Ityóka-pityóka".'

Bartók's understanding of folk music and its musical possibilities was strengthened when he began to learn something of the art of Debussy.

> When, in that very same year (1907), Kodály urged me to study Debussy's works, I was very much surprised to find that pentatonic turns identical with those found in Hungarian folk music played a prominent part in his melodic construction,

he wrote in his autobiography.

The wheel had come full circle: in Debussy's music the melodic world preserved by the Hungarians through long ages now merged into a new era of European music, having no connection with the late products of German Romanticism. Later, in 1931, Bartók wrote of Hungarian folk music:

> In form, this peasant music is the most perfect and most varied. It has an amazing force of expression, and besides, it is completely devoid of any sentimentality or superfluous embellishment.

And in a pamphlet entitled *A magyar népdal* (The Hungarian Folk-Song) (1924) he also wrote that folk melodies

> in their own small-scale way, are just as perfect as any large-scale musical masterpiece.

71

Bartók's recognition of what was truly valuable in music made him all the more impatient with 'the insufferable exaggerations of post-Romanticism'; it also gave an added significance to his social outlook. First of all, he acquired an ever deepening knowledge not only of peasant music, but also of the peasants themselves and the conditions under which they lived. For music was an integral and inseparable part of every aspect of their daily lives and could not be understood without an intimate knowledge of how they lived. There are innumerable emphatic warnings on this subject in Bartók's later works on the science of folk music. His new-found knowledge of peasant conditions also sharpened his criticism of the Hungarian upper classes. He identified the trivial, pseudo-national popular folk-art songs with the upper classes who continued to favour them, just as he identified what had become for him so supremely significant, the true Hungarian folk music, with the people who had preserved it and made it a part of their lives. His earlier outbursts against the Habsburgs were now directed increasingly against the Hungarian upper classes. While exploring the values upheld by the peasants it became clear to Bartók that it was they who were the true guardians of the nation's treasures: it was from the peasants that the nation could receive its cultural heritage, and not from the middle class with its preference for the gypsy tunes of the cafés, nor yet from the ' "highly-esteemed" Hungarian audiences' that he and Kodály had so roundly condemned in the preface to *Hungarian Folk-Songs*.

Thus Bartók's social views emerged as a result of his study of folk music. The nationalism he had proclaimed during his years at the Academy now acquired real content through the recognition that the problems of the peasants were related to the problems of the nation as a whole. His musical studies led him logically to that state of social and political consciousness reached by Ady and his associates through their own daily struggles in the field of literature and politics. In the documented biography by János Demény the author compares the development of Bartók and Ady, and when he comes to discuss the historic events of 1905, he emphasizes particularly the Russian Revolution and the political atmosphere in Europe at that time. He also quotes Ady's famous article of December 29, 1905: 'Mighty Russia has been horribly shaken . . .' There is no way of knowing how closely Bartók followed the international class struggles of the period. The probability is, however, that he became aware of the events of the Russian Revolution and of the various national proletarian movements only indirectly, as a result of his cultural interests and by observing the attitudes and activities of the most progressive members of the intelligentsia.

We must concede that János Demény was quite right to link Bartók's sojourn among the peasants of Békés County with his experience of Paris. Nor was the connection merely one of chronology. Like Ady before him, Bartók acquired in Paris a breadth of vision that enabled him to recognize the sorry state of petit-bourgeois provincialism so prevalent in Hungary. He gave expression to his youthful feelings of rebellion by wearing a summer shirt without collar or cuffs when invited to dinner at the Vecseys', and later by ostentatiously wearing worn shoes; but his rebellious feelings developed into sincere revolutionary beliefs which he upheld in times of grave crisis and which were the basis of his alignment with the noblest causes of his times.

4 'Nietzsche's disciple'. Philosophical, creative and personal crisis. New ideals: folk music, the world of the peasants, and nature

As Bartók continued to extend and develop his philosophical outlook, he arrived quite logically at a point when he inevitably found himself in the most profound opposition to the most widely accepted personal and social beliefs. His commitment to clarify his relations with individuals and society, to come to terms with the natural and moral order, imposed an ever greater burden on him.

His experiences in Paris inevitably affected this progress towards maturity. His failure in the Rubinstein competition, his multifarious impressions of the metropolis, the bustling crowds in the streets, all combined to arouse oppressive memories of his loneliness as a child.

> As for myself, in spite of the fact that I have my meals in the company of 20 people—Cubans, North and South Americans, Dutchmen, Spaniards and Englishmen—and go on outings with Germans and Turks, yet I am a lonely man! I may be looked after by Dietl or Mandl in Vienna, and I may have friends in Budapest (Thomán, Mrs. Gruber), yet there are times when I suddenly

become aware of the fact that I am absolutely alone! And I prophesy, I have a foreknowledge, that this spiritual loneliness is to be my destiny. I look about me in search of the ideal companion, and yet I am fully aware that it is a vain quest. Even if I should ever succeed in finding someone, I am sure that I would soon be disappointed.

Although the state of peaceful resignation and the perennial quest are irreconcilable, nevertheless I have quite grown used to the thought that this cannot be otherwise, that this is how things have to be. For solace, I would recommend to anyone the attempt to achieve a state of spiritual indifference in which it is possible to view the affairs of the world with complete indifference and with the utmost tranquillity. Of course, it is difficult, extremely difficult—in fact, the most difficult thing there is—to attain this state, but success in this is the greatest victory man can ever hope to win: over other people, over himself, and over all things. Sometimes I feel that for a brief space of time I have risen to these heights. Then comes a mighty crash; then again more struggle, always striving to rise higher; and this (cycle) recurs again and again. The time may come when I shall be able to stay on the heights.

This moving excerpt is from a letter addressed to his mother and dated September 10, 1905. At the beginning of the letter he dwelt on the moral and social problems inherent in the relations between men and women; he favoured the view that the same rule of conduct should be applied to both sexes. The idea of 'rising to the heights' reveals that he had been studying Nietzsche and in a letter to Irmy Jurkovics dated August 15, he stated directly that he was a 'follower of Nietzsche'. It was Bartók's familiarity with Strauss's *Zarathustra* that led him to a study of the German philosopher whose extreme individualism was arousing interest not only among young Hungarian writers but amongst intellectuals throughout the world. From Nietzsche came the idea of living an individual life beyond the claims of society, but the bankruptcy of such a philosophy was recognized by the greatest minds of the age, including Bartók.

In the same letter from Paris dated August 15, Bartók goes on to express other thoughts which confirm his rejection of Nietzsche's ideas: thoughts which contrast strangely with those expressed in the excerpt quoted above, for they show Bartók as a materialist whose beliefs were founded in the principles of the natural sciences.

The inner tension resulting from Bartók's personal loneliness and his struggle to solve these problems of ideology reached a point of crisis two years later when he fell in love with Stefi Geyer, an emotional experience that was to have a lasting effect on his personality. Stefi Geyer, who later became a world-famous virtuoso violinist, was at that time a remarkably beautiful girl of nineteen, a talented pupil of Jenő Hubay. According to Kodály, the crisis was provoked by the fact that she did not return Bartók's love. But two long letters written in the autumn of 1907 reveal how profoundly incompatible were their beliefs. In these letters Bartók expounds in detail his materialist and atheist convictions. Kodály has said that Bartók was swept 'to the brink of non-existence' (au bord du néant). In many of his letters from Paris there are lengthy descriptions of the sepulchral atmosphere of a night-club called Le Néant. In other letters written during the autumn of 1907, there are indications that Bartók at times contemplated suicide.

Among the crowds of the large cities, with their urban civilization, he was oppressed by loneliness. He could find solace only in the solitude of nature, which inspired him to write the beautiful descriptions contained in his letters both from Paris and from Transylvania. In Bartók we see revived the pantheism of the Romantic poets which later found its way into his compositions. It was in similar fashion that Debussy fled from the 'dubious handclasps' of the metropolis to the solitude of the seacoast.

> The banks of the Seine are so beautiful that I would call the Parisians a happy people simply because they can glory in this sight at any time,

Bartók rhapsodized to his mother, while to Irmy Jurkovics he was inspired to praise the beauty of the Parc Monceau. He was most profoundly affected by nature, however, when the scene was totally undisturbed by the presence of man. After staying in some of the lively and fashionable spas, he found this unadulterated peace in Argentières in July 1908.

> It's beautiful here! At last, no rows of 'Grand Hotels', no hordes of idle, time-wasting Englishmen, no network of cogwheel-railways ready to take you anywhere,

he wrote to Etelka Freund, using almost the same words as those used by Debussy in his unceasing complaints about the English and the Americans who were to be found everywhere spoiling the beauty of the coast. On September 2, 1908, Bartók was at last able to write, 'I have reached the *ne plus ultra* of my desires: the sea . . .' In the south of France, he swam in the sea for the first time, walked barefoot on the sands and even saw a mirage. All these experiences were contained within a space of two hours during which he encountered no other human being.

Wherever he went, he found a similar delight in nature. Near Balán-bánya (now Bălan), in the midst of the Transylvanian mountains, he could imagine himself in Salzburg, Székelykő reminded him of Mount Grand Salève near Geneva, while in the account of his Transylvanian tour in January 1911, he wrote: 'It is as good as a winter trip to Semmering or the Tátra Mountains.'

As he travelled about the world Bartók showed himself to be equally adaptable in his response to nature and to the arts. There was for him a close relationship between the beauty of the Swiss mountains and the majesty of the Transylvanian hills; in his letter from Paris he had already mentioned the connection he felt between the treasures of the Louvre, the work of the greatest of the European composers and the folk music of Hungary. In his own country and during his travels abroad, he was searching for a world he could call his own, literally and figuratively; using his fixed principles as a yardstick he discovered a personal scale of values.

In his approach both to nature and to folk music we can discern one of the most profound of the principles by which he was guided towards the formation of his philosophical outlook. His views on what he considered to be the intrinsic nature of the creation of folk music were given in greater detail in 1921 when he wrote:

> In a narrower sense, peasant music is the result of the reshaping work of a natural force operating unconsciously: it is the instinctive creation of a human mass without artificiality. It is a natural phenomenon, just like the various forms of the animal or vegetable kingdom. As a result, its individual organisms —the melodies themselves—are examples of the highest artistic perfection.

He escaped from the superficial Hungarianism of the hybrid productions of the entertainment industry which were rife in the urban areas, and discovered in folk music an anchorage worthy of his artistic gifts. His chosen path led him away from the loneliness of crowded cities to the solitariness of nature and also to the peasant community which had created and preserved a folk art that seemed to have originated in nature.

After the hectic concert seasons, he would spend his summers among the peasants. Their way of life was the only one he could accept as natural, and he knew how to overcome their distrust of city dwellers. In July 1907, Bartók commissioned a desk to be ornamented with folk carving from György Gyugyi Péntek, a Körösfő carpenter, and at the same time became acquainted with 'Gyugyi Péntek's people'. He wrote:

> Now, I'm quite at home with them (his house consists of a kitchen and a very small workshop with a leaking roof).

In her book *Bartók Béla a népdalkutató* (Béla Bartók the Folk-Song Researcher), Júlia Szegő quotes the recollections of Bartók's peasant acquaintances and of the Transylvanian singers he met during his tours before the First World War. In 1954, after a span of fifty years, György Péntek's son, Ferenc, could still remember Bartók quite clearly, and was able to describe him with affectionate familiarity as a kindly man who inspired trust and confidence. 'He was a simple man, and popular,' said Ferenc Péntek. There is nothing to surprise us in this statement, and it is therefore all the more astonishing to find that Ferenc Péntek went on to describe Bartók as 'a gentle, smiling little man, always in good humour'. It would seem that the young composer, who at that time was wrestling with the philosophy of Nietzsche and the problem of existence and non-existence, became serene and even gay in the company of the peasants of Körösfő. In their midst, as in the midst of nature, he could relax. In Portugal he had similar experiences to those in Transylvania.

> Today I was greeted for the first time by Portuguese peasants,

he wrote to his mother on April 11, 1906.

> It was dusk, and I was walking in the meadows of Coimbra. They were coming home from work and may have taken me for a priest; they said: *Bom noite* and I answered the same. So I have spoken Portuguese!

Bartók's experience of country life and his discovery of folk music combined to give him what he was searching for—on the one hand, a music that was Hungarian in character and of artistic merit, and on the other, a source of inspiration for his philosophy of life. This polarization of his vision and creative energies resulted in his rejection of everything that was unnatural, especially the pseudo-civilization of the cities, and he began to esteem more and more highly all that he considered to be natural, genuine, sincere and true. These happier experiences soon expelled from his mind the memory of the discomforts of his firsf collecting tours and in 1928 prompted him to write a moving account ot his deep affection for the peasants:

> We had to live in the most wretched villages, in the most primitive conditions . . . and we had to make friends with the peasants and win their confidence. And this last, in particular, was not always easy, for, in previous times the peasant class had been too thoroughly exploited by the gentry, and in consequence was very suspicious of anyone who appeared to belong to this class. Yet in spite of all this, I must admit that our arduous labour in this field gave us greater pleasure than any other. Those days which I spent in the villages among the peasants were the happiest days of my life.

Certainly there were two sides to Bartók's ideology, and it cannot be denied that it contained a great many features which were reminiscent of the pantheism of Romantic art and also something of the Romantic Utopianism in which a hatred of capitalism found expression in the condemnation of urban civilization. These features were most evident during the first part of his life and career as a composer. But his close association with the peasants had its basis in the reality of the political situation. During the grim years which preceded the Second World War, and even more so during the war itself, it was the genuine nature of this association which fed his humanism, clarified and sharpened his criticism of society and guided him in his study of war and peace, nationalism and internationalism.

The two years between 1905 and 1906 were a formative period in the development of Bartók's views on existence and non-existence, nature and society, man and the world he lives in.

> If I ever crossed myself, it would signify 'In the name of Nature, Art and Science,'

he wrote to Stefi Geyer on September 6, 1907. It was Diderot who had associated nature with his personal Holy Trinity: Truth, Goodness and Beauty. Bartók's new faith was inherited from materialist predecessors.

It was in August 1907, that Bartók, writing from the Gyergyó Mountains, informed Etelka Freund that he was busy orchestrating the fourth movement of his *Suite No. 2* which at that time he called his 'Serenade'.

CHAPTER V

FOLK MUSIC INSPIRATION AND ITS FIRST GREAT CREATIVE PRODUCT. BLUEBEARD'S CASTLE. 1907–1911

1 APPOINTMENT AS TEACHER IN THE ACADEMY OF MUSIC. LESSONS
DRAWN FROM MUSICAL FOLKLORE AND FROM THE MUSIC OF DEBUSSY.
A NEW APPROACH TO THE UNDERSTANDING OF LATE LISZT WORKS

Bartók's interest in Hungarian folk music determined not only his whole outlook and way of life and his attitude to society and his own art, but also committed him irrevocably to Hungary as the scene of his labours. When Professor Thomán retired from his post at the Academy of Music and Bartók was appointed to succeed him, this merely confirmed him in a decision he had already made and provided him with a means of livelihood in Hungary where he was involved in research into folk music. As a pianist whose talent was beginning to be acknowledged all over Europe, and with the assistance of his many acquaintances, there would have been innumerable opportunities for him to live abroad. Dohnányi, after all, had done so for many years; nor was Bartók particularly attracted to teaching. All his life he looked upon teaching as a nuisance, and we can see from his letters that from the very start he complained of the inconvenient and demanding nature of the work. But he had to consider the appointment also in relation to his interest in folk music. He wrote in his autobiography:

> In 1907 I was appointed professor at the Academy of Music and I particularly welcomed this appointment because it gave me an opportunity to settle down at home and pursue my research in folk music.

But a gulf of time separates the moment of complete understanding of a given truth with all its scientific and moral implications, and the moment when an artist can incorporate that truth into a work of art. Bartók had been deeply immersed in the study of folk music for a long time, and had made considerable progress in the development of the vision in which folk music was to play an essential part, before he made his first attempts to apply the lessons of folk music to his creative work.

The new music which Bartók discovered was fundamentally different from the German-Romantic concept of music with which he had been familiar since childhood. His attention was arrested and his imagination stimulated by certain novel features which, however, faced him with the problem of their musical treatment. He has explained in his autobiography the musical significance of his discovery:

> It was decisively important for me to study all this peasant music because it showed me how to be completely independent of the universally prevailing major and minor scale system. For the majority—and most valuable—of the melodies I collected during my research tours, moved in the old church tonalities, that is, in the Greek and certain other even more primitive (pentatonic) modes, and show the most varied and freely changing metrical and rhythmic patterns performed in both rubato and 'tempo giusto'. It is now clear that the ancient scales, that are no longer used in our folk-art music, have lost none of their vitality. Their application has made possible new types of harmonic combinations.

When, in a lecture given in the United States in 1928, he explained in detail how the melodic intervals characteristic of folk music, and the tonality logic of its diatonic scales, were condensed into the harmonies of twentieth-century Hungarian music, he was in fact summarizing what he and Kodály had with such difficulty achieved in their own compositions during the previous twenty years. Writing in 1931, he frankly admitted the difficulties:

> One of the most difficult tasks is to know how to deal with folk melodies. I dare say it is as difficult, if not more so, than writing a large original work. We can readily understand one reason for these difficulties if we remember that we are bound by the very nature of any given melody. Another difficulty arises from the peculiar character of these melodies. This has to be recognized, assimilated, and then enhanced, and not obscured, by the arrangement. One thing is certain: inspiration is just as necessary for the arrangement of folk music as for any other kind of composition.

This is worth remembering when attempting to assess the true significance of Bartók's folk-song arrangements of 1907. The piano version of *Three Folk-Songs from the County Csík* and the first of the *Eight Hungarian Folk-Songs* completed ten years later, reflect memories of the composer's collecting tour in Transylvania in 1907. The close relationship between the two works is shown by the fact that the third of the Csík County folk-songs is the same as the fifth of the *Eight Hungarian Folk-Songs*.

Later, in 1931, Bartók defined the four phases of the influence which it is possible for folk music to have on the work of a composer. He mentions first the method of harmonization as illustrated in his works of 1907 in which

> the peasant melody is given an accompaniment or perhaps inserted between a prelude and postlude with only slight, if any, variations in the melody.

We can find innumerable examples of this mode of harmonization, or 'the first phase' as Bartók called it, particularly among the piano pieces composed in the years after 1907; masterly 'frames', to use Bartók's own description, into which he fitted 'the main thing, the peasant melody, like fixing a precious jewel into its setting'. The pieces in the cycle *For Children* are examples of these miniature masterpieces with their wonderful harmonic accentuation of the character of the melody. Examples of this mode of harmonization may also be found in pieces which are quite different in character—the *Fourteen Bagatelles*, the *Ten Easy Piano Pieces* and the *Sketches* in all of which there is the realization of new ideas. And all of them illustrate the composer's determination only to use settings worthy of folk music.

A comparison between the rigid, scholastic harmonies which Bartók and Kodály used in 1906 in their settings of the folk-songs included in the volume entitled *Twenty Hungarian Folk-Songs* and those of the *Three Folk-Songs from the County Csík* of 1907, reveals immediately a fundamental transformation in harmonic thinking. The compositions of the latter spring from the modal-pentatonic intonation of folk music and are imbued with the very essence of folk music; the works mentioned earlier are even lovelier examples of Bartók's achievement. The impetus to find a method of composition adequate for his purpose was provided in the first place by the folk-songs themselves. Bartók was further stimulated in the same direction when he first became acquainted with the music of Debussy.

This did not occur during Bartók's first visit to Paris in 1905. His visit took place in the late summer when the theatre and concert season had ended. Furthermore, in 1905, the music of the French master was not the daily fare of even the most sophisticated of Paris audiences so that it would have been difficult for a young man wandering about the metropolis to come upon it by chance. It was to be Kodály who introduced Bartók to the music of Debussy. For Kodály spent a much longer period in Paris in 1907 and when he returned to Budapest he talked to Bartók about his musical experiences, mentioning particularly the work of Debussy. It is probable that Bartók lost no time in learning to appreciate the beauty of Debussy's music and in assimilating with characteristic thoroughness the new ideas it contained.

It was a most favourable moment for him to become acquainted with Debussy's work. It stimulated his development in the musical direction already given it by his preoccupation with folk music. He was surprised to recognize in Debussy's music a realization of the same melodic and harmonic characteristics that he had found in Hungarian folk music. Debussy had by that time used the modal and five-tone melodic turns to create a mature world of harmony that was all his own, and Bartók was overjoyed when he discovered that he could identify his own conclusions with those of Debussy. In 1928 he wrote an account of this discovery:

> This fact, as early as 1905, led me to end a composition in F-sharp Minor with the chord: F sharp—A—C sharp—E. Hence in this closing chord, the seventh figures, as a consonant interval. At that time a close of this kind was something quite out of the ordinary. Only in works by Debussy, of approximately the same period, could a parallel case be found, namely, the following closing chord: A—C sharp—E—F sharp.

Nor can we wonder at these similarities if we consider that to achieve his solutions Debussy drew from the same sources of inspiration as Bartók; for Debussy was influenced both directly (and also indirectly through the works of Borodin and Mussorgsky) by the folk music of Eastern Europe and Asia.

But even nearer home there was available to Bartók another source of inspiration for the creation of a new world of harmony and its use in a music based on folk music. That source was Zoltán Kodály. The volume of folk music which the two composers had published together in 1906 clearly illustrates how much further Kodály had advanced in this partic-

82

ular direction. And Bartók was influenced by the music of Debussy not only directly but also indirectly through the work of Kodály. Later, under the influence of his own creative logic, he moved in a different direction. But the influence of his first fresh encounter with a new French music always persisted and continued to determine the basic tone of a great many of his simple and informal arrangements of folk-songs. At the same time these songs contain those features of his art which are most akin to the work of Kodály and this basic tone is fused with the vision of village life embodied in his music. Debussy's attraction for him may be seen in his choice of works for concert programmes made throughout his life, which often included works of the great French master.

Finally, Debussy's music provided Bartók with the encouragement he needed and demonstrated how to throw off the tyranny of German-Romantic music. Writing about Ravel in 1938 he formulated very clearly the significance of this new sense of direction:

> It is well known that Hungary has suffered for centuries from its close proximity to Germany, both politically and culturally. The most highly educated of our citizens, however, have always rebelled against this unhealthy situation, recognizing that they had a closer spiritual link with the Latin races, and especially the French, than with the Germans . . . It is obvious and understandable, that this recognition of kinship should find an expression in music, in opposition to the German music which until the end of the nineteenth century had dominated the musical world in Hungary. New ideas were released and the emergence of Debussy signified the replacement of German music by French music as a source of inspiration. By the turn of the century, young Hungarian musicians, of whom I was one, had already been attracted for some time towards other fields of French culture. It may be readily imagined just how much significance they attached to Debussy: their discovery of his art awakened them to a knowledge of what French music had to offer.

It will be appreciated that such a statement, made in the year in which Hitler occupied Austria, was not without political content. But these words also implied a change that was significant in the history of music. The new direction of Bartók's personal development not only accelerated his disenchantment with the music of his former ideal, Strauss, but again directed his attention toward Liszt.

As a student at the Academy in 1902, Bartók's creative powers had been stimulated by Richard Strauss's *Zarathustra*. Then, at a deeper level of inspiration, as he composed first the *Kossuth Symphony* then the *Rhapsody*, he found that he was turning to Liszt. For Liszt, who perpetuated and bequeathed the heroism and profundity of Beethoven, and who, by disintegrating the tonality logic of the musical idiom of his time, proved to be even more significant as an innovator than Wagner.

For Bartók, Debussy's music threw light on another, less well-known and less spectacular aspect of the legacy of Liszt: his contribution to the early stages of the diatonic developments leading to Debussy, and his incorporation of the Renaissance heritage and the modal and pentatonic melodic turns of Russian and East-European music. Bence Szabolcsi informs us that Liszt was the first to arrive at the pentatonic cadential chord, which Bartók considered in relation to Debussy. This type of harmony was perhaps first used as a cadential chord in 1876, in the sixth piece of Liszt's *Christmas Tree* series. It appears later as an experiment in the works of Percy Grainger of Australia and Cyril Scott of England. It became a regular feature of Debussy's music and every music lover in Hungary is familiar with it as a result of hearing Bartók's piano piece *An Evening with the Székelys*. In the dance music coming out of England and America in the nineteen-twenties and thirties it was finally degraded into a cheap and hackneyed mannerism.

These diatonic melodic and harmonic features of Liszt were the first musical formulations of the lyrical impressionism found in descriptions of nature in poetry and painting at the close of the century.

Bartók's admiration for Debussy enabled him to rediscover Liszt:

> We find a surprising relationship between certain kinds of the works of Liszt, for example parts of the Années de Pèlerinage and the Harmonies poétiques et religieuses, and some of the compositions by Debussy and Ravel, the two outstanding figures in the new world of French music. I am convinced that without Liszt's Jeux d'eau de la Villa d'Este and similar works, it is hardly conceivable that the two French masters could ever have composed in a similar vein,

wrote Bartók in his study of Liszt in 1936. In his autobiography he summarized his views on Liszt as reached in this study:

> I became fully aware of the real significance of this master and from the point of view of the development of music I felt his works to be more important than those of Wagner and Strauss.

In his works dating from 1907–8, Bartók resolved and gave musical expression to his intellectual difficulties, inner conflicts and tensions experienced during the period when he was still struggling to formulate a philosophy of life. This is the meaning of Kodály's reference, made in 1921, to the finest and most complete of Bartók's works composed in 1908, the *String Quartet No. 1*; for he wrote that 'it contains an inner drama, a man's return to life after travelling to the very borders of non-existence.'

Bartók composed one work after another without interruption until 1911, the year when he composed *Bluebeard's Castle* and the *Allegro Barbaro*. Indeed, because of the nature of its content and form, *The Wooden Prince*, a ballet composed much later, can be classed together with this group of works. The two compositions he began working on again in the summer of 1907—the *Suite No. 2* which had been laid aside and the unique folk-song arrangement for piano written at the same time as the last movement of the *Suite*—are almost symbolic expressions of his basic musical aspirations of that period: to criticize, appraise and sift the heritage of European classical music, to create new forms based on his discovery of folk music, and finally, to synthetize these two aims. These three rules which lay at the root of his creative methods were to determine the whole of his life work and order his development as a man who was both a scientist and an artist.

His piano works were the laboratory in which he worked out his ideas. Some of the series, such as the *Fourteen Bagatelles* (op. 6) and the *Ten Easy Piano Pieces*, were composed almost simultaneously, during May and June 1908. The volumes *For Children*, originally a series of eighty-five short piano pieces, confirm that he was composing almost uninterruptedly at that time (1908–9). This is not the case with some of the other series. Nearly two years elapsed between the two sections of the *Two Elegies* (op. 8b)—February 1908 and December 1909. The first piece of the *Sketches* (op. 9b) also dates from 1908, and the third is dated August

1910. *Quarrei*, November 1908, was not followed by *Molto Vivo*, *Capriccioso* until 1910, and the two were rounded out with *A bit drunk* in May 1911 to form the *Three Burlesques* (op. 8c). The *Eight Hungarian Folk-Songs* for voice and piano were begun in 1907 and completed only in 1917. Of the later works, the *Two Romanian Dances* (op. 8a) and the *Four Dirges* (op. 9a) composed around 1910, are largely made up of pieces that are similar in kind.

The orchestral compositions are to some extent the means of tidying up earlier efforts, works such as the *Violin Concerto* in two movements (1907–8) dedicated to Stefi Geyer, perhaps in 1914, and the latter part of the *Suite No. 2* which is so frequently mentioned. Stefi Geyer kept the unpublished score of the *Violin Concerto*, which was not performed until May 30, 1958, in Basle, after her death, and it was only then that it was published. At some time between 1908 and 1916, however, Bartók took the first movement of the concerto and added an orchestral version of the fourteenth bagatelle, thereby creating one of his most famous works, the *Two Portraits* with its two sections, *The Ideal* and *The Distorted* (op. 5). The next orchestral work, *Two Pictures* (op. 10), was composed after an interval of two years, in August 1910, and already belongs to the early period of his mature vision.

Of all the pieces of that period, the *String Quartet No. 1* (op. 7), merits a special mention. On a postcard dated January 28, 1909, Bartók informed Etelka Freund that he had completed it on the previous day. This work marks one of the recurring peaks of Bartók's composing activity from which the unity of his work as a whole is most clearly visible.

Bartók's fascinated interest in folk music turned him sharply against the Hungarian-type folk-art songs that were so popular at that time. Some decades later, certain types of the *verbunkos* dance became an integral part of his music. His turning against Romanticism, to which he quite often referred, manifested itself differently in his attitude to German-Romantic music. In this connection, folk music and French music combined to influence him not so much towards a rigid isolation but rather towards selectivity and crystallization of his ideas. During this period, a type of melody developed in Bartók's works that was clearly reminiscent of Strauss and ultimately of Wagner. This melody soars upwards, aspiring to the heights, then plunges down only to turn upwards but with intervals every now and again of one second before sinking to an even greater depth than before. There is a tendency to split into parallel thirds, the rhythm becomes drawn out and ethereal, and the metrical limits are effaced by syncopation. In the prelude to the third act of *Tristan*, such a melody is a particularly fascinating musical expression of eternal longing without rest and the search only for annihilation.

In some of his works, as in the first movement of the *String Quartet No. 1*, we find the unmistakable descending intervals which preserve the elaborately drawn-out thread of a Wagnerian melody. The broken seventh intonation of the ascending thirds also derives from Wagner. This is to be found here in one of the most significant melodic nuclei in Bartók's music, one which was to occur throughout his works both in the form of ascending and descending broken chords, with major and minor third. He wrote this down in the form of notes in a letter written in the autumn of 1907, as a leitmotif in the *Violin Concerto* then in preparation (he took the German term from Wagner experts). The major form of the motif appears at the beginning of the 'ideal' portrait with its programmatic meaning, and is turned into a funeral march in *Bagatelle No. 13*: 'Elle est morte', runs the title of the piece. In the 'distorted' portrait the same theme is transformed into a grotesque waltz-scherzo.

While writing about this type of melody, we must also mention that it could readily be used in the highest positions of the strings in the music of both Wagner and Bartók. The relationship between its descending version and downward turning large intervals is obvious if we consider the first and last notes of the broken seventh chord omitting the notes in between.

In order to understand the meaning Bartók wished to convey, we must again take Wagner's aesthetics as our starting-point. In *Tristan* and *Parsifal* this type of melody, with its characteristic soaring then falling only to soar yet again, is used to express eternal yearning and ceaseless suffering before rest, annihilation or redemption. It would be difficult to find anywhere else, either in Wagner or in Bartók, such heavenly sounds in major tonalities expressing the immanence of supreme bliss and redemption, as those found in *Parsifal* and the 'ideal' of the *Two Portraits*.

There are only one or two comparable passages, and these occur in Bartók's piano works such as the *Dedication* or *Dawn* in the *Ten Easy Piano Pieces*. In them we can recognize 'Nietzsche's disciple' who for one moment believes that he has reached a state of bliss in which he is indifferent to all disturbing influences.

But with the passage of time the ascending type ceases entirely and there is an increasing number of variants expressing restlessness, continuous suffering and the search for relief. The artistic expression of the theme of love and death in *Tristan und Isolde* had a far-reaching effect on Bartók's works; its influence may be seen in those sections of his compositions in which melody is used to express the feminine aspect of the relationship between man and woman. Sighs of longing quicken with impatience and become determined and resolute as in the first of the *Sketches*, *Portrait of a Girl* and also at the end of the fourth. A characteristic feature of this melodic realm is the widening and sometimes very nearly impossible extension of the intervals. In these details we can see in embryo the movements of Judith, pounding, shrieking, struggling, embracing and repulsing, in *Bluebeard's Castle*.

The female features of the melody, first inspired by Stefi Geyer, later became generalized and were frequently used by Bartók to express feminine characteristics. In the first of the *Sketches*, composed for Márta Ziegler, later Bartók's wife, we can find a harmonic summary of the typically female features of the melody.

The same themes are given a dancing rhythm, and later are fused together with the waltz-scherzo found in some of the works succeeding the 'distorted' portrait; they are also to be found incorporated in the musical character sketch of the princess in *The Wooden Prince* and that of the girl in *The Miraculous Mandarin*. But it also approaches the melodic world of folk music. One of its forms is identical with that particular pentatonic four-tone chord that we have already mentioned as a closing chord. In this way a tense, dramatic break-up of a four-tone chord flows into the serene idyll in the last bars of *Portrait of a Girl*. This is what Bartók heard in the melody of 'They Killed a Poor Lad', the thirteenth piece of the first book of *For Children*, in which he places a special harmonic emphasis on the descending pentatonic four-tone chord.

This type of melody has inherited not only the musical legacy of the most expressive features of German Romanticism, but also its meaning. But just as in the development of his philosophy, in which he was influenced only indirectly by Schopenhauer through the works of Nietzsche, so too in his musical development we can see that after his experience of Wagner it was only indirectly through the work of Richard Strauss and later Max Reger that he approached this melodic realm. The influence of Max Reger is revealed primarily by the less chordal and looser polyphonic texture of the melody, as in the first movement of the *String Quartet No. 1* and in the music of the 'ideal' portrait.

One of the most important sources of Bartók's use of tonality can be found in an interesting type of melody which stems from Wagner, whose musical image for a cycle of endless suffering is well known through the wonderful English horn solo in the prelude of the third act of *Tristan*.

The stubbornly sustained accompaniment in the *Qualvolles Ringen* in *Ten Easy Piano Pieces* reflects this Wagnerian melodic cycle. Even in the title there is some link between the two passages. For Bartók, however, it was the relationship of the four tones which provided him with the most exciting problem of tonality. From this moment onwards, right to the end of his life, the two ways of dividing the octave, using the perfect and the diminished fifths, became a means of creating tension. The contrasting of the two kinds of fifths is one of the most conspicuous of the new features which are already to be found in the tonality framework of the *String Quartet No. 1*, especially in the construction of the last movement. This kind of shrinkage and expansion of the fifth interval was to become one of the most important characteristics of later tonality combinations. Another example of this occurs in the second of the *Bagatelles*.

Fragmentary melodies harmonized in different tonalities provide further evidence of the broadening of Bartók's tonal thinking, while the first piece of the *Bagatelles* and the second of the *Sketches* brought into the open the problem of the simultaneous use of double tonalities. It was only after some decades that Bartók again attempted to solve this particular problem, in *Mikrokosmos*. Meantime, in his works written between 1908 and 1910, Bartók was pursuing another line of development in his harmonic thinking. The chromatic usage of half-tone intervals, as it is traditionally called, the attraction of the leading note and the principles of functional logic gradually gave way to a manner of thinking and composing that might be more aptly called not chromatics, but rather diminished interval diatonics. This path of musical development led to the emergence of an independent application of half-tone intervals by means of which he hewed a way towards the achievements of Schoenberg's circle in Vienna; and these intervals with their hovering tonalities paved the way for atonality.

One of the most important lessons to be drawn from Liszt's musical teaching was the possibility of dividing the octave into equivalent intervals consisting of the diminished fifth together with the augmented fourth, or by the use of major and minor thirds. At this time, the basic features of Bartók's formal construction were beginning to be determined by these new divisions, as evidenced in the large-scale framework of the *String Quartet No. 1* and in the slighter character piece, *Bear Dance*. But characteristically, the minor third division is no longer the traditional diminished seventh chord, but a piling up of minor thirds, none of which is an augmented second. The sigh of the C sharp descending to B flat in the last of the *Four Dirges* is the same minor third that was to blare forth the appearance of the Mandarin ten years later, and is a traditional augmented second merely in the way it was written down.

These contrasting character pieces form a musical pattern which is similarly evident in the system of meanings and expressions derived from German Romanticism. After the manner of Liszt and Berlioz, Bartók used only one theme for both the transfigured happiness of the 'ideal' and the grotesquerie of the 'distorted' in his *Two Portraits;* and he used the same technique in the last two of the *Fourteen Bagatelles*, the one a funeral march and the other a grotesque waltz-scherzo. In the *String Quartet No. 1*, however, Bartók turned back to the profundity of Beethoven in the analytic way of development, in a manner worthy of his mature period. From these early beginnings, Bartók approached the firmest foundations of the patterns of European music construction; and throughout the rest of his life he exerted the greatest possible care when working out the proportions of large units and also when polishing even the minutest detail. In the last movement of the *String Quartet No. 1* we find something that was to appear again in his later major works:

the clarity with which he showed at the crucial points of construction the basic tonal pillars.

At the same time, however, his interest in folk music was enriching his work with a blossoming undergrowth of musical meanings, characters and types. The folk-song harmonizations, apparently so simple, are not insignificant exercises in harmony, but are in fact masterly character pieces in miniature. We have only to turn the pages of the volumes of *For Children* to gain some idea of the wide range of emotions expressed in the folk-songs. We can see from the titles in the Slovak volumes and from the tempo markings which, in the Hungarian volumes, indicate the atmosphere of the pieces, Bartók's incredible depth of understanding, as well as the creative sympathy with which he recognized, accentuated and enhanced in his artistic arrangement the original character of the folk-songs. His love and skill cast a spell over the simple songs, transforming this Cinderella form into a royal art; he wove them into his own poetic imaginings, honouring each song according to its merit. From the world of folk music came the beautifully innocent nursery songs, the jokes, the ballads of the outlaws, the dirges, the instrumental fantasies, the drinking songs and the love songs, the idylls and the dramas. They brought within the compass of great art the wealth and wisdom inherent in the life of the people that had not previously been recognized.

From the very beginning, these songs appeared side by side with another type of work which also owed its inspiration to folk music. In Bartók's own words,

> the composer does not use genuine peasant melodies, but devises instead
> something imitating a peasant melody.

One of the best-known and loveliest examples of such a creation is the village scene in *An Evening with the Székelys*, peerless in its beauty among all the works inspired by folk music.

Here too there are endless possibilities of classifying the types in contrasting pairs. There is the duality provided by the folk music itself: slow and fast, parlando and giusto, narrative and dance. In *An Evening with the Székelys* these are gathered into a five-part rondo structure, but the successive pieces of the series also contrast with each other or are arranged progressively in smaller groups, which are virtually little suites.

Folk-songs and ballads with a weightier content and harsher, more tragic harmonies began to take shape as the counterpart to the funeral marches appearing in the other branch of Bartók's realm of melody. This is exemplified in the eighth movement of the *Ten Easy Piano Pieces*, 'They say they will not give', which anticipates the later tragedy of Borbála Angoli in the ballad movement of the *Fifteen Hungarian Peasant Songs*. The unbridled abandon of the waltz-scherzo of the other branch of Bartók's melodic development finds its counterpart in the *Bear Dance* in which the music is at times grotesque and at times quite frightening; here too we may find the stubbornly repeated sounds heard in the galloping last movement of the *String Quartet No. 1*. Later, in various individual pieces, we find an independent development of the different types of melody: demoniacal or grotesque, awe-inspiring or droll and jovial. By 1911 the first of these types had developed into the overwhelming onslaught of the *Allegro Barbaro* which anticipates Bartók's later terrifying creations, the wooden puppets and the Miraculous Mandarin. There is an additional differentiation in the droll and jovial types of melody. These are characterized on the one hand by the grotesquerie used to portray the staggering hero of *A bit drunk* in the second of the *Three Burlesques*, a preliminary study for the scene with the dismembered wooden puppet and the old suitor; on the other hand there is also the development of an atmosphere reminiscent of Bruegel in the scenes of village festivity such as the second piece in *Two Pictures*, *Village Dance*, or many years later, *Village Joke* in the *Mikrokosmos* and in the second movement of *Music for String Instruments, Percussion and Celesta*.

Looking back at Bartók's personal and intellectual development analysed earlier, it cannot be doubted for one moment that the musical expression derived from Wagner through Strauss and Reger, which, in this new and great duality, had its philosophical counterpart in the thought of Schopenhauer and Nietzsche, is united with spiritual solitude, introversion, individualism and subjectivity. In the duality of man and woman it expresses at the same time the female principle. In his music there is an intimation of continual suffering, will, aspiration and self-consuming energy; it is the embodiment of uncertainty, transcendentalism and mutability. The methods he uses are extension of tonality, melody, harmony and rhythm.

On the other side, the newly-discovered world of the people stood for all that was peaceful, enduring, natural and manly. Bartók moved towards it with purposeful and deliberate movements. The stability and certainty of his melodies, harmonies, rhythms and tonality are based on the familiar world of nature, self-confident, powerful and reassuring.

These moods are at first expressed independently, opposing one another, in the compositions dating from 1907–8. In the last movement of the *Suite No. 2* the first pentatonic melody is wedged into the fabric of the whole work as one independent line of a folk-song, as if it were a quotation. In the same way, in the last movement of the *String Quartet No. 1*, the early, pentatonic antecedent of the peacock melody is merely a pause, an episode. The opposition is sometimes stressed by an accentuated contradiction, as at the beginning of the *Ten Easy Piano Pieces*. The first piece, the unnumbered *Dedication*, with its programmatic application of the leitmotif, is undoubtedly intended to reflect a mood of spirituality akin to that of the ethereal 'ideal' portrait. Immediately following this, as the first of the numbered pieces, comes the *Peasant Song*, stark in its simplicity, a new style of folk-song without harmonies. The contrast between these two pieces anticipates the portraits of the prince and princess in the later ballet.

In the longer series such as the *Bagatelles*, the *Ten Easy Piano Pieces* or the *Sketches*, the two moods are for the most part quite separately expressed in different pieces. But there are important features which pave the way for an imminent synthesis and closer interdependence. Although the *Bear Dance* was inspired by folk music, it is related to the more complex world of great music through the melody and rhythm, for it features a complicated structure of thirds, harsh bitonal harmonization and a rondo-like arrangement. This encounter leads to a new type of music, as does the later *Allegro Barbaro*. Similarly, above the *Tristan* inspired accompanying figures in the *Qualvolles Ringen*, the melody hints at the line structure of the folk-song. And again, in the sixth of the *Bagatelles* we may hear in its half-tone, broadly-sweeping melodiousness a hint of the syllabic and linear structure of the folk-song.

In this connection, the *Four Dirges* deserve special mention. In their fluidity we can detect the search to link the relaxed rhythm, movements and declamatory tone of a melody that comes from the world of *Tristan* with their counterparts in the parlando of a folk-song. This duality, for which a different solution is explored in each of the four dirges, is the germ of a new kind of slow movement which developed in the later works. The second dirge is particularly interesting and worthy of attention because the first line of its pentatonic melody is used to begin the formulation of the basic melody in *Bluebeard's Castle*. In its powerful development, it anticipates the figure of Judith, and in the pounding of the repeated, syncopated chords of the accompaniment, there is a similar foreshadowing of her emotions. As the first theme returns to close the piece we can hear above it in the diminishing sound of these chords as they die away, the very atmosphere of the scene in which Judith takes her place among the living dead—Bluebeard's former wives. The opening line in unison is repeated in the manner of a folk-song, and each time it is left open; when this occurs for the second time it is done in such a way as to enable the other melodic idea to unfold in the middle of the work, declamatory, intense and full of pathos. Finally, the introductory melody returns twice in the bass, while, culminating and dying out above it, we hear the melody of the middle section, this time ended in an enclosed form. This five-part arrangement, with its extended middle section and synthesis of two elements, is a miniature version of the later opera.

The *Evening with the Székelys* had already demonstrated the symmetry of such a five-part arrangement. This rondo-like symmetry is a development of a similar, though very much simpler, arrangement seen in the *Suite No. 1* and it is also an anticipation of the great works to come, among them two superbly constructed stage works now imminent. The first of the *Romanian Dances* is one of the most wonderful realizations of a triple division in this symmetry. Here there is a synthesis of folk-music material and great classical music not only in the sense that the whole work consists of a detailed analytical way of development but also in that it contains the break-up, repetition and inversion of a single motif. In the slow, central section, the same basic motif is broadened and expanded into parlando.

In the composer's musical expression of a dualistic vision made up of opposing elements, there are now ever clearer indications of the unity of opposites; the material is ready for the first great synthesis.

94

3 THE START OF COLLECTING SLOVAK AND ROMANIAN FOLK MUSIC.
THEIR INFLUENCE UPON MUSICAL WORKS AND BARTÓK'S SOCIAL VIEWS.
NEW HUNGARIAN MUSIC AND THE PRESS. COMPOSER RECITALS BY
KODÁLY AND BARTÓK. THE WALDBAUER QUARTET

At about the same time as the pieces inspired by Hungarian folk music there also appeared some piano works which had their roots in Slovak sources. The fifth of the *Bagatelles*, for example, is an arrangement of a Slovak folk-song; so too is the third of the *Ten Easy Piano Pieces*, 'Slovakian Boys' Dance' while the eighth piece in the latter volume is based on a folk-song for which there are both Hungarian and Slovak lyrics, 'They say they will not give'. The series of works inspired by Slovak folk music reaches its peak in the third and fourth volumes of *For Children*. Here Bartók expresses, just as vividly as his earlier portrayal of Hungarian village life, the world of Slovak folk poetry in which he had so deeply immersed himself.

It was not long before Bartók added to these works the creative results of his study of Romanian folk music. The fifth of the *Sketches* bears the title *Romanian Folk-Song* and a footnote gives the place of origin as the Belényes region, while the sixth piece, *Oláhos*, is stated to be Wallachian. Although this series of pieces inspired by Romanian material comes to an end for the time being with the *Two Romanian Dances*, nevertheless a similar musical atmosphere continues to make itself felt in the second of the *Two Pictures*, in the *Village Dance*.

In the preface to his collection of Slovak folk-songs in the German-language edition, Bartók describes why he extended his researches to include Slovak and Romanian folk music:

> I began my researches into folk music in 1906 by investigating and collecting Hungarian peasant music. I had scarcely begun this work when I realized that a knowledge of the Hungarian material was in itself insufficient for any scientific purposes and that it was essential to have a most thorough familiarity with at least the folk music of the neighbouring peoples. That is why I embarked on collecting Slovak folk music in 1906, and continued to do so, though with some considerable interruptions, until 1918.

According to the records, he began his Slovak research in Gömör County. In August 1906, he first started at Gerlicepuszta, and later, in

October, he went on to other villages. On November 3, he wrote from Pozsony to Lajos Dietl, describing his findings with all the enthusiasm of a 'zealous collector', though he also had to find time for practice on the piano he had brought with him to Gerlicepuszta. Again he wrote,

> After spending every evening for 3 weeks in Slovakian villages, I have not been able to get down more than 150 songs; I phonographed 80.
> Could you come to us for a few days at Christmas? I invite you to a song-collection excursion in the neighbouring villages. It's very interesting, especially the phonographing. Your knowledge of Russian (!) might be useful to us among the Slovakians.

There is no evidence to show whether this Christmas expedition actually materialized; but from the dates of the songs published in a later collection we do know that in March and November 1907, in October 1908 and in January 1909, and possibly on a further occasion in that year, he was collecting in Nyitra (Nitra); and we know of songs noted down in Trencsén (Trenčin), in August 1909.

It was during the summer of 1909 that he also started out on his Romanian tour. For two weeks from July 18, he was collecting in Bihar County, around Belényes. After a short excursion to Styria, he was again to be found in Bihar, and at the end of August he went as far as the Mezőség to collect Romanian folk music. He continued his research in Bihar in February 1910. During the latter part of 1910 and the beginning of 1911, between Christmas and Twelfth-night, he continued his work in Torda-Aranyos and Fehér Counties. The card from Topánfalva mentioned earlier, in which he compared the Transylvanian mountains with Semmering, also dates from this period.

In these new territories Bartók came across various types of instrumental folk music. On a card to Etelka Freund dated August 31, 1909, he noted down a Romanian instrumental melody; and in November, 1910, he took part in a bagpipe and horn competition among the herdsmen in the Ipolyság. On the card from Topánfalva he also referred to a good deal of instrumental music, to peasant fiddlers and women and girls who played the alphorn.

As a result of his contact with this broader stream of folk music there accrued to his own creative art yet another new and significant feature. One characteristic of Slovak, Romanian and Transylvanian folk music is a type of melody which forms a Lydian scale with its augmented fourth, and is often coupled with another modal scale, the Mixolydian, with the minor seventh. One section of this scale is identical with a part of the whole tone scale, and either in the whole tone or the Mixolydian–Lydian form, serves as a bridge connecting Bartók's folk-music discoveries with the music of Debussy. It is this that gives an unmistakable character to the tonal effect of *L'Après-midi d'un Faun, Première Nocturne*, and *La Mer*. The higher partials of the acoustical scale were assuming ever greater significance even in the years preceding the turn of the century, in the music of, among others, the Russian composer, Alexander Scriabin. It is part of the importance of this musical development that it shows a close affinity with the response to nature found in the poetry of late Romanticism. It is similarly important as a significant feature of Bartók's musical vision for it constitutes the third major element of his music, the other two being the use of the expressive half-tone and pentatonic melody inspired by folk music. This feature may have appeared for the first time in the remarkable *Bear Dance* in the first half of 1908, and it persisted as a characteristic of his work throughout his life being frequently referred to as the Bartók scale.

Bartók's research among the neighbouring peoples also helped him to clarify his political and social outlook. His experiences in the villages while collecting Hungarian peasant songs had already opened his eyes to the condition of the people. His collecting tours in Slovakia and Romania served to strengthen his impressions of the peasant's lot. Later, in 1933, he described the 'medieval' conditions prevailing in the Romanian villages in Transylvania.

> The villages are full of illiterate people; there is no railway anywhere in the vicinity, often there are not even roads; every basic necessity is produced at home if possible; the people never leave their immediate locality, except when absolutely necessary (military service, court matters).

These primitive, 'natural' conditions provided Bartók with the perfect background for his ethnological studies of folk music; but, as a student of society and politics, he was made to realize even more clearly than hitherto the true meaning of the 'national' policy of the ruling classes; this he now saw in the light of the dual oppression of the nationalities. It was only decades later that he expressed in his writings this realization that the real contradictions existed not between the nations but between the classes. But the first stimulus which enabled him to achieve such a realization dates from this early contact with the peasants. 'There is peace among the peasants,' he wrote in 1943, 'hatred for their brothers is fostered only by the higher circles.'

These experiences helped Bartók to evaluate his own sense of national responsibility and brought home to him the true significance of his statement at Gmunden in 1903. His intention to support the cause of Hungarian independence and to serve the Hungarian people was now broadened to include 'the brotherhood of all the peoples'. This was not expressed until twenty years later either, but even as early as 1910 his deeds were a witness to his dedication to this cause. The preserving diligence with which he studied the Slovak and Romanian languages, could have been merely a means used for ethnographic purposes. In 1905, he had studied French with the same persistence, and later, when he was doing research work in Eastern Europe he undertook to learn Russian, Arabic, Turkish, the Southern Slav languages and, towards the end of his life, English. In each case he managed to acquire as much of the language as was necessary for his work, although, according to Kodály, he had no talent for languages. He corresponded in Romanian. Much later, during a difficult and troubled period of history, his life-long friendship with János Buşiţia, a secondary-school teacher in Belényes, became a symbol of fraternity between the nationalities.

Unmistakable proof of his convictions may be found in the third and fourth volumes of *For Children*. The whole collection indicates that Bartók fully realized the immense significance of cultural policies and the importance of musical education for children. It also reveals that he found in the imaginative world of folk music and in that inhabited by children a natural world with similar meaning. In this work Bartók expresses the cultural emancipation of the national minorities, and the volumes were by no means to the taste of the ruling classes among whom there existed at that time an ever growing imperialism and when the mood of the public was in general chauvinistic. The significance of this work was not in fact recognized until 1925 when it was mentioned in a Prague paper.

Finally, in 1910, Bartók took the first steps to establish a system of co-operation between the folk-music research workers of Hungary,

Slovakia and Romania. In April of that year he wrote a letter in French to Dimitrie G. Kiriac, a Romanian composer and student of folk music, offering the whole of his Romanian collection (four hundred songs from Bihar and two hundred from other regions) 'to a public library in Bucharest', and for possible publication. In June he wrote a similar letter to the Turócszentmárton Könyvnyomda Részvény-társaság (Turócszentmárton Book Publishing Company) offering 'the manuscripts of a collection of Slovak folk-songs'. The Romanian Academy of Sciences accepted his Bihar collection for publication on May 11, 1911, and it appeared in 1913, printed in Romanian.

He was at this period too deeply engaged in the work of composing and of collecting folk-songs to have either the time or inclination to give many public recitals. It is true that there were certain spectacular performances here and there when he played concertos by Saint-Saëns, Volkmann or Liszt. And he even ventured, for the first and last time in his life, into the sphere of conducting: On January 2, 1909, he conducted the Scherzo movement of his *Suite No. 2* in Berlin. During these years, however, he was most frequently prompted to appear in public by the urge to perform his own works and those of Kodály, and to disseminate a knowledge of the new music and its exponents. And fortunately these occasions grew in number.

The influence on Hungarian political life of the Russian revolution of 1905 was not to be denied. The Russian example provided a strong impetus both to the advocates of a bourgeois democratic revolution and to those engaged in the organization of the working class. It stimulated progressive activities in literary and artistic circles, while the magazine *Nyugat* became the mouthpiece for a group of the younger generation of writers who were influenced by Parisian intellectuals. Hungarian culture was revived by this current of fresh air which had a similar effect on the musical life of the nation.

Bartók's works were performed one after the other. The première of the complete *Suite No. 1* was conducted by Jenő Hubay on March 1, 1909, and *Suite No. 2* received its first performance, conducted by István Kerner, on November 22. The first performance of the new version of the *Rhapsody op. 1* had taken place only one week earlier, on November 15, again with Hubay as conductor and Bartók as soloist.

The fame of Hungarian music was carried abroad by the works of Bartók and his contemporaries. In Vienna, Ferruccio Busoni was delighted by the *Fourteen Bagatelles*. *'Endlich was wirklich neues!'* he exclaimed after hearing it played by the composer. And in the following January, Bartók was encouraged by Busoni to conduct the Scherzo of his *Suite No. 2*. The composition aroused violent controversy among the Berlin audience and the music critics. In Paris, the introduction of new Hungarian music was organized by Sándor Kovács, the outstanding young pianist, teacher and theoretician, who arranged a Festival Hongrois at which there were performances of the music of older composers as well as that of Bartók, Kodály, Dohnányi and Leó Weiner. On May 28, Bartók performed in Zurich where he played the piano part of his *Rhapsody* at a celebration concert of the Allgemeiner Deutscher Musikverein.

The most significant dates in the calendar of concert performances of new music are March 17 and March 19, 1910. On those dates the works of Kodály and Bartók were presented consecutively. The significance was recognized by Géza Csáth, a writer and critic who died at an early age; in the April 1st issue of *Nyugat* he gave a concise evaluation of the two concerts. In a statement which is also quoted by János Demény he commented that 'we should make a note of the dates of these two concerts when these two young men, hand in hand like comrades, indeed like comrades-in-arms, stepped onto the podium'. The list of works performed at these concerts was indeed impressive, including the *String Quartet No. 1*, the *Sonata for 'Cello and Piano*, and several piano pieces by Kodály, Bartók's earlier *Piano Quintet* as well as a number of piano pieces, and also his fascinating *String Quartet No. 1*. But these concerts were also memorable in that they marked the date from which Bartók and Kodály were recognized as composers to be reckoned with in the musical world. As a result of his recital, Kodály gained for himself the recognition of the musical public of Budapest.

Another notable result of the concerts was the success accorded to the Waldbauer Quartet whose members were all very young. Oddly enough, their ages ranged with the parts they played. Thus Imre Waldbauer, the first violinist, was eighteen; János Temesváry, the second violinist, was nineteen and Antal Molnár, the violist, was twenty. The doyen of the ensemble was the twenty-five-year-old 'cellist, Jenő Kerpely. These four young players undertook to achieve, and indeed successfully achieved, something that was no longer within the capacity of the older generation, whether on account of age, position or musical thinking. They took the trouble to steep themselves in the spirit of new music, to study the methods of performing it, and just as so often before in the history of music, they created a style suitable to the music they were endeavouring to interpret, and they developed their own technique parallel with the development of the music. In December of that year, when Debussy was visiting Hungary on a concert tour, they delighted him with an authentic and masterly interpretation of his String Quartet. The two famous concerts at which Bartók and Kodály played their own compositions set the ensemble on the road to world fame. These young performers always showed a particular talent for the interpretation of new work, especially that of Bartók. It was Imre Waldbauer who played the violin solo of the first piece in Bartók's *Two Portraits* when this was first performed on February 12, 1911.

At both these concerts Bartók took the lion's share of the programme by playing the piano himself. Throughout his life he maintained a friendly, or, to quote Géza Csáth, 'comrade-in-arms' relationship with the Waldbauers. He gladly undertook to play the piano parts of chamber works at their concerts, and often played together with members of the quartet.

It was largely on account of the works of Bartók that the new music received support from the critics. New voices could be heard in the Hungarian press; young writers on music explained and propagated the music of Debussy, Bartók and Kodály. One of the first to do so was Géza Csáth who wrote an appreciation of the *Fourteen Bagatelles* in the issue of *Nyugat* dated January 16, 1909. He was gifted with more musical insight than any of the critics of the older generation, who were often, however, full of goodwill. His subtle ear perceived the twelve-tone harmonic tendencies in Bartók's music. Although, in the fashion of the age, he approached the content of Bartók's work from the point of view of the psychology of the individual, he nevertheless maintained that 'it had reason, musical content, Hungarian character and a future.'

Sándor Kovács wrote a number of studies of Bartók's music in which he quite rightly recognized the composer's polyphonic experiments, though at that time these were not yet inspired directly by Bach and Renaissance polyphony as he thought, but rather indirectly through Reger. His misconception was shared by Géza Vilmos Zágon in an article dated June 1911, but all credit is due to Kovács for his insight and for drawing attention to the relation between Bartók's music and that of Liszt.

In his capacity of aesthetician in the field of music, Antal Molnár, at that time the violist of the Waldbauer Quartet, also took up the cause of the new music. In a lengthy study published in *Zeneközlöny*, on March 1, 1911, he analysed Bartók's *String Quartet No. 1*, and from that time on, throughout his successful career as a writer, he remained one of the most understanding advocates of the new art. Shortly afterwards, he joined Bartók and Kodály on their expeditions to collect folk-songs.

Compared with their elders, these young people had a much clearer understanding of the essentially Hungarian characteristics of music. Lajos Szirt revealed in *Zenevilág* that he was well aware that the group of ardently Hungarian musicians who had acclaimed the *Suite No. 1* were disappointed by *Suite No. 2*. It was Géza Csáth's acknowledgement of this disappointment that led him to conclude his account of the *Bagatelles* so sadly: 'In Hungary, now as before, they rebuke and ridicule those who carry on the work of their predecessors instead of merely imitating it.' While Aurél Kern applauded the two young composers at the end of their 'composer's concerts' with all the wild enthusiasm of a Turanian chauvinist, Béla Reinitz recognized the social significance of the new music. Unlike Sándor Kovács, he did not go so far as to discern a socialist content in Bartók's works, yet in a magnificent article on Kodály, in the March 18 issue of *Népszava* he sensed the 'manifestation of the soul of the real Hungarian people . . . springing from the blood of György Dózsa' (a reference to the martyred leader of the Hungarian Peasant War of 1514). In his review of the 1911 première of the first 'portrait', Reinitz no longer showed any antipathy towards Bartók. He recognized in the tone of this work a kinship with the *String Quartet No. 1* and looked upon it as a preliminary study for the quartet. Recalling the first performance of the quartet which took place during the previous year, he wrote in a reconciliatory and appreciative fashion.

Bartók too wrote a number of musical studies. His review of Strauss's *Elektra* in March 1910, signalled the end of the spell in which he had been held by that composer, and in his famous article written in 1911 and entitled 'Liszt's Music and Today's Public' he expounded a fundamental basis of his own development as an artist and composer and revealed how intimately his work was related to that of Liszt. In the same article, Bartók also gave his view of the significance of Liszt in the history of music in general, and in the history of Hungarian music in particular.

By embarking on these artistic and scientific projects, Bartók's whole way of life was changed. Having renounced his career as a pianist, a career which necessitated journeying all over the world, he accepted the appointment as a professor at the Academy of Music and settled in Budapest. Shortly afterwards, his mother left Pozsony and joined him in the capital where for a time they lived in Teréz körút. His passionate love of travelling was by no means abated but could only be indulged during his holidays. It was then that he went on collecting tours, visited the great cities of Europe and, later, did most of his composing.

Marriage was one of the signs of his new-found security and decision to settle down. In the autumn of 1909, he married a former pupil, Márta Ziegler, to whom he dedicated the first piece of the *Sketches* in 1908, the *Portrait of a Girl;* later he dedicated to her the *Three Burlesques,* and in September, 1911, his opera, *Bluebeard's Castle.* In 1910 their son Béla was born. In the spring of the following year they moved to Rákoskeresztúr where they lived until 1920 in what was later known as Rákoshegy, first in Jókai utca, then, from 1912, in Teréz utca.

The years of search and doubt had by now left their mark on Bartók, both in his features and in his demeanour. The optimistic look in his graduation portrait, the openly defiant and rebellious expression of the composer of the *Suite No. 1,* had now been exchanged for an air of introspection, thoughtfulness and gravity. Once talkative and gregarious, Bartók now became taciturn. His manner has been vividly described by Antal Molnár: 'When in 1910 I was entrusted by Kodály to collect folksongs in Transylvania, I was on several occasions received by Bartók in his home in Teréz körút where he lived together with his mother. Since I was unfamiliar with the technique of collecting, he had to give me instructions. He spoke as matter-of-factly as a locksmith showing his tools to a new apprentice, but with a flattering brevity. Otherwise he stared at me with wide questioning eyes, quite often silent for fifteen minutes at a time. And since I did not dare to break the silence, we just gazed at each other without saying a single word. On one occasion, he suddenly sat down at the piano and played his first string quartet from beginning to end. Then again we were silent for half an hour. We were communicating silently, and, as I felt, eloquently!'

The time had arrived when his creative vision, which until then had shown itself only in single characteristics, movements and paired character pieces, was to be expressed in a larger work in which all these elements would be united. The first great synthesis of these elements achieved artistic form in his opera, *Bluebeard's Castle*.

4 'BLUEBEARD'S CASTLE'. BÉLA BALÁZS, THE LIBRETTIST. LAYERS, DRAMATIC STRUCTURE AND TONAL CONSTRUCTION OF THE MUSIC. 'ALLEGRO BARBARO'

He worked on the opera for a period of six months, entering it for a competition organized by the Lipótvárosi Kaszinó.

> I set the mystery play Bluebeard's Castle to music between March and September 1911. This was my first vocal composition, as well as my first composition for the stage,

he declared at the première, a statement which was published in the May 24, 1916 issue of the *Magyar Színpad*.

The author of the libretto, Béla Balázs, who came from Szeged, was three years younger than Bartók, and was one of the most talented members of the younger generation of writers. His poems were published, together with those of the best of his contemporaries, Endre Ady and Mihály Babits, in the pioneer anthology, *Holnap* (Tomorrow). But he has a very special and honourable place in the ranks of Hungarian artists of the twentieth century for he alone assumed responsibility for the development of modern Hungarian music from its earliest beginnings, and considered it to be his own particular task to provide modern librettos of a high quality to promote the music of Bartók and Kodály. His comments on the subject appeared at about the same time as Bartók's statement of 1918: 'I wrote the mystery play *Bluebeard's Castle* eight years ago for Béla Bartók and Zoltán Kodály because I wanted to give them an opportunity to write works for the stage. (My ballet *The Wooden Prince* was also written specifically for Bartók).' In 1947, when he returned from the long emigration, Balázs paid tribute to Bartók's memory by writing for the stage a dramatized version of the *Dance Suite*. And he appeared on the stage for the last time together with Kodály as co-author of the ballad of *Cinka Panna* at the première in 1948. He died in 1949.

Béla Balázs had met Kodály many years previously when they were students together at the Eötvös College and it was probably through Kodály that he became acquainted with Bartók. An article he wrote in 1922 throws an interesting light on the period of their early struggles and reveals some of the problems that occupied Bartók's mind at that time. The article supplements Bartók's covert confession made in his auto-biography concerning his doubts about his appointment to the staff of the Academy of Music, and the possibility of undertaking folk-music research as an alternative to settling down at home. According to Balázs, Bartók at that time was bent on leaving Hungary at all costs. 'He was convinced that his work was in vain. The stubborn way in which he continued his struggles was an awe-inspiring sight. Without hope or faith, and yet with a bitter and icy resolve—out of duty—and at that time it was I who kindled his belief in himself. I talked to him about the great Hungarian cultural renaissance, the necessity for a Hungarian contri-bution to the development of European culture, and I encouraged him . . . But I had never before observed in anyone the tight lips and unchanging deathly pallor with which Béla Bartók listened to me . .' quotes János Demény from the *Bécsi Magyar Újság*. 'My mystery play was born out of the faith we shared in common when we were both young. It was not meant to be a libretto. After all, it was also played without music at one of the *Nyugat* matinées. The poem was written for Bartók only in the sense that one of two parched and exhausted wanderers might strike up a song to encourage the other, more weary even than himself, to sing too. For singing can carry you on for a time even when your feet are no longer willing. And he was encouraged. He joined me, but with song the like of which had not been heard in Europe since the time of Beethoven . . .'

In Béla Balázs's vivid description we can recognize the Bartók who was 'driven to the brink of non-existence'. Although the composer's dawning awareness of a new calling and purpose in life received its most profound stimulus from his discovery of folk music and the resulting transformation of his thought, nevertheless he must have been greatly helped by the faith of staunch friends like Béla Balázs. And Béla Balázs's mystery play provided him with an opportunity to synthesize his new-found vision for the first time in a large-scale creative work.

The Bluebeard legend is an ancient one; the story of a man who has killed seven wives. It is in fact closely related to the legend of Don Juan and is one of the most variously elaborated themes of European art. The attraction of these stories may be explained by the fact that they deal with fearful and extraordinary happenings told in the mysterious style of a fairy-tale and because the principal theme centres on one of the basic problems of society—the relation between man and woman. As in a fairy-tale, the central theme is simplified so that the stories have a general significance. The story is freed from the fetters of history, time and space, like the heroine of János Arany's ballad 'Vörös Rébék' who is transformed into a bird and thus freed from her own body. So too this legend has travelled through the ages, recognized and welcome wherever it is found. The characters and details of the story and the conceptions embodied in it vary with every age and country in which artists have given it form.

Intellectuals and artists in the disintegrating and alienated bourgeois societies of the nineteenth and twentieth centuries have been happy to identify themselves with the figures of Don Juan and Bluebeard; anguished by their own sense of isolation from society, they turned to these beings as fellow-sufferers who, however, seemed to have the power to tear asunder the established social and moral laws. Kierkegaard, whose thought in some ways anticipated existentialism, hailed Mozart's Don Juan as a hero whose demoniacal energy enabled him to break the cords of social bondage. In this figure he modelled the precursor of Nietzsche's 'superman'. Wagner, at that time a pupil of Schopenhauer, created Tristan and Isolde, the lovers who in the agonizing rapture of desire find fulfilment in dissolution and dissolution in fulfilment. Psychological research based on individualism sought to find in their passions that lost paradise in which society did not suppress the basic human instincts, while the symbolists bemoaned the fate of the lovers as an example of man's inevitable solitariness, a prisoner without hope of escape, the helpless victim of a tragedy decreed by Fate.

Béla Balázs, highly educated, a poet and writer well versed in philosophy and psychology, was able to appreciate the full significance of the theme. The most immediate influence exerted on him was that of the French symbolists. The opera *Ariane et Barbe-Bleu* by Paul Dukas was presented in Paris in 1907. Earlier versions of the story are carefully enumerated in György Kroó's book, *Bartók's Stage Works*. The drama on which this opera was based was written by Maeterlinck, who also wrote the libretto for Debussy's opera *Pelléas et Mélisande* first performed in 1902. The relationship between the Tristan legend and the Bluebeard story may be clearly recognized in the opera *Pelléas et Mélisande*. The aging Golaud, jealous of his younger brother Pelléas, kills him and drives his child wife, Mélisande, to her death. But the stage setting for the opera is full of symbolic imagery. The dark forest, which is the setting of the first scene in which Golaud finds Mélisande, may be found in literature from the time of Dante if not earlier. Even more significant is the dark and gloomy castle which is the background for the rest of the story. In it Mélisande's smile is the only ray of sunshine which penetrates the darkness. The figure of Mélisande haunts much of the Hungarian poetry of that period: in one of Ady's poems he refers to her as 'the white lady of the castle' and in Béla Balázs's drama which became Bartók's opera, her name is Judith.

In Anatole France's short version of the story Bluebeard is transformed from the lecherous murderer of the legend into the innocent victim of a tragicomic misunderstanding; and in Béla Balázs's mystery play he personifies the tragedy of man's impenetrable solitariness. The universe itself is the stage on which the medieval mystery plays were enacted, with the fall and redemption of man as their subject; but the symbolists, equipped with a knowledge of modern psychology, turn into a stage set the microcosm of the human soul. The prologue asks the question, 'The curtain which is our eyelashes is raised and we ask: Where is the stage —within or without?' The answer is inherent in the question: within. Bluebeard's castle is no less than the impregnable human soul itself. Ady supplies us with the key to this idea in his *Új Versek* (New Poems) when he writes, 'My soul is an ancient, spell-bound castle, moss-grown, impregnable and deserted.'

Balázs interprets the legend to signify that we are ourselves Bluebeards held captive in the castle of our irrational fears, robber barons every one, building a home for ourselves out of the souls, tears and blood of others from whom we have stolen their treasures. We guard our blood-stained treasures behind the closed doors of our dark castle, and we can be released from this prison of our own making by the selfless and self-sacrificing love of another (like, as Antal Molnár reminds us, the flying Dutchman in Wagner's opera). But to receive the gift of a selfless love we must open wide the doors of the castle, revealing all our treasures to our redeemer. And when all has been revealed to the redeemer and he has assumed possession of our castle, he too is trapped within its walls, becomes one of its dark secrets and joins the previous would-be saviours as a prisoner. The bleak castle stained with blood and tears, and the prisoners within it, are once again plunged into darkness without hope, enclosed in a circle of enchantment from which the captives cannot escape.

Even this brief account of the legend suffices to explain the fascination it held for Bartók and accounts for his choice of Béla Balázs's drama in his most significant creative period. To approach the play from the single point of view of the conflict between man and woman would be to over-simplify its meaning. Undoubtedly Bartók had very vivid memories of the personal crisis he had passed through in 1907–8 and saw in the play a generalized artistic expression of the problem he had so recently solved. Though the love motif is dealt with in a profound and sensitive manner, this was only one single factor which contributed to the crisis from which he emerged with a whole new vision of the world. A Hungarian, yet also a member of the wider social group of Europe, equipped with a cultural heritage from many sources, Bartók used this crisis as a starting point for his creative work. As members of a living social community, our daily lives are affected by the past as well as by present happenings.

Béla Balázs was Bartók's contemporary. The circumstances of his life were identical to those of Bartók, for he lived in the same community and grappled with the same problems. As we see from the reminiscences quoted above, he looked upon himself as Bartók's companion in a joint venture, and he had the right to do so. In his drama their common problems are given artistic expression in a modern idiom which entirely corresponds to Bartók's own outlook. In the nightmare solitude which he imagined, there is the memory of Nietzsche's philosophy and Strauss's *Zarathustra*, while for Bartók there was the reminder of Tristan and Isolde in the voices of the two lovers as they yearn for each other but meet only in the solitude of infinity. The opening bars of *Bluebeard's Castle* provide us with a musical description of the dark castle which vividly evokes the memory of Golaud, Pelléas and Mélisande in Debussy's opera, and although the music is very different, we are reminded of Debussy's forest music. Any comparison with Debussy must indicate the contemporary flavour of the genre. In 1911, a few months before the completion of *Bluebeard's Castle* the great French master had finished his tremendous stage oratorio, *The Martyrdom of St. Sebastian*, based on the mystery play by D'Annunzio. *Bluebeard's Castle* may be thought of as the successor to this work for it has more of the characteristics of an oratorio than an opera.

The poems of Endre Ady, which held an increasing fascination for Bartók, sprang from the same roots as these mystery plays. And it was Ady who brought out in his work the wider artistic significance of the man–woman relationship in the mystery plays. Ady's Margita, loved by three Hungarian youths, seen against the background of Paris, is intended to personify Hungarian society in the process of renaissance. The Bluebeard in the drama by Balázs epitomizes the author's own complex relation to his people, the social order and the national culture. This is even more strikingly evident in the character created by Bartók in his music. This would explain why Balázs stylized his symbolic drama in the tradition of Hungarian folk poetry. From no other source could he have found the inexhaustible surge of his octosyllabic verse. 'I was looking for a Hungarian style of drama,' he wrote in the Viennese memoirs quoted above. 'I wanted to magnify the dramatic *fluidum* of the Székely folk ballads for the stage. And I wanted to depict a modern soul in the primary colours of folk-song. I wanted the same thing as Bartók. We had the same will and the same youth.'

The octosyllables represented one of the most difficult problems in the treatment of the lyrics. Had there been a well-established precedent for the treatment of the lyrics it would still have been difficult to avoid monotony, for the verses were uniform throughout and for that reason did not easily lend themselves to music. Bartók therefore had to invent a musical idiom and also adapt the Hungarian text for his stage works. He could not use Ferenc Erkel's iambics which sprang from the dotted rhythms of the historic Hungarian dance and march music, the so-called *verbunkos* which distorted out of all recognition the stress of the Hungarian language. Nor could he resort to Mihalovich's Wagner-inspired experiments with declamation. It was the influence of Debussy, the folk-music parlando, and above all the early songs of Kodály, that enabled Bartók to create for the first time an original language for the stage that was Hungarian to the core and which accommodated every nuance of the text just as faithfully as it responded to the art of stage delivery. There is a hint of Wagner's declamatory style with its larger intervals in the treatment of the more turbulent passages of the text. 'Bartók has begun the task of liberating the language and of intensifying natural intonation into music, thereby greatly enhancing the development of Hungarian recitative. This is the first Hungarian musical stage work in which the vocal line is unfalteringly Hungarian,' wrote Kodály in a review of the première in 1918.

Another feature of Béla Balázs's drama that made it peculiarly suitable for musical transcription was the clearly articulated, easily comprehended symmetry of its structure. As the castle opens and is gradually revealed in the light only to close and disappear again in darkness, the circle of the action is complete. From the Beethoven of the late string quartets and from the works of Liszt, Bartók had learnt how to hold within the iron embrace of symmetrical structure of form the tensions inherent in the extreme contradiction of internal drama. His attraction to vast symmetric structures with an uneven number of sections had already been demonstrated in the *Suite No. 1*, and it continued to find expression, though to a lesser extent, in for instance *An Evening with the Székelys* and in the structure of the first *Romanian Dance*.

The opening of the fifth door marks approximately the structural centre of the drama and the axis of its symmetry, balanced on either side by the two arches, ascending and descending, the ascending one with its two pairs of doors. But within the symmetry of this vast outer arch, the text offers the musical realization of another structural axis—the culmination of the dramatic conflict between the two characters which grows in intensity until the moment when they stand before the seventh door. The contradiction between the two structural principles is indicated visually by leaving the sixth and seventh doors standing open while the castle grows darker instead of lighter. Again Beethoven was Bartók's model for the simultaneous musical formulation of two distinct principles. Beethoven could reconcile dual culmination points with inimitable artistry even within the space of eight bars of a sonata theme.

This structural framework also determined Bartók's choice and arrangement of sounds intended to be directly expressive or descriptive. The outermost layer of the musical devises employed by the composer to convey specific sounds and produce specific effects, closely follows the main lines of the structural units. These sounds include, for instance, Judith's sighs, her poundings, the creaking of locks and the sound of footsteps. The significance of the doors is conveyed by means of a deeper and more programmatic layer of music. In order to achieve the visual and dramatic effects necessary for a stage work Bartók made brilliant use of the possibilities of the large orchestra employed by Strauss. He conjures up the red glare and crackling fire of the torture chamber, evokes the martial sound of trumpets amidst the armoury and the cool peace of nature in the secret garden, while at the opening of the fifth door a tumultuous succession of major chords from the entire orchestra illustrates the dazzling rays of the sun which illuminate the vast empire of the castle. The stillness of the pool of tears is interrupted only by an occasional run of liquid notes heard against the diminished sounds of the orchestra.

The music accompanying the scenes at the doors has much of the melodiousness and tonality of folk music. The trumpet sound of the armoury scene falls into a pentatonic scale, while the light from the third and fourth doors is expressed by means of the Lydian-Mixolydian scale with augmented fourths which Bartók first encountered in Debussy's nature music and also, at almost the same time, in Romanian and Slovak folk music.

As the scene changes from one door to the next, the plot of the drama is developed by means of dialogue, conflict and discourse that is almost quarrelsome. It is in these scenes that the music most closely resembles the expressive melodies of Wagner but Bartók's music is interwoven with the parlando of Hungarian folk music as in the *Four Dirges*. In the story, it is Judith who takes the initiative. The musical sphere through which she moves, conveys an impression of gasping, howling, gesticulation and embracing movements; in Bartók's aesthetics, developed after 1907, such music conveys what was for him the meaning of the female principle. On the same musical plane we find the familiar leitmotif of the *Violin Concerto* of 1907–8, and the break-up of major and minor four-tone chords. The leitmotif with its programmatic meaning runs through the musical fabric of the opera, mostly in the descending, minor version. This provides a musical formulation appropriate to Judith's first word and the sighing castle, while plaintive string glissando links the first and last sounds of the chord in the scene by the pool of tears. Again it emerges from the sighing runs which represent the pool of tears, appearing now in the same notes as those of the *Violin Concerto*—B sharp, G sharp, E, C sharp.

There is a gradual abatement in the urgency and violence of this melodic realm with its impression of wild and threatening gestures; instead we begin to hear a quiet note of lament, the sound of a tearful voice which introduces the basic music which characterizes the Duke himself and the castle—the laconic music of a five-tone Hungarian folk-song. The melodic accompaniment to the scene by the pool of tears is similarly quiet and lamenting in character. So too is the music heard during the scene at the final door with the sad group of former wives. Here there is no specific musical illustration of the scene; the music is almost identified with that which characterizes the Duke and his castle—the four-line F sharp pentatonic folk-song that is heard as an entity set apart and unapproachable at the beginning and end of the opera.

The tonal pattern of the work reveals a planned order that is similarly fascinating and is the result of the development of a unified system of tonal thinking that began in earlier works, primarily the *String Quartet No. 1*. Just as we can find in the second *Dirge* a model for the structural elements of the opera, so in the *Allegro Barbaro* of the same period we find the counterpart of its tonal structure. Both works are based on the same tonal duality—the simultaneous use of the F and F-sharp tonalities. (It is interesting to note that we can find the same F, G flat, or, in Bartók's transcription, F, F-sharp duality, in the English horn solo in the third act of *Tristan*.) This tonal network which characterizes the opera consists of a dual tonal base, one centred on the traditional relations of perfect fifths, the other on a tritonal relation of fifths, the two being closely interlaced. This complex network is vitally linked to what one may think of as a dual spinal column, one section of which is the traditional family of perfect fifths, the other the tritonal relation of fifths which cross and are related to each other. From the latter comes the division of the octave into the series of minor thirds—F sharp, A–B sharp, D sharp. (Ernő Lendvai would refer to this as the axis of the tonal structure.) This system of various tonal relationships, related to and intersecting each other, might well be called, after the fashion of polytonality, a polyfunctional system.

In the case of Bartók, this tonal network is no mere experiment in form and technique, but is an important aspect of his method of constructing a work that would convey the significance of the content, just as the classical masters used the system of traditional tonalities as the basis of the forms they devised. In the opera, the F sharp tonality represents the Duke and his castle while the F tonality characterizes Judith and the captive women. Judith's first note in the opera is F, and the two extreme notes of her descending leitmotif link the two tonal poles, F and F sharp. In the prelude and in the finale, the musical image of the castle is depicted by means of an F sharp pentatonic melody. This marks the beginning and the end of the plot: we are left in the same darkness from which the first scene emerged at the beginning of the opera. The climax of the opera is marked by the solemn sounding of the opposing polarity of C major. This C major is at the same time the traditional upper fifth of Judith's tonality. The radiant melody of this realm is heard three times and on each occasion it is harmonized in a different tonality. These are, as they occur consecutively, C, A flat, and F major. Together they make up the basic minor triad of Judith's F tonality. The women at the seventh door also bewail their fate in a C tonality, but this time it is a minor one. In the music characterizing the individual doors both before and after the musical climax at the fifth door, the doors are linked by tonality in pairs, two pairs before the climax and one following it, and there is also an internal relationship between these tonalities.

The simultaneous sounding of the two tonalities reflects the conflicts at the crucial stages of the drama. When the initial F sharp melody returns to convey the image of the castle of tears, it is veiled by the F minor sighs of the women. At the closing of the seventh door there is a tensely drawn-out opposition between the notes F–F sharp and C–C sharp, marking the 1st flare-up of the strife between Bluebeard and Judith. The harsh minor second of the 'blood' motif which appears at the end of each scene is one element of the tonal structure and also an undisguised illustration of the clash between the two protagonists. At the same time it is related to the sphere of direct musical portrayal.

In the second half of the opera, there is an interesting change of note: as Bluebeard's longing to be loved grows in intensity he sings more and more frequently in Judith's F tonality, while as Judith tries more and more desperately to discover the secrets of the castle the more closely she approaches the F sharp tonality of Bluebeard. When, before the open seventh door, Bluebeard has recounted the story of his previous wives and turns to the fourth, Judith, he declares his love for her in a sweeping F major key. This is the moment when there is the fleeting possibility of reconciliation, when their antagonism might have been transformed into a union of love. But it is too late, Judith's role changes and she joins the other women as one of the secrets of the castle. She remains only as a painful memory, represented by the sigh of the F major chord which is faintly heard after the last note of the concluding F sharp pentatonic melody.

The former system of relationships between notes and keys had disintegrated, and a new and logical order had evolved and been developed on the basis of new principles; this was the result of the synthesis of a less rigidly applied European tonal system and a folk music that was strictly and similarly disciplined. The logic of the system enabled Bartók to find a way of expressing his vision of the world in which we find the crystallization of all that he had learnt and appreciated in the field of folk music. The individual elements of the complex material which came from so many different sources preserved something of their original significance though their content is modified so that they can be incorporated smoothly within the unity of a new framework. The transitions, or bridge structures, in the musical images in the opposing pairs of movements found in the earlier works, are also developed in

Bluebeard's Castle where they serve to create the unity of contradictions. The solid basis of the whole system is folk music, and it is the artistic expression of the value which Bartók attached to the conception of nature in his mature outlook. The passages in the opera which are concerned with human solitariness are identified with folk music, signifying that for Bartók this symbol transcends the sphere of human relations and represents also the relationship and contest between man and nature. Here there can be no solution because any direct contest between man and nature, without the mediation of society, can lead only to tragedy.

Bartók's entry was awarded no prize in the competition. However, he resigned himself neither to the failure of the opera in the competition nor to the necessity of a tragic ending to the conflict represented. The funereal *Bluebeard's Castle* was followed by *Allegro Barbaro* with its traditional diabolic scherzo, which testifies to the stern and intensified resolution with which he was prepared to continue his battles. In this work, the minor third expressing Bluebeard's despair is transmuted into the sounds of a condensed unit which signifies combat. Although in the central section we can still hear Judith's sigh, faint as if after the passage of time, the rest of the work constitutes a powerful experiment in evolving new syntheses.

CHAPTER VI

YEARS OF SILENCE. FOLK-MUSIC COLLECTIONS AND THE ANXIETIES OF WAR. THE WOODEN PRINCE. 1911–1917

1 Struggle for the recognition of new music. Disappointment and withdrawal. 'Four Orchestral Pieces'. Folk-music collections in Bihar and the Romanian collection in Máramaros

> My works, from Opus 4 onwards, naturally aroused considerable antagonism in Budapest. One reason for this lack of understanding was that the performance of the newer orchestral pieces was by no means perfect. We had neither an understanding conductor nor a suitable orchestra. At the height of the battle, some of the younger musicians, including Kodály and myself, tried to form the New Hungarian Music Society in 1911. This had as its avowed aim the organization of an independent concert orchestra that would perform the newest and freshest musical creations in an acceptable manner.

This extract from Bartók's autobiography indicates the largely negative reasons for setting up the organization which became known as UMZE. Bartók himself was personally affected by the fact that his work could not be performed in a worthy manner, and it is not to be wondered at that he should have contemplated such action. Any attempt to extend the horizons of the national musical culture was hopelessly impeded by the inadequate organization of Hungarian musical life. But, as we have already seen, there were on the other hand some advocates of the contemporary trends in European music who were ready to support these same trends in Hungary. The Waldbauers proved by their own performances that a good rendering could reveal the true worth of this music. Favoured by a temporarily milder climate of social and cultural opinion, the Waldbauers stimulated by their example the development of a movement which gradually achieved a unity acknowledged in the concert halls and in the press.

As the strength of the existing forces diminished and that of the attacking forces increased, a number of signs appeared to indicate that the time was ripe for the establishment of UMZE. In the issue dated April 15, 1911, the *Zeneközlöny* published a draft scheme for the organi-

116

zation of the society and Sándor Kovács appealed for subscribers, laying special emphasis on the pressing need for an orchestra. From the very beginning, this article aroused disagreement among those in authority and the state subsidy necessary for the organization of the orchestra was withheld. The series of five chamber-music and solo recitals with which UMZE was launched, was a more modest endeavour than anything that had been anticipated.

It was not a very promising start to the enterprise, as we see from Bartók's outburst on the postcard sent from Szabadka (now Subotica, Yugoslavia) to Etelka Freund on November 24:

> Well, this UMZE has been such a nuisance that I would like to consign it to the depths of hell.

Yet, three days later, he undertook a major share of the first UMZE concert in the Royal Hall. There were performances by only one solo recitalist, Dezső Róna, an opera singer, who in both the first and second parts of the programme sang some of the folk-song arrangements by Bartók and Kodály; Bartók, however, played the piano throughout the evening. Most of the works he played were by Scarlatti, Couperin and Rameau, a fact which provides striking evidence that through his research into folk music he had come to recognize, like Liszt, Debussy and Ravel before him, the Baroque sources of twentieth-century musical thinking. He also took part in the second UMZE concert, held on December 12, when he played works by Debussy, Ravel and Leó Weiner. At the next two concerts, however, held on January 12 and March 27, 1912, he did not play, nor were his works included in the programme; the fifth of the proposed series of concerts did not take place. UMZE had failed. This failure, in conjunction with other failures of a more personal nature, caused Bartók, around 1912, to 'withdraw completely from public musical life'.

The failure of UMZE cannot be attributed wholly to the unsatisfactory organization and inadequate administration of the society. These were factors which merely reflected the underlying cause of the failure—public indifference to the cause of new music in Budapest. The experiment was a painful demonstration of the fact that contemporary music was appreciated only by a few of the younger musicians whose minds were open to new ideas but who were at that time still unable to enlist support from even progressive writers and artists. Their knowledge and enthusiasm counted for nothing beside the apathy of the Budapest audiences. In a review of the first concert organized by UMZE, one critic wrote in *Zeneközlöny*, 'Unfortunately, the interest shown by the audience was minimal, although here they were being given an opportunity to hear music the like of which is not easily found anywhere . . .' This particular critic was still hopeful that 'the basic reason for the failure was not so much the antagonism of the audience itself but rather the novelty of the organization' and he believed that it would only be a matter of time before audiences would come 'to know and appreciate such music, and finally find that they could not live without it'. After the second concert any such charitable explanation had to be abandoned. The review in *Egyetértés* provided an answer to the hopes expressed in *Zeneközlöny*: 'The audience shows no sign of interest in these undeniably interesting programmes. Indeed, the second concert held this evening in the Royal Hall was attended by only a proportion of the small group of subscribers whose support we had counted on after the first concert. Yet, had they filled every seat in the hall, and had there been nothing more to fulfil their expectations, these would have been amply rewarded by the brilliant virtuosity of Béla Bartók's piano playing and the first performance of Leó Weiner's three compositions.'

This open indifference, coming after a temporary period of awakened public interest, was the result of political gloom and uncertainty. During the elections of 1910, István Tisza's so-called Labour Party which followed the policy and therefore enjoyed the support of Vienna, gained a majority in Parliament. The earlier coalition had now been replaced by an openly extremist and reactionary government bent on stamping out every vestige of internal resistance to their plan to strengthen the armed forces and conduct an imperialist war. With all the conscientiousness of a medieval chronicler, János Demény had recorded the increased interest in music that became evident during the years 1910–11 at this time of change in the political climate—of which one characteristic symptom was the formation of the racist Turan Society. In fact, however, the new political atmosphere favoured the kind of musical life which did not develop for some time. The interest in music to which he referred was due to the delayed effect of the relaxed cultural atmosphere of the earlier liberal period. One of the last noticeable results of this period of liberality was the musical confidence expressed in the activities described above; there followed a destructive period of sabre-rattling when power lay in the hands of landed reactionaries who were intoxicated by chauvinist dreams and illusions of grandeur.

The failure of UMZE occurred under repressive conditions and the threat of war. On April 22, 1912, István Tisza, backed by Vienna, became Speaker of the House. On April 23, a mass demonstration of protest was crushed by the police. Tisza also resorted to force in Parliament where, by forcibly removing the opposition members, he achieved an artificial majority which enabled him to push through a bill to increase the armed forces. If the short-lived enthusiasm for UMZE left any doubts as to the true nature of the forces behind the cultural activities of the times, these were quickly dispelled after the first performance of Bartók's *Two Portraits* conducted by István Kerner on February 26, 1913. It is true that Béla Reinitz, writing in *Népszava*, praised the new Bartók composition; and in the columns of the *Zeneközlöny* there was an attempt to remain faithful to the principles of UMZE by printing a favourable review containing a preliminary assessment of the work, and in *Magyarország*, Andor Merkler paid tribute to the composer; but in general, the occasion provoked a renewed outburst of criticism from most of the influential conservative papers. The music critics were only too happy to be able to justify their condemnation by referring to the hissing by which a certain section of the audience had expressed its disapproval. 'Bartók's work is a pathological phenomenon rather than art,' wrote one anonymous critic in *Világ*, and in the *Budapesti Hirlap* there appeared for the first time the charge of treason that was to occur again and again thereafter, whether openly or in some veiled form; it is interesting to note that on this occasion the accusation came from the pen of Emil Haraszti, author of later books on Bartók. One quotation from his article suffices to remind us of his attitude: 'We should like to know why Béla Bartók, a professor of the National Hungarian Royal Academy of Music has now assumed the role of a musical Scotus Viator. Can it be that he is no longer interested in Hungarian music of any kind? He has become the apostle of Czech, Romanian, Slovak and God knows what other kind of music—any kind except Hungarian . . .' These remarks were inspired by the tense atmosphere of the pre-war years of international crises, when the problem of national minorities had not been solved and István Tisza was about to become premier. Haraszti was referring to R. W. Seaton-Watson's articles signed *Scotus Viator* (Scottish Traveller), in which the question of the minorities was considered from the point of view of Entente imperialism. In any such accusation there was an element of danger to Bartók.

At the beginning of 1912, having recognized the failure of both UMZE and *Bluebeard's Castle*, Bartók made no more public appearances and withdrew from the musical life of Budapest.

His withdrawal was complete and all-embracing. Some of the reasons which led to his decision are revealed in a letter he wrote to Géza Vilmos Zágon on August 22, 1913;

> . . . a year ago sentence of death was officially pronounced on me as a composer. Either those people are right, in which case I am an untalented bungler; or I am right, and it's they who are the idiots. In either event, this means that between myself and them (that is, our musical leaders: Hubay, etc.) there can be no discussion of music, still less any joint action . . . Therefore I have resigned myself to write, for my writing-desk only.
>
> So far as appearances abroad are concerned, all my efforts during the last 8 years have proved to be in vain. I got tired of it, and a year ago I stopped pressing for that, too . . . My public appearances are confined to *one sole field:* I will do anything to further my research work in musical folklore! I have to be personally active in this field, for nothing can be achieved in any other way; while neither recognition nor public appearances are required for composing . . .

In 1912, Bartók wrote *Four Old Hungarian Folk-Songs*, folk-song arrangements for male chorus, and also *Preludio, Scherzo, Intermezzo* and *Marcia Funebre*, which together constituted *Four Orchestral Pieces* op. 12. This work was indeed composed for his writing desk only. Nine years later it had still not been orchestrated and it was not performed until January 9, 1922. 'This long delay speaks volumes about our musical conditions,' wrote Kodály in the *Zeneközlöny* after the première.

Kodály's assessment of the *Four Orchestral Pieces* is entirely in accordance with its date of origin for he wrote of it as an example of the creative phase between the production of *Bluebeard's Castle* and the composition of *The Wooden Prince*: '. . . The work is reminiscent of both.

120

The *Marcia Funebre* is as if it were a tragic echo of the opera and an elegiac reverberation of the *Intermezzo*. The *Preludio* and the *Scherzo*, on the other hand, herald the sunnier realm of *The Wooden Prince*.' The structural edifice of the *Four Orchestral Pieces*, however, is based on a grander and more comprehensive design. This was Bartók's first attempt, after the period of crisis through which he had passed in both his personal life and in his artistic development, to compose a symphonic work that would portray the world. In his search for a means of expression he turned, not to *Bluebeard's Castle*, but to his earlier work. This was one of those occasions on which he made a fresh start and which from time to time draw our attention to the homogeneous nature of the problems he faced in all his works and also of the ways in which he attempted to solve them.

The most striking feature of this particular composition is the use of paired contrasts in the manner of Beethoven which Bartók became aware of and learned to use through his study of Berlioz, Liszt and Wagner; here, even more sharply contrasted than previously, we find the Scherzo and the funeral march paired in a new setting. The fact that the work ends with a funeral march reminds us of the *Kossuth Symphony* but the later work sounds a more passionate and tragic note. The turmoil of the fourteenth *Bagatelle* and the second 'portrait' with their unevenly numbered beats and Mephistophelian intonation, is intensified in the Scherzo into a veritable witches' Sabbath. And it is also true that these features can be found in the dance of the Princess. But the *Intermezzo*, with its slow waltz and veiled siciliano-tone, is perhaps even more significant and points still further into the future. Here is the raw material from which Bartók wove the delicately coloured fabric of the music portraying the girl in *The Miraculous Mandarin*. The cool, quivering landscape of the *Preludio* not only reminds us of the flower-garden of the castle and the 'In full bloom', the first piece of *Two Pictures*, but also prepares the way for the nature music of the ballet to follow, *The Wooden Prince*.

It is in the middle section of the first movement that we find the most powerful reminder that there are shadows beyond the sunlight; the clouds seem to gather above some lonely wayfarer who finds oblivion beside a pool of tears. The sighing notes of the leitmotif have already been heard in *Bluebeard's Castle*.

By using the symphony as a means of expression Bartók was again faced with the same problems he had attempted to solve earlier, and most agonizing of them all was the old problem of contradictions. The title of the third movement, *Intermezzo*, is in itself an indication that it is a bridge between two tragic and dramatic movements that belong together and are interrelated. The connection between the two movements is too loose and provisional for the work to merit the title of symphony or even suite. Nevertheless the fact that the work has four distinct sections makes it reminiscent of the *Suite No. 2*, and it was as a suite that such outstanding connoisseurs of Bartók's music as Aladár Tóth liked to regard it. However, the real significance of *Four Orchestral Pieces* is best realized if we consider it in relation to the long series of works that followed, all of which ended with a slow movement.

During the following year, Bartók composed only the shorter series of piano pieces included in the *Piano Textbook* that Bartók edited together with Sándor Reschofsky. In the little pieces *For Children*, we can see signs, as in the earlier *Bagatelles* and *Sketches*, of the later *Mikrokosmos*. The year 1914, however, appears to have been quite unproductive and we know of no work completed during that year.

During these years, however, he became even more engrossed than previously in folk-music research, and, as he himself confirmed in a letter written to Géza Vilmos Zágon in 1913, his activities in this field were ceaseless. Though from time to time he collected Hungarian folk music, he was for many years mainly preoccupied with Romanian folk music. If we trace on the map the route of his collecting tours we can see that he used Bihar as a centre from which to make a systematic survey of the methods of music-making and the melodic styles of the Romanian peasants living in the eastern parts of Hungary.

He travelled eastwards towards the very heart of Transylvania. For instance, he made one expedition in March 1910, to Kolozs County, in November he was collecting songs in Szolnok-Doboka and between December of that year and January 1911 he went to Alsó-Fehér and Torda-Aranyos Counties. In April 1914, he again spent some time in this area, visiting Maros-Torda County where he was accompanied by his wife, Márta Ziegler, who collected forty songs. It is believed that the source of his first notes on the southern areas was his birthplace, Nagyszentmiklós, in Torontál County, which he visited in January 1910. He returned to Temes and Torontál in March 1912, and again in November and December of that year, and in February and March 1913. A successful tour of Hunyad County in December 1913 completed his researches in these southern areas. He also made several trips to Szatmár County in the north, as for instance when he visited Bereg in April 1912, to collect Hungarian material. The collection he made in Máramaros, however, was much more significant than his previous discoveries. It would appear from one of his references to Máramaros that he had already been there in 1912; this may have been at the time of his trip to Szatmár-Bereg. However, most of the three hundred and sixty-five melodies which constitute the Máramaros material, was recorded in eleven villages between March 5 and March 17, 1913. In Máramaros he was assisted by Ion Bîrlea, a priest of Jod. Meantime he returned at frequent intervals to his beloved collecting centre, Bihar, where he was helped by János Buşiţia; between December 1911 and January 1912, and again in February 1914, he stayed there, making expeditions to collect Hungarian folk-songs in such regions as Maros-Torda. This brief summary of his journeys may give some idea of the well-nigh incredible range of his research work.

For the most part, Bartók arranged his tours to take place during the school holidays, during the summer, at Christmas and at Easter. A good many of the folk customs are connected with the religious festivals of Christmas and Easter, and these were especially interesting to Bartók. During his tour he was particularly concerned to note down the peculiar genre known as *kolinda* that was associated with the Christmas folk customs. Nearly everywhere he went, he came upon precious examples of these songs with their elaborations of various historical and mythical legends as well as the story of the Creation as told in Genesis. He published his discoveries concerning the musical dialects of Romanians living in the Bihar, Máramaros and Hunyad districts, and much later he also published a separate collection of Romanian *kolindas*.

The cares of publishing were an added burden to him during this busy period of travelling and collecting. For, together with Kodály, Bartók did his utmost to ensure that the fruits of his scientific work should be made known to the public. His Bihar collection was published in Bucharest, and it was also in conjunction with the Romanian Academy of Sciences that he prepared his material from Máramaros. On March 18, 1914, under the auspices of the Ethnographical Society, Bartók gave a lecture on his discoveries in the Hunyad area. This lecture was published later that year in the *Ethnographia* under the title *A hunyadi román nép zenedialektusa* (The Musical Dialect of the Rumanian People in Hunyad). The lecture was accompanied by musical illustrations provided by Romanian peasants whom Bartók brought specially from Cserbel (Cerbal) to sing and dance. He took great pleasure in showing them the sights of Budapest and wrote an amusing letter to János Buşiţia describing their adventures in the city.

Bartók and Kodály jointly sought help from a distinguished literary society so that they would be able to publish the results of their scientific work. After summarizing what had already been accomplished in the field of folk-music research in Hungary, they prepared their own Hungarian collections for publication. The text of their appeal was printed in the October issue of *Ethnographia*, but they waited in vain for a response. Bartók did not live to see the first attempt to publish his work in a comprehensive and systematic way.

As he became involved in the study of folk music in so many different places he began to realize the possibility of undertaking more extended researches. He thought the time was ripe to undertake, for scientific purposes, a comparative study of the melodies of various regions and even peoples. In an article written in 1912 he wrote of such a study as a new science of 'comparative music folklore'. The comparisons he made and the similarities he noted were at first seemingly accidental. A melody heard in Máramaros in 1912 revived his long-standing interest in Arab music, and this in turn may have been aroused merely as a result of his trip to Africa made in the course of his concert tour of Spain and Portugal. In 1911 he visited Paris in connection with his study of Arabic folk music and in June of 1913 he realized his plan to visit North Africa. On this journey he was accompanied by his wife. There he laboured indefatigably in the intense heat, collecting the folk music of non-urban Arabs. He wrote to Buşiţia that he found the work very interesting but that his health was suffering and that he had been barely able to endure the heat even for one week. He was forced to leave the country, though he planned to return to the Kabyle tribe the following year. In October he wrote to Bîrlea informing him that he had already bought a Kabyle grammar.

2 POLITICAL TENSION, THWARTED FOLK-MUSIC PLANS. OUTBREAK OF WAR. COLLECTING WORRIES AND FAMILY TROUBLES

One by one, however, these important and ambitious plans were shattered by the approach of war. Kodály has recorded that '... around 1912 he began to study Russian in connection with his plans to make a Chuvash-Tartar study trip to Russia ... This tour did not materialize because of the threat of war. It is hard to imagine just how much more we would now know about the music of our Eastern relatives had he succeeded in getting there.' Bartók's other plans had to be similarly abandoned, for instance his projected visits to Kabyle and Moldavia in 1914 and a scheme to revisit Biskra in 1915.

The political atmosphere abroad had for some time been poisoned by the threat of war while at home the prevalence of chauvinistic hatreds and prejudices was making life in Hungary well-nigh unendurable. Already in February 1913, when Bartók made an application through the Hungarian foreign ministry for a note of recommendation from the French to the Algerian authorities so that he could continue his work of collecting Arab music, he met with little encouragement. The note was not provided. Finally, Zágon came to his aid and it seems that it was he who managed to secure some kind of letter of recommendation for Bartók in Paris. By this time it had also become more difficult to maintain friendly relations with our neighbours. It was not possible to publish the Máramaros collection until after the war, in 1923. The publication of the collection of *kolindas* was delayed in Munich until 1935. The first note of Romanian chauvinism was sounded in the spring of 1914, in an article in a Moldavian magazine, *Sezâtoarea*, in which the writer accused Bartók of falsifying some of the melodies of his Bihar collection. The author of this article did not accept these melodies as Romanian, attributing them to sources contaminated by 'Hungarian influence'; in like manner, there were Hungarian chauvinists and dilettanti who rejected the Hungarian folk-songs as 'Romanian' or 'Slovak'. Bartók lost no time in writing to the *Convorbiri Literare* of Bucharest to refute these charges; but the article in *Sezâtoarea* proved to be only the first of its kind. And it was on the basis of Bartók's account of his Hunyad collection that he was denounced in the post-war years by Hungarian racists.

This growing number of obstacles to friendly relations with our neighbours made Bartók all the more determined to overcome them and to learn more about the different nationalities so that he could justify and maintain his political views. His friendship with János Buşiţia became even closer. Hardly a year passed by without a visit to Belényes. Everywhere he went Bartók made a point of sending a card or a letter to the secondary-school teacher in the small town of Bihar County. In the course of the summer of 1912, Bartók wrote from both Lapland and from Africa. He showed the same care and solicitude in corresponding with his Romanian friends, the composer Kiriac, a librarian in the Academy, Bianu, and the priest at Máramaros, Bîrlea.

His experiences among the Romanian peasants greatly strengthened his political convictions and conduct. In the course of his explorations he visited remote districts which from the point of view of collecting folk music were 'model villages' but which were completely neglected communities of impoverished Romanians living in isolation, without roads or schools. One such village was Máramaros where in 1907 the exploited Romanian peasants took up their scythes in revolt, and Vaskoh in Bihar where there were epidemics of pellagra caused by malnutrition and famine. Bartók's clear-sighted understanding of the situation is shown in the very first letter he wrote to Buşiţia in the Romanian language, dated January 1912, the time when he was suffering setbacks as a composer. The last paragraph of the letter is worthy of quotation:

> I'm sending you a book of poems by Ady who is our youngest poet, but the most respected since Petőfi and Arany. I suggest that you read those particularly on pages 30, 34, 38, 43, 49, 88, 106, 115. The first, one says that Hungarians, Romanians and Slavs in this country, should all be united, since they are kindred in misery. We've never had a poet who would dare to write such things.

The volume which Bartók enclosed was *Az Illés szekerén* (On the Chariot of Elijah) published in 1908. Demény lists the poems included in the first edition as follows: 'Magyar jakobinus dala' ('Song of the Hungarian Jacobin'), 'Magyar fa sorsa' ('The Fate of the Magyar Tree'), 'Miért is

126

tettem' ('Why Did I Do it'), 'A téli Magyarország' ('Hungary in Winter'), 'A magyar vigasság' ('Hungarian Merry-making'), 'Nekünk Mohács kell' ('We Need a Mohács'), 'A grófi szérűn' ('In the Count's Barn'), 'Akit én csókolok' ('The One I Kiss'), and 'Májusi zápor után' ('After a May Shower'). This letter assumes even greater significance when we recall the political atmosphere of the period when it was written, a period when the Tisza regime was becoming more powerful, when the Czech Parliament had been dissolved by Austria, the Croatian Parliament by Hungary and the various leaders of the national minorities were being brought to trial.

On November 3, 1912, Bartók wrote a brief postcard to his mother from Bucharest:

> I am on a short expedition to the Balkan Peninsula! I have made friends with some Romanians (since I cannot make friends at home).

These few words provide the clearest possible indication of his feelings as well as the clarity of his political outlook. After his return to Paris Bartók wrote to Buşiţia on July 18, 1914, informing him that he had been able to 'arrange several things connected with Romanian affairs'. A few days later he arrived back in Budapest only just before the outbreak of the First World War.

The catastrophe that shook the world came also as a great shock to Bartók.

> I have wanted to write to you for a long time, but I have been so upset by world events that my mind has been almost completely paralyzed,

he wrote to Buşiţia at the end of September. There was an unusually long period of silence before his next letter to Belényes written on May 20, 1915. He excused this seeming neglect on the grounds of

> depression due to the war—a condition which, in my case, alternates with a kind of devil-may-care attitude.

As well as being disturbed by 'universal human issues' he had to contend with the more personal troubles connected with the difficulty of continuing the task of collecting folk music. 'But no matter what happens,' he wrote in a letter dated September 1914,

I shall remain faithful to the work I have begun. I look upon it as the main purpose of my life to continue and complete my study of Romanian, or at least Transylvanian, folk music . . .

This thought occurs again, like a recurring refrain, in the letter of May 1915, when he writes,

... nothing matters, but to remain good friends with Romania; it would be a grievous thing to me to see my beloved Transylvania devastated, besides greatly hindering my prospect of finishing, or rather continuing, my work.

His way of life was very little affected by the war, and he was able to go on with his work, though he had to curtail to some extent the range of his activities. He was not called up for military service as he was found to be under-weight—he weighed only ninety-nine pounds, and was therefore classed as unfit for active service. He confessed that he would

find it a bit of an effort to do big marches or quick advances (or retreats?), and with a great load on my back, too.

For some years he had been accustomed to accept invitations to appear in public only on rare occasions of absolute necessity. As early as on April 20, 1912, on the occasion of his first concert in Transylvania, held in Marosvásárhely (Tîrgu-Mures), he did not play his own works. We have already noted that this was also the case on the occasion of the UMZE concerts. On February 1st, 1913, he gave a concert in Kecskemét, where it is believed that he gave the first public performance of the *Allegro Barbaro*. The next public appearance which has been reported is the piano recital which he gave on March 18, 1914, on the occasion of Thomán's twenty-fifth anniversary as a teacher. There followed another lengthy period before his next appearance; this was on October 17, 1915, during an exhibition of paintings by József Rippl-Rónai when Bartók gave an afternoon recital of some of his own works, and possibly also something from his book of *Fifteen Hungarian Peasant Songs*. The programme also included an appearance by Zsigmond Móricz who read one of his short stories.

These appearances were of little significance when compared with the numerous recitals he had given in earlier years, playing week after week in Hungarian towns and also the capital cities of many different countries.

Now, however, there were no more journeys abroad to collect folk-songs, no more of the globe-trotting that he so much enjoyed: his travels had come to a halt. The daily walk between his apartment in Rákoskeresztúr and the Academy of Music where he was teaching could scarcely compensate for the loss of his trips to Paris and Africa. And in his own country he was still not accepted as an artist of any great merit. After a performance of only part of his *Suite No. 1* there were hypocritical notices in the press, deploring the 'aberrations' of the genius who had once been capable of writing such a work. In fact the performance was a repetition of an earlier performance by the Hungarian Philharmonic Orchestra in Vienna when Bartók had written to protest against the mutilation of his work and to forbid the orchestra ever to play his work again.

His excursions to collect folk music were therefore a source of refreshment as well as an escape from the oppressive atmosphere of Budapest. He wrote to Bușiția:

> It is hard to imagine, that anyone could go on collecting folk-songs in times like these. But it can be done. The amazing thing about it is that you can do it exactly as in peace time. The peasants are so merry and light-hearted, one might think they don't care a hang about the war.

For the time being he had to suspend his visits to Romanian peasants

> because of inconvenient transport facilities; but I did some collecting among the Slovaks, first in my own locality (Rákoskeresztúr) and then in Zólyom County, for a week around Easter!

He continued his researches in Zólyom County during July and August. This time he took his family with him for the summer holiday, and his son, Béla, remembers the experience to this day: 'I recall the collecting tour in the summer of 1915 when we stayed in Hédel, in Zólyom County, where the first night we slept on makeshift beds on the benches of the elementary school . . .' Bartók was at that time still working on Slovak material, and his discoveries are recorded in notes dated November and Christmas, 1915, and Easter, 1916. It was during these tours that he discovered traces of a type of Slovak melody known as the *valašská*. This Mixolydian melodic type, mostly instrumental in nature, was, in

Bartók's view, extremely important in the history of Slovak folk music; indeed he believed it to be the oldest and most original of its kind.

But a period of still greater difficulty was approaching when the Bartók family began to be affected more closely by the hardships of war. The most severe blow fell when Romania came into the war at the end of August 1916. Mrs. Bartók and her son were in Transylvania at the time of the Romanian invasion and for three weeks nothing was heard of them. It is possible that it was during her escape that Mrs. Bartók suffered the pulmonary lesion which later affected her health. In 1917, she went to the Tatra mountains for treatment, although—as Bartók complained to Buşiţia in 1917—

> what she needed was the strict régime of a place like Davos, but no one can get to those places now. She is still not fully recovered, and I don't know what will happen. At Keresztúr there is neither butter nor milk nor anything else.

Besides these family troubles Bartók also had to bear all the cares of a frustrated folklorist.

> The steadily worsening world situation which, it seems, has ruined my career (collecting folk-songs, I mean), for the most beautiful regions of all, Eastern Europe and the Balkans, are completely ravaged—this in itself has depressed me enough. How my heart bled when I heard that the inhabitants of Fogaras, etc., had left their homes to go with the Romanian army. Will they ever come back again, and if they do, what sort of condition will they be in?! Shall I ever be able to do any collecting there?! How I grieved for the Székelys of Csík and Gyergyó, for I was there, too. Later, of course, it came out that it was not the 'enemy' who caused them so much suffering but—but I'd rather not write it; anyway, you know who.

And finally, in drawnig up the balance sheet of the war years, he wrote,

> I have gone through more trouble in the past year and a half than at any time in my life before.

STIMULUS PROVIDED BY ROMANIAN AND SLOVAK FOLK MUSIC, SMALLER FOLK-SONG COMPOSITIONS. 'THE WOODEN PRINCE'. LIBRETTO, DRAMATIC AND SYMPHONIC CONSTRUCTION. 'PIANO SUITE' (OP. 14), SONGS. 'STRING QUARTET No. 2'

And yet after the first bout of war depression had somewhat eased, Bartók, like Debussy in those same years, began to compose again and returned to the old problems of the tormenting creative work without which he could never exist for any extended period. 'I have even found the time—and ability—to do some composing,' he wrote to Buşiţia on May 20, 1915, mentioning his renewed activity for the first time.

The fruits of the work accomplished by Bartók during these years of retreat are of two kinds reflecting the two branches of his life-work, original composition and folk-music research. His study of folk music resulted in a long series of works which were direct adaptations of newly-discovered folk music; parallel with these works there appeared those compositions which sprang from his experience of human solitariness and his attempt to resolve the inner conflicts of the past ten years. For many years to come these two branches of his life-work remained apart, with no visible link, yet there was always present the hidden relationship that is dependent on a shared source of life.

Those of Bartók's compositions which are most closely akin to folk music accurately reflect the musical experiences of his collecting tours. First, in 1915, he formed several short series based on the songs of the Romanian tours. The first of these, as in his earlier work of a similar nature, were composed for the piano and included the *Sonatina*, the *Romanian Folk Dances* consisting of six pieces, and the two cycles of the *Romanian Kolinda Melodies* (comprising, respectively, nine and ten pieces). These were supplemented by the unpublished *Two Romanian Folk-Songs* for female voices and *Nine Romanian Folk-Songs* for voice and piano. The new compositions to which Bartók referred in his letter to Buşiţia are presumably the piano pieces and the six little dances with their dedication in Romanian. In its original form and transcription it is still one of Bartók's most popular compositions.

The songs collected among the Slovaks were arranged later. The first part of the future *Three Rondos on Folk Tunes* for the piano originated at that time too. In 1917, Bartók composed *Slovak Folk-Songs* which consisted of five songs for male voices, also *Four Slovak Folk-Songs* for mixed voices and piano (though according to János Demény the latter was composed during the previous year, for he believes that it was performed on January 5, 1917, by Emil Lichtenberg's choir).

In the meantime, Bartók continued to produce adaptations of Hungarian folk-songs, including *Four Old Hungarian Folk-Songs* for male voices written in 1912. In 1917, he completed a series of songs which he had begun sometime earlier and which became known as the *Eight Hungarian Folk-Songs* for voice and piano. The first of these pieces dates from 1907. In like fashion, during these years of war, he found time to reap the harvest of his work throughout the previous years by completing a series for piano, *Fifteen Hungarian Peasant Songs*. It is probable that the last section of this work, *Old Hungarian Dances*, was in fact written first.

Superficially, these works would appear to be quite simply a continuation of the earlier folk-song series such as *Three Folk-Songs from the County of Csík* and *For Children*, but closer scrutiny reveals that they have been profoundly affected by his experiences during the intervening years. The changes are discernible primarily in the rounding out of structural forms and to a much lesser extent in the methods of harmonization which retains more or less faithfully the open, serene and simple tone of similar works written earlier. In his later folk-song arrangements Bartók searched assiduously for diversified ways of applying the formal possibilities inherent in folk music. The cycles, originally put together as a random selection of pieces, developed more and more into close-knit units. One indication of this is the manner in which Bartók selected individual works written earlier, added to them and so formed complete series. Another indication of this method is the experimental development gradually introduced into the *Fifteen Hungarian Peasant Songs*. In places, the folk melodies fit into classical patterns and become paired dances in a trio, a rondo or a sonata movement. The range of dance types, colourful and varied though it may have been, becomes even richer and the fast closing dance movements of the cycles become full-bodied, firmly established sections. Their predecessor was 'The Swineherd's Dance' in *For Children*—the source of the splendid folk dance finales in the *Romanian Folk Dances*, the *Four Slovak Folk-Songs* and above all, the *Fifteen Hungarian Peasant Songs*.

Parallel with this gay and lively group of works which owe their inspiration to folk music, was another series of weightier pieces which presented greater difficulties to the composer. Bartók did not mark the folk-song cycles with opus numbers, only the 'great' works. These were the compositions into which he poured his creative genius, in which he expressed his vision of man and the world about him; in them he indicated his beliefs as an artist and formulated a condensed expression of his philosophy. In these works we find the tormenting legacy of Bluebeard's meditations.

When any one work by an artist fails to evoke a response from the public, that work acts as a barrier, blocking the path to his future development. In Bartók's case, the failure of his opera acted as just such a barrier. No one could know so well as he the epoch-making significance of the work and its importance in his own artistic development. Very understandably, its rejection caused him to retreat.

However, he did not give up the struggle. He did not abandon the idea of having his opera performed, and he did not despair of his future development. No such course was possible, for that would have been to believe that he had already solved the problems involved in his first attempt to synthesize in his work the paired contradictions of his own world of music. All things considered, *Bluebeard's Castle* is more in the nature of a question than of an answer. The more unrelenting was his definition of the human condition as one of unmitigated solitariness, the more desperately did he seek an answer to the question as to whether in the bourgeois society of the twentieth century it was possible for man to arrive at some satisfactory relationship with the world. Could it be that there was no way to bridge the gulf between one individual and another, between man and woman, the individual and society, man and nature? Bartók was concerned to know if it was indeed an ultimate and inviolable law of nature that the human soul should remain for ever solitary, imprisoned—as he had conceived it in his opera—behind seven doors; or could it be that there was in this very solitude the promise of a nirvana of happiness beyond anything that man could achieve within the confines of society? In the allegorical terms of the ancient legend

Bartók was asking whether the darkness of the castle masked, or even dispelled forever, the vision of peace glimpsed through the fourth and fifth doors, or whether there was the possibility, even necessity, to release this all-destructive darkness and expose it to an all-destructive light.

These questions, though differently formulated, had occupied bourgeois philosophers for the greater part of the nineteenth and twentieth centuries. Bartók had begun to ask them when he first came under the influence of Nietzsche. He saw his own dilemma as the choice between the tragedy of solitariness and the equally tragic condition of detached indifference to all things and all mankind. It was through folk music that he found a personal solution to this dilemma. The search for a way of solving these problems in his creative work, however, was more prolonged and tormenting. But this was the task he had set himself, and he did not give up the struggle when he had finished *Bluebeard's Castle*. Indeed, it was precisely because the final judgement in the opera appeared to be 'Now it will be always night', a grim belief that seemed to block any way of resolving contradictions, that Bartók was stimulated to resist such ideas and struggle to find new solutions to his problems. In the *Allegro Barbaro* and the *Scherzo* of *Four Pieces* for orchestra, the dominant tone was one of protest. The *Allegro Barbaro* showed a new aspect of Nature —her unbridled power, and the forces she could bring to man's aid were she to become his ally.

The new libretto by Béla Balázs, *The Wooden Prince*, gave promise of a new way of passing beyond the crisis induced by the earlier opera; it suggested new solutions to theoretical problems and to the problems of stage production. The proposal to produce a ballet was first made in 1913.

> The Opera House does not want to perform my opera at all. However, they've so far defied official opinion, by asking me for an hour-long ballet,

wrote Bartók to Zágon. In composing the ballet he was spurred on continuously by the knowledge that his opera had been neglected. At the première he said,

> I liked my first opera so much that when I received the libretto for the ballet from Béla Balázs, I immediately thought the ballet with its spectacular, colourful, rich and varied scenes would make it possible to have both works performed on the same bill.

134

Balázs's libretto was printed in the Christmas issue of *Nyugat* in 1913. The story tells of a prince who finds in the heart of a forest a flower garden through which flows a stream. On the banks of the stream he sees a princess who is now being chased into her palace by a fairy who is the guardian of Nature. The prince, unable to cross the stream or penetrate the forest, tries and fails to reach the princess. He then tries to attract her attention by carving a wooden puppet which he clothes with his own mantle and crown. Finally, he cuts a lock of his hair and hangs this on the puppet's head. The trick works and the princess is enticed out of her palace by the gaudy puppet, who gains her affection at the expense of the lovesick prince now standing deserted and forlorn without his princely raiment. A command from the fairy brings life to the puppet which begins a frightening and demoniacal dance in which it is joined by the princess. Nature takes pity on the heart-broken and despairing prince. This time the fairy commands the trees and flowers to bow before him and he is given a garland for a crown and a new mantle of flowers. Meantime the puppet begins to dance more and more slowly, staggering like a clockwork toy that is running down, and the princess loses interest in him. Now she notices the prince and would go to him; but the forces of Nature hold her back; she will only become worthy of the prince's love when of her own free will she gives up her crown in repentance. But there is a happy ending to the story when Nature looks with favour upon both prince and princess.

After the première, Béla Balázs made a statement in which he explained the symbolism of the ballet. His intention was to express 'the tragedy of the artist... The wooden puppet, which my prince makes in order to attract the princess himself, symbolizes the creative work of the artist, who puts all of himself into his work until he has made something complete, shining and perfect. The artist himself, however, is left robbed and poor. I was thinking of that very common and profound tragedy when the creation becomes the rival of the creator, and of the pain and glory of the situation in which a woman prefers the poem to the poet, the picture to the painter.'

But in using the libretto as the starting point for his music, Bartók achieved something far more profound and universal than would appear from Béla Balázs's interpretation of the story. The critics, each in his own particular way, sensed something of this duality. Izor Béldi, a lawyer who was also greatly respected as the music critic of *Pesti Hirlap*, found that 'a vast musical apparatus, a frightening mass of musical pyramids, masses of sound accompany and illustrate what is merely an idyllic pastoral play. On stage, a charming puppet play with bucolic scenes as in a fairy tale; but in the orchestra, a cosmic hurricane!' István Gajáry, a composer as well as critic, expressed similar disappointment in *Az Ujság*. He criticized the music because it had none of the sentimental quality he associated with romantic love and dismissed it as unsuited to the 'easily comprehensible little tale ... We are looking for other sounds to express love and happiness than those Bartók gives us,' he wrote. 'On hearing his sharp dissonances we think of anything except the tender lyrical emotion the music is intended to convey.'

In fact, just as in the mystery play *Bluebeard's Castle*, Bartók was again expressing the most profound doubts experienced by man. In the opera he had expressed through music his sense of the tragedy of man's solitariness and isolation from the rest of the natural world; he could not attempt anything less ambitious in the ballet. The work is on an equally grand scale, this time a hymn to the creative power of man seen against the universe itself.

In this he was encouraged by the similarity of the formal structure of the two works. Béla Balázs constructed *The Wooden Prince* in a symmetrical shape like that of *Bluebeard's Castle*. In the latter the lowest point of the structure is represented by the dark castle at the beginning and end of the opera, the peak of the structure being the scene at the fifth door. The ballet, on the other hand, begins and ends in the warm glow of a rural scene, the peak of the structure being the dark scene when the prince is shown sorrowful and deserted. This structural similarity enabled Bartók to link the two works in a manner that could not easily be apprehended from a study of the dramas themselves. The very first sounds reveal that the landscape before our eyes is related to that glimpse through the closing doors of Bluebeard's castle. The vast realm of Nature, to which we all belong, is shown with all the richness of the flower garden in the scene at the fourth door and all the brilliance of the scene at the fifth door. In this same atmosphere the prince and the princess find peace at the end of the story. The framework of the system of tonality is also similar to that of the opera. In the latter, F sharp minor was the last tone of the cycle of keys, with C major as the tonality of the fifth door, while in the ballet, C major is the tonality of the framework. The nature scenes in the ballet lend themselves to the radiance of the major tonalities, and it is only at the mid-point of the structure that the sorrow of the deserted prince is sounded in C sharp minor. The C–C sharp bitonality of the ballet is at the same time a continuation of the F–F sharp duality in *Bluebeard's Castle*.

It was this remarkable relationship between the two works that Kodály forcibly brought to the attention of the critics after the first joint performance in 1918. 'The ballet balances the grief-stricken adagio of the opera with a playful, animated allegro,' he wrote in his review. 'The two together stand as the two movements of a giant symphony. And those who consider Bartók's main achievement to be atonality, should finally realize that both works have basic recurring tonalities just as in a Mozart opera.'

Even at the time of the first performance, Bartók had already mentioned the symphonic conception of the piece.

> The music of the ballet is a symphonic poem danced by the various characters Three parts are clearly distinguishable, and these in turn can be further divided into smaller units. The first part extends to the end of the dance between the princess and the wooden puppet. The second, considerably calmer than the first, bears the typical characteristics of an inner movement and lasts till the reappearance of the wooden puppet. The third is actually a repetition of the first, but here the order of the Sections is reversed, as is demanded by the text.

After completing the opera, the composer has set himself the task of creating a work of a symphonic nature. The *Four Orchestral Pieces* was part of this plan. His work on the ballet did not cause him to put aside this project; indeed his immediate aim in composing it was to continue his symphonic work, enriching it with all the possibilities offered by the ballet stage. Long ago, when Michelangelo planned to create sculptures, his patron, the Pope, commissioned him to paint frescoes on the ceiling of the Sistine Chapel; Michelangelo painted statues in the frescoes. In the same way, the libretto offered Bartók symphonic possibilities. The clear articulation in Béla Balázs's method of literary construction permitted the addition of music in almost the correct proportion, while his libretto for the ballet was well adapted to a symmetrical arrangement of symphonic movements.

Examples of similar structures may be readily found in the history of symphonic music. Bartók himself had used just such a structure in his *Suite No. 1.* In that particular composition he inserted the Scherzo movement between two slow movements, as Beethoven had done in the Sixth Symphony. In the case of the ballet, in order to achieve a symmetrical division of the three central movements, it was necessary to employ a new method—that of inserting the slow movement between two dances. In most of the examples of this structure we find the slow movement inserted between two minuets in the genre of classical divertimento.

The motif for employing this construction was therefore by no means absent from the libretto, and there was every justification for a symphonic work as dramatic as the stage production. But compared with the possibilities offered by the construction of the libretto, the dramatic content of Balázs's script was weak. It is true that he gives us a life-like and combative hero, but this princely hero is in no way matched by the princess who certainly cannot be looked upon as a heroine. Destructive and unaware, she resembles a mischievous child and it is only at the end of the play that she becomes aware of herself.

At the very beginning of the ballet we are given a hint of the contradictions implicit in the characters. Bartók represents the princess by using the components of the waltz music (a faster version of which may be found in the last of the *Bagatelles*) and in the 'distorted' version of the *Two Portraits*. In the slowest moments of the rhythm there is a memory of the heel-clicking embellishments of the *verbunkos* dance. In those days it would scarcely have been considered suitable for Bartók to use *verbunkos* music for the portrayal of a sympathetic character. On the other hand, the prince enters to the measured sounds of a folk-song in unison. The contrast between this and the affected dance of the princess is as great as that between the *Peasant Song* in the *Ten Easy Piano Pieces* and the *Dedication*. The ballet, however, allows no possibility of the development of this contradiction through the dramatic action. The musical material which represents the princess is in the nature of a recurrent quotation, and there is no development of the music representing the prince's journeyings.

One way of providing a second force in opposition to the prince would have been to confront him with the power of Nature, or at least the fairy guardian of all natural things. But in that case his struggle would have been with supernatural, non-human forces, for his battle with the stream and the forest has no basis in reality, the outcome being determined at the whim of the fairy. The end of the ballet shows the prince at peace with Nature, but it is not the peace that comes from victory over Nature, it is the peace found when Nature has taken pity of her victim. Such an opposition therefore could offer no possibility of true dramatic conflict. Any hint of such a conflict between prince and Nature springs from the music and has no basis in the libretto.

The figure of the prince, confronted by Nature and an unalterable destiny, reminds us of Judith in the opera. Just as the prince battles with Nature, she too, as the active partner in the contest with Bluebeard, was shown as being engaged throughout in a hopeless struggle with a supernatural opponent. This link between the two characters is expressed in the music, for Bartók chose to express the prince's despair in the slow movement of the ballet, not by means of the Bluebeard theme, with its derivation from a closed, unbreakable pentatonic unison folk-song, but rather through the material used to accompany Judith's expression of her grief, violent, plaintive, wild or threatening. The use of folk-song to express this sense of doom, as in the Bluebeard theme, does not occur again in Bartók's dramatic realm. The musical image of sorrow was to develop into the musical features found in the *Four Dirges*.

Bartók then was faced with the task of finding another figure to oppose that of the prince. There was only one possibility left to him—to breathe life into the wooden puppet, which was merely grotesque and ridiculous in the libretto, and make of it a rival worthy of the prince. It is at this point that Bartók adds a new dimension to Balázs's story. In the play, the wooden puppet is no more than a tool in the hands of the fairy. Bartók, however, actually animates the puppet so that we believe it to be the embodiment of unleashed and menacing natural forces. In its first dance, the crudeness of the second of the *Two Pictures*, *Village Dance*, has been intensified into the frightening, threatening, wild galloping of the *Bear Dance*. This interpretation gives a more profound and general meaning to Balázs's original conception of the artist rivalled by his own creation. Bartók's music makes us believe that the artist has created something from which springs a power greater than his own, and beyond his control.

In its second dance, the puppet, which had previously shown only frightening qualities, now seems pitiable and grotesque. The musical features of his dance remind us of the second of the *Burlesques* and the portrayal of the stumbling, staggering figure in *A bit drunk*, at the same time they foreshadow the portrayal of the elderly suitor in *The Miraculous Mandarin*. Had the prince been allowed to defeat the wooden puppet, this would have offered the possibility of an organic development towards a symphonic finale in which the cause for which the hero fought would have been made clear. But Bartók could not alter the libretto to that extent because at that time he himself had still not worked out the musical conception of such a solution. Instead of allowing the music to develop to a dramatic climax, he added a broadly impressionistic framework within which he set the contradiction between the three inner movements —the slow movement inserted between two scherzos.

The concept of the prince's apotheosis through Nature is still that of a disciple of Nietzsche who resolves solitude by rising above the world. Its musical image in no way resembles a Beethoven hymn to mankind victorious, liberated and at one with Nature, a kind of continuation of the finale of the Sixth Symphony, but rather evokes the nirvana of Wagner's romantic pantheism, the idea of nature found in the *Rheingold*. Bartók, however, was no fatalist; nor were his heroes. He could not look upon nature as a power of a different order from that of mankind, whether higher or lower in degree: man had to seek alliance with nature through his own struggles. His impressionistic portrayal of ecstasy found in nature was not an organic part of the content and structure of the work, but merely an outer shell in which he enclosed the inner tensions. This experimental work remained as it were a poetic episode, a fairy-tale incident in Bartók's creative career. Later, he lost any illusion he may have cherished as to the possibility of romantic realization of his problems, and in other works he achieved symphonic fulfilment by developing the realistic dramatic core of the inner movements. Bartók worked on *The Wooden*

Prince over a considerable period of time. He began it before the outbreak of war in 1914, then put it aside and did not take it up again until 1916. By that time, however, he was interested in other ways of achieving musical solutions. The opus markings also indicate the lapse of time during the composition of the ballet. The ballet is opus 13, while other pieces written at the same time or even earlier carry higher opus markings. The *Suite* for piano op. 14 was composed in February 1916, and two of the *Five Songs* (posthumous) op. 15 (the identity of the authors of the lyrics is not yet known) date from February and August 1916. *Five Songs* (texts by Ady), op. 16, are dated February–April 1916. And finally, this series ends with the *String Quartet No. 2*, op. 17, written between 1915 and 1917.

All these works have one feature in common: like *Bluebeard's Castle*, they end with the dying notes of a slow movement. But there is a more human atmosphere in the dramatic ending of the *Four Orchestral Pieces;* this is very different from the idea of eternal imprisonment conveyed by *Bluebeard's Castle* and the concept of heroic defeat in the funeral march of the *Kossuth Symphony*. A new type of slow movement was also taking shape. This no longer expresses a grief that is full of pathos, represented by wild, theatrical gestures, as in the *Four Dirges,* the opera, the ballet or even the last of the *Four Orchestral Pieces*. Now the grief is more introverted and full of anxiety. The lament is suppressed and interwoven with a type of veiled slow waltz representing the figure of the girl in *The Miraculous Mandarin*. In each of the five songs by Ady there is a variation of this nature; indeed they might almost be studies for an opera that was never written. Closely related to this type of slow movement is the last movement of the *Suite* for piano, and a more meditative and polyphonic type is to be found in the third movement of the *String Quartet No. 2*.

At the same time as he was developing this introverted and solitary mood in his slow movements, Bartók was also composing scherzos that were ever wilder, more abandoned and intense, developments as it were of the *Allegro Barbaro* to the point at which they lost altogether the character of a scherzo. The scherzo in three-quarter time in the second movement of the *Suite* for piano is followed by a fiery 'allegro molto' which has its origin in the *Allegro Barbaro* and also anticipates the central 'allegro molto capriccioso' and still later, the pursuit dance in *The Miraculous Mandarin*. After 1913, Arabic folk-music elements were absorbed into this type of barbaric dance with its quick, galloping rhythms. It was characteristic of Bartók's usual methods that his knowledge of Arabic folk-songs did not change the character of his works, but rather enriched the types already in existence. In the fiery dance of the *Allegro Barbaro* he had already created the basic type of an unbridled, duple-metre ostinato dance. Highly original in character, this was made even more striking by the drumming rhythm and exotic oriental melodic motifs newly adopted from Arabic folk music.

The *Suite* for piano is an interesting record of further aspects of the problems with which the composer was faced. Originally, the comfortable Allegretto dance was followed by a slower Andante movement, a slow waltz, related to certain Ady songs. Thus, the *Suite* would have become a unique, five-part cycle, with two Scherzos between two slow movements. The keys of B flat–F sharp–B flat–D–B flat would have followed each other in a symmetrical system, framing the central B flat tonality with a major third above and below. By abandoning one of the slow movements, Bartók fashioned a four-movement cycle with a slow closing section which bears a slight resemblance to the *Four Orchestral Pieces* for orchestra in that the 'barbaric' dance is enclosed in the middle of the work. At the same time, by coupling uneven and duple-metre scherzos of European and 'barbaric' origin, he shaped a structure similar in its proximities to the second and third movement in the *String Quartet No. 1*. This structure is also used at the dramatic climax of *The Miraculous Mandarin*, in the girl's waltz and in the mandarin's dance of pursuit; and it occurs again later, this time in reverse order, in the second movement of *Music for String Instruments, Percussion and Celesta*. Finally, in the *String Quartet No. 2* he evolved a pure, unadorned example of the slow–fast–slow arrangement of contradictory inner movements which lies at the heart of the five-part symmetry he devised later, in which the inner conflicts are totally exposed.

In full knowledge of the *Mandarin* story we can safely assert that the demands made by the plot for this particular arrangement of the movements are in accordance with the rhythm inherent in the chosen form. In this play we see the last flare-up of the life force in a man in whom this has for long lain dormant but smouldering, so that now it finds expression in violence and destruction; here too we find a poetic image of the will which finds fulfilment in death.

By now, the preconditions for the form and content of *The Miraculous Mandarin* are by and large complete.

CHAPTER VII

THEATRE SUCCESSES. THE MIRACULOUS MANDARIN.
1917–1919

1 Premiere and success of 'The Wooden Prince'. New artistic atmosphere towards the end of the war. Performance of 'Bluebeard's Castle'. Contract with Universal Publishers

The Wooden Prince was written in extremely difficult circumstances. These were described to Buşiţia in the letter dated May 6, 1917, in which Bartók also expressed concern about his wife's health.

> With so many troubles on my mind I only just managed to finish a one-act ballet for the Opera House. It would have been a big job even in peace time, with all these troubles. And when, with great difficulty, I had got it done, then the real struggle began: you've no idea what a senseless and frustrating battle I've had with the Opera House. What is the Royal Opera House anyway?! An Augean stable; a dumping-ground for every kind of rubbish; the seat of all disorder; the pinnacle of confusion, where only one man is respected and has the right to make decisions, however trivial they may be: the Government Deputy; but this otherwise well-disposed V.C.P.C. (Veritable Confidential Privy Councillor) hardly ever looks in at the theatre. Now the first night is May 12th; and this is the last week of rehearsals. People are already sharpening their claws against me.

Further information about the preparations for the ballet are to be found in Béla Balázs's memoirs. For many months he undertook to act as go-between for Bartók in his dealings with the Opera House authorities. He tells us that after the composer's painful experiences in connection with the rejection of *Bluebeard's Castle*, Bartók refused to speak to 'those people', his term, according to Balázs, for the Opera House administration. 'He stipulated that he would not go near the Opera throughout the period of rehearsals. Let them do what they want, he said. And whatever the goings-on I was not to tell him anything about it.'

Count Miklós Bánffy, the Government Deputy, was in fact strongly in favour of the composition and performance of *The Wooden Prince*. According to Balázs, however, this was not because of any enthusiasm

144

for Bartók's music. But he was himself a writer and designer of stage scenery, and as he was interested in the sets of the ballet, he urged on the production. This merely increased the antagonism of the 'trained' artistic personnel. 'The director refused to undertake the assignment, holding that "it was not ballet" and declaring that he wanted to "cut half of it out . . ." The ballet master, a Swede called Zöbisch, a kind of teacher of rhythmic gymnastics, did not understand one beat of the music. And what could a ballet corps, which never got beyond Coppelia and Sylvia, make out of a piano arrangement by Bartók!' These reminiscences by Béla Balázs of events that took place five years earlier appeared in the *Bécsi Magyar Ujság* in May, 1922.

Balázs undertook to be responsible for the direction and coaching of the corps de ballet, 'because,' as he said, 'I would rather learn the ballet profession myself than allow a single note of this music to be left out.' In February, the rehearsals were in full swing, and on February 22, Bartók wrote to his mother that 'the first and second ballerinas are dancing gaily to my music.' And Balázs wrote, 'I lost thirty pounds in the space of three months (during which the critics hovered around us, croaking like the ravens over a dying man), and then at last, battle was declared.'

The first performance belied all the dire prophecies. Its success was without parallel in the history of the Opera House, arousing applause 'that, according to the old ushers, had not been heard in the Hungarian Royal Opera House since the premiere of Madame Butterfly'. Thirty years later Béla Balázs could still vividly recall how the applause had resounded in his ears. Some time after his return to Hungary he described the occasion in the magazine *Fórum:* 'After the last bars, there was a deathly silence in the audience lasting for several seconds. There was not one sound of a clap, a hiss or a whistle. It was as if an invisible scale of gigantic proportions was being tipped first one way then the other . . . Then the applause broke out in the galleries, and like an avalanche, swept down to the boxes and the stalls, carrying before it all the rabble of the press. Many reviews had to be rewritten that night.'

Bartók also saw clearly this 'tipping' of the scales. In his own more measured and objective phrases, he too recorded in his autobiography:

> The year 1917 brought a decisive change in the attitude of the Budapest audiences towards my works. I lived to see, at last, one of my bigger works,

the ballet The Wooden Prince, given a musically perfect performance under the leadership of the conductor, Egisto Tango.

The success of the performance was in fact very largely due to the outstanding Italian conductor of the Hungarian Opera, Egisto Tango. (Kerner refused an invitation to conduct the work.) Tango first studied the score by himself for several weeks, then successfully battled his way through thirty rehearsals. Such a thing had never happened before at the Opera House. In his letters, Bartók expressed his admiration for the Italian artist in words that were for him unusually warm: 'the best conductor' he had so far worked with. The tireless way of working, together with the magnetism of his personality, enabled Tango to achieve miracles. Some of the members of the orchestra had written beside their parts 'not necessary to tune up'; and Balázs has described how during the performance these men looked at each other, 'pale with excitement, as if asking whether it was possible that they had played so well. How had it come about, they seemed to be wondering . . .' Contemporary reviews also included favourable comments about the principal dancers, Anna Pallay, Emília Nirschy, Boriska Harmat and Ede Brada.

The skill of the orchestra at the first performance of *The Wooden Prince* did for Bartók's orchestral music of a symphonic nature what the Waldbauer Quartet had done for his chamber music at the composer's concert in 1910—it provided, for the first time, a mature style of performance worthy of Bartók's music. Since that evening in 1910, the Waldbauers and other members of their generation who were connoisseurs, admirers or performers of new music, had reached maturity. Géza Csáth, Sándor Kovács and Géza Vilmos Zágon were all to meet a tragic death in 1918. But at the first performance of *The Wooden Prince* a new generation had its say in the development of Hungarian culture. Among these young people were the ballerinas, who, according to Balázs, 'trembled for the fate of the work' and the audiences in the gallery 'where in the utter silence you could almost hear the beating hearts'. The first applause came from this new young intelligentsia; the first response was in their hearts, and the jubilant ovation came from their throats, not those of the snobbish occupants of the boxes who had come 'to witness a scandal', nor from the critics in the stalls who, 'with the sole exception of Béla Reinitz, had written an account of the failure of the ballet the previous evening'.

Eight years previously, it had been the journalists, already initiated into the appreciation of the new music, who were faced with the task of explaining this to their readers. Now the journalists were carried along the tide of public approval first felt and expressed by the audience, or rather, a section of it—the gallery.

This change was symptomatic of something more than the shifting outlook of a new generation or a straightforward controversy as to the value of the music. It was an unmistakable sign of a change in outlook that was spreading amongst all the peoples of Europe, not merely in cultural matters but first and foremost in regard to the heaviest burden they had been asked to bear—the burden of the war. Nationalist enthusiasm for an imperialist war, a feeling stirred up by ruling circles everywhere, was by this time on the wane throughout Europe. Day by day, more and more people were finding to their cost that war was not a firework display but an endless experience of suffering and privation. They had had enough of war and longed passionately for peace. As the atmosphere became more and more revolutionary, the leaders struggled to maintain their own positions and to prosecute the war for their own advantage. Lenin himself, in January 1917, described these efforts as a political change 'from imperialist war to imperialist peace'. Bartók's own life at this time was marked by the strange duality of carrying out the feverish preparation for the première of his new work during the months of the most terrible tribulations of the war.

An even more tense situation was developing for the Austro-Hungarian Monarchy as a result of a series of military defeats. News of the bourgeois revolution in Russia gave added impetus to protests in Hungary. The workers, on whose shoulders fell the heaviest burdens of the war, organized strikes of increasing severity, and in the days preceding the première of *The Wooden Prince*, for the first time since the beginning of the war, hundreds of thousands of people in Budapest celebrated May Day with a work stoppage.

Progressive Hungarian artists also joined together to present a broad front on the question of the call for peace. This anti-war front of writers and artists was largely made up of progressive bourgeois intellectuals, but they were led by a small group who advocated a socialist revolution. Anyone worthy of being known as a member of the Hungarian intelligentsia belonged to this group, with the possible exception of certain self-styled writers with extreme nationalist views who were loyal to the Court. The progressive intelligentsia was united through membership of the *Galilei Kör* (Galilei Circle), the progressive artists rallied around the *Nyugat* and the *Ma*, and the organ of the most left-wing members was the magazine, *Tett*. Their ideas found expression in the daily press in the pages of the *Világ* and the *Népszava*. The group known as 'The Eight' (A nyolcak) was composed of painters and sculptors and had been in existence since 1911.

Very little has so far been discovered about Bartók's relations with the progressive writers and artists of the time. Slowly the details are being collected from which we will be able to gain a picture of the various stages of his career as an artist, but the day-to-day occurrences of his life, especially during the war years, are still shrouded in an obscurity impenetrable to the biographer. And yet it is through these everyday happenings that great personalities are linked with the age in which they live. There must be many documents in existence which have yet to be brought to light before we can gain a clearer picture of these aspects of Bartók's life. A few facts, however, have been established.

It is true that in his retreat at Rákoskeresztúr he led a rather isolated life. According to one of his letters, he read the newspapers only sporadically. Yet there are several indications that he kept abreast of cultural developments. His matinée-recital during the Rippl-Rónai exhibition is one link in the chain of his contacts with other progressive artists as well as with Rippl-Rónai himself. The Austrian composer Egon Wellesz, a member of Schoenberg's circle, who visited Budapest in 1911, first heard of Bartók through some of the progressive painters with whom Bartók had become acquainted on his visits to the exhibitions of 'The Eight'. It was on one such visit that he first met Ady. In August 1917, Bartók sent to Buşiţia, together with the verses in *Bluebeard's Castle*, a novel by Móricz entitled *Az Isten háta mögött* (Behind God's Back), recommending it as 'the best Hungarian novel.' He sent these books to his Romanian friend 'as tokens of a happier Hungarian–Romanian relationship in the future'. He continued:

This friendship for the moment—as a result of Apponyi's 'blessed' activities—is delayed, but its time will come when the long-bearded old men have gone, and their place has been taken by the young people of today, the people of *Világ*, *Nyugat* and *Ma* (!)* get their chance.

(Count Albert Apponyi was for long the most influential representative in Hungary of a conservative, nationalist cultural policy.)

It was during this period that the magazine *Ma* reproduced a portrait of Bartók painted in 1913 by Róbert Berény, a member of 'The Eight'. This is possibly the finest of the portraits of Bartók: the artist has captured, in flaming reds with black shadows, the Petőfi-like glint in the composer's eye. Bartók himself must have thought well of it for he expressed a wish to send it to Buşiţia together with the books. In the letter quoted above he apologizes for the omission:

> I have not been able to get the Berény picture I promised you, for I hardly ever go to Budapest these days.

In the world of music also there were more signs of this changing climate of opinion. It may well have been because he sensed the first breath of this new atmosphere at the time of the performance of the *Two Portraits* in April 1916, that Bartók resumed work on *The Wooden Prince*. At the very first sign of encouragement he lost no time in abandoning the self-imposed exile he had endured with such bitterness. On January 5, 1917, there was a performance of some of his Slovak choral works, probably the *Four Slovak Folk-Songs*. After the successful premiere of the ballet, Bartók was certain that the Opera House would include *Bluebeard's Castle* in their programme for the coming season, and that this would be given on the same evening as the ballet, as part of one programme, in accordance with his own wishes. On October 17, Dohnányi played selections from Bartók's compositions, and on November 18, Hungarian musical circles acclaimed the concert given by the newly reorganized Waldbauer Quartet. Bartók also took part in the concert, playing Debussy's Sonata for 'Cello and Piano together with Kerpely. Kodály, as music critic for *Nyugat*, had already analysed the significance of the chamber recital: 'The Waldbauers were also swept away on the tide of war, which halted them on their path to world fame, a fact which

---

* It is a play on words as the title of the review *Ma* means today.

is of much greater significance than the personal loss suffered by four individuals. When they were forced to withdraw from the musical life of Budapest, there came to an end the kind of activity through which Hungarian audiences were gradually becoming educated to appreciate the highest kind of music . . . Those who still have the capacity to rejoice can be happy to think that these musicians are together once again. Their performances reached the technical perfection of their earlier performances, and in inner refinement surpassed them. Yet this performance was the result of practice during only a few days of leave from military duties and the odd days of holiday when, by travelling from one end of the country to the other, they managed to achieve a meeting. The road to the highest perfection is open to them; to reach this goal they require nothing more than the opportunity to devote weekdays as well as holidays to their work . . . The piano part of the sonata was played by Béla Bartók, a name which for the past ten years or so has been linked with the first performance of the most interesting new music for piano.'

At the beginning of the following year, on February 11, 1918, a Budapest audience heard the first performance of the orchestral version of the *Romanian Folk Dances*, on March 3, the Waldbauers introduced a new Bartók work, the *String Quartet No. 2* and on May 7, a recital of his own works by Kodály recalled the days in 1910 when he and Bartók set out together along their chosen path. These distinguished performances by Kodály and Bartók, the Waldbauers and Oszkár Kálmán (the singer in the title role of *Bluebeard's Castle* then in rehearsal) maintained the high standard set at the recital given eight years previously. In Béla Reinitz's review which appeared in *Világ*, there was all the fervour of a comrade-in-arms in his references to the art of Kodály.

This series of performances reached its climax at the première of *Bluebeard's Castle* on May 24, 1918. The two parts were sung by Olga Haselbeck and Oszkár Kálmán. Bartók's long-cherished dream was realized when Tango produced both the opera and the ballet in one evening.

> The reviews of Bluebeard were better than those of The Wooden Prince. With the exception of the *Pesti Hirlap* and the *Ujság* all the papers wrote about it favourably, especially the two German-language papers, the *Neues Pester Journal* and the *Pester Lloyd*,

he wrote to Buşiţia on June 6. Only one other paper, the *Vasárnapi Ujság*, should be mentioned, in addition to those listed by Bartók, as showing no understanding of the work. Some appreciation of the opera was shown, though in varying degrees, in all the rest of the more important dailies, apart from *Nyugat* which carried the review by Zoltán Kodály.

Bartók, however, did not regard this as his greatest success of the year compared with another achievement he recorded: 'I have succeeded in reaching a long-term agreement with a first-rate publisher.' He was referring to the Viennese firm, Universal Edition, which from then until the outbreak of the Second World War continued to publish Bartók's works. 'This is a splendid thing,' he continued in his letter to Buşiţia,

> because thanks to the neglect of our publishers at home, for a period of six years or so, not one of my works has been published, and perhaps no other Hungarian musician has been given such an opportunity by a foreign publisher . . . at any rate, this contract counts as my greatest success as a composer so far.

The good old pre-war days seemed to have returned. It was even possible to collect Romanian folk-songs once again in Transylvania and to spend the pleasant summer months in Bihar. In July, together with Tango, Bartók visited Belényes, then Örvényes. Fearful of a shortage of food because of the war, Tango fortified himself with salami. Unfortunately he had not been there very long before he contracted typhus and had to stay with the Buşiţias in Belényes until he was well enough to travel. During his convalescence he played parts of *Bluebeard's Castle* on the piano. Bartók continued his researches in Havasdombró or, in Romanian, Dumbravita (or Dumbraviste) de Codru. According to Julia Szegő, the author of a biography of Bartók, who lived in Kolozsvár (Cluj), Bartók had also visited this small mountain village before the war and had planned to compile an ethnographic monograph on the area. A few melodies recorded in Doboz and Vésztő, in the vicinity of his brother-in-law's home in Békés County, may be found among his collections of Hungarian folk music.

He encountered a number of difficulties in the preparation of a concert programme of army songs current under the Monarchy. This task was sponsored by the Musikhistorische Zentrale in Vienna. In a letter to

Bușiția dated January 12, 1918, Bartók gave details of the stupidity of the military officials, their bureaucratic or 'Imperial and Royal' reasoning when they tried to prevent the concert from taking place. The occasion, however, provided Bartók with the opportunity to collect material that proved to be very useful in the scientific study of Hungarian folk music. The importance of the occasion did not lie in the fact that arrangements of Hungarian and Slovak folk-songs by Bartók and Kodály were performed in Vienna, nor in the fact that Ferenc Székelyhidy sang Kodály's *The Ballad of István Kádár*. The true significance of the event lay in the fact that it had occasioned Bartók to supplement his collection with songs heard among the soldiers when he was preparing for the concert, and, even more important, he had been interested enough to write concert programme notes in German entitled *Die Melodien der madjarischen Soldatenlieder*. In these notes, he outlined for the first time the classification of Hungarian folk-songs which he worked out in detail later in his book *The Hungarian Folk-Song*. This work is based on the study published by Zoltán Kodály in 1917, the first scientific publication made in connection with their joint research into the oldest pentatonic strata of Hungarian music.

In the summer of 1918, he made his last journey among the Romanian peasants at Belényes, and in August he went for the last time to the Slovak region of Nyitra. This was not because he considered that his collection of Romanian and Slovakian folk music made over the last decade was now complete, but the collapse of the Monarchy and the political changes brought about by military defeat effectively prevented him from visiting those places for the rest of his life.

2 'THE MIRACULOUS MANDARIN'. LIBRETTO BY MENYHÉRT LENGYEL, BARTÓK'S ADAPTATION. MUSICAL TYPOLOGY, DRAMATIC CONSTRUCTION AND MUSICAL IDIOM OF THE WORK. BARTÓK, MEMBER OF THE MUSIC DIRECTORY OF THE HUNGARIAN REPUBLIC OF COUNCILS

The long years during which he met no kind of success by no means modified his profound attraction to stage works, and the success of the joint performance of his opera and ballet served to stimulate this kind of creative activity. He entertained some hopes of receiving a libretto from Sándor Bródy, one of the most distinguished writers of his generation, but he waited in vain, and in September 1918, he wrote to Bușiția,

> Bródy did not send the libretto, so I have begun to set Menyhért Lengyel's libretto to music.

This was the libretto of *The Miraculous Mandarin*.

The text was printed in *Nyugat* on January 1, 1917. On January 17, in the *Esti Ujság*, there was a report to the effect that at the time of the guest performance in Budapest in 1912, Diaghilev had asked Lengyel if he could have it for his own corps de ballet which was already world-famous. But Ernő Balogh, later a member of Bartók's circle of friends in New York, remembers otherwise. He says that the author did not intend this work for the stage. There is unfortunately no evidence to support or refute either of these claims, mentioned in the book by György Kroó, an authority on Bartók's stage works; his version of the first story is based on a study by Géza Körtvélyes, an expert on the art of the dance.

Presumably Bartók read the text in *Nyugat* and was sufficiently interested to want to set it to music. His son, Béla, recalls that Bartók was introduced to the author by István Thomán who invited them both to lunch one Sunday around the beginning of 1918. This may have been the occasion when Bartók received Lengyel's permission to set his 'pantomime grotesque' to music.

The author's description of the plot is succinct and terse as befits the genre. In fact it consists of a series of stage directions. The essence of the story had been given by Bence Szabolcsi in his study of Bartók's work: 'In an Apache den in a great western city, three vagrants force a girl to stand in the window and lure passers-by into their room. A shabby old gentleman ventures to enter, then a poor young man, but they are thrown out because they have no money. The third visitor presents a peculiarly awe-inspiring appearance, a Chinese mandarin who has strayed into the great city. At first the girl is too frightened to play her part but then her enticing dance arouses his passion and he begins to pursue her wildly. The vagrants throw themselves upon him, rob him and attempt to kill him three times in succession. But after each attempt they find that he is still alive. They strangle him, stab him and hang him—but in vain. Their victim cannot die until the girl has given him the kiss he longs for.'

Bence Szabolcsi's restrained summary is the result of much sifting of the original text. And Bartók had already removed some of the naturalistic and blood-curdling details. He had, for instance, deleted a number of crude stage directions such as 'the skin cracks', 'the body slumps', 'the knife comes out of the mandarin's back', and so on; he had also omitted a fourth murder—by shooting. This modified story was the one summarized by Szabolcsi, yet, in spite of his reserve and good taste, even the summary conveys something of the *grand guignol* horror of the original melodrama.

From about 1910 onwards, European art began to be populated by inhuman horrors and apocalyptic monsters. These were the creations of a bourgeois world in which man's imagination had been deeply affected by political crises, wars, and the threat to life inherent in bourgeois society.

To the ever-present fear of internal revolution and the 'spectre of communism' was added the threat of revolt by the colonial peoples, the constantly increasing numbers of 'the barbaric masses'. The pleasantly idyllic exoticism expressed in a keen interest in and sympathy for the culture of the Far East was transformed at the time of the Russo-Japanese war into a mood of hysterical fear of the 'yellow peril'. Civilized Europe awaited its destruction at the hands of the barbaric masses. The machine of civilization itself had grown into a threatening monster and its technology seemed to have turned against man, its creator, master and guardian; now, it seemed, it was becoming the willing tool of one section of mankind only, the workers, who were no longer prepared to use it in the service of their so-called betters. But most frightening of all was the blood-thirsty scavenger eating his way into the very minds and hearts of men themselves. More and more openly he was baring his teeth, his savagery thinly disguised by a veneer of culture, education and morality, waiting only for the opportunity to seize by the throat more venomously than any primitive barbarian his 'fellow human beings'.

During the last century, the arts temporarily succeeded in keeping at bay this spectre which nevertheless continued to grow in secret. Men of culture fostered the hope that they would be able to cure society of its ills by means of realistic social criticism expressed in authentic and sober tones and also by indulging at the same time in some of the illusions and taboos that would allow them to ignore the realities of the situation. It was as if no one had yet caught sight of the waiting monster of Edgar Allan Poe's horrific story 'The Fall of the House of Usher', a work that Debussy tried hard to set to music in the first decade of the century. The atmosphere was that of a house in which the very foundations are being eaten away by dry rot, when the crumbling of the whole structure is imminent. From 1910 onwards, figures such as Golems, Draculas, Alraines, werewolves and miraculous mandarins, which had been found only in worthless tales of bandits and detectives, now began to appear frequently in serious literature. World catastrophe was depicted everywhere and the forces of terror shown ready to destroy all European culture. In these books, the masters of the world were attacked in much the same way as the Olympian gods suffered at the hand of the giants and centaurs of mythology.

This exposure of latent horror and hidden danger and crime, together with an attempt to portray these evils in all their apocalyptic magnitude, was an expression of protest by twentieth-century artists against the obsolete ideals and inhumanity of contemporary civilization. In his study of *The Miraculous Mandarin* Bence Szabolcsi has stated that feelings of 'anger and despair' were largely responsible for the artistic protests which channelled all the furious currents of indignation. The avant-garde of the artistic communities, especially during the war, considered no method too garish or shocking for use in their attempts to draw attention to their eleventh-hour warnings and cries for help. They cast aside all previous notions of propriety in order to dispel the illusions which prevented people from seeing what was really happening in the world and so make some contribution to the destruction of the bourgeois order.

There were, however, significant differences between different groups of artists, whose aims were no less varied than the methods by which they demonstrated their beliefs. There were those whose exposure of inhumanity served only to liberate and glorify it; this was so in the branch of futurism which advocated war and destruction and which eventually became linked with fascism. Others believed that after the period of destruction which seemed unavoidable there would arise new possibilities for more honesty and humanity in human relationships.

This was the branch of futurism with which in its early stages Maia-kovsky was associated and which later became identified with socialist revolution.

The great majority of radical Hungarian intellectuals recognized in the imperial war the legacy of a hateful past and opposed it with all their might. In March 1916, in the magazine *Tett*, Lajos Kassák denounced the policy of the pro-war group of Italian futurists. It will therefore be appreciated that Béla Bartók's social and artistic outlook caused him to be attracted towards those Hungarian writers, painters and sculptors who held revolutionary views and were totally opposed to the mainte-nance of the old order. These were the ideas which possessed his mind when he came to read Lengyel's libretto.

It is easy to recognize in Lengyel's characters some reflection of the spectres haunting the imagination of the age—crime, eroticism, barbarism and the mysteries of the Orient. The social criticism implicit in the text and its bitingly satirical style are undeniable. But there is an intrusive and pervading note of naturalistic brutality which arouses horror and revulsion and serves to conceal the object of criticism. The girl, who symbolizes humanity in the story, is caught in a conflict between two kinds of barbarity which it is left to her to resolve if she is to end the horror of her situation. Once again Bartók was expressing his hatred of the inhumanity of urban civilization. He does not see the mandarin as a grotesque monster but rather as the personification of primitive, barbaric force, an example of the 'natural man' to whom he was so strongly attracted. Thus in Bartók's version of the story the girl is not compelled to choose between two evils, but rather to demonstrate her support for the humane qualities that are concealed behind the frightening and grotesque appearance of the mandarin. In this situation, the end of the play signifies for her a catharsis.

In their analysis of the plot, Bence Szabolcsi and György Kroó rightly emphasize the humane character of Bartók's conception and execution of the work. Such an interpretation alone could enable us to understand why the composer spoke of this exciting and horrible story as 'mar-vellously beautiful' when he was interviewed by a correspondent of *Színházi Élet*. This concept must be the starting point for any appreciation of the dramatic structure and musical characteristics of the work and is equally necessary if we are to understand why Bartók changed the original libretto.

The boldly outlined plot of Menyhért Lengyel's pantomime in fact offered the possibility of an excellent libretto. It provided a basic dramatic situation in which clearly drawn characters reacted in well defined conflicts. There is an impressive assurance shown in the way the author allows his characters to be swept forward by the dynamism of the stage action, as if borne on the current of a swift-flowing river, to reach the astounding finale. The author had a mistrust of 'literary' verbosity which enabled him to offer the composer the ground plan of a work eminently suitable for further abstraction and generalization of the characters and plot, as well as the possibility of giving the characters new life in his own medium. This is a basic rule in the relation between any librettist and composer. The final significance of a new work when it has been set to music and has been produced on the stage, must depend on the moral outlook of the composer and his power to realize it in his art.

The airless den of the Apaches in the original story was transformed by Bartók into a stage set of cosmic significance. He it was who rounded out the character of the girl who had been driven to prostitution by the force of circumstances, turning her into a symbol of feminine tragedy, perhaps even of any defenceless being longing for salvation. Menyhért Lengyel gave her the name of Mimi. In Bartók's work she is simply The Girl. Through the power of Bartók's imagination the three Apaches were transformed into the devils that inhabit the inferno of the metropolis. It was Bartók who straightened the back of Lengyel's grotesque gnome—lonely, exotic, a lustful maniac from the East. Bartók developed this character until he had created a symbol of the elemental impulse of the Life Force in Man, an awe-inspiring judge of inhumanity and a liberator of the humane feelings man has repressed. In Bartók's work, these characters are made to act out the martyrdom of the kindly impulses which have for so long been ridiculed in man. Szabolcsi sees these characters as protagonists in the conflict between the opposing forces of the age, symbolic figures who 'step on the stage almost naked, with allegorical simplicity, as in a medieval morality play or in the tragi-comedies of the Baroque era'.

As a result of this imaginative feat, Bartók was able to treat the characters, thus generalized and developed, as if they were his own creations. He incorporated them into his own artistic vision which rested on his own system of values, and enlisted their support for his own ideas. He drew them into the huge family of his own created characters and entrusted them with parts to live and live again, carrying on their battles and continuing always to search for some way out of the vicious circle of man's destiny.

He fashioned the musical representation of these characters out of types and characteristics found in his earlier orchestral and stage music. The different characters, with their numerous movements and gestures, provided an excellent basis for his task. The lapidary structure of the libretto and sharp etching of the characters made it possible for Bartók to emphasize and intensify qualities already present. It would be highly instructive to consider the progress of this strange 'transmutation'.

There were no precedents in Bartók's music for the characters of the three vagrants. They are children of the great city and their musical characterization emerges appropriately enough out of the clatter of the opening music, continuing it with tense monotony. As this sound picture of the streets continues unrelentingly, we become more and more convinced that it holds some further meaning.

Superficially, it is undoubtedly related to the fashionably naturalistic noises found in the music of the period. To its function of creating atmosphere, however, there is added a new significance. The trombone signals which, when we first hear them, sound like motor-car horns, soon reveal a relationship to the convulsive, stubborn rhythms heard during the forest struggle in *The Wooden Prince*, and immediately we are enveloped in the inhuman atmosphere of a desperate struggle between life and death.

This city clatter remains throughout as an ostinato framework. We hear it whenever the vagrants come out of their hiding places to attack their victims and divide the loot. Its constant nature illustrates the idea that this world does not change, that there is no hope for 'development' until a greater force comes to overpower it.

In fact it is out of this world that the musical figure of the girl emerges. The first shrug of her shoulders resembles the violent gestures of the quarrelling bandits. But at the very beginning, when she is first compelled to lure in the passers-by, there is a strange hint of suffering in her manner, and this is conveyed by the sigh of the descending broken four-tone chord inherited from Judith, or, if we trace it even further back, from the heroine of the *Two Portraits*, though by now it has undergone several transformations. Her gesture of resignation also has its predecessors, among them the gestures of the tormented prince. But never previously have these longing, horror-stricken or fleeing gestures cast such long and ghastly shadows, which here, elongated into insubstantial pictures, express the terror of the girl.

Bartók developed the character of the girl in some detail, and she is also the most clearly defined character in Menyhért Lengyel's original version of the story. She is constantly on the stage and she has to meet all the other characters. In each of her encounters a different side of hers is revealed. Of all the characters she is the most truly human, and it is her human qualities, human frailty and virtue, human desires and fears, which are embodied in Bartók's music.

In the first two episodes she meets the Old Gentleman and the Youth. The hapless old man, as jaunty as he is penniless, comes in with the same jerky movements as those of the wooden puppet when it has lost favour with the princess. Here, the relationship between the old man and the girl is established immediately: the girl behaves towards the old man in exactly the same way as the princess when she ridicules the wooden puppet.

The girl is physically attracted to the shy youth who is the second visitor, but her feelings are undirected and almost impersonal. The youth is hesitant, the girl tactful. From the outset, their mutual attraction seems to be without hope of fulfilment. There is also no precedent for the music of this scene. The melody of the slow dance in five-fourths time, with its blurred rhythm, takes the same uncertain, spiral path of the melody found in *Qualvolles Ringen*. There come also to mind more remote precedents, among them the sound of the English horn as Tristan waits for death; while its descendants include a piece in the *Mikrokosmos* entitled 'On the Island of Bali'. The stifled eroticism of this dreamy yet evocative scene makes it one of the most exotic parts of the ballet.

Bartók's superb portrayal of the girl is one of the finest examples of his awe-inspiring powers of musical characterization. As she dances round the mandarin she is made to reveal her innermost self and essential femininity. It is here that, in the waltz-scherzos, she proves her kinship with the 'women of the past'. Her timid, embarrassed movements are shaped into a slow, reserved waltz. We are reminded of the *Intermezzo*, the resigned third movement in the *Four Orchestral Pieces*, or the first and last of the *Five Songs* op. 16. Later the waltz accelerates, and the girl is swept into an ecstatic dance of death which is a continuation of the long series of old waltzes and witches' dances. The last of the *Bagatelles* gave us the dance entitled 'My lover is dancing' (Ma Mie qui danse). This developed into the 'distorted' of the *Two Portraits*. The same tone flashed out as one feature of the musical characterization of the princess and reaches a peak of violence in the second movement of the *Four Orchestral Pieces*. The basic motif of the great waltz in *The Miraculous Mandarin* is a three-tone chromatic musical gesture, one described by György Kroó as 'the theme of the girl', and which links her with the sphere of the vagrants. Perhaps it is of more than passing interest to note that this motif together with some other characteristic intonations of the music of *The Miraculous Mandarin*, also occurs twice in the last of the songs op. 16. The title of this song is 'I cannot go to you' and the 'theme of the girl' runs through the refrain 'I am dying' on each of the two occasions when this is heard.

A theme of such intensity is necessary since it must stir the mandarin to set in motion his own irresistible dance. This dance is a savage, drumming march, a kind of new *Allegro Barbaro*. It has at its core an oriental type of melody, with augmented second intervals, which partly follows the pattern found in all the themes which revolve at the centre of the work, and which, with its narrow intervals of minor thirds, has some affinity with the 'barbaric' family of the scherzos. Its most immediate predecessor is to be recognized in the fast movement of *String Quartet No. 2*, and not long afterwards its descendants were to appear in the first and second movements of the *Dance Suite*. The third movement of the *Suite* for piano op. 14 is closely related to it, and yet another descendant was to appear as 'The Chase' the last piece in the cycle *Out of Doors*. The minor third motif is inseparably associated with the monumental figure of the mandarin. At his very first appearance, the orchestra plays this motif as resoundingly as the call of the bugles for the

Last Judgement. And when, at the very end, he makes his last longing movement towards the girl, an unseen chorus repeats, with a great blast of human sound, the minor third now differently placed.

We are already familiar with the minor-third root of the wild, unbridled scherzos in duple metre. It must therefore come as no surprise to find that this now becomes the voice of the mandarin, representing his unconquerable will to live and his passion that cannot be allayed. It is therefore strange to find that a grotesque variation, almost a caricature, of this motif accompanies the dance of the old gentleman. But if we can recognize with certainty that the old gentleman is the descendant of the failing wooden puppet, it is not far-fetched to think of the mandarin, not as the prince, but rather as the embodiment of the demoniacal primitive force with which the wooden puppet was at first invested. One branch of the duple-metre scherzos extends from the *Bear Dance* through *Village Dance*, to the first dance of the wooden puppet, while the other branch was composed of the scherzos closely linked with the *Allegro Barbaro*.

György Kroó reminds us that the mandarin inherited from the prince only those pentatonic features which expressed his kindliness. The tormented gestures of the prince were inherited from heroines, primarily from Judith, and now in this ballet they again found a more suitable place in the characterization of the girl. The mandarin was cast in a different mould from that of the prince who, in spite of his imposing appearance when he first set out to court the princess, would not have been equal to the life-and-death struggle of the later ballet. Here it was necessary to embody in a human being the elemental force seen earlier in the wooden puppet; for now it was necessary to show a human being strong enough to overcome the hell of inhumanity, and, through his love and death, to make the enslaved woman who was his predestined mate, aware of him and thus able to discover her own true identity.

The inner dramatic tensions of the story are faithfully reflected in the structure. Thus there is no concealment of the conflicts in the slow–fast–slow movements, that is, the scherzos and funeral marches; these are not hidden at the centre of an arching structure as in *Bluebeard's Castle*, nor are they similarly enclosed within a circling framework like the Wagnerian nature scene of the earlier ballet. *The Miraculous Mandarin* takes its place among the works which end with a funeral march. Its immediate predecessor is the *String Quartet No. 2*, in which the 'barbaric' *Scherzo* with its rushing minor thirds is similarly enclosed between the slow movements.

Toward the middle of the ballet, the two main characters are jointly depicted by a double scherzo. The waltz-scherzo represents at one and the same time the Girl, an urban atmosphere and, as so often in Bartók's works, feminine neurosis. The other scherzo conveys the elemental power of nature. There would be a hiatus between the two were it not for the link provided by the prior entrance of the mandarin and his presence during the girl's dance. This has the effect of heightening the tension of both. The structure of the work is symmetrically designed: three times the enticing gestures of the girl attract the three vagrants, one after the other; next comes the double scherzo at the centre of the structure; lastly, the work is balanced by the three successive murders. It was in order to preserve this balanced structure that Bartók omitted the fourth murder.

The dramatic strength of *The Miraculous Mandarin* lies in the fact that each of the characters has to fight his own battle, bloody as it is, without recourse to outside help. There is no one to rescue them, neither the inevitably approaching Fate of *Bluebeard's Castle* nor the pantheistic miracles of *The Wooden Prince*. The tragic ending of the ballet provides a realistic dramatic solution, a veritable catharsis which could only be realized through the preceding stages of horror. This is therefore the only genuine drama among Bartók's stage works; hence its direct and shocking effect on the audience. And the message of the ballet is as timely now as it was when it was first produced nearly fifty years ago.

The musical idiom of the ballet faithfully demonstrates Bartók's musical thinking at that time. We have no way of knowing whether Bartók had any direct experience of the music of his great Viennese contemporary, Arnold Schoenberg, during the war years. Our present limited information suggests that he had none. Even so, there is no cause for wonder at the similarity of their music and their aims. Both composers had to work their way through the school of late German Romanticism. Both had to find a way along the difficult paths of spiritual development and musical expression through the tangle of an expressive musical language characterized by tenuous, apprehensive or plaintive melody, at a time when the world of harmony was only just being liberated from the restrictions of tonality. One trend of Bartók's musical thinking led to a free application of the twelve half-tones, and a complete relaxation of the restrictions of traditional tonality, just as Schoenberg, only a short while afterwards, laid down the equal usage of half-tones as a rule of composing technique. Signs of this trend had already appeared in Bartók's works written as long as ten years before. His melodic world since 1916 had tended toward a stringing together of intervals in a certain alternating system, toward the establishment of interval patterns, as Ernő Lendvai calls them, while in 1918, the *Études*, composed as companion pieces to *The Miraculous Mandarin*, mark an important experiment with the sounding of the twelve half-tones in series. An article which was published in the German music magazine *Melos* in 1920, indicates his interest in atonality, dodecaphony and serial construction. In this article he gave full consideration to the possibility of a new line of musical thinking, and the effect of the simultaneous sounding of tones not on a principle of pitch but on a principle of dynamics.

The loosening of the tonal system of the great bourgeois musical culture was the inevitable accompaniment in music of the disintegration of the whole bourgeois world outlook and system of values. The establishment of the twelve-tone scale and the serial as a method and principle of composition was a direct reflection of this process, but it was in no way a solution. Though an illusion of supreme objectivity may be created through the intellectualization of the new order of tones by external standards, the actual content, when it becomes identical with the aesthetic principle, is removed from the battle of ideas and constitutes a retreat from social activity into the sphere of abstract moralizing.

The greatest of his masters, Schoenberg, Berg and Webern, never applied this method rigidly, nor did they identify technique, their means of expression, with the aesthetic content of their art. Their whole life-work testifies to the fact that they always regarded technique as a means to an end, and each of them shaped it to express his own personality and artistic ideas. By 1920 Bartók was no longer treading the same path. A thorough analysis of the ballet bears out the claim, made later by the composer, that even at that time, his music had not discarded certain forms of tonality. The musical fabric of *The Miraculous Mandarin* is arranged round certain tonality focuses which constitute a firm skeletal structure for the work. The so-called complementary technique, that is, the complementary use of smaller groups of the twelve tones arranged in a certain order, is the sign of the new tonality cells, and heralds a method of composition found only much later in the works of Bartók's Viennese contemporaries.

On the other hand, Bartók never made exclusive use of dodecaphony to express his vision. In the article written in 1920 and mentioned above, he made it clear that it was not his intention to give up the traditional musical intonations for the sake of new possibilities: the true significance of these was, in his view, to supplement and enrich traditional musical thinking.

This principle, as expressed in his writings, was splendidly realized in his creative art. Throughout this period there was an intensification of the dualism of his musical world in which, ever since the encounter between the expressive, late Romantic style on the one hand and folk music on the other, the former had signified the oppressive and the unnatural, while the latter represented all that was natural and humane. This is exemplified by two parallel groups of his works—those marked by an opus number and those without; and it is also demonstrated by the musical dramaturgy of *The Miraculous Mandarin*. At this stage of his development as a creative artist, it was inevitable that there should be a meeting between the two aspects of his musical thinking, that which involved the most radical disintegration of tonal melodic and harmonic order, and that which involved all that he had discovered in relation to the oldest and most rudimentary melodic germs of folk music. In Bartók's musical idiom, the latter indicated the boundary within which a conscious analysis of traditions could nevertheless remain constructive and musical. In his scale of artistic values, it also represented the force of nature within man himself and upon which man could rely in his struggles, the force which, in the tragic story of the mandarin, was responsible for a moral victory over the opposing forces of inhumanity.

According to contemporary accounts, *The Miraculous Mandarin*, at any rate in the piano arrangement, was completed in the summer of 1919. 'The new ballet is finished, Béla is already orchestrating it,' wrote

164

the composer's wife to her mother-in-law in Pozsony, on Whit Monday. Sometime in July (opinions vary as to whether it was at the beginning or at the end of the month), the composer played it to a small group of invited guests at the home of István Thomán. But before the first stage performance, there was to be an interval of many years, years of great trial for the composer, years during which the ballet was quite neglected. The orchestration was not completed for many years, and even after the première in Cologne in 1926, Bartók changed certain details over and over again. He did not live to see it performed in Budapest.

In 1919, throughout the period of the Republic of Councils, Bartók remained true to his friends, his principles and himself. Like Béla Reinitz, Kodály and Dohnányi, he served in an advisory capacity to the members of the cultural administration of the proletarian dictatorship responsible for a music policy. In the statement mentioned earlier, made when he was being interviewed by a correspondent of *Színházi Élet*, in March 1919, he spoke about prospects for musical education such as had not previously been dreamed of. There were also plans to establish a music museum. 'Kunffy has already signed the authorization,' he wrote to his mother on June 9. Later the plans were modified. It seemed a better idea to 'set up a department of folk music within the existing museum'. But these ambitious plans could not be realized. After the defeat of the workers' state, there was a change in the political atmosphere, and Bartók found himself quite differently placed. He was forced to alter his way of life and adapt himself to new working conditions so that his creative talent began to develop in yet another direction.

CHAPTER VIII

INTERNATIONAL SUCCESSES AND NEW CREATIVE IDEALS. 1919–1923

1 COUNTER-REVOLUTIONARY CHANGES IN HUNGARY. DISCIPLINARY IN-
VESTIGATION AT THE ACADEMY OF MUSIC. PLANS FOR EMIGRATION,
GATHERING OF INFORMATION IN BERLIN

The changes in Bartók's way of life brought about by the political events of 1919–20 once again confront the biographer with the difficulty of correctly marking the various periods of his career. The story of his life as a boy and as a young man during the first two decades of the century has already demonstrated that the twists and turns of his outward life by no means coincided with the changes of style, content and characteristics found in his works. Bartók himself, in later statements and in his writings, always emphasized that the year 1926 marked the division between two periods characterized by different creative methods. This date is confirmed by research workers and indeed by the works themselves.

It is a striking fact, however, that in the outward circumstances of his life, the most fundamental changes took place, not in 1926, but considerably earlier, in 1919–20. Yet it is scarcely possible to classify so rigidly the events of a man's life on the one hand, and on the other, his development as an artist. It is more likely that the events of 1919–20 and their impact on Bartók were to some extent responsible for the fundamental transformation of Bartók's artistic outlook which became evident some years later. In the same way, as we have already seen, the creative period which began in 1907, owed its inspiration to political, ideological and personal influences dating from 1905 or even earlier. The political events of 1919 and the early years of the nineteen-twenties had the effect of completely altering the course of Bartók's life and this in turn affected his creative work: after the fallow years of 1924–25 came the rich harvest of the piano compositions of 1926. A study of the relationships between Bartók's life and his work shows that in the compositions written between 1920 and 1923 there are some early indications of the coming transformation of his artistic outlook.

Bartók's ideas were not those of an avowed socialist. As in the case of most bourgeois intellectuals, his entry into the Republic of Councils did not result from membership of the working-class movement. But, during the previous decades, his own struggle to realize his social and cultural ideals and to win freedom and independence for the Hungarians and other nationalities had taken place side by side with members of this section of society. He rightly looked upon the policies of the workers' state as a victory for his own ideals which were now, as a result of his own efforts, suitably incorporated into the plans of the Music Committee of the cultural administration of the Republic of Councils. In the task of planning and implementing this new cultural programme, he found himself joined by old friends. It was during past years of hardship that Kodály, Dohnányi, Béla Reinitz and Béla Balázs had become his friends and comrades. Though there were many issues on which Bartók did not agree with Dohnányi, he never questioned his artistic capabilities or status. During these years they were drawn together even more closely by their common effort to realize the cultural ideals to which they were both dedicated, and also, for a time, as a result of persecution by the counter-revolutionary government. In such circumstances, their ideological and moral differences temporarily lost much of their significance.

The few months of the proletarian dictatorship were for Bartók too a period of feverish activity in many enterprises. But all his endeavours were doomed to failure at the end of July 1919, when the Entente Powers took advantage of the weak organization and lack of experience of the workers' government to intervene with armed forces, so that with the aid of internal counter-revolutionary forces, they overthrew the Hungarian Republic of Councils. The Revolutionary Governing Council resigned on August 1, and immediately, the counter-revolutionary forces, sheltering under the wing of the social democratic government and the occupation armies, elected as their Governor Archduke Joseph von Habsburg. In the capital, members of the right-wing parties allocated to each other the various positions of governmental authority, and negotiated with the Entente armies of occupation, while in Transdanubia the people suffered the bloody retaliation of Horthy's notorious officer contingents. In the autumn, disciplinary committees were set up, and on November 16, Horthy made his triumphal entry into Budapest.

During these decisive weeks, Zoltán Kodály was the director of the Academy of Music. Early in 1919, when he reached the age of seventy-six, Ödön Mihalovich, who had succeeded Ferenc Liszt as director of the Academy, retired from this post and became life president. The Károlyi government then appointed Ernő Dohnányi as director and Zoltán Kodály as his deputy. During the summer of 1919, Dohnányi gave a series of concerts in Norway and he was still abroad at the commencement of the school year of 1919–20. He was not in Hungary at the time of the political changes, and when he returned home at the beginning of October, he found that he had been suspended for one year 'so that his appointment could be reconsidered'. During this period the counter-revolutionary press put forward the name of Jenő Hubay as a suitable director for the Academy, and fostered the idea that such a position would be a suitable reward for a man who had been persecuted by the workers' government.

Fourteen members of the staff of the Academy registered their protest against Dohnányi's enforced leave of absence by going on strike.

> After a few days, 2 of them turned blackleg, then the rest also resumed their duties,

wrote Bartók to his mother in Pozsony, on October 23. According to János Demény, five of them—Kodály, Kerpely, Dr. Géza Molnár, Antal Molnár and Imre Waldbauer—had earlier been subjected to disciplinary action by the Ministry for their conduct during the Republic of Councils. 'And now the whole affair is fizzling out,' continued Bartók.

> There was to have been a disciplinary investigation into the activities of Zoltán and the others, but it's always being postponed—it is evident that the whole business was a farce. They continue to draw their full salaries, of course, only they do no work. In a word, they come off better than the teachers against whom no disciplinary action has been taken.

On November 25, Jenő Hubay's appointment to the post of director of the Academy of Music was announced in the press. Bartók gave his own account of the affair in a letter to his mother dated November 28:

168

Mr. Hubay has made his festive entry into the halls of the National Academy of Music (with an *Einzugsmarsch* which was probably self-provided for the occasion). He is now busy giving interviews to the representatives of every kind of newspaper and handing out statements right and left. Some 2 weeks ago, for instance, one of his pronouncements appeared in the columns of *Budapesti Hirlap*. 'I certainly count on having the support of Dohnányi and Bartók in my great work'. And the other day, in *Az Ujság*, he made a statement to the effect that I could not be expected to show an interest in piano-teaching; that some sort of post would have to be created specially for me to make it possible for me to add to our national heritage of music in perfect freedom, as and when I could. That's all I know, as I haven't of course met Hubay as yet. Still, it should be enough to convince you that no one is persecuting me or stirring up trouble against me personally. You know, of course, that I have for a long time now wanted to give up teaching and do some other kind of work, e.g. in a museum. Hubay and his friends are equally well aware of this fact and must have in mind something like that.

But Hubay could not count on the immediate support of Dohnányi either. Hubay tried to persuade him to stay on at the Academy as a professor, but Dohnányi agreed only on condition that there should be no penalization of his colleagues. This condition was not honoured. Dohnányi meantime made a number of appearances both as a pianist and as a conductor on the concert platforms of Budapest. With remarkable consistency he included one of Bartók's works in every programme. During his piano recital at the Academy on October 8, he played *An Evening with the Székelys*, *Bear Dance*, and *Allegro Barbaro*. On November 3, he conducted the *Two Portraits*. On December 29, he conducted the *Rhapsody* for piano and orchestra at a concert given by the Philharmonic Society, with Bartók as the solo pianist.

The events of these few months reveal clearly the dual nature of cultural life at that time. To understand what Bartók meant by the phrases 'fizzling out', 'farce' and 'postponement' we have only to collate the various measures proposed, the statements made and opinions offered in the press. It then becomes clear that the cultural administration of the counter-revolutionary government was by no means self-confident. In Bartók's letter of October 23, there is a vivid description not only of his own circumstances, but also by implication, of the general atmosphere:

> ... I am not badly off here, and I'm not being persecuted (not because they have no cause to—they have no qualms about acting without good cause nowadays—but because they dare not).

At the first concert he gave after returning home, Dohnányi was showered with bouquets. He was elected as resident conductor of the Philharmonic Society. And while disparaging comments on Bartók's music continued to appear in the press, some of the more enlightened personalities, including Géza Molnár, a noted critic and aesthetician, and Miklós Radnai, later the director of the Opera, rallied to his support. Miklós Radnai records that at his concert of December 29, Bartók 'was received with a lengthy burst of applause as soon as he appeared on the platform'.

In a letter to Pozsony dated November 28, Bartók was able to write:

> Nothing more has been done about taking disciplinary action against Zoltán and the others.

The full force of the counter-revolutionary attack on the representatives of cultural progress did not make itself felt until the first half of 1920; then it became open, unmistakable and relentless. On January 10, disciplinary action was taken against Kodály as a former member of the Music Committee. It was more difficult to take action against Dohnányi and Bartók since there was always the possibility of rousing the antagonism of their admirers abroad. Nevertheless, the two men immediately announced their support for Kodály. Within a few days, first Dohnányi, then Bartók, had written indignant letters of protest to the ministry councillor, Baron Gyula Wlassics Jr., who was the president of the disciplinary committee.

> I have only just learned that 'membership of the Directory' is one of the charges now being made against Zoltán Kodály for disciplinary investigation of which you are chairman,

wrote Bartók on February 3.

> Having myself participated in the executive functions of that body in precisely the same way as Kodály, I must protest against his bearing alone any responsibility, either for the mere fact of former membership or for anything else he may have done to which objection is now raised.

170

On January 28, Dohnányi had written, 'Kodály is being made responsible for things that he cannot be held responsible for, things for which I alone, as director of the institution, can be held responsible . . .'

Bartók was not directly involved in the turmoil that surrounded the affairs of the Academy. At the beginning of September, Kodály had submitted to the ministry a request that Bartók should be granted leave of absence for six months. This had been granted, and in December Bartók had asked for an extension so that he would not have to teach during that school year. In the original application in September, Kodály had referred to Bartók's poor state of health. 'It is a matter of the first importance to our national culture,' he wrote, 'that Bartók, our country's most outstanding composer, one who is recognized throughout Europe, should regain full working capacity . . . In the last twenty years, in addition to teaching, he has carried out an exhausting task of the utmost significance, as shown by the compositions, concerts and ethnographical studies that have resulted from it. Even if his constitution had not been impaired by physical strain and serious privation during the past months and years, he would still be in need of a period of rest and special consideration.'

This was indeed the case. Bartók was badly in need of rest. But it was not for this reason that he asked for leave of absence. He was planning to emigrate and wished to be in a position in which he was free to seek information. Further extracts from his letter of October 23 provide evidence of his anxious state of mind.

> As for me, I keep waiting and waiting. So long as we remain isolated and continue to find ourselves in what amounts to a state of siege, it will be impossible to do anything. But I have been making what enquiries I can in 3 different countries about the chances of making a living . . . For the next ten years at least it will not be possible to do any work, i.e. the kind of work I am interested in (studying folk music). In other words, if I have a chance to do this kind of work abroad, I see no point in staying here; and if it's impossible to make a living from this kind of work abroad either, it would still be better to teach music, in Vienna say, than in Budapest; for there at least they have good musical institutions (orchestras, opera, etc.), whereas everything is being ruined here because our best musicians, our only ones—Tango, Dohnányi, etc.—are being hounded out of their posts.

With the defeat of the revolution, Bartók's most gifted colleagues had been forced to emigrate. Balázs fled to Vienna. Reinitz, once released from prison, went there too. Dohnányi led the peripatetic life of an artist whose engagements were world-wide, and for years he returned to Budapest merely for concert engagements. Tango, after being driven out of the country by the right-wing administration of the Budapest Opera House, found a temporary refuge with the Kolozsvár Opera. Thus, as we also learn from the same letter, it was not merely in order to pursue his career as a musician, that Bartók sought information about the possibilities of emigrating to 'Transylvania, Vienna or Germany'. It was of course true that his publishers lived in Vienna and that Bartók had been in constant touch with the musical life of the city ever since his student days. It was true that he had given recitals in Berlin on many occasions, had spent many months there as a young man, and that his friend and ardent admirer, Ferruccio Busoni, still lived and worked there. It was in the German language and with the German culture that Bartók always felt most at home. As for Transylvania, he admitted to his mother in the same letter that it would feel more or less like Hungary to him.

> Of all the territories that lay within the former boundaries of Hungary, that was the one I liked best anyway.

But apart from such links, he was more profoundly drawn to Transylvania, Vienna and Germany by a feeling of solidarity with his friends in exile. During the Horthy era, the trail of the emigrants led first to Vienna and Berlin, and Bartók seized every opportunity to throw in his own lot with that of his friends. A dedication to Béla Reinitz, then in prison, appeared on the title page of the manuscript of *Five Songs* op. 16 (texts by Endre Ady) published in 1920. When, on February 20, 1920, in the right-wing paper *Szózat*, Bartók's name was printed among the list of members of the Music Committee enjoying the favour of the counter-revolutionary government, he replied on the very same day,

> . . . I would not even wish to be a member of a Music Committee from which the finest musicians in the country have been excluded.

In February, Bartók visited Berlin, his first trip abroad since the war. He was to have played the piano solo of his *Rhapsody*, with Scherchen conducting, at the fifth orchestral concert of the Neue Musikgesellschaft on February 28. But it would appear from a notice printed in the March 3 issue of *Vossische Zeitung* that the orchestral scores were not available for some reason. Bartók therefore played one of his *Elegies, An Evening with the Székelys* and the *Allegro Barbaro*. On March 8, he gave another recital at the concert of chamber music arranged by the same society. On that occasion he played the piano part of Kodály's Sonata for 'Cello and Ravel's Trio. He also played a number of his own short piano pieces. In the *Vossische Zeitung* on March 6 there appeared a lengthy appreciation of Bartók's music written by one of his former composition pupils, Gizella Selden-Goth, who was living in Berlin at that time.

Since there is no evidence to suggest otherwise, it would seem that Bartók made no further appearances in Berlin that season. Nevertheless he remained in Berlin until the end of the month, and probably until the beginning of April. He could not leave Berlin earlier—as we know from László Somfai—'because of political and transportation disturbances caused by the Monarchist Kapp-Putsch'. (*Documenta Bartókiana*, II.) On March 30, he wrote from Berlin to his old friend in Belényes, János Buşiţia, for there was still no normal postal service between Hungary and Romania. From this letter we learn that while he was in Berlin, Bartók was considering the possibility of settling there.

> At home, the outlook is pretty bleak; I have come here to have a look round and see what may be done. I have been pleased to find that I am greatly respected here. At any rate, it would be possible for me to settle here too.

News of these discussions soon reached Hungary. In the March 30 issue of *Szózat*, the music critic, Viktor Papp, wrote that he understood that Reinhardt, the world-famous theatrical producer, had commissioned Bartók to write the music of his play Lysistrata, and added the alarming conclusion, 'So Bartók is to remain in Berlin!' The few documents referring to the circumstances and details of the commission hardly reveal anything. Even the genre of planned stage music was uncertain. The sources speak of a pantomime, or choruses, or accompanying music for choruses. From László Somfai's above-mentioned statement it is clear that the thought of music for 'Lysistrata' occupied Bartók very seriously, and it was only around the time of his home-coming that he rejected Reinhardt's offer.

Bartók, however, did not remain in Berlin. The reason may be found in a later passage of his letter to Buşiţia.

> ... as you know very well, my interest in folk-songs would hardly allow me to go to the west; it can't be helped, they draw me to the east.

He returned home in April by way of Pozsony where he visited his mother and friends. He also gave a recital there on April 16. He played some of his own works, probably *Fifteen Hungarian Peasant Songs* in their final, complete form. He played the piano part of his *Rhapsody* accompanied by his former pupil, Sándor Albrecht, who played an arrangement of the orchestral score on a second piano. It was probably not until the end of April or the beginning of May that Bartók arrived back in Budapest.

He now made his home in Budapest proper. For some ten years he had lived with his family in Rákoskeresztúr, and it was there that he had composed his stage works, but immediately after returning to Hungary he moved into the villa owned by the banker, József Lukács, father of the philosopher, György Lukács, in Gyopár utca. During these difficult years, József Lukács gladly provided a place of refuge for artists and scientists sympathetic to the ideals of the revolution, thus deliberately continuing the best traditions of the broad-minded members of the bourgeoisie who had lived in Pest at the turn of the century. One of his guests, who stayed with him for some time, was Aladár Tóth who returned from exile in the country only to be persecuted by the White Terror. Thomas Mann also visited him, and under his roof first met Béla Bartók. Professor Albert Gyergyai, who was at that time tutor of the younger Lukács children, has given us a delightful account of Bartók as a member of the household. Writing in 1955, he tells us that as far as he can remember, the Bartók family lived in Gyopár utca for about two years. Then in the spring of 1922 they moved to No. 4 Szilágyi Dezső tér.

As a result of his trip to Berlin, German translations of two of his earlier essays on folk-music research were printed in the 1920 volume of the influential Leipzig journal of musicology, *Zeitschrift für Musikwissenschaft*. These were *Der Musikdialekt der Rumänen von Hunyad* and *Die Volkmusik der Araber von Biskra und Umgebung*. The important letter dated October 23, 1919, describes how the text of these essays, and others too, were sent to Germany in the autumn of 1919:

> A university professor who has 'emigrated' to Germany has taken with him a German translation of all my papers on folk music (they deal with Hungarian, Romanian and Arab folk music), and he is trying to do something for me in there.

The 'emigrating' professor was Géza Révész, a music psychologist. It seems that it was as a result of his efforts that the Máramaros collection was eventually, after many earlier futile attempts, successfully printed in German in 1923 as the fourth volume of the *Sammelbände für vergleichende Musikwissenschaft*, published by the firm of Drei Masken.

Although the two former essays had been published earlier in Hungarian—some of the sections about Arab folk music appeared in 1917, the essay on the Romanian folk-music dialect of Hunyad as far back as 1914—some chauvinistic circles in Budapest only then noticed some of Bartók's conclusions about Romanian folk music. The Treaty of Trianon had only just brought home to the Hungarians the full and bitter realization of what it meant to them to have lost the war and suffered the suppression of their revolution. Soon after he returned home, in May, the time seemed ripe to these chauvinists for the initiation of a campaign to persecute Bartók as a traitor. The following is a brief summary of the account of a libellous press campaign and Bartók's reply to it.

The dominant note of the attack was struck by 'dr. e.s.' (Elemér Sereghy) in the May 19th, 1920 issue of *Nemzeti Ujság*. His argument is strangely similar to that of Emil Haraszti when he introduced the scathing reference to 'Scotus Viator' some seven years previously. Claiming cultural 'superiority' for Hungary, Sereghy stated that in the German version of

The Romanian Folk-Music Dialect of Hunyad Bartók 'piled tendentious data, one fact after another, such as we cannot accept'. Sereghy, attempting to demonstrate his own superior knowledge, expressed contempt for Bartók's research into Romanian folk music, saying that it was without significance. It was his opinion that Bartók's 'lengthy scientific analysis' was of no interest to 'anyone in the world', and that 'its publication would be superfluous and valueless even from the point of view of the Romanians were it not for a couple of hints between the lines in which the political slant is unmistakable'. His chief accusation against 'the royal Hungarian professor' was that he had 'advertised' as areas of Romanian culture 'Máramaros, Ugocsa, Szatmár, Szilágy, Beszterce-Naszód, Bihar and Hunyad as well as districts further to the south and east'. He concluded his attack with the query: 'What can have happened to Bartók, the man who three years ago was claiming as Hungarian even Slovak and Romanian folk-songs, yet now is endeavouring to trace back to a Romanian origin every one of our Transylvanian songs? It would be highly desirable if the Minister of Culture, before the expiry of Bartók's leave, would give him an opportunity to state more clearly which nationality he belongs to.'

Two days later, this libellous article was answered in *Uj Nemzedék* by 'a Professor of Music at the Academy'. The 'professor' coolly explained the real meaning of Bartók's essay and the circumstances of its publication, and in conclusion effectively undermined Sereghy's political accusations by pointing out the fact that the Romanian folk-songs had been collected in Transylvania and not in Romania and provided 'such excellent proof of our own cultural superiority that I would like to submit this data to the Peace Conference'.

Sereghy, however, was not to be deterred. He suspected the 'Professor of Music' was really Kodály. (This in fact was not so, and to this day the 'professor's' identity remains unknown.) Enraged by the fact that his attack should have met with such a cool response, he accused Kodály of being 'Bartók's evil spirit' and spoke of Bartók's essay as 'unpatriotic poison'. He contended that Bartók had deliberately timed the publication of his essay so as to arouse public sympathy in Romania. He was shocked and reproachful that Bartók should have allowed his Romanian collection to be published in Bucharest, and refused to acknowledge that his incriminating study on the Romanian folk-music dialect of Hunyad had appeared much earlier. In conclusion he added, 'Those who think us naive, and would like to offer this article to the Peace Conference, are either deranged or collaborating with the enemy.'

At this point the editor of the *Szózat* intervened by printing an interview with Jenő Hubay. Hubay of course did not adopt the uncouth tones used by Sereghy, and introduced his remarks by emphasizing that he had enjoyed for a long time 'a close and friendly relationship with Béla Bartók', and considered him to be a man 'of remarkable talent . . . something I never fail to recognize'. Nevertheless, he went on to say that in his opinion the publication of the German translation of the essay was 'most untimely, even unfortunate', and that Bartók's 'lack of foresight' was to be deplored. Hubay gave ample proof of his own complete ignorance of the matter under discussion, concluding his statement by stressing that maintenance of territorial integrity should be considered before 'a question of detail in musicology that is of little significance in any case'.

On the very next day, May 26, Bartók's own reply was printed in *Szózat*. He utterly rejected Hubay's accusations, commenting as follows:

> It is not I who trace Transylvanian songs back to a Romanian origin; it is Director Hubay who accuses me by saying, 'By mistake, he has taken over many Romanian musical motifs in his collections of Hungarian folk music' . . . My researches over the past decades have made me immune to such 'errors,' more so than Mr. Hubay who, as far as I know, is not familiar with either my Hungarian or other collections, and has never shown any interest in them. Let Director Hubay specify the songs I have falsified if he wishes to stick to his assertions, or let him name the songs he imagines to be Romanian and prove that they are actually of Romanian origin.

Bartók ended his letter with the query:

> Who is it who can be said to be unpatriotic? The one who over the past decade has spared no energy in becoming acquainted with Hungarian folk music, or the one who welcomes this research with indifference, even with hostility and false accusations? Finally I ask if the term 'poisoner' should not rather be applied to one who out of ignorance, malevolence and the wish to mislead others, has had the audacity to level a trumped-up charge of lack of patriotism based only on an essay which in fact serves the cause of the Hungarian?
> Respectfully, Béla Bartók.

On the same day, the matter was discussed at a committee meeting of the Hungarian Ethnological Society. Scientific arguments were advanced which caused the committee to decide that it 'would not identify itself with an attack which had no objective foundation, and would protest against it in the name of freedom to undertake scientific research'. But Hubay, offended by Bartók's harsh tone, declared that he would continue to maintain that 'in the tragic situation of Hungary at that time', the publication of the article was 'ill timed and unpatriotic'. With these words the debate in the press came to an end.

These expressions of political spite, narrow-minded and ignorant as they were, would scarcely be deserving of half the space accorded them were it not that they are but one of a number of indications of the social antagonism that was developing towards Bartók and his music. The tone of the attacks and the slogans used were similar to those employed by the same reactionary groups of nationalists who had slandered him in the years before the war. It was not Bartók but they, his dilettante accusers, who, whether ignorant or conscious of what they were saying, had 'three years before' regarded 'Romanian and Slovak folk-songs' as Hungarian. Nor could it have been otherwise, since these 'nationalists' were for the most part familiar only with the folk-art songs which they thought of as Hungarian. Yet Jenő Hubay now demonstrated his own bias and incompetence by hastening to substantiate Sereghy's accusations. He declared that Bartók had mistakenly included a great many 'Romanian folk-music motifs' in his collections of Hungarian folk music. This was one of the final blows in an attack which had started in 1914 in the Şezâtoarea. Romanian chauvinism was by now an accurate reflection of the Hungarian variety: Romanian reactionaries would not admit that their folk-songs were indeed Romanian, they regarded them as Hungarian and maintained that they had been falsified when recorded by Bartók.

It is comforting to turn to the reviews written at that time by the ever-faithful Pongrác Kacsóh who continued to have unfailing confidence in Bartók's ability. Yet those who had not understood the composer's work a decade earlier were still expressing their doubts. After the composer's recital on January 7, 1921, Izor Béldi made the arrogant boast in *Pesti Hirlap* that 'he could not praise every work without reservation'. To his ear, the *String Quartet No. 1* completed twelve years previously was nothing more than a 'kaleidoscopic variation of motley musical colour effects'. He was better able to appreciate the *Piano Quintet*, with its more customary intonations, while his scepticism allowed him to attribute the success of the shorter piano pieces only to Dohnányi's 'virtuoso performance'. Two weeks later, on January 21, he mentioned the new arrangement of the *Suite No. 2* but failed to make any comment.

After the first performance of the *Four Orchestral Pieces* on January 9, 1922, he could no longer restrain himself: 'Those who, like the writer of this review, advocate an absolute beauty in music, must regretfully confess that they cannot support Bartók in this new musical gospel; his work had the same effect upon us as if it had been played from back to front.'

Once again we find among the critics two familiar names, on the one hand that of Emil Haraszti who had neither learnt nor forgotten anything, and on the other, that of Aurél Kern who, after the performance of the *Suite No. 2* in January 1921, had hoped that 'the time will come when Bartók will be understood', in spite of the fact that 'the public remains puzzled by the relentless modernity and wild abandon of the work with its gigantic and weighty construction'. However, Kern too considered the *Four Orchestral Pieces* to be an 'aberration of a great poetic spirit . . . The *Suite* is the work of a genius,' he admitted. 'It is superfluous to say it . . . It is not complicated,' he continued with astonishment, 'I have heard it twice, I can already perceive the whole fabric—and yet I do not understand it.' A week later, after hearing the *Improvisations*, he admitted that the failure was his. 'Even though I have been on many occasions astounded by his bold, wild, merciless modernity, my assessment of Béla Bartók's work has always been facilitated by the fact that I invariably found in his music something engaging, and some examples of his superb genius which I could enjoy and praise with complete honesty. But now I am beginning to find myself in deep water when I consider his later works. I must confess that I do not understand them.' Nor did he trust the enthusiastic reception given them by the audiences. 'I do not quite trust the good faith of the audiences which today filled the hall to capacity and applauded so noisily. These young people who rally round the banner of the *ars nova* show a capacity for worship that is a bit decadent as well as blind, and perhaps even deaf. I wish their cause every success, but I think the pace of Bartók's militant advance is somewhat too hasty.'

Though some members of the audience may have applauded for the wrong reasons, the enthusiasm was genuine and the audience was not in the main either decadent or dishonest. People like Aurél Kern were suspicious simply because they could not understand why the audience appreciated Bartók's art. Aurél Kern was quite right when he said that the audience consisted mainly of young people: it consisted of those whose applause five years previously had ensured the success of *The Wooden Prince*. Their applause on that occasion had started in the gallery and spread to the stalls and boxes. Even at that time they had understood that Bartók's music was more than an example of a passing musical trend: they realized that his music was a battle ground for the struggle between reaction and progress. Influenced by the enlightened views current at the time of the revolution, these young people could not but be aware that the stormy atmosphere surrounding the Bartók concerts was indicative not only of the composer's position in the front ranks of the cultural struggle but also of the conflict between revolution and counter-revolution that was making itself felt in every sphere.

During this period of oppression, the Hungarian intelligentsia made use of cultural weapons in the revolutionary struggle, and it may be that Aurél Kern was not fully aware of just how right he was to think of Bartók's music as a banner at the head of the revolutionary movement. These demonstrations of solidarity and enthusiasm on the part of the politically conscious members of the intelligentsia had been noticeable at Bartók's concerts ever since the autumn of 1919. This live support was the reason why Bartók did not retire from the concert podium at this time, for wherever he played one of his own works, he could feel how greatly his music was needed.

According to János Demény, Bartók's works were performed on eight occasions between the autumn of 1920 and January 1922, and Bartók himself gave several piano recitals. This is no insignificant number if we bear in mind the general political situation and more particularly Bartók's withdrawn way of life. He was in fact once more teaching at the Academy during the school year of 1920–21, but a contemporary statement by

Dohnányi refers to the fact that 'he merely holds classes and has no contact with anyone'.

The concert he gave in Szeged in November 1921 had repercussions which are very revealing of the mood of the country as a whole. At this concert he played works by Scarlatti and Kodály and also some of his own songs and piano compositions. 'The ice has been broken,' began the review in *Szeged*. 'The audience not merely sensed, but actually knew that Béla Bartók is one of the leading representatives of Hungarian music.' In two of the reviews of the Szeged concert his name was linked with that of Ady. And it was probably at that time that his music inspired the poet Gyula Juhász to write a poem about him.

It was therefore much to be deplored that certain reviewers were carried away by their enthusiasm and put too much emphasis on what they termed 'the Hungarian racial' characteristics of Bartók's music. Obtuse as they were, it is not surprising to find that Aurél Kern, Viktor Papp and other seasoned nationalists should have distorted Bartók's internationally significant creations into something that was old Turanian Hungarian. Their inveterate nationalistic Hungarianism would not allow them to realize what a long way Bartók had had to travel since the days when he affected a Hungarian cravat to the time when he could create the *String Quartet No. 2*. Indeed their chauvinism had hardened with the passage of time and had become incorporated within an obstinate allegiance to the cause of Hungarianism which at the same time allowed them to compromise with the forces of reaction. It is much more tragic that between the two wars, in the admiration for Bartók's music felt by a considerable section of the Hungarian intelligentsia, there was an element of nationalism, and that though their respect for him was sincere and basically well-meaning, they perverted him into the apostle of 'ancient primitive force'. It was soon after 1920 that the germ of this misinterpretation first became active.

But the more clear-sighted members of the left-wing intelligentsia began to voice their support for Bartók more and more clearly in the Budapest press. In *Nyugat* one of the great music critics of the day, Aladár Tóth, boldly contested Kern's distorted, anti-Semitic 'music policies', and the 'great' musicians officially honoured by the right-wing administration he branded as the suppressors of Hungarian musical life.

181

In his reviews—profound, analytical and European in outlook—for twenty years he fought with all the might of his pen for the cause of Bartók, Kodály and the advancement of Hungarian culture as a whole. István Péterfi, who had been silenced for some time, soon joined forces with him in *Világ*. Reviewing the première of *Four Orchestral Pieces* he quoted Ady. 'Bartók will never be the "violinist of the nonentities",' he wrote. And in 1922, *Magyar Írás* printed an article by another admirer and disseminator of Bartók's art, Sándor Jemnitz, who had studied under Reger and Schoenberg and who later became an influential critic in the columns of *Népszava*.

These disciples in Hungary were not alone in their admiration for Bartók. At about that time, the name of the composer once again began to become known throughout Europe, his works were performed more and more frequently, and there were more general attempts to analyse his art. His *Suite No. 1* was heard in London, and his *Suite* for piano op. 14 was given a notice in an Italian music magazine. In 1920, a lengthy study of Bartók by Cecil Gray appeared in the British paper *The Sackbut*, and in March 1921, Bartók's fortieth birthday was honoured by nearly every group of people interested in progressive music throughout Europe. The *Musikblätter des Anbruch*, which was closely associated with Universal Edition, published a special issue to mark the occasion, and the *Revue Musicale* carried a summary of Bartók's career by Kodály. Bartók was now mentioned as one of the world's greatest living composers.

Bartók's opponents in Hungary were forced to take note of his success abroad, and make some attempt, however unwilling, to conceal their resentment. By the time the official cultural policy was sufficiently consolidated for its leaders to think of settling their account with Bartók, his supporters in Hungary, strengthened by his fame abroad, had become so powerful and well organized that the Horthy regime, which had already aroused international indignation with its abuse of the law, was anxious to avoid any scandal connected with Bartók that might assume international proportions. Even if Sereghy had felt that the time was now ripe for prosecuting Bartók, the more well-informed members of the cultural administration would have been very embarrassed to have the true nature of their feelings towards Bartók exposed to the world. This is shown by the tone of Hubay's statement, and especially by the fact that the whole question was dropped completely after the resolution of the Ethnological Society.

It is certain that had Bartók's position appeared to be one fraction less assured, he would have been called to account and forced to defend himself, as Sereghy had demanded in the first of his articles. At the Opera House, the 'defenders of the nation' did not hesitate for one moment to prevent the return of Egisto Tango, the outstanding conductor of *The Wooden Prince* and *Bluebeard's Castle*, two achievements that were consistently held against him after 1920. Even more instructive is the case of Kodály. Although after the disciplinary investigation he was allowed to retain his teaching post, he was told to stay on leave until February 1921, and this 'leave' was prolonged by Hubay for the second term. Meantime, Hubay made every effort to secure his compulsory retirement. 'They never want to see him again within the walls of the institution,' Dohnányi told a correspondent of *Az Ujság* on January 25, 1921.

There is no doubt that the way in which Kodály was treated was partly due to personal antipathy on the part of Hubay. But Hubay's dislike of Kodály was not in itself sufficient motive for the campaign against the composer in which his enemies were encouraged by the fact that he seemed more vulnerable than Bartók, an altogether easier target, and more suitable for exhibition as a warning to others. While making repeated efforts to win over Bartók, they at the same time tried to isolate Kodály and turn him against his friend. This deceitful policy became especially overt after the première of Kodály's *Song of Faith* and the Ady songs in January 1921, when some of the critics abused him as Bartók's parasite, a careerist without individual talent. As on all such occasions, Bartók struck back immediately. The very next day, in *Magyarország*, the paper in which the abusive article had appeared, he refuted the critic's allegations. Some time later, he wrote an article which appeared in *Nyugat* to make known the true relation between him and Kodály. The following quotations from the article will suffice to put in perspective the depressing accusations made by Kodály's critics.

> The most important event of this year's concert season was the première of Kodály's two songs given by the Philharmonic Society on January 10. A considerable section of the press 'acknowledged' this event by making the most

severe criticisms of Kodály's competence as an artist *(Pesti Hirlap, Budapesti Hirlap, Pesti Napló, Az Ujság, Magyarság)*, and one of these papers *(Magyarország)* has even launched a personal attack on him.—I cannot allow such systematic persecution to pass without comment.—For some time now, certain musical circles have shown a particular delight in playing me off against Zoltán Kodály. They want to make it appear as if Kodály was using our friendship to his personal advantage. That is the basest kind of lie.

In the next paragraph, Bartók, with a conciseness to be wondered at, explains how his own music and that of Kodály is linked by their common source of inspiration, folk music, and with equal clarity he explains the differences between their compositions. He emphasizes the value of Kodály's creative work, adding:

And there are some people who, ill-intentioned as they are, want to trample upon these treasures of the Hungarian soil. The man who was not moved to the depth of his being by the setting for Ady's 'Sírni', is either as deaf and insensitive as a puppet, or full of prejudice and malevolence.

This then is my opinion of Kodály's music, the opinion of a man whom Kodály's attackers have recently liked to refer to as 'the greatest Hungarian composer'. It is possible that I do not know much about these things, but in that case, how could I be such a 'great' composer? It is obvious that these gentlemen are badly mistaken on one count or the other. (At any rate, I am willing to accept any demotion from them.)

Fortunately, the Kodály question will be decided not at home but abroad. Thanks to a publisher in Vienna, those works by Kodály which have so far been buried alive, are to appear in rapid succession in the very near future, so that soon we shall hear foreign opinions of them. And then we shall again witness the peculiar phenomenon which we observed a short time ago in connection with another 'question'—those gentlemen who have so far been hurling abuse for all they are worth, will turn into meek lambs, or, perish the thought, into enthusiastic admirers.

I can almost hear their reproachful comment that I am speaking 'with a friend's bias'. But here again they are mistaken in their view of what comes first—I do not respect Kodály as the best Hungarian musician because I am his friend but because (quite apart from his grand human qualities) he is in fact the best Hungarian musician. The fact that it has been I myself and not Kodály who has profited most from this friendship, is further proof of his superb qualities and unassuming selflessness. In the course of my career, in which a need to struggle was never lacking, he has always stood bravely and openly by my side, unsparing in his efforts to help me on my way. It is due to his lightening judgement, astoundingly infallible, that the final version of many of my works is so much better than the original version. Is it not strange

184

that as a teacher this 'quantité négligeable' as Kodály is now referred to should have so greatly influenced 'the greatest Hungarian composer'? . . .

And it is this man, to whom Hungarian culture owes so much, who is being attacked from every quarter, now by those in public office, now by the 'critics'. In every way that is open to them, these creatures without talent, these do-nothings and nobodies, try to make it impossible for him to work unmolested, and all the while, they rant about the superiority of Hungarian culture.—That is all I wanted to say . . .

And Bartók's prophecies about the future were surprisingly accurate. When Kodály's reputation as a composer continued to increase, and it became known that Universal Edition of Vienna had contracted to publish all his works at the beginning of 1921, Jenő Hubay found that there was nothing to prevent him from co-operating with Kodály at the beginning of the following term. Kodály returned to his post at the Academy.

It is much to be regretted that the memory of Jenő Hubay, a great violinist, master of a Hungarian school of violin that was of epoch-making significance and teacher of many world-famous artists, should be sullied by his petty and biassed political activities in the field of culture. At the invitation of Liszt he had returned home from Brussels where he had been head of the violin faculty to take up a position on the teaching staff of the Budapest Academy of Music. But in times of crisis he showed himself to be an unworthy successor to Mihalovich, who followed Liszt as Director of the Academy. Mihalovich, rising above any personal and artistic limitations, had always attracted the best musicians to the Academy because of his breadth of vision, and he had made it into a great institution.

In 1922, Dohnányi left to give a concert tour abroad.

3 TOWARDS A NEW SYNTHESIS OF FOLK MUSIC AND MODERN ART-MUSIC
    IDIOM: 'IMPROVISATIONS'

The new political situation brought many changes in Bartók's life and in the cultural life of Hungary in general, and it has been necessary to describe the period in some detail so that the reader would be in a position to understand the history of the next two decades. But now let us return to Bartók's work-room to discover what he had been working on during these difficult times.

It was his work in folk-music research that suffered most in the conditions then prevailing. His letters contain bitter complaints and expressions of his longing to be able to spend the pleasant summer months in collecting folk-songs; he longed especially for Transylvania and felt nostalgia for the weeks he had spent in the villages, or as he wrote later, for 'the happiest period of my life'. It would seem from his *Önéletrajz* (Autobiography), of which the German version appeared in 1921, and the Hungarian version in 1923, that he became resigned to his changed circumstances.

> The situation even today makes it impossible for me even to think of continuing my folk-music research. Our own resources do not permit us this 'luxury', and besides, research work in territories now torn away from the former Greater Hungary, has become impossible for political reasons as well. And more distant foreign countries are quite out of reach . . . And anyway, there is no genuine interest in this branch of musicology anywhere in the world—so perhaps it does not have the importance that some fanatics attribute to it!

His interest in folk music, however, continued unabated, and even if he could not collect it, he could at least systematize, arrange and publish the material he had gathered earlier. From this time on, his scientific work became more specifically a matter of the summary, synthesis and theory of folk music. On March 15, 1921, together with Kodály, he finished the preparatory work for their joint collection of one hundred and fifty Transylvanian folk-songs, entitled *Erdélyi Magyarság, népdalok. Közzé teszik Bartók Béla és Kodály Zoltán* (Hungarians of Transylvania. Folk-Songs published by Béla Bartók and Zoltán Kodály. This appeared in 1923). Six months later, in October 1921, Bartók completed his comprehensive work, *The Hungarian Folk-Song*. In the lengthy introduction Bartók developed the system he had outlined in the programme notes of the 1918 Concert of Soldiers' Songs in Vienna, expanding it into the first scientific survey of Hungarian vocal folk music. He cited three hundred and twenty folk-songs to serve as examples of a classification that in its main features is still valid for the principal types of Hungarian folk-songs. The guiding principle in making this classification was the accentuation of the kinship between folk-songs based on content and style; this principle superseded any formal, glossary arrangement. The resultant order is so convincing that modern research workers are constantly applying it to their own work. There is an Appendix in which Bartók added three Cheremis songs to illustrate melodic similarities with the Hungarian songs.

This book, published by Rózsavölgyi, did not appear until 1924, one year after the publication of the Máramaros collection in German, *Die Volksmusik der Rumänen von Maramures*, in Munich.

Another reason why the year 1920 may be said to mark a turning point in the history of Hungarian musicology, is the publication in that year of one of Kodály's most significant studies, *Árgirus nótája* (The Song of Árgirus) in the journal *Ethnographia*. 'This study,' wrote Bence Szabolcsi, when it was reprinted in 1955, 'with its principles, methods and achievements, paved the way for all contemporary Hungarian research into the history of music (and to some extent the history of poetry too).' In this study, Kodály revealed his discovery of a close relationship between verse-chronicles and folk-music tradition; he thus exposed the living processes of a cultural heritage made evident in the written down word or by word of mouth at this meeting point in the history of literature and music. This study marked a definitive differentiation between the methods employed by Bartók and Kodály and between their respective views on folk-music research. Bartók concentrated on an exploration of the ethnographic, and as it were horizontal, aspects of folk music, and sought to understand folk-song as part of the living organism of folklore as well as to systematize it within the context of peasant conditions. He had already become deeply immersed in the task of arranging and processing his material when the shock of political events opened his eyes to the possibility of a more far-reaching scientific project which would also embrace the study of other peoples. Kodály, on the other hand, concentrated on what may be termed the vertical relationships of our musical heritage as a whole, and on the attempt to broaden folkmusic research to include especially the historical national aspects, and also to ensure the perpetuation of folk music.

The complaints quoted above from the conclusion of Bartók's autobiography were not confined to the restrictions on his folk-music research.

> These disturbances, which lasted for about eighteen months, were not exactly conducive to calm, serious work,

he wrote, a statement illustrated by the short list of compositions completed during that period. The *Suite No. 2*, performed in January 1921, was a rearrangement of a composition written thirteen years earlier, and the *Four Orchestral Pieces for Orchestra*, written in 1912, did not achieve a public performance with new orchestration until ten years later. It is therefore not to be wondered at that in the new orchestration of the *Four Pieces*, especially in the Scherzo movement, we can find conspicuous references to the orchestral effect of *The Miraculous Mandarin* which was still fresh in his memory after its long period of gestation. A piano piece entitled *Eight Improvisations on Hungarian Peasant Songs* (op. 20) and written in 1920, reveals more clearly than anything else just what it was that was engaging Bartók's attention at that time.

During the war it had seemed as if folk-song arrangements and compositions in their own rights were to develop as two quite separate sections of Bartók's œuvre. The former, insofar as their harmonic means and musical idiom were concerned, broadly retained the manner evolved in 1907–8, which was based on a pattern of modal intonation acquired under the direct influence of Kodály, and indirectly from Debussy. The folk-song arrangements developed towards larger, cyclical forms and broad dance finales. In the compositions marked by opus numbers, Bartók sought inspiration from folk-music sources which presented no obstacle to their fusion with the musical idiom of Viennese contemporaries, primarily Schoenberg with his tendency towards atonality. This explains the presence of the exotic folk-music motifs in the *Piano Suite*, *String Quartet No. 2* and *The Miraculous Mandarin*.

The synthesis of Hungarian folk music and his own experiments in composition first emerged in a novel form in the *Improvisations*, but this was only after some earlier attempts in this direction. The two articles written by Bartók during his stay in Berlin in the spring of 1920 provide interesting evidence that he had already considered some of the problems involved. It may be that Bartók wrote these articles in German in the first place, for it was in *Melos*, the paper of the avant-garde German composers, that they appeared. In one of them, he considered the possibilities of atonality and their reconciliation with traditional tonalities. The other article is even more interesting. In this he raised the idea of the possible congruity of folk music and atonality and of a synthesis between the two. It seems probable that the idea came to him in connection with the analysis of Stravinsky's *Pribaoutki* (Peasant Songs) with which he probably had become acquainted a short time before.

But traces of earlier experiment can also be found in the works. According to the established chronology of Bartók's works, the composition of the *Fifteen Hungarian Peasant Songs* dates from somewhere between 1914 and 1917. Not long ago, however, Endre László called my attention to the fact that some of the pieces in this volume were in fact collected in 1918. A glance revealed that the songs that were collected later are not included among the *Old Hungarian Dances* numbered 7–15, but in the previous series numbered 1–6. A more thorough examination revealed that there is a difference of harmonization in the two groups. In the arrangements of songs 1–6, there is a heaviness, a more intricate tonality and a closer affinity to the *Improvisations*. It is the unique, dramatic variations of 'Angoli Borbála' that stand out most distinctly from the *Old Hungarian Dances*, representing the earlier level of arrangement. Therefore, it is probable that the series of the *Old Hungarian Dances* was completed earlier, that Bartók had performed them separately during the war years and only later added to them so as to form a more comprehensive cycle showing the outlines of a four-movement arrangement (*Four Old Dirges*, 1–4; *Scherzo*, 5; *Ballade*, Tema con variazioni, 6; *Old Hungarian Dances*, 1–14). The broad folk-dance finale already fits into the plan of the later great compositions.

The three folk-songs that appeared in the Paderewski memorial volume may also have formed part of the experiment in a new method of folk-song arrangement. This would make it probable that their date of origin is in fact later than that which appears in the records (1914–17).

In his treatment of the folk-songs in the *Improvisations* Bartók showed more freedom and independence than in his earlier arrangements. He did not add accompaniments to the original, unaltered form of the folk-song, but composed original works for the piano in the very spirit and with all the character of the original melody, though this sometimes necessitated a repetition or even change in parts of the melody, lines or motifs. This was in marked contrast to his earlier arrangements in which 'the accompaniment and the pre-, post- or interlude are of secondary importance, merely a frame for a peasant melody, like a precious jewel

189

in its setting'. Later he wrote an essay in which he described his new method:

> The peasant melody only plays the role of a motto and the most important thing is what is placed around and below it. The two types are linked by innumerable transitional stages. Sometimes it cannot even be decided which element prevails in the arrangement. It is always imperative to remember, however, that the musical raiment of the melody should always spring from its own character and from the open or concealed traits inherent in the melody . . .

A parasztzene hatása az újabb műzenére (The Influence of Peasant Music on Modern Art-Music).

The *Improvisations* emerged from the application of these principles. The eight masterly character pieces of this work reveal Bartók as a composer capable of speaking with complete confidence in his own modern musical idiom—an idiom that is at the same time that of folk music. 'Again we have to deal with folk-song arrangements, the brightest peaks of Bartók's epoch-making work in this field,' commented Aladár Tóth after the first performance on January 18, 1922. The seventh piece of the series is a deeply moving lament; the lullaby 'Beli, fiam, beli' provides the foundation for this superb lament dedicated to the memory of the great French composer Claude Debussy who died in 1918, and who had himself, in his lullaby, *Berceuse héroïque*, mourned the fate of Belgium in the First World War. It seems that Bartók played this piece as an individual item in the programme of his composer's matinée on February 27, 1921, for this one piece alone provided the subject for Aladár Tóth's review in which he wrote, 'The "*En Hommage de Debussy*," that has become world famous, is the most magnificent "piano adagio" written since Schumann.'

Improvisations contains the first examples of the method of folk-music arrangement which Bartók was to employ during the nineteen-twenties. In the three major works that followed, the two *Sonatas* for violin and piano and the *Dance Suite*, a newer synthesis of folk music and composing techniques gave promise of yet more significant achievements.

190

4 HAPPY CONCERT TOURS IN TRANSYLVANIA, SUCCESSES IN ENGLAND AND PARIS. TWO SONATAS FOR VIOLIN AND PIANO. EUROPEAN ORGANIZING ACTIVITY OF DISCIPLES OF MUSICAL PROGRESS. THE SLOVAK COLLECTION

From the end of 1919, Bartók had frequently thought of emigrating and among the list of places he considered there always occurred the name of Transylvania. Yet it was not until 1922, two years after his exploratory visit to Berlin, that Bartók was able to go there. He was already making plans to go there in 1912, and in his letters to János Buşiţia we find the dates he suggested. 'I may arrive between July 7 and 14,' he wrote on June 14. On July 4, however, he was writing in a more hesitant tone,

> Unfortunately, it is still uncertain whether I can come, because it is unimaginably difficult to get a visa . . . One thing is certain: I shall not arrive before the 15th.

Two weeks later, his hopes were dwindling.

> My guess was correct, the visa is not to be had, or rather only at the expense of such dreadful effort and only after several weeks, so that I must give up any plans for an excursion this year.

But at last his hopes were realized when he was allowed to make a concert tour of Transylvania from February 15 to February 28, 1922. In the preliminary correspondence, he had negotiated for a longer period, and was to have arrived in Kolozsvár (Cluj) on February 5. Performances in Nagyvárad (Oradea), Brassó (Braşov), Temesvár (Timişoara), Arad, Sepsiszentgyörgy (Sfîntu Gheorghe), and Máramarossziget (Sighetul Marmaţiei) were also mentioned. But in the end the duration of his visit was reduced to barely two weeks and the number of towns to be visited was also limited. 'I played three times in Kolozsvár (Cluj), and once in Szeben (Sibiu), Szászsebes (Şebişul-sasesc), and M.vásárhely (Tîrgu Mureş)', he wrote to Buşiţia on the 27th, the day of his last concert in Kolozsvár.

It is typical of Bartók that in the preliminary correspondence he should have selected with great care the programmes he considered to be most suitable for a particular place and audience. And the letters again provide evidence of his remarkable and meticulous attention to detail, as when he was careful to write,

Let me note here that these pieces by Scarlatti and Debussy are not the same as those I played in Marosvásárhely in 1913.

One striking feature of his recitals is that the works performed were, apart from his own compositions and those of Kodály, mainly sonatas by the eighteenth-century composer, Scarlatti, and selections from Debussy's *Preludes*. In view of Bartók's reference to the concerts he gave in 1913, it would be logical at this point to compare his programmes with those selected for the UMZE concerts: we find that on both occasions all the emphasis was on Baroque and twentieth-century music.

The fact that it was possible for János Demény to collect so many press cuttings on the subject of Bartók's concert tour of Transylvania, indicates how much this was publicized at the time. From the tone of the advance notices, interviews and reviews it is clear that the people of Transylvania were overjoyed to see Bartók once again. At the same time, there was now and then a note of pride in the consciousness that, unlike the officials in Budapest, the Transylvanians could recognize and appreciate Bartók's stature as a world-famous musician. There was also no attempt to hide their condemnation of Bartók's enemies in Hungary.

It was with the joy of one who has returned to his own home that the famous guest revisited the towns of Transylvania. In this post-war visit his strong attachment to the country was rekindled and more than ever before was he overcome with nostalgia. The picture of Bartók which emerges from the interviews and reports is that of a more relaxed and communicative man than had been known for years at home. He ended his farewell postcard from Transylvania with the words,

I think I can come back at the end of October, then I may even stop at Belényes. Now I am going home and from there to London and Paris.

It is possible that the reader is not mistaken in discerning in these lines some reluctance on the part of Bartók to visit London and Paris. Again, on March 4, he wrote to Ion Bîrlea, the colleague in Máramaros, 'I have to go to London and Paris,' as if he were impatiently waiting for the month of October when he would be able to return to Transylvania after fulfilling his engagements in the concert tour of Western Europe.

But if the prospect of the trip to London aroused any feeling of reluctance in Bartók's mind, this must certainly have been dispersed by his reception.

> People had shown a good deal of interest even before I arrived, and I had a very warm welcome,

he wrote to his mother.

> The day before yesterday, I gave a 'private recital' in London, at the Hungarian Minister's (or Consul's?) residence; it was arranged by the Arányis. Although it was not open to the public, *The Times* printed a review on the following day, and a very favourable one, too. My arrival had already been reported—in the *Daily Telegraph* and the *Daily Mail*, and in 2 musical periodicals.

The letter was dated March 16, and posted from Aberystwyth,

> on the west coast of England, or rather, of Wales. The 2 huge windows of my room look out over the sea—down below the waves roar, and it is marvellously sunny. Aberystwyth is a little university town with a pop. of 10,000, and it's here that I am playing tonight... My public recital in London has been arranged for March 24...

The way had been paved for his reception in England partly by the fame of his works and the analytical studies which had been published by Cecil Gray and others, and partly by the kind offices of his old acquaintances, Jelly and Adila Arányi. If we cast our minds back to Bartók's years as a student at the Academy, we will recall the prominent position in Budapest society held by the Arányi family. The two sisters had been living in London for some time and it is certain that they were at pains to introduce Bartók into musical circles there. As we learn from a review which appeared in *The Times* on March 15, the Arányi sisters performed a Spohr duet, while Jelly and Bartók performed his *Sonata No. 1* for violin and piano at a 'private concert' given by Hedry, the Hungarian *chargé d'affaires*. The *Sonata* had been completed in the previous December in readiness for this occasion and was dedicated to Jelly Arányi. The sonata was also played at a public concert held in the Aeolian Hall, London,

> at which I introduced a series of my piano pieces and some works by Kodály,

as he said later to a correspondent of *Zenei Szemle*. 'The audience particularly applauded the Sonata,' he added. At home in Budapest, he first performed the *Sonata No. 1* on December 20, together with Imre Wald-bauer.

Bartók played at two other private concerts, one at the home of the singer Dorothy Moulton, and one in Liverpool. These guest performances met with unprecedented success. A final assessment of their importance was given by Aladár Tóth in *Nyugat* when he wrote, 'The private concert had already aroused enormous interest. *The Times* gave two accounts of it, on the second occasion devoting a whole column to the *Sonata* for violin and piano. In six other dailies Bartók was mentioned as one of the greatest geniuses of modern music. His big public concert was held in the Aeolian Hall and was reviewed in nineteen daily papers; even the most conservative critics acknowledged him as a master.' Aladár Tóth's account, taken in conjunction with Bartók's own remarks made to the correspond-ent of *Zenei Szemle*, provide sufficient evidence that Bartók had been discovered and appreciated by the British press, and that Bartók's music had served to introduce the whole entity of modern Hungarian music.

From these and other signs, Bartók judged that the English and French intelligentsia were appreciative of the Hungarian people, sympathizing with them as victims of Germany's aspiration to the rank of a great power in the recent World War. This discovery naturally moved him deeply and when he was interviewed by a correspondent of the *Keleti Ujság* in Kolozsvár, in the autumn of the same year, he was still emphatic on the subject. But in recalling his appearances in London, he was also reminded of the tremendous reception he personally had been given as an artist. In the interview printed on October 31 in this paper, he is reported to have said,

> At the end of my violin sonata, I was surprised, and almost confused, by the waves of applause rising up to the platform from an English audience which is generally described as cold and reserved.

On April 3, he crossed over to Paris, where on April 8 he gave a concert with the same programme as that given in London. The *Sonata No. 1* for violin and piano was again performed together with Jelly Arányi. 'She outdid herself that evening,' wrote Bartók to his mother on April 15. But more important than this concert or the other two private recitals given during his stay in Paris was the dinner given after the concert by

Henri Prunières, the editor of *Revue Musicale*. This occasion provided Bartók with an opportunity to become acquainted with most of the significant composers of the age including Ravel, Stravinsky, Szymanowski, Roussel and the 'Six' whom he described in a letter to his mother as 'a few young (notorious) Frenchmen whom you would not know'. In the statement printed in *Zenei Szemle* mentioned above, he also included the names of Honegger and Milhaud among the list of composers he had met. Aladár Tóth has recorded that the host made the remark, 'Only Schoenberg is missing'.

Though there were not so many press notices of Bartók's appearances in Paris, the tone of the reviews that were printed was just as appreciative as those in England. In the issue of *Revue Musicale* which appeared on May 1, there was a review of the *Violin Sonata No. 1* by Prunières which was so penetrating that it might well be classed as a scholarly study of the piece.

When he was in London, Bartók had written to an acquaintance in Kolozsvár that he intended to travel from Paris to Amsterdam and thence to Frankfurt. But the journey to Holland was postponed for one year. However, there are accounts of his stay in Frankfurt. Denijs Dille tells us that on April 24 he performed at a chamber concert as a member of a quartet. The conductor, Jenő Szenkár, had planned a first performance of *Bluebeard's Castle* and *The Wooden Prince* to take place in Frankfurt during Bartók's stay in the town. Bartók's original intention was to leave Frankfurt on April 26 and to return home by way of Pozsony. But it seems that he stayed on for the première which did not take place until May 13.

A card written to Etelka Freund on May 9 indicates that he did not derive a great deal of pleasure from it.

> Everything went without a hitch in England and France. But not so in Germany. Here, everything is falling apart. Impossible conditions ... What bad violinists, and what a bad opera company to spoil my works. I can only look forward to a disastrous première. Well, thank you very much, but I don't want to have anything to do with Germany. My foretaste of the event is quite enough for me, in fact too much. There is only one man here who is worth anything at all and that is Szenkár from Budapest.

This is a surprising statement to come from that same Béla Bartók who only two years previously had thought of settling in Berlin. But force of circumstance had quite changed his plans to emigrate. One might say that he did in fact emigrate, not to any one European capital, but to Europe as a whole. To be more exact one should add that this was the Europe where he could meet the most progressive and well-organized musicians of that time. For all over Europe there were groups of musicians who represented through their art the progressive ideals of the bourgeoisie, as for instance, the Anbruch circle in Vienna, the group of musicians centred round *Melos* in Berlin, the Prunières and other supporters of *Revue Musicale* in Paris, and such men as Edward J. Dent and Cecil Gray in England. The artists who sponsored *Melos*, for instance, arranged a series of concerts for February 6, 8, and 9, 1923, at which Bartók's works were performed and in which Bartók himself and the Waldbauers participated.

It was through the activities of these groups that it became possible for those who advocated the new music in various parts of Europe to unite in support of their common aims. In April and again in May 1922, Bartók's works were performed, both in the concert hall and on the stage, in Frankfurt, and when a festival of modern music was held there in August, the participants decided to establish the International Society for Contemporary Music, as proposed by Edward J. Dent. It was not long before the Society included as members both Czech and Hungarian musicians, and the first festival of modern chamber music was held in Salzburg in August 1923.

It would be instructive at this point to glance back at earlier attempts made by the advocates of modern music to form themselves into some kind of organization. The first group of this nature was formed in Paris before the First World War, and soon afterwards, Hungarians who had visited Paris and who had been influenced by this group, formed the organization known as UMZE (New Hungarian Music Federation). In the conditions prevailing in Hungary at that time UMZE could not survive but, as we have seen, the anti-war campaign led by Hungarian artists and intellectuals became part of an international movement which grew in strength during the second half of the First World War. For just as the imperialists and the bourgeoisie began their preparations for another war immediately after the official ending of the first holocaust, so too the democratic and progressive forces joined together in an attempt to prevent another such tragedy. Thus, in a new and this time international music organization, Bartók was able to continue, at a higher level, the battle he had been fighting for so long. From this time on, until the outbreak of the Second World War, he regularly gave recitals throughout Europe, and nearly all his works, from the *Violin Sonata No. 1* onwards, were, with very few exceptions, introduced abroad. Meantime, his admirers at home remained faithful to him in what virtually amounted to his emigration.

Bence Szabolcsi poses the question that must arise in all our minds —amidst all these feverish activities in which he never paused between 1920 and 1930, did Bartók have any rest at all? Szabolcsi has only one explanation for Bartók's powers of endurance; that he was able to find relaxation in the very variety of those activities which included teaching, composing, giving recitals and doing scientific research. When he was exhausted by travelling on concert tours and making public appearances, he could always spend time arranging his collections of folk-songs, and it must have been a great solace to him to return thus to his old peasant friends, even if only in thought. Since he had finished editing his collection of Hungarian folk music, he turned in 1922 to his Slovak collection, and in the summer of that year, he systematized and finally completed the first volume of melodies for the Matica Slovenská. This collection became the subject of endless correspondence and the objective in a distressing tug-of-war. He did not live to see its publication, for it was not until 1959 that the first volume of the complete series was finally published under the auspices of the Slovak Academy of Sciences.

Bartók's second post-war tour of Transylvania, to which he had been looking forward ever since the spring of 1922, was made between October 24 and 31 of the same year, and proved to be both enjoyable and restful. He stayed at Belényes, Nagyvárad and Kolozsvár, and once again he was able to meet his old friend, János Buşiţia. In his farewell letter written from Kolozsvár on October 31, Bartók used the second person singular, a rare sign of informality, and the seal set on a friendship that had lasted for more than a decade. Meantime, the Hungarian newspapers continued to print lengthy reviews of his tours of England, France and Germany; and these were still written in tones of appreciation. A month later, between November 20 and November 22, Bartók visited Szatmár (Satu-

Mare) and Máramarossziget (Sighetul Marmației), but this time no concert was arranged at Nagyvárad.

There was another pleasant interlude when, together with Imre Waldbauer, he gave a concert at Kassa (Košice) April 5, 1923. This was the result of bold, local enterprise, and took place beneath the dim lights of a provincial stage, with creaking chairs huddled together on the steps leading up to the apron.

> In one part of the Sonata, Imre forgot to remove the mute.—The violin sounded fainter and fainter and fainter—and still he didn't notice anything; there was a *fermata* during which he could have removed the thing, but he didn't—and he was getting dangerously near to an *f*, in fact an *ff*. My God, I wondered, what's going to happen here! And at last I had to shout at him: 'Take off your mute!' To crown all, the page-turner finally knocked my music off the stand and had to pick it up from the floor. By that time I was near to bursting with laughter,

he wrote in a letter to his mother immediately after the concert.

But he could not stay to enjoy the intimate and lively atmosphere of country concerts. By the end of April, he was already in Holland, and en route for England. On May 7, he again appeared with Jelly Arányi in London, this time performing both the *Sonata No. 1* and *Sonata No. 2*. The latter had been completed during the previous summer and had been given a first performance in Budapest on February 27, with Ede Zathureczky as the violinist.

5 THE FOLK-DANCE FINALES: SIGNS OF A NEW CREATIVE APPROACH AND NEW ARTISTIC IDEAS. 'DANCE SUITE', FIRST LARGE-SCALE MUSICAL EXPRESSION OF THE IDEA OF THE 'BROTHERHOOD OF PEOPLES'

Though the prospect of settling in Transylvania must have been very tempting to Bartók, especially as he now had so many memories of idyllic summers spent in the villages there, any such retreat from the crowded cities of Europe to take up the peaceful task of collecting folk music was not for him. It was not so much the pressure of external circumstances that allowed him no rest, but rather a compulsion from within. However exhausted he might be by the constant demands of his work, however much he might long for peace in which to indulge his passion for collecting folk music, he was only able to live a life of seclusion for a very brief period before being driven back amongst the crowds by the very force of his creative genius and dedication to the search for truth, even though it should cost him his life. These were the forces that led him to remote villages and these were the forces that drew him back into the world to hold up for all to see the truth he had discovered there, the humanity which it is possible for men to show to one another in the very midst of their struggle for survival. The logic of reality compelled Bartók to summon his knowledge of this truth to further his development as an artist. It had long been obvious to him that in order to make an important contribution as a composer, he must resolve in his works the contradiction between the serenely isolated mood of his folk-song arrangements written during the war years, and his deeper need for commitment. After the *Improvisations,* the two *Sonatas* for violin and piano represent the next significant stage in the process of synthesis. The first of these achieves its intention by means of the traditional three-movement form. The second is composed of a slow and a fast movement, a structure which revives memories of the two-part works of his youth, but which also presages the slow–fast of the rhapsodies to follow in the succeeding years and there is even some hint of the first version of *Contrasts.*

But it is the closing movements of the two sonatas that are most striking. In the course of twenty years, the slow and tragic quality of his last movements, the dramaturgy of his ethereal or tragic but always slow finales, and a particular range of content in these movements, had become typical features of Bartók's work. Now, in 1921 and 1922, two cycles were completed one after the other, both ending in a fast, unrestrained dance. The predecessors of these fast movements were the closing dance images, independent finales which developed out of the folk-music arrangements of the war years but which far surpassed the earlier achievements. The basic material of these finales is not true folk-song, but an individual creation of melody in the spirit of folk music and peasant dances. There is a close kinship between the fast closing movements of the two sonatas. But without a knowledge of the earlier *Improvisations* it would be difficult to imagine such an elaboration of folk-music material, expanded by free, rhythmic accent and melodic variations. In his very early works, for instance the first of the *Two*

Romanian Dances for piano, one may find examples of a similarly consistent solution of the dance movement constructed freely yet with firm logic, out of homogeneous musical material. This is another indication that in the years immediately ahead Bartók was to return to many experiments that had been abandoned in the prolific years of 1908–10.

The fact that the finales were created out of the musical material of folk dances is particularly striking when these are compared with the preceding movements which are quite different in style and content. The first movements of the sonatas are linked to the late Romantic, Expressionist aspects of Bartók's world by their melodic texture—fine as a spider-web and as ethereal—by the relaxation of bar limits, and by the hovering rhythm and tonality references which are reduced to a few supporting notes. It would be possible to recognize in these movements the sphere of the Girl who loathes yet longs for the mandarin, the atmosphere of death found in the *Five Songs* op. 16, with texts by Ady, and the free, twelve-tone phantasy images of the *Etudes*, even without the characteristic, descending minor seventh chord, bitonal tensions, typical melodic turns and harmonic recollections that evoke Bartók's torment and suffering between the composition of *Bluebeard's Castle* and *The Miraculous Mandarin.* It would scarcely have been possible for Bartók to express this emotional world more definitively than he does in the two *Sonatas* for violin and piano. The second movement of the *Sonata No. 1*, with the reminiscing monologue of the violin, and the solemn harmonies of the piano, is one of the most beautiful slow movements which Bartók composed. In some ways it recalls the *String Quartet No. 2*, but it also offers a promise of the serene harmonies that would eventually emerge out of the tempestuous works to come.

Even in the hovering texture of some of his early works there was the muscular quality of folk music. In the aesthetic structure of the *Piano Suite*, the *String Quartet No. 2* and *The Miraculous Mandarin*, he had for the most part made use of the wild, throbbing quality of Arabic folk music to convey the note of defiance and rebellion, and to express the elemental forces of nature. These expressions of revolt, however, were preceded and followed by movements expressing anguish; they achieved only a temporary ascendancy, representing the briefly flaring passion of 'those who are always too late' (Ady) and who could find fulfilment only in tragedy. In the finales of the two *Sonatas* for violin and piano, however, we find both contrasts and unity between the elements of East-European folk-dance music and the music which expressed the self-destructive torment of suffering. The composer András Mihály draws attention to the fact that these sturdy melodies, firmly modal, diatonic and with narrow intervals, had a contrary significance not previously found in Bartók's world of ideas. Whereas in the earlier folk-music arrangements, the voice of the East-European peoples could be heard only in relation to their own national background, in these closing movements the folk-music elements convey the composer's vision of a possible solution for the problems of mankind everywhere. Folklore thus becomes an artistic treasure which is the heritage of all mankind, an expression of the belief that the humanity found in the lives of village folk and their ability to live together in peace may also be fostered throughout the world.

We might well be accused of exaggerating the significance of the content of the two sonatas, as outlined above, were it not for the confirmation so clearly provided by the great orchestral composition which followed, the *Dance Suite*. We owe this work to the celebrations held in Budapest during the year 1923. A letter written by Bartók to his mother on August 13, while he was on holiday in Radvány, contains lengthy references to the *Dance Suite*. He had almost finished work on it at that time, though it had proved to be no light task.

> I had to do a lot of work on the score (you know what I am talking about —those orchestral dances which will be performed at a gala concert in Budapest on November 19); the score has to be finished by the end of August so that the orchestral parts can be done in Vienna.

The concert mentioned in this letter was held on November 19 to celebrate the fiftieth anniversary of the unification of Pest and Buda. Bartók, Dohnányi and Kodály had all been commissioned to write compositions in honour of the occasion. The concert began with a performance of Dohnányi's *Festival Overture* and this was followed by two epoch-making masterpieces of twentieth-century Hungarian music— Kodály's *Psalmus Hungaricus* and Bartók's *Dance Suite*.

The basic ideas of the *Dance Suite* become more apparent if we compare this work with the *Psalmus*. Kodály chose to base his work on the chronicle poem by Mihály Kecskeméti Vég which was Biblical in tone, for it was his intention to evoke in his music memories of a tragic period in the history of Hungary while at the same time expressing the bitterness and suffering he had himself experienced. At the same time, he wanted to expose the moral standards and social conditions of the capital as they really were. Aladár Bálint, the critic who wrote in *Népszava*, recognized the contemporary relevance of the text. 'The psalm is most apt, so much so that it might serve as a motto for the gala concert,' he wrote on the day after the concert, and he quoted a few lines from the text:

> *Violence and strife rage fierce in the city,*
> *Mischief and malice, envy and sorrow,*
> *Boasting of riches, pride of possession;*
> *N'er in all the world saw I such deceivers!*

Béla Bartók's *Dance Suite* evokes a delightful vision of festivity in which all men are brothers. With this work he regaled the audience at the gala concert, his offering for the edification of the ill-willed chauvinists who were the masters of Pest-Buda. The work expressed an ideal which he did not openly advocate until 1931, but it had been the guiding principle of his scientific research and in the development of his creative work ever since 1908. This was the only 'historical lesson' that Bartók could give to his compatriots. The *Dance Suite* achieves a marvellous apotheosis in which it seems that the peoples of the world are united in one dance. In the first movement, rhythm and beat are created out of one- or two-tone melodic fragments followed by a series of sharply delineated dance melodies evoking the tone of Hungarian, Arabic, Romanian and Slovak folk dances respectively, which are united in the ecstatic whirl of the finale. The significance of this work lies in the fact that it represents Bartók's first conciliatory gesture towards national historical popular music; thus, at the end of the various types of dance movements in the ritornelle, he makes sympathetic use of the *verbunkos* for the first time since his encounter with folk music. In this way yet another musical tradition became incorporated into his widening vision.

The power of Bartók's genius enabled him to synthetize old and new forms in the *Dance Suite*, with an assurance that must inspire us with awe. The musical material he used, necessitated a return to a much more close and firm frame of tonality. 'An atonal folk music, in my opinion, is unthinkable,' he wrote a few years later.

> Since we depend upon a tonal basis of this kind in our creative work, it is quite self-evident that our works are quite pronouncedly tonal in type.

The basis of the tonal structure is the same tense half-tone bitonality as that found in *Bluebeard's Castle*. There an F, F sharp duality determined the relation of keys in the particular parts, here the basic duality hinges on G, G sharp. In the feature of the new period which can be traced back to the *String Quartet No. 1* is the total exposure of the skeleton structure found in the fourth movement of the *Dance Suite*—a languid Arabic melody based on G sharp is accompanied throughout the movement by a series of veiled fourth chords based on G. The reticulation of soaring melodies by means of colourful divisions was to become a characteristic feature of Bartók's later style.

The six movements of the *Dance Suite* rest upon a monumental three-part structure. The first allegro section consists of the first three dances together with the two ritornelles placed between them. The structure of the individual dances becomes progressively more intricate. The fourth movement constitutes the slow mid-section. It is linked by a ritornelle to the fifth movement, a bridge form of incredible intensity which quickens in tempo and becomes more dynamic as it nears the three-part finale which follows without any break.

There is a remarkable similarity between the structure of this work and that of *The Miraculous Mandarin*. There too, in the first part, the exposition, we find a similar use of ritornelles—in this case a succession of dance images placed between the scenes where the Girl lures her victims to their fate. In the ballet, three ritornelles surround two episodes—the Old Gentleman and the Youth, while in the *Dance Suite* two ritornelles are flanked by three dance images. The slow movement and the ensuing bridge section in the *Dance Suite* correspond to the waltz of the Girl and the pursuit dance of the mandarin in the ballet. And the pursuit dance ended in the reprise of the triple death scene just as the fifth movement of the *Dance Suite* ended in the triple closing movement. But the comparison also reveals a fundamental change—in the ballet and in the preceding *String Quartet No. 2*, two slow movements enclosed a fast one, while in the *Dance Suite*, the slow section is surrounded by folk-dance allegros, in accordance with tradition. In contrast to the open-ended structures used in his previous period, Bartók here stressed the enclosed nature of the structure by using identical material in the opening and closing movements. But he did not use the material in the same way as in *Bluebeard's Castle* or *The Wooden Prince*, where a final recapitulation closed the circle of the composition. A further characterization of the new period in Bartók's music is the repetition and rounding out in the recapitulation of the initial ideas, this time on a higher plane, so that 'the enchanted circle' of the earlier works is transformed into progress in an ever ascending line (Ernő Lendvai).

There can be no doubt but that the *Dance Suite* bears many times over the imprint of the musical impressions gained by Bartók during his recent travels in Europe. In the more traditional enclosed and strict three-part structure it may be possible to trace some elements of Baroque influence. Indirectly this indicates that Bartók was transferring some of his interest from Schoenberg to Stravinsky, and especially to the latter's *Sacre du Printemps*. But there are also more direct indications of this fact —the dogged repetition of fragments of motifs, the further enrichment of rhythmic invention, the highly individual use made of wooden wind instruments such as the oboe and the English horn and the effectiveness of the increasingly independent brass ensembles. These features also heralded the approach of a new period in Bartók's music.

It is quite possible that these changes were scarcely noticed by the Budapest audience at the concert on November 19. The orchestra of the Philharmonic Society was conservative and was rarely capable of conveying the essence of Bartók's music or any other music of the twentieth century. The people of Pest did not discover the *Dance Suite* until 1926, when Václav Talich, the prominent Czech conductor, gave it a worthy performance with the Prague Philharmonic Orchestra,

This transformation of Bartók's inner vision and creative outlook was once again accompanied, as in 1909, by changes in the external circumstances of his life which in this case resulted from important personal experiences. During the summer of 1923, he divorced his first wife and late in August married his pupil, Ditta Pásztory, with whom he later gave a number of joint recitals.

CHAPTER IX

PAUSE IN CREATIVITY—ACTIVE CONCERT PROGRAMME.
OVERTURE TO A NEW CREATIVE PERIOD. JOURNEY IN THE
U.S.A. 1923–1928

1 RECOGNITION IN ROMANIA. FULFILMENT OF CAREER AS PIANIST. DIS-
COURAGEMENT AS A COMPOSER. OBSTACLES IN THE PATH OF THE
PERFORMANCE OF 'THE MIRACULOUS MANDARIN'

After the *Dance Suite*, Bartók composed nothing more for three years.
Only one work remains from this period, a series of Slovak folk-songs,
Five Village Scenes, written for female voices with piano accompani-
ment.

This pause in his creative work is adequately accounted for by the
rapid increase in the number of his concert engagements which occurred
at that time. In the foregoing chapters we have closely followed the way
in which Bartók resumed his career as a concert pianist during the post-
war years, we have watched his rise to world fame, and we have seen
how, once the barriers created by the war began to crumble, he became
so well known, both as a composer and as a pianist, that even his opponents in Hungary were forced to refrain from attacking him. These
concert tours, though tiring, afforded him many new and interesting
experiences. Although he looked upon recital-giving as an unavoidable
nuisance, travel had been his passion since early youth. 'He was always
pleased to go to new places on concert tours,' recalls his son, Béla,
'and his return home was always a great pleasure both for him and for us.
He would come back laden with frozen reindeer meat, grapefruits, photographs and all sort of other gifts.'

But during the years that followed the première of the *Dance Suite*,
Bartók undertook so many concert tours abroad that we must now be
content to give them only a brief glance.

Scarcely a week after the historic date of November 19, 1923, Bartók
started out for England. There he gave concerts until December 12,
and on his way home, he played in Paris on the 15th, and in Geneva on

the 20th. At the beginning of the following year, in February 1924, he gave concerts in Slovakia, on the 5th in Komárom, and on the 9th in Losonc. On February 24, he attended an international music conference in Zurich, and on March 21, he played in Temesvár (Timişoara), the first concert of a tour of Transylvania. After a few days during which he gave guest performances in Nagyvárad and Lugos (Lugoj), we find him in Rimaszombat (Rimavská Sobata) on the 19th, and at the end of April, in Northern Italy.

Bartók began the following season with another series of concerts in Romania: October 9, Arad; October 10, Temesvár (Timişoara); October 11, Nagyvárad (Oradea); October 15, Kolozsvár (Cluj); October 17, Brassó (Braşov). This time, however, he brought his tour to an end in Bucharest. There a tremendous reception awaited him, organized by leading figures in the musical life of Romania. On October 19, the Association of Romanian Composers, to which he had earlier been elected as an honorary member, invited him to become chairman of the adjudicating committee for the George Enescu prize. That same evening he gave a piano recital, and for the following day the Association had arranged a concert of chamber music in his honour. On this occasion he played the *Second Sonata* for violin and piano together with Enescu. The response of the public was so enthusiastic that the Romanian government decided to bestow upon him the Bene Merenti Order (first class). This was perhaps the only decoration that Bartók felt proud to have been awarded. 'You know, don't you,' he wrote to Buşiţia on May 15, 1925,

> that since I last saw you I have been awarded the 1st class of the order of merit known as *Bene Merenti!*

His first foreign tour of the year 1925 took him to Prague where on January 10 he gave a piano recital. On March 2, he played in Brno, and on the 10th, he gave the first of a series of concerts in Italy; this was in Milan, after which he went on to play in Rome on the 12th, in Naples on the 13th, and in Palermo on the 14th. On December 7, he made an appearance in Trieste, and in March 1926, he set out on another tour of Italy that took him to Bergamo, Cremona and Florence. Six months later, he described these experiences in a letter to Buşiţia dated September 18, 1926:

> ·I must continue to give recitals (though this is not necessary financially speaking) . . . Last winter I played in Amsterdam, Berlin, Florence, Trieste, and even in such small Italian towns as Cremona and Bergamo . . . Perhaps you know that I also gave a concert in Bucharest during the winter (one of my 'Hungarian' rhapsodies with the Georgescu Philharmonic—there are so many *csárdás* in this rhapsody, I don't think so many have ever been performed before in Bucharest . . .)

By collating this letter with the careful accounts given us by Denijs Dille and János Demény, it is possible to fill in still further the details of Bartók's concert engagements. His appearance in Amsterdam mentioned in the letter took place on October 15, 1925, at the last concert arranged for his tour in Holland. This was given by the Concertgebouw Orchestra with Pierre Monteux conducting, and the programme included the *Rhapsody* op. 1 and the *Dance Suite*, the former with Bartók as soloist. The concert in Berlin took place on January 18, 1926, when Bruno Walter conducted the Berlin Philharmonic Orchestra and Bartók again played the piano part in the *Rhapsody* op. 1. Three days later he played in Baden-Baden once again. Finally, on February 22, he set out on another tour of Romania during which he gave performances in Kolozsvár and Arad, before giving his last recital in Bucharest on February 26.

These tours represent a tremendous undertaking, for they were made in addition to his teaching responsibilities at the Academy and the task of collecting folk music during the summer holidays. But this was not all. For he also took part in the SIMC festival at Prague at the end of May 1925, gave a joint recital in Pozsony on September 25 which was not mentioned in his letter to Buşiţia, and he performed at numerous concerts held both in Budapest and in the country.

It is time-consuming for an artist to keep a fresh approach even if he includes in every programme one particular work or one particular type of music. Bartók, however, included in his programmes, from time to time, various new selections as well; this was particularly the case when he played at concerts held in his native country.

Bartók's silence as a composer during this period can undoubtedly be attributed in part to his preoccupation with his career as a pianist, but there was an additional cause, for added to the strain of work was the weight of Bartók's own melancholy. Nor did conditions in Hungary change during these years; he was still only partially accepted as a composer and indeed there was now an even sharper division of opinion between the prominent figures in the musical world who were enthusiastic about his work and the officials who opposed it. Bartók did not achieve world fame first and foremost because of his virtuosity as a pianist; this came primarily through the performance of his works abroad. The enthusiastic reception of his compositions in other countries was reported regularly in the Hungarian press, especially by Aladár Tóth, and for some people at home Bartók's success abroad held a depressing significance. Perhaps the most successful of all his works at this time was the *Dance Suite*. It was introduced to the public of Cincinnati by Frigyes Reiner on April 3, 1925, was heard in Prague on May 19, and achieved a great success with Václav Talich as conductor at a festival given by the International Society of New Music. Six months later, when the Prague orchestra made a guest appearance in Budapest, the audience compelled the orchestra to play the whole piece over again. Emil Haraszti commented in his review of the performance that in Germany alone the work had been played in fifty places in one year. But some of Bartók's other works were heard all over the world. On April 2, 1925, there were performances of *Bluebeard's Castle* and *The Wooden Prince* in Weimar. That same year saw the première in New York of *Two Portraits*, introduced by Ernő Dohnányi who was appearing there as guest conductor. Bartók's compositions had already met with success in Moscow at the end of 1923 during the exhibition and festival arranged by the Association for Contemporary Music. In those days, musical life in the Soviet Union was closely related to that of Europe and avant-garde activities were followed with interest. Bartók's scores were shown at the exhibition together with those of Schoenberg, Hindemith, de Falla and Ravel, and in the Moscow press there were wildly enthusiastic notices of the two sonatas for violin. The two string quartets were introduced by the Stradivarius Ensemble at the beginning of 1925 and were very well received.

His name began to appear with increasing frequency in the international press and he was also attracting more attention as a scientist. In 1924, sixty-two of his articles were edited for inclusion in the Dictionary of Modern Music and Musicians, a musical lexicon published by J. M. Dent and Sons in London in that year. One year later, in 1925, he began negotiations with Oxford University Press for the publication of the collection of Romanian *kolindas*. Thus the most outstanding music critics of the time followed his development with respect, ensuring for him the devotion which was his due.

He was similarly respected and admired as an outstanding interpreter of piano music. For many years, before and during the war, he had scarcely performed in public so that when he started to make regular appearances once again, his impact as a pianist was all the more considerable. In this sphere, he was already much more than a merely occasional interpreter of his own works. He who had been known as the child genius from Pozsony returned to the concert platform as a mature artist interpreting the masterpieces of the world whether Baroque, classical or the piano works of twentieth-century composers. After a piano recital given on November 6, 1923, Aladár Tóth wrote: 'It is the fate of many artists that while the audience applauds their virtuosity as pianists, it forgets their creative activities as composers. This fate, which overtook Bach and Liszt, has in some miraculous fashion failed to touch Béla Bartók in whose gigantic artistic personality the composer gradually overshadows the virtuoso pianist. The general public has so far forgotten Bartók's early achievements as a pianist, although a career equal to that of Busoni was predicted for him by his teacher, that now when he has reappeared on the concert platform after so long an interval, it is as if we must rediscover his peerless talent for interpretation.' And after the recital of sonatas, given jointly with Emil Telmányi on January 29, 1925, he wrote: 'As a virtuoso pianist, Béla Bartók deserves to be ranked with Busoni. Indeed in one respect Bartók surpasses everyone else: When he sits at the keyboard, we feel from his interpretations that he must be ranked with Kodály as one of the greatest and at the same time most poetic musical personalities of our times. Though there have been great interpreters of music, we have not known the spell cast by a truly great musical personality since the time of Beethoven (the last musician of genius with the touch of a poet). An uncompromising honesty lies at the root of Bartók's art as a performer. He always starts from the work

209

itself to which he never insinuates anything superfluous. He finds riches enough in the form of the work as it is and he merely tries to explain the inner content of the work within this form. To reach the essence of the music he in no way dissolves the basic structure, but rather uses the original structure as a starting point from which to make his way direct to the inner meaning. It is because of this that we have never heard more definitely outlined phrases, strong rhythms and cleaner tones than in the playing of Bartók. And how right Bartók is! Between the performing artist and the work performed there is a puritanic relationship which releases immeasurable richness, variety and colour.'

And truly, the aesthetic, disciplined tension, passion and adherence to truth shown in his performances, enraptured all who heard him play. According to some of Bartók's contemporaries who are alive today, it was István Thomán's opinion that Bartók and Busoni were the two pianists who approached most nearly to the technique and style of Liszt.

Standing out all the more sharply against such a background of enthusiastic approval were the unpleasant political incidents provoked by official circles. On December 23, a report of an interview given by the music critic József Wágner, appeared in *Zenei Szemle* and contained his statement that Bartók had been attacked because he had recently dedicated his *Five Songs* op. 16 to Béla Reinitz. At the beginning of 1924, the press reported the scandalous circumstances surrounding the award of the Greguss prize, a very important music prize in Hungary. Bartók's opera and ballet were judged to be far superior to any works that had appeared for many years, yet the prize was not given in respect of these works because the lyrics had been written by Béla Balázs, who had been forced to emigrate. When Bartók gave a piano recital in Sopron on March 8, 1924, 'A Sopron Friend of Music' noted that 'while official Sopron, which diligently attended every ball and reception in the Carnival season, and appeared to a man at the concert at the Prohászka soirée held on Sunday evening [Bishop Prohászka was politically and ideologically on the side of the counter-revolution], was nowhere to be seen at the Bartók concert with the exception of the police captain and the judge.'

Finally, we learn from the issue of *Erdélyi Hirlap* dated April 25, 1924, that a Hungarian political party had pressed for disciplinary action against Bartók because he had given concerts in Transylvania. The

Minister of Culture started the proceedings. (This particular charge was later dropped.) The response made by the Romanian government was to refuse Jenő Hubay permission to enter the country to give the concerts planned for April and May 1924; they remembered that in the debates on the subject of Romanian folk music in 1920, Hubay had opposed Bartók.

But when Bartók gave concerts in Italy, Aladár Tóth was able to note with astonishment, 'It seems that under the Italian skies, Hungarians are liberated from the effects of the ancient—or as they now have it, "Turan" —curse. After Bartók's recital in Milan, the Hungarian consul, Villányi, and other of his compatriots in that city gave a reception and banquet in honour of the composer.'

It may also be illuminating to quote one more passage from one of Bartók's letters, this time written on May 20, 1925,

> Not long ago I received from Prague a copy of an article which had appeared in a Czech newspaper and which expressed wonder and enthusiasm at the idea that it should have been possible for me, a Hungarian composer living in Horthy's Hungary, to publish my own collections of genuine Slovak folk music under a Czech title and including Czech songs. (Viz. Book Three and Book Four of For Children which actually did appear in that manner, but in 1912, so that this extraordinary occurrence took place before Horthy's time.)

And yet it was neither these political provocations nor the general atmosphere of narrow-mindedness that most disheartened him. Such provocations were expected, this atmosphere he knew, and even when he had been obliged to spend all his time at home after the war, he had learned to rise above disturbing conditions. He was chiefly worried about the fate of his works, and perhaps especially so when he realized that in spite of everything he had an audience at home, he had his followers and he felt that he had a mission to fulfil.

It is therefore not to be wondered at that when he was interviewed by a representative of *Erdélyi Hirlap* in Temesvár, Bartók spoke more freely and sincerely than to the press at home. At that time there were close connections between Budapest and Temesvár and the *Zenei Szemle* was published in the latter town. It will be instructive to quote at length from the account of an interview with Bartók printed in *Erdélyi Hirlap* on November 13, 1924:

'We looked up the distinguished artist to inquire why he had not completed the score of his opera (sic) *The Miraculous Mandarin* the libretto of which had been written by Menyhért Lengyel.

' "I have not been composing for some time," Bartók told us. "I have no time for it, nor have I the urge to continue. I am giving a good many recitals. I have just returned from Romania; before that I was in London, Paris and Switzerland, and I will be leaving for Prague shortly. Indeed, I have already signed a contract with a concert manager for the coming season. I will be going to America where I shall play works by Hungarian composers."

' "Is that why you have no time, maestro? But why is it that you feel no urge to compose?"

' "All right, I will tell you. Two years ago, the Pest Opera wanted to revive two of my works. The rehearsals were well under way when the directors received an anonymous letter: it contained threats not only to me personally but also to the management if we dared to put on my "un-Hungarian pieces" . . . So my works are looked upon as un-Hungarian . . . and I have lost interest. But I have no desire to compose. Why should I compose foreign music?"

' "Before we left," the composer added, "I was also attacked for allowing the Romanian government to publish the Romanian part of my folk-music collection. In fact, together with Zoltán Kodály, I offered the whole collection to the Hungarian government. I could not help it if there was no money to have it published. The Romanians themselves asked me for permission to publish the Romanian songs. Was it wrong to agree? Should I have left the entire collection to gather still more dust? The Romanians were grateful . . . There may come a time here at home, too, when I shall be recognized as a Hungarian composer. Though perhaps by that time I shall no longer be alive." '

It is always difficult to find out later what exactly was said at the time of the interview. Journalism has its own rules, and the person interviewed tends to be quoted as giving the answers expected of him. There can be no doubt, however, that the statements attributed to Bartók were in fact his own. It is true that there was some talk of reviving *The Wooden Prince* after the war, and it is also true that in the right-wing press there were vehement protests that such a production would be unwelcome because the libretto was the work of Béla Balázs. Gyula Wlassics, intendant of the Opera House, wrote to Bartók on October 1, 1923, assuring him that it was only because of circumstances beyond his control that he could not put on the opera (sic) and ballet. Should it be possible to remove the familiar obstacles, he would lose no time before including the pieces in the scheduled programme. That was his dearest wish. He urged Bartók to complete the score of *The Miraculous Mandarin* so that he would be able to give it a premiere during the season 1924–25.

On May 27, 1924, Wlassics repeated his request that Bartók should complete the score, and to this letter Bartók replied on June 5. He promised to complete the score in two sections, the first to be ready by July, the second by August 15. Meantime, Antal Molnár also used his influence to further the production by writing an open letter to Aladár Tóth in the *Zenei Szemle*, urging him to promote the date of the premiere at the Opera House.

On October 10, one month before the interview printed in the *Erdélyi Hirlap* of Temesvár, and quoted above, a statement by the composer appeared in the Brassó papers.

> Forty pages of the score of The Miraculous Mandarin are already complete, and about 12 pages remain to be done. I am just finishing the orchestration now. Unfortunately, I have had very little time for it over the past 5 years.

The long delay before the first production of the pantomime, which the composer had already named in the interview mentioned above as *The Miraculous Mandarin*, was not entirely due to the fact that Bartók had not completed the orchestration. An analysis of the various arrangements and a comparison of the manuscript versions show that Bartók himself was not satisfied, that the work had not reached its final form for many years. The musicologist Aurél O. Nirschy has attempted to trace the stages of development through which the composition passed before achieving its final form and his discoveries confirm for the most part the statements in the letters and in the interviews quoted above. In 1921, Bartók had already handed in to the Opera the first version of the work written for the piano. It was in September 1924, as seen above, that Bartók handed in the first forty pages of the orchestrated score, and the rest followed soon afterwards. This score, however, differed in many respects from the original piano abstract. There were alterations in many sections and the finale was completely different. Bartók had already made these alterations to the original piano score. Obviously he expected this version to be used for rehearsals at the Opera.

There was also a piano abstract for four hands which Bartók took to Berlin in 1923 and played together with Árpád Sándor, but it is not known for certain which of the versions this represented. And it is difficult to establish which version was published by Universal Edition in 1925. It is, however, quite certain that even the 1925 version was not the final one. In connection with the orchestral suite, which was based on the work, Bartók gave further instructions to the publishers on February 3, 1927. After the dismal failure of the production in Cologne, he tried to adapt as much of the music as possible for concert performance according to John Vinton's quotation which appeared in *The Musical Quarterly* in January 1964. Denijs Dille discovered that during the rehearsals for the performance in Budapest in 1931, Bartók made changes throughout the score. Finally, John Vinton tells us that it was in a letter dated January 29, 1936, that Bartók mentioned for the last time certain changes that he still wished to make. It was in this letter that he instructed Universal publishers to make the changes indicated on the last pages of the score, which have been preserved in the piano abstract for four hands and in the short score. (These are not identical in all respects.)

The fate of *The Miraculous Mandarin* became a matter of great concern to Bartók. It was no wonder that the calvary of the pantomime in Hungary disheartened him. During the course of these events he had the opportunity to observe that any attempt to support him on the part of the more liberal and sober members of the government was always defeated by the reactionary nationalists of the right wing. But together with the negative fact of his silence as a composer, we must mention the positive and much more important fact that during this same year his art reached a new level of maturity.

We know enough of the enquiring nature of Bartók's mind to realize how eagerly and with what an unquenchable thirst for knowledge he sought information concerning everything that was new, whether by reading, observing for himself, or listening to others. We are sadly lacking in evidence to demonstrate the ways in which he acquired information. He himself spoke about it very little. It is therefore particularly noticeable that during the post-war years he made frequent references to the musical experiences he had enjoyed during his travels. These comments alone indicate how important it was to Bartók that he should have had so many opportunities of observing the musical life of Europe after his years of isolation during the war. With the help of these statements, his writings, and above all his compositions, as well as comments made by others and the evidence of his concert programmes, we can now attempt to describe the development of his outlook during the nineteen-twenties.

There are a good many indications that of all his contemporaries it was Stravinsky who interested him most. Denijs Dille tells us that he was already familiar with the *Sacre du Printemps* at the time of the rehearsals of *The Wooden Prince* in 1917. It is also clear that during his first tour abroad after the war he must have become acquainted with other works by this composer, for he wrote an article for *Melos* in 1920 in which he analysed *Pribaoutki*, while at a concert held on April 23, 1921, he played the *Piano Rag Music* as well as pieces by Debussy and Schoenberg. When Bartók returned from his first post-war visits to England and France, his tour was described in great detail in *Nyugat* by Aladár Tóth who also reported the composer's opinion of the western capitals. The report was written in the form of an interview and it is noticeable that the name of Stravinsky occurs most frequently in Bartók's statements. When interviewed by a representative of the Brassó papers for the account printed on October 18, 1924, he mentioned both Stravinsky and Schoenberg.

In my opinion among composers living abroad today, there are two geniuses
—Stravinsky and Schoenberg. Stravinsky stands closer to me—think of the
Sacre du Printemps—which I consider to be the most grandiose musical opus
of the past 30 years.

According to later statements, Bartók was particularly attracted to the
music written by Stravinsky at a time when the latter was influenced by
folk music; it is undoubtedly true that it was Stravinsky's music that
exercised the most profound effect on Bartók during the years of his
maturity.

Bartók also esteemed very highly the music of Debussy whose works
always figured prominently in his concert programmes. His acquaintance
with the younger composers of the war generation, 'The Six', was not
limited to the social contact made during his evening with the Prunières.
As early as April 1920, he played Milhaud's *Le Bœuf sur le toit* with
Sándor Albrecht in his flat in Pozsony. Later, especially during the SIMC
festivals, he had further opportunities of hearing Milhaud's works and
discussions about his achievements. It was also at these festivals that he
first took note of Hindemith, and in 1922, Aladár Tóth quoted Bartók's
comment that 'his three orchestral pieces barely rise above the level of
Pfitzner.' In May, 1925, on the other hand, he mentioned Hindemith
as a talented younger composer and classed him with Křenek, who was
twenty-five years old at that time.

These occasional references to the work of other composers are interesting signs of Bartók's increasing awareness of new musical phenomena,
and also indicate indirectly his progress towards a mature creative
outlook. But they are merely indications and nothing more; the full
story of his development can only be conveyed by an analysis of the
general situation in the field of music in Europe at that time, by a discussion of the works that mark the beginning of Bartók's next period,
by a study of Bartók's style and also that of his Hungarian contemporaries.

From the year 1916 onwards, there developed an ever closer link
between artists of the avant-garde in various countries, and in the post-
war years their sense of unity found expression in the foundation of the
international association for the promotion of new music. However, by
the time this association had become an organized body, the original

sense of unity which had led to its foundation, had been lost. With the cessation of hostilities at the end of the war, there occurred tremendous changes in the social structure of the defeated powers and in the political relations between all the European countries. It followed naturally from these various changes that in each country the beliefs and attitudes of members of the different classes were completely transformed, and in the work of creative artists these beliefs and attitudes were reflected in a variety of forms.

One of the slogans commonly heard at that time expressed the belief that men had now lost their former illusions about the world they lived in or advocated the suppression of all romantic sentimentality, but beneath these slogans were many different and indeed contradictory beliefs of varying social significance. In their creative endeavours widely differing social forces made use of the means of expression available to modern art. Where the world cataclysm brought about the end of the state apparatus of semi-feudalism, there the working-class movement became stronger. Socialism was victorious once for all in the Soviet Union, and also achieved a compromise or transitional form in Germany and the territory of the Monarchy. In these countries all those artists who support-ed the cause of the working class hoped that bourgeois illusions would be shattered by the power of the party of the working class and placed at its disposal the stylistic methods of the earlier rebel artists. This was the basis for the feeling experienced by artists and musicians in the Soviet Union and in other European nations, especially Germany and Austria, that they were fighting the same battle.

In this connection it is relevant to note here that in the writings of the music historian János Maróthy, our attention is drawn to the brutal quality of certain music characterized by barbaric ostinatos signifying the noise of machines and the terrifying march of labour. The composers who were in sympathy with the working-class movement sought to find the authentic note of the people, even in the cheap street music heard in the great cities, a form exploited by Ernst Křenek in his jazz opera, *Johnny Strikes Up.* (This opera was still being performed in the Soviet Union when Bartók went there as a guest artist in 1929.) A daring rejection of traditional forms was counted as a declaration of war against bourgeois philistinism.

Some bourgeois radical elements of this view had existed when the flag of 'The Six' was unfurled. Some members of the group who were loosely associated, and did not always agree with each other, turned their attention from the fleeting mood of Impressionism and the self-consuming nature of Expressionism, to something blatant, prosaic and more generally comprehensible.

The compromise solutions and transitional solutions favoured between the two world wars eventually developed into ideas which constituted an early form of fascism. In the aesthetics which recognized the necessity for an urban society there was always the danger of fostering inhuman and anti-human concepts, and indeed these were present from the very start in both the theory and practice of Futurism. A pseudo-radical rejection of the humane historical traditions of art was evident in new experiments made during the so-called RAPP period of Soviet art. After the war, this danger was first realized because of the activities of those who propagated fascism in Italy. Some ten years later, under the German version of fascism, the content of dehumanized art took on exactly the opposite form: it was neither destructive nor pseudo-revolutionary, but assumed a mask of 'sober, healthy, popular, optimistic conformism' and its purpose was to conduct a holy crusade against what fascism denounced as 'degenerate' art characterized by modern trends which expressed progressive and socialist ideas.

On the other hand, after their experience of the horror of war and of the social upheavals which followed, the majority of the bourgeoisie were swept along by the current of hedonistic nihilism. This cult of frivolity, as it came to be described later by literary historians, denied not only traditions that were admittedly obsolete, but all tradition, not only romantic sentimentality, but all emotion; it denied not only hypocritical bourgeois morality but the very concept of morality, and it condemned not only the former social order, but the structure of society in general. A thousand different aspects of exhibitionism, egoism, brutality and the perverse pursuit of pleasure found expression in both art and aesthetic theory. The extravagant craze for dancing so characteristic of the early nineteen-twenties, the mammoth fortunes (acquired in an instant and lots as quickly in the economic slump that followed the post-war boom), a senseless squandering of money and craving for amusement, were all symptoms of this inhuman outlook.

The highest level of creative work resulting from this denial of the social and moral basis of art, rested on an aesthetic theory of 'objectivity' according to which art is nothing more than a series of technical tricks, acquired with understanding and cleverly applied: without content, created without emotion, intended to give only momentary amusement, and by successfully achieving this, to give pleasure alike to artist and onlooker. Artistic tradition was considered to be of value only insofar as it was conducive to the acquisition of a reliable craft technique. Thus the artists of the Baroque period were admired because they seemed to be untrammelled by what were now looked upon as the ridiculous moral and philosophical scruples which held back the Romantic artists: well satisfied with their own respectable craftsmanship, they were content to execute the commissions demanded of them. The steady, albeit mechanical, flow of his allegros, demonstrates the confidence felt by the Baroque musician in his own knowledge and superior technique in the construction of traditional forms. Thus Baroque music was held out as an example to the composers of the nineteen-twenties.

This was the current of ideas that influenced Stravinsky when he revived the music of the Baroque period just before the beginning of the nineteen-twenties, and which influenced Hindemith a few years later when he became interested in the objective craftsmanship of classical construction. His motto was *Neue Sachlichkeit*—New Objectivity. And though in the years to follow, Stravinsky, with his superior virtuosity, pursued his way through the great historic styles, he in fact denied the essence of style that springs from content. The good parlour *causeur* can amuse his audience at a very high level of performance in every style from Baroque to jazz without really saying anything. The story of Stravinsky's development is tragic yet human, because his search among the past styles was really a search for himself, an attempt to put together the broken pieces of his own shattered features, an aim he pursued diligently, secretly and with great elegance.

It cannot be denied that a good many of the excesses due to dilettantism were exposed as a result of the new endeavours by those who turned their backs on subjectivity and the cult of genius associated with the

Romantics. Professional knowledge, which had been discredited, was once more respected, and young musicians were confronted with such awe-inspiring examples of superior skill as Stravinsky's gift for composition. But there was only one Stravinsky, and the barren neo-Baroque disciples tried in vain to follow in his footsteps.

It was the victorious countries that were particularly notable for their frivolous and hedonistic movements. The defeated nations, especially the Czech and Austrian provinces of the monarchy, became the traditional home of a certain type of progressive intellectuals of the bourgeois class. This group of intellectuals, especially those among them who were artists, for the most part descended from the semi-feudal class of the court officials. Members of this class had never won political freedom for themselves and had always allowed themselves to be governed by the wishes of the great aristocratic landowners. They very early renounced the idea of revolution in favour of conformity which under the rule of Emperor and King gave them, at any rate in times of peace, a comfortable feeling of well-being. They bequeathed only a sense of their own inferiority to the intellectuals of this class who survived the war and who now in their turn, with much searching of consciences and all the torture of self-doubt, devoted themselves to an ascetic search for an abstract truth. The musicians who came from such a background were honest and imbued with good intentions, as may be seen from the fact that they never rejected bourgeois humanism and idealism and that socially they were orientated towards the working class. This was so in the case of Anton Webern. And similarly, in times of crisis, they stood on the side of humanity, as did Schoenberg. In the nineteen-twenties, however, in their search for an artistic habitat, they drew back from the masses and instead sought for truth in the isolation of Nietzsche.

Pioneers, like Honegger, who sought for traditions among the masses as they united, were few and far between. But Bartók, through the change in his style that took place between 1923–26, was already moving in this direction.

Yet it is questionable whether we should speak of the transformation that took place as a change of style. It does not resemble the spectacular change of style effected by Stravinsky. In the case of Bartók, it was not a question of discarding an old-fashioned style for something newer and more ornamental, but rather that his work developed organically because of his power to observe creatively and because of the individual methodology that was integral to his work. This transformation, far from necessitating any revision of his principles, either artistic or as a human being, in fact tended to strengthen them.

His new experiences undoubtedly stimulated and determined the progress of this transformation. It would be absurd to deny that he was influenced by practical considerations. He was urged on not only by the need to satisfy his own enquiring mind and by his fervent desire for some kind of rejuvenation, but also by the demands of the world market for modernity. The need to devise suitable programmes for his recitals spurred him on to compose the series of his piano works. It became necessary for him to replace the *Rhapsody*, written twenty years ago, with a new piano concerto for inclusion in the orchestral programmes. Károly Kristóf, the contemporary journalist who reported Bartók's activities throughout his life, quoted Bartók's remarks made during an interview on November 22, 1925. 'I must compose a piano concerto,' said Bartók. 'This is sadly lacking. This will be my next work.' He also felt the need for new piano pieces to add interest to his solo recitals.

At this point in Bartók's career, the forces of necessity combined happily with his own deep instinct for creative method. Piano composition remained for Bartók the most natural and intimate means of expression. The period of rejuvenation from 1907–10 began with the composition of piano works and now again the commencement of a new period starting in 1926 was marked by an impressive series of works for the piano. During 1926 there appeared in June *Sonata*, in June–August *Out of Doors* (in two volumes), in October *Nine Little Piano Pieces* and between August and November he wrote *Concerto No. 1* for piano. This series concluded with the two great string quartets produced during the following years: *String Quartet No. 3* in September 1927, and *String Quartet No. 4* in July–September 1928.

The fact that he lived at a distance from the pressures to conform to modern styles exerted by the western market, allowed more time for his new sources of inspiration to become absorbed and united with his own traditions. These had by now become part of his very blood, a compound of the feverish experiences of his youth, the constant practice of his art through several decades and above all his determined aesthetic convictions. Through the mediation of the great music of the Romantics he remained enough of a pupil of Beethoven to appreciate the significance of aesthetics. And his development as an artist owed nothing to the rewards of success but had always been stimulated by what he had learned with such difficulty and self-sacrifice through being prepared to assume responsibility. No one in Hungary ever contemplated the possibility of achieving an early success by composing music that was both competent and new. Such a path was open only to the artist with a firm belief in himself and the truth that was in him. By education, circumstance and habit, Bartók was happily prevented from succumbing to the temptations of aesthetic 'objectivity'.

Bartók was confronted with this temptation when he met the greatest exponent of 'objectivity', Stravinsky, in Paris in 1922. In the memorable account of this meeting printed in *Nyugat* Aladár Tóth wrote, 'Stravinsky explained to Bartók that his music was as objective and absolute as possible, and did not describe, symbolize or express anything, had no relation to emotion, and was only line, harmony and rhythm. He (Bartók, that is) did not in any way identify himself with the theories of Stravinsky, but he firmly believed that the great Russian musician was possessed of such an original talent that this could not be injured by any kind of aesthetic arguments. We must always remember that there is true poetry in Stravinsky's *Sacre du Printemps* (according to Bartók, his greatest work).'

In his discussions with the writer Dezső Kosztolányi three years later, Bartók reached similar conclusions. He agreed with those who turned against Romanticism in all its exaggerated forms.

> With the music of Wagner and Strauss, the off-shoots of Romanticism have become unbearable.

Kosztolányi observed, however, that 'every art is necessarily human and cannot be made independent of man, feeling and the object of feeling.' To which Bartók replied in agreement.

> This is natural because otherwise music becomes the music of machines. Bach also expressed something—some moments of life.

Some years earlier, in 1919, when he was energetically attacking Romanticism, Stravinsky had discovered a model for his endeavours in Baroque music, and this he publicized with all his customary love of ostentation. Yet he was not the first to have made the discovery, the latest musician to have done so being Debussy who even at the beginning of the century had incorporated in his piano music the traditions of the French masters of the Baroque. Stimulated by this example, Sándor Kovács, in about 1910, became interested in the works of Baroque composers and published some of their compositions. It is not impossible that it was through his activities that Bartók came to love the Baroque style. At any rate, in 1911, he played works by Scarlatti, Couperin and Rameau at the concerts organized by UMZE; and in 1912 he wrote an article for *Zeneközlöny* on 'the performance of works written for the clavecin'. When he resumed his career as a pianist at the beginning of the nineteen-twenties, Baroque music occupied a prominent place in his programmes. He prepared for publication certain pieces of Italian Baroque music for harpsichord, and in 1922, during a visit to England, he listened to a harpsichord recital by Wanda Landowska.

It is true that he sometimes treated the Baroque pieces included in his programmes somewhat in the manner of the Romantics, who had influenced him earlier, such as Busoni. But in spite of an occasionally arbitrary interpretation of these pieces, he respected the traditions of Baroque music and did not depart from them. The method of composition employed in his works dating from 1926 shows traces of his study of Baroque music.

> In my youth, Bach and Mozart were not my ideals of the beautiful, but rather Beethoven. During the past few years, I have been occupied with pre-Bach music and I think that traces of these studies are revealed in the *Piano Concerto* and the *Nine Little Piano Pieces*,

wrote Bartók sometime during the nineteen-twenties to Edwin von der Nüll who was the first to analyse his music. The sources of this inspiration and the results achieved by Bartók in following the Baroque example were, however, quite different from those of his western contemporaries. The latter merely abandoned content and were left with nothing more than technical ingenuity, while their imitation of the Baroque manner was little beyond a trifling with style. Bartók, however, assimilated what

223

was best in the Baroque style so that he experienced a renewal of his sense of responsibility as an artist. He became the strong and superior master of a school which helped him to achieve a more perfect and disciplined expression of his artistic ideas.

> As a man grows more mature, it seems that he has a greater longing to be more economical with his means, in order to achieve simplicity,

we read in a statement given to the American press in 1941 (F.F. Rothe in *The Etude*). And in the same interview he said,

> As far as I am concerned, I think I have developed logically and in one direction, at least beginning with 1926, when my works became more contrapuntal and simpler in general.

Indeed, it is because of their contrapuntal artistry that the compositions dating from 1926 are so very important in relation to the structure of Bartók's works. The 'dialogues' in the first volume of *Nine Little Piano Pieces* are really contrapuntally constructed inventions. The renewed tendency towards polyphony was a reminder of his youth and the works before 1910, but *String Quartet No. 1*, the first of the *Two Portraits*, and some of the pieces in the *Bagatelles* with their loose linearity become strict counterpoint in the works of the mature Bartók. The relation between the early compositions and those of 1926, also the differences between them, were immediately recognized by Aladár Tóth at a composer's recital held on December 8, 1926, for the critic was gifted with unerring judgement in such matters. He commented in *Pesti Napló*, 'Bartók's counterpoint now differs in essence from that of his former works, for instance the String Quartet No. 1. The fugue-like sections in the quartet spring rather from the spirit of Beethoven's polyphony in the last quartets, while the new piano pieces are reminiscent of the polyphony of Bach and the pre-Bach Italians. We can discern the forerunners of the little piano pieces in some of Bartók's Bagatelles and Sketches; indeed, the Dialogues and the Menuetto give the impression of being a continuation of earlier short polyphonic piano works in their form, and yet, in the strict and rigid contrapuntal system of present-day polyphony, we can hail an entirely new Bartók style.'

In the *Etudes*, the first developments of twelve-tone atonality are held together by the complementary counterpoint fixed in bitonality as in the first movement of the *String Quartet No. 3*, 1927 (note that the appearance of the two-part complementary bitonality and its method of construction call to mind the earlier works and refer to the beginning of the first of the *Bagatelles*). János Kárpáti reminds us that in the *String Quartet No. 1* there is a suspicion of the influence of Alban Berg's Lyrical Suite. (Bartók introduced his *Piano Sonata* in 1927 on July 26, at the same concert in Baden-Baden at which Berg's work written for string quartet was first heard.) But it was through the mediation of Berg's composition that Bartók assimilated the spirit of Baroque counterpoint. The dodecaphony of the Viennese school became fixed at this time in the strict contrapuntal system of serial technique.

The Baroque example did not, as in the case of Stravinsky, result in any startling stylistic changes in Bartók's works. Nor did he now reject the folk-music sources in his music; on the contrary, all that Bartók had acquired from Baroque music became, together with folk music, an organic part of his most profound and individual traditions. We could also add that another effect of the Baroque example was to inspire a new and more profound method of composition initiated in the realm of folk music.

The second movement of the *String Quartet No. 3* is perhaps the best example of how a disciplined use of Baroque polyphonic artistry was used to express Bartók's own ideals of folk music. This movement has one single theme at its nucleus and this is developed through a marvellous use of every device of counterpoint. At the central point of the symmetrically soaring structure of this masterpiece we find a meeting between the theme—transformed, widening, narrowing, reversed and in a mirror image—and the fugue which is built out of it. The intonation of the slow movement of the *Sonata No. 1* for violin and piano with its echoes from the past, is attached as an accompaniment to the first figure of the theme. But is not this clever transposition executed with such ingenuity, the very life principle of folk music? Did not Bartók, following the example of the masters of Baroque, observe the inner dynamics of folk music and condense them into compositions that are without equals?

> The melodic world of my string quartets does not essentially differ from that of folk-song, only the framework is stricter,

said Bartók in February 1927, in response to a question posed by Denijs Dille. He continued,

> It must have been observed that I place great emphasis on the work of technical arrangement, that I do not like to repeat a musical idea without change, and I do not bring back one single part in exactly the same way. This method arises out of my tendency to vary and transform the theme. I am not merely playing when I reverse the theme at the end of my second piano concerto. The extremes of variation, which is so characteristic of our folk music, is at the same time the expression of my own nature,

said Bartók. In this method of construction it is easy to recognize one branch of his early development as found, for instance, in the first of the *Romanian Dances*, which is built formally round the theme.

In the works that appeared immediately after 1926, even in those which outwardly appear to be abstract, folk music is the key to all the phenomena so ingeniously created by the composer, as for example in the relation between the two Scherzos of the *String Quartet No. 4*. The melodic models on which the two movements are built are identical, but the first movement is built up on half tones, the second on whole tones. Bartók explains this in the preface to the *Jugoszláv népdal gyűjtemény* (Collection of Serbo-Croatian Folk-Songs): it seems that there are many northern diatonic variations of South Slav half-tone melodies in which the diatony became 'compressed', and narrowed 'chromatically'.

One of the little piano pieces, 'Musettes', is an interesting and characteristic example of the fusion between folk music and Baroque form. Those who are familiar with the history of music will recognize in it the stylized dance movements of Baroque suite music. In Bartók's piece, however, the title regains its original meaning when we hear his quotation from village bagpipe music. The fast movements of the *Concerto No. 1* and the *Sonata* for piano, with their evenly pulsating allegros, were inspired by Baroque music, but we can hear something beyond the musical apparatus of Baroque music discovered by Stravinsky. Contained within them is all the natural strength and abandon of folk dance such as may be found in the *csárdáses* written by Liszt in his old age and which found new expression in the *Allegro Barbaro* and the *Bear Dance*. The inclusion of some elements of the Arabic folk idiom contributes to produce an even wilder effect, also evident in the *String Quartet No. 2*, the mandarin's dance and the *Dance Suite*.

Contemporary critics who heard Bartók play are unanimously agreed that there was a tension in his playing, and that the hardness with which he struck the keys was worthy of any performer on a percussion instrument. In the works he composed after 1926, he also emphasized the percussive nature of the piano keys. But anyone who has heard the *Old Hungarian Dances* played by the composer himself, will recognize in these renderings not only an adherence to the Baroque method of piano playing but also the rhythmic tapping sounds of the cimbalist when he accompanies a dance played by the village band.

In his theoretical studies and in the lectures he gave at this time Bartók revealed that he was conscious of a renewed relationship with folk music in his compositions. It is noticeable that Bartók, who had previously scarcely ever spoken about the way he worked, from this time on began to make a conscious and confident analysis of the inner laws of his own music and that of his contemporaries. The first occasion on which he did this was during his lecture tour of America in 1927–28 when he gave illustrated lectures on 'Hungarian Folk Music' and 'New Hungarian Music'. During this period, his efforts in both the theory and practice of composition may be summarized as an attempt to achieve synthesis.

According to his theoretical analysis, folk music is not simply a model for melody. It is not an arrangement or imitation of the enchanting sounds of nature whose world of intonation and novelty instinctively becomes part of the composer's idiom. It is not a motto, as in the *Improvisations* to which the composer ingeniously adds his own invention.

It is the ultimate and deliberately assumed principle of musical thinking and construction, whose realm also prompts the composer to a more tonal style of writing. The relationship between melody and harmony begets strikingly new melodic turns, scales, harmonies and structures.

Questioned by an American journalist in 1941, Bartók stated the essential prerequisite for a style system arising naturally out of folk music:

> The most important thing for a composer is to grasp the spirit of that music, to incorporate it with his entire output, allow it to permeate his whole being and outlook.

When speaking to Denijs Dille he expressed the same idea though he put it rather differently,

One must know folk melodies as we know them.

This transformation of folk music into a 'mother tongue' was the only way in which he could free himself from its limitations and so that his own principles could be fully expanded to allow for the accommodation and development of the traditions of European music.

It was in fact during this period that the duality of folk music and Western traditions ceased to be present in Bartók's music. The synthesis which Bartók began to seek in the violin sonatas was now fully realized. In the earlier work the two worlds were present but in separate movements; from 1926 these worlds were united in Bartók's work. At the time of the American tour mentioned above, he deliberately differentiated between the innovations which he and Kodály had introduced into their music and those made by his Western contemporaries.

Of course, many other (foreign) composers, who do not lean upon folk music, have met with similar results at about the same time—only in an intuitive or speculative way which evidently is a procedure equally justifiable. The difference is that we created through nature, for: the peasant's art is a phenomenon of nature.

As an individual and as a scientist he continued to oppose city civilization throughout his life. In his music, however, the concept of a society based on the brotherhood of peoples turned more and more from a romantic myth to living reality. In one of Bartók's recently discovered letters, there is an interesting and seemingly contradictory documentation of the relationship between folk music and art-music as found at a still higher level. The letter was written on December 16, 1924, and was addressed to Ernst Latzkó in Weimar, 'the city of Goethe, Schiller and Ferenc Liszt,' in the words of the journalist who wrote about it in *Magyarország* at the time of the rehearsals for *Bluebeard's Castle* and *The Wooden Prince*. According to the account which appeared in this paper, Ernst Latzkó was to give a lecture entitled 'Bartók's Significance in the Musical Scene' during the afternoon of the première on April 2. When Bartók wrote to him during the previous December he mentioned, among other things, his hope that Dr. Latzkó would not lay too great an emphasis on the role of folk music in his works. This would appear to be in contradiction to his folk-music compositions and theoretical outlook. However, the explanation may lie in the fact that, as we have already had occasion to observe, those features of his work that were inspired by folk music were often described in the press, both at home and abroad, as 'racial' or 'of ancient barbaric force', something exciting, exotic and strange. But for Bartók, as a man and as a composer, folk music ranked equally with music in the historical traditions of Western Europe, and he accepted it naturally as part of his musical heritage like any other kind of music. The fact that Bartók had already been misrepresented in this way no doubt caused him to fear that Dr. Latzkó might not, when lecturing, show a correct understanding of his use of folk music, and so fail to demonstrate to his audience that for Bartók folk music was not a curiosity but a natural means of expression. It was undoubtedly this concern which prompted the composer to write to the lecturer in these terms.

There is also a strange contradiction in the fact that at the very time when the inner principles of folk music were permeating his works, he sadly lacked any opportunity to collect folk music or to refresh himself through direct contact with the peasants. However, it was during this period of Bartók's life that he set about the gigantic task of systematizing and summarizing his collections of folk music. The folk melodies brought back to his mind the memory of his tours and his experiences in distant villages, and this concentrated recollection most certainly played a part in his achievement of synthesis in composition and his further development towards maturity.

By the autumn of 1923, Bartók had finished most of the preparatory work in connection with the publication of his collection of Slovak folk-songs. And one year later, at about the time that he wrote the letter quoted above, this renewed inspiration of Slovak folk music resulted in the appearance of the first version of the five-part *Five Village Scenes* written for voice and piano. This is like a strange little island rising between the two continents of works written before 1923 and after 1926, and is a worthy link between them. Each of the Slovak folk lyrics describes one episode in human life: 'Hay-making', 'At the Bride's', 'Wedding', 'Lullaby' and 'Lads' Dance'. This work was in part a supplement to its great forebear of 1917, the *Four Slovak Folk-Songs*. The method of arrangement synthetizes the more developed and freer technique of the *Improvisations* with the ostinato technique of *Les Noces* by Stravinsky, a choral work with piano accompaniment, also with a wedding theme. But in the Bartók work we see again and in a more definite form the type of five-part movement system which in the core of the structure hold together two slow movements with a fast one, and which may be recognized here as an early forerunner of the *Concerto No. 2* for piano and orchestra and the *String Quartet No. 5*. Thus the *String Quartet No. 2* has now come into its own in a position of even greater importance at the centre of a work on a much larger scale, though drawn behind the protection of the more general movements of a communal character.

An analysis of the *Village Scenes* cycle brings to our notice the problems connected with the disposition of the movements in the larger works of the new period. Through our knowledge of Bartók's earlier work we have become accustomed to the fact that the individual pieces in any one series, even when the connection between them is apparently quite loose, are not assembled by accident. In the two volumes of *Out of Doors* the relationship between the various pieces is similar to that in both the original arrangement of the five movements of *Village Scenes*, and also the later choral version. The latter version, written for solo voice and piano accompaniment, consists of three movements only of the original version. The first volume of *Out of Doors* consists of three pieces, 'With Drums and Pipes', 'Barcarolla' and 'Musettes'; the second volume consists of two pieces, 'The Night's Music' and 'The Chase'. The first volume therefore consists of an andante enclosed between two fast movements, a unit comprising three movements as in the second version of *Village Scenes*. In the second volume we find the well-known contrast so often found in the early works—the slow–fast pairing of two movements. But the two volumes together constitute two slow movements which become increasingly dynamic, a five-part unit exactly like the first version of *Village Scenes*. The five pieces of *Out of Doors* appeared in two volumes merely for convenience of publication, but the division nevertheless arises naturally from the inner logic of the work.

In the structure of the third and last volume of the *Nine Little Piano*

Pieces we find the same pattern—two movements, slow–fast, paired together. A Preludio is followed by a movement consisting of variations of the new-style folk-song. Each of the two preceding volumes consists of a four-movement unit: the four Dialogues in the first, Menuetto, Air, Marcia delle Bestie and Tambourine in the second. Bartók referred to his testing of the construction when he made a statement on October 3, 1940 to a correspondent of *Magyar Nemzet*, Miklós Szentjóbi. He spoke of the origin of *Mikrokosmos* and traced the idea for these six small books to a little piece written in 1926.

> As a matter of fact, it was originally written as the tenth of the *Nine Little Piano Pieces* but was somehow left out.

This 'somehow' was Bartók's modest description of the way in which he carefully and consciously selected the movements. He omitted the tenth piece from this work just as deliberately as ten years earlier he had discarded one of the movements of his *Suite* for piano, leaving only four in the final version. Before returning to the new period, let us look backwards once more, this time to compare the *Suite* for piano with another work prepared at about the same time, the *Four Slovak Folk-Songs*. These two works might well be called the 'Five Slovak Folk-Songs', for they are related in the same way as are the two later works—the five pieces of *Out of Doors* and the first version of *Village Scenes*. The two four-unit movements in *Nine Little Piano Pieces* were left behind by the main stream of Bartók's works in which there recurred constantly two-, three- and five-movement structures. The works consisting of three movements now finally settled into the closed structure of fast–slow–fast movements inherited from the Baroque tradition. The *Sonata* for piano and the *Concerto No. 1* for piano are clearly built on the three-part system. The relationship between the three parts is much more enclosed and comprehensible than in the *Sonata No. 1* for violin and piano where the second movement was wedged between two supporting movements.

The first two string quartets of this new period, the *String Quartet No. 3* and the *String Quartet No. 4* are particularly worthy of note. The *String Quartet No. 3*, in which there is a curious repetition of the slow–fast paired movements, is shaped into an unbroken unit of four movements and is thus related to the violin sonatas. But it is no less closely related to the Baroque 'concerto grosso' which consists of a similar unit of four movements. The *String Quartet No. 4* is in five movements, two of them Scherzos. The enclosed nature of the structure is emphasized by the presence of related themes in the first and fifth movements and also in the second and fourth movements, thus maintaining the symmetry of the arching structure. The slow middle movement is enclosed by two movements with related themes, thus: 1–2–3–4–5. In one of János Kárpáti's studies, he refers to the relationship between Bartók's string quartets and Beethoven's last quartets. And it was in fact in the quartets that Bartók most clearly demonstrated his fidelity to Beethoven, and this at a time when Baroque music was being revived. This structural hardening that was becoming evident in his compositions and the development of a symmetry that is reminiscent of Haydn—the sensitive core of the slow movements always protected by the hard sheath of those on either side—were not qualities achieved through imitation of the Baroque models but resulted naturally from the inner organic development of Bartók's music. It would be possible to follow this development from its beginnings in the two sonatas for violin, and continuing through the *Dance Suite*. It is to the consideration of Bartók's slow movements that we must always return when attempting to trace the path by which he arrived at the aesthetic vision which lies at the heart of the new system of composition. This new type of slow movement marks the birth of 'The Night's Music'.

The first piece of the second volume of *Out of Doors* earned the enthusiastic praise of a number of the critics after the première on December 8, 1926. Here again, Aladár Tóth's aesthetic judgement has proved to be more accurate than that of any of the other critics. Let us quote what he had to say about the work: 'We could hear in these sounds a distant, wandering note, the cry of birds, the calm music of the stars, the transcendental melody of the majestic hymn of the night—any vision it is possible to conjure up without the aid of sounds which attempt to imitate the crickets, birds, or stars; these sounds evoke the reality of a night beyond the realm of the earth, Bartók's own night. This is one of the most marvellous masterpieces to capture the poetry of nature in Hungary. This grandiose picture of the night must be placed side by side with Kodály's work for female choir, Mountain Nights, as worthy of a place beside the greatest of Hungarian poems, even when we remember that both Petőfi and Vörösmarty wrote poems to the stars.'

We have no way of knowing when the time sequence of 'day, night, day' was taken from nature as a dramatic unity to give shape and significance to a play with three acts or a symphony with three movements. This sequence was used by Shakespeare in *A Midsummer Night's Dream* and by Wagner in *Lohengrin, Tristan* and *Die Meistersinger*. And Tamino, in the recitative of the great duet in *The Magic Flute*, also follows, from C major to C major, the course of the chariot of the sun. He goes into battle with confidence, endures the night of fear and the hell of terror, and emerges with renewed hope: a gay, warm-hearted youth, after a period of trial and tribulation, becomes a man.

But instead of giving more examples, let us recollect the great triptych of Debussy's *Iberia*. In this work we are reminded first of the noisy clamour of a working day in a Spanish city; next comes the enchanted atmosphere of an evening full of the secretive rustlings, wisps of sound and fragrances evoked in Baudelaire's famous poem 'Harmonie du Soir'; and the third section brings us the even greater clamour of the street sounds at the dawn of a day of festival.

It was therefore in the era of Romanticism that we first find this type of 'night intermezzo' and these two extreme forms of the central nocturne. The one represented solitary musing, the other the descent of night in which man is enchanted by nature; the one was expressive, the other impressive, but both expressed the attitude of a man who is cut off from the society in which he lives. Bartók, logically enough, chose to employ the first of these two inherited types. It is true that earlier, like his young hero in *The Wooden Prince*, he had turned to nature when looking for a solution to his problems. But it was not the sensual Impressionism of Debussy for which he was searching; he was feeling his way towards the Expressionism through which Schopenhauer and Nietzsche expressed a pantheistic philosophy, and which was also used by Wagner in *Tristan* and Schoenberg in the *Verklärte Nacht*.

We must remember that it was only as an experiment that Bartók introduced the Nature solution into *The Wooden Prince*. In the slow-fast–slow dramaturgy of the succeeding works, the prince rebels, driven on by the elemental forces of Nature to attempt to escape, albeit unsuccessfully, from the constricting bond of inhumanity. The whirling, barbaric and militant Arabic dances found in the *Suite* for piano, the *String Quartet No. 2* and *The Miraculous Mandarin*, were followed by music that was broken and funereal.

One might very well question whether Bartók's approach to nature and creative method had turned upon itself in his 'The Night's Music'? There was some danger that he might now achieve nothing more than sensual imitation of natural sounds—the sound of crickets, insects or frogs. The sound impressions in this work undoubtedly resemble those found in the middle sections of Mendelssohn's *A Midsummer Night's Dream* and the music in which Debussy conveys his impressions of the suffocating heat, rustling movements and fragrance of the Spanish nights. At this time Bartók added to the musical devices at his command a quality that came very near to noise. In one of his articles in a 1920 issue of *Melos* he discusses the possibilities of sound groupings and effects not according to level of key and harmonic tonal values but according to their creation of an effect of space and strength. In 'With Drums and Pipes' and 'Tambourine', the dance movements of the *Nine Little Pieces*, and in his employment of percussion instruments to give an effect of mysticism in the slow movement of the *Concerto No. 1* and later in *Music for String Instruments, Percussion and Celesta*, the *Sonata for Two Pianos and Percussion* he widened the range of his expressive methods by the use of noise. And in the string quartets composed after 1927 he also made increasing use of pizzicatos, glissandos, muting and other effects of the strings.

Nevertheless, 'The Night's Music' and the slow movements composed during the same period bear only a superficial resemblance to the impressionistic compositions created by apparently similar techniques in which there is deliberate imitation of natural sound, and equally superficial is the resemblance to the futurist compositions fashionable at that time in which there was a deliberate use of noise. Here again Aladár Tóth's judgement proved to be correct. Bartók's new music in which he evoked the spirit of night was inspired by quite different aesthetic experiences. The rustling quality and mystic atmosphere which now became part of Bartók's musical world was a direct development of earlier features—parlando, emphatic slow movements, funeral marches and dirges. The earlier laments and complaints and the moments of dramatic pathos are felt with all the more intensity now that they are heard through the suffocating clutch of the sordino. Bartók achieves an effect of even greater tension when in his use of noise he reduces speech to a whisper, a wail to a sigh, a gesture of desire to abortive longing. A veil of noise is used to conceal the wilfulness of Judith, the struggles of the prince. The horror-music of the female character in the *Mandarin* broadens into infinity, becoming like a fog or spider's web. Thus, nocturnal sounds for Bartók are not noises on this side of music, but as abstract, strangled reductions, go beyond it.

The veils of the fourth chords in the third movement of *String Quartet No. 2,* were the first to drape the until then audible funeral march in black. From then on, it belongs to 'the night's music' type, appearing in the Arabic night in the slow movement of the *Dance Suite,* in the slow movements of the *Piano Concerto No. 2,* and the *Divertimento.* The monotonous frog-music of the piano notes was first heard in the accompaniment of the last piece of *Five Songs,* op. 15: 'Here in the valley...'. A section of the text unmistakenly betrays the content of the basic aesthetic concept: 'Walking in the fog I feel as if I am the only one alive on earth'.

This then is a new nature experience in 'the night's music': the surrender of a man left alone with nature. He does not rebel against nature, nor does he seek redemption from it, or oblivion in the intoxicating rapture of the starry night, but sinks mutely, abandoning his individual existence. The gestures and cries of woe are superfluous. Who would he direct them to? Who can see him? Who can hear him? Nature is no longer a mask for kind or cruel spirits and fairies as in myths, but a merciless, objective and impersonal state of being. 'Where is the stage, outside or within?...' we could ask together with the bard of *Bluebeard.* For the man going through the experience of the night's music it is rather within than outside. Along with nature, his attention is turned inwards. It no longer matters whether the prince hears from without the monotonous words of the toads or whether it is from within his own mind that he hears the Homeric voices of the dead. In the timpani glissandos of the slow movements of the *Sonata for Two Pianos and Percussion* there is perhaps more certainty of the inward source of the rhythmic noise, for this evokes the idea of a beating heart and pulsating blood.

Yet we can also feel the possibility that humanity and conscience, apparently dormant in mankind and withdrawn into nature, may still survive, just as Petőfi's candle burned on through his dark night (in those days the very symbol of conscience and patriotism). The voice of conscience breaks through mere vegetative existence with a melody that is infinitely remote, sad and clear, as heartrending in its sadness as the distant murmuring of the chorus heard during the action of *The Miraculous Mandarin*.

Again we are reminded of Vörösmarty when in his later years he describes the music he heard and the visions that came to him during his own night of sorrow:

> Whose was the muffled sigh
> What howls, cries in this wild stampede,
> Who thunders across the sky,
> What sobs like a mill in Hell?
> Fallen angel, broken-hearted soul,
> Defeated armies, or daring dreams?
> (Vörösmarty, 'A vén cigány' [The Old Gypsy])

This comparison with Vörösmarty is more than a pleasing poetic parallel, for throughout the ages these subjects—the descent into Hell, the myths of resurrection (both of which have found musical expression), the notion of the Sun God who daily traverses the heavens, the myth of Osiris imprisoned within the sheath of a mummy, or of Demeter and Persephone in the underworld—all have been similarly used as a philosophical basis for symbolic works of art. The comparison becomes especially close if we recognize in Bartók's version of this theme of so ancient a lineage, a modern variation of the old *nóta* (art-song) which conveys the infinite solitariness of twentieth-century man in the Europe between the two world wars.

It was because of similar social circumstances, a common history and closely related artistic precedents, that Bartók, following the road of German Romantic Expressionism, approached the musical realm of his

Viennese contemporaries, Schoenberg, Berg and Webern—ascetics searching for truth—to the greatest degree, especially in his music of solitude. The Scherzo movement and the two new-sounding slow movements also underwent the same kind of sound transformation around 1927–28. From the demoniacal shrieking of the ride of the Valkyries and the Mephisto waltzes there developed the nightmare dances of the string quartets and the *Concerto No. 2*. The function of these latest types of movements, their new dramatic significance in Bartók's symphonic works and the extent to which these compositions represented a world outlook more advanced than that of his Viennese contemporaries, was to be revealed in the works to come.

3 NEW ADVENTURES OF 'THE MIRACULOUS MANDARIN'. DELAY OF THE
   BUDAPEST PREMIERE. PREMIERE IN COLOGNE. GRADUAL ISOLATION
   FROM HUNGARIAN PUBLIC LIFE. SUCCESS OF 'STRING QUARTET NO. 3'
   IN PHILADELPHIA. CONCERT TOUR IN THE UNITED STATES

The history of the composition, production and reception of *The Miraculous Mandarin*, and the story of its survival through adverse circumstances, is not yet concluded. And the later chapters of this story make just as sorry a reading as our account of the earlier frustrations which Bartók encountered. The ballet may be said to have been 'murdered' repeatedly like its own hero, the mandarin, before finally achieving the tragic victory of a first stage performance. For it was indeed 'murder' when, time after time, the ballet was announced, only to be postponed. On January 24, 1926, *Új Nemzedék* gave out that 'the world-famous composer has been working on The Miraculous Mandarin for a considerable time and has now reached the point when rehearsals can very shortly begin.' Three days later it seemed that *Pesti Napló* also had information to the effect that the date of the first performance had been fixed for March 22. There was no such première. On March 28, *Budapesti Hirlap* announced that the première would take place 'in the Opera House, at a later date, when the leading parts would be played by Gyula Csortos and Gizi Bajor' (two of the most prominent actors of the day). The name of Gyula Csortos was again connected with a part in *The Miraculous Mandarin* in *Az Est* on October 16, 1928. At the same time the *Budapesti Hirlap* announced that a piano version of the ballet music would be broadcast by Budapest Radio on April 8, played by the composer himself and one of his former pupils, György Kósa. According to a more detailed programme only selections of the music were to be played.

This prolonged delay associated with the première of the ballet at the Budapest Opera House once again reflected the various groups and forces at work in Hungarian cultural and political life. And the most likely explanation of the numerous announcements of a production that failed to materialize, is that these were made as part of a campaign conducted by the composer's most faithful supporters. An introductory paragraph to an interview given by Károly Kristóf on June 27, 1926, gives a clear indication of the prevailing division of opinion in cultural matters: 'For a number of years the Opera House has been planning to put on a pantomime entitled The Miraculous Mandarin by Béla Bartók and Menyhért Lengyel. Because it has been under consideration for such a long time, the work is always scheduled for the end of the season and is always postponed because of "unforeseen difficulties". It should be noted that this is not a work requiring elaborate apparatus. It is a one-act masterpiece that lasts for only twenty minutes. Admirers of the nation's greatest composer have had to wait many years to see this twenty-minute work. Unfortunately, the première has not taken place during the present season either, and this in spite of Radnai's directorship which has been so energetic in other ways. It has been postponed again from the end of this season to next season, and even then it is scheduled only for the latter part of that season, too. It is to be regretted that this latest postponement may very well deprive the Opera House of the great honour of securing the première of a work by our greatest composer for the stage. According to the German newspapers, the Cologne Opera House has obtained the performing rights and plans to stage the work next season.'

The Budapest Opera House did indeed rob itself of the 'great honour' of the first performance. Bartók's ballet was shown in Cologne and many other cities before it was seen in his own native land. The performance in Cologne had already been announced in the *Pesti Napló* on April 8. It was then assumed that the date of the première would be some time during the second week of May. Bartók himself believed that the arrangements were definitive, and in one of his letters to his mother he made it clear that a visit to Pozsony was dependent on the date of the première.

> I may well decide to go to Cologne for the première of the Mandarin. But I do not know yet when it will take place. I am waiting for a reply. But if it should take place immediately after Whitsuntide, then I shall be forced to delay my visit to Pozsony until June.

The 'second week of May' became 'sometime in October', then 'November 20' and the première in Cologne did not finally take place until November 27, and then primarily as a result of the initiative of its conductor, Jenő Szenkár.

In the December issue of *Anbruch* the work was reviewed by Dr. Max Unger who began his account with the words, 'Cologne, the city of cloisters and churches, glorified by Heinrich Heine...' received the work with hypocritical horror. On the following day, Jenő Szenkár was summoned to the presence of the Mayor of Cologne who reprimanded him in no uncertain terms and banned all further performance of the work. Thus the work suffered a preliminary death, like that of its own hero.

The demise of this production of *The Miraculous Mandarin* was but one incident in the continuous battle which raged in Cologne between the progressive theatre and reactionary public opinion:'... the hissing, whistling and stamping continued for several minutes and did not diminish even with the appearance of the composer, and when he stood with the conductor in the aperture of the safety curtain, the noise became an uproar,' wrote Max Unger in the review quoted above. He mentioned that similar scandalous scenes had occurred sometime previously at the première of a prose work. 'The press, with the exception of the left wing, protests, meetings are held by the clergy of both faiths, the Mayor of the city... steps in with dictatorial powers, and the work is removed from the repertoire.'

Unfortunately, the political activities organized by the right wing had a range of influence that extended far beyond Cologne and the borders of Germany. The Cologne affair was reported in the *Pesti Napló* on December 14, when Károly Kristóf noted that the incident had attracted the attention of those 'in high places' and that officials of the Ministry of Culture had notified the Opera House that before beginning rehearsals it would be necessary 'to submit the libretto of *The Miraculous Mandarin* to the Ministry where it would be decided whether or not the performance of Béla Bartók's dance-pantomime would be permitted to appear on the stage of the Hungarian Royal Opera House'.

The suite that was extracted from the ballet music was first performed on October 14, 1928, by the orchestra of the Philharmonic Association conducted by Ernő Dohnányi. On this occasion more references to a performance at the Opera appeared in *Pesti Napló*. In response to questions posed by this newspaper, Miklós Radnai, the director-manager of the Opera, stated that because of Gizi Bajor's many commitments, the main role had been given to the soprano at the Opera, Rózsi Walter, who also undertook parts that required acting ability. He also stated with evident determination, '*The Miraculous Mandarin* must be performed and I intend to have it performed. When will that be? I hope that it will definitely be shown during the second half of this season. As far as the "daring" libretto is concerned, it is true that we shall have to tone it down, but that will not involve us in many difficulties.'

Meanwhile, in the opposing ranks, the Hungarian Royal Ministry of Religion and Public Education continued to maintain the view that the work was not suitable for public performance and on one occasion, in 1930, this body was instrumental in preventing a performance from being given abroad. This action, however, merely served to discredit Hungarian musical culture, for those cities in which there were no conspiratorial links with the clerical and otherwise reactionary forces, began one after another to include it in their programmes. It was the Prague première which finally launched the work on February 19, 1927, from which time it became steadily more and more successful.

The modest fig-leaves of official tribute would hardly conceal the naked reality of quiet but continuous isolation at home. The official records showing that Béla Bartók alternated with Jenő Hubay as representative of the Academy of Music in the Upper House of Parliament are not likely to be read by any but the most diligent of researchers. It was not a distinction about which he could feel any inclination to boast and he declined all official invitations resulting from this office. Hubay and Bartók were both elected in January 1927. In a letter dated May, 1926, he wrote to his mother:

... The day before yesterday, I received an invitation to take 'tea, on Tuesday at 22 hours, with the Hungarian Royal Prime Minister and Countess Bethlen'. You can imagine how pleasant this is for me. The same thing happened just a year ago when I declined on some pretext or other. Now I don't know what I should do. This kind of fuss is very painful to me.

Bartók's growing alienation was further confirmed by the fate of his next works when these were introduced to the public. On July 1, 1927, the *Concerto No. 1* for piano and orchestra was performed at an I.S.C.M. (International Society for Contemporary Music) festival in Frankfurt-am-Main, when Furtwängler conducted the orchestra and the composer himself was the soloist. (An analysis of the work by Antal Molnár appeared in *Melos* a few days before the première.) On July 16, Bartók introduced his *Sonata* for piano, also in Frankfurt-am-Main. Thereafter, the *Concerto No. 1* was to be heard in many foreign cities before it was finally performed in Budapest. It was performed in London on October 10, in Prague on October 16, in Warsaw on October 21 and on November 6 the composer played it in Vienna at one of Anton Webern's famous symphony concerts for the workers. He intended it to be the opening work in the programmes planned for his American tour, but it was *Rhapsody No. 1* that he in fact played once again. The concerto was performed only once during the tour on February 13, 1928, at a concert of Hungarian music given in the Carnegie Hall, New York, when the Cincinnati Orchestra was conducted by Frigyes Reiner. Bartók also played it in Boston on February 17, 18, with Koussevitzky, and again a week later in Cincinnati. It was only after all these performances had taken place abroad that the work received a première in Budapest on March 18, at a subscription concert given by the Philharmonic Orchestra. Scarcely a weak later, on March 23, 24, he played the work in Cologne with Abendroth and again on April 19, 20 in the Kroll Opera, Berlin, with Kleiber. Here we should add the dates of performances in Amsterdam and The Hague—November 8, 10, 1928, with Pierre Monteux conducting the Concertgebouw Orchestra.

The choral and chamber orchestra version of the cycle *Village Scenes* was also first heard in New York and only later in Budapest. The American performance took place on February 1, 1927, the Budapest performance on February 14 of that year. We could add to these examples of neglect the history of the *String Quartet No. 3* dating from September 1927. The people of Budapest first heard of this work on October 2, 1928, when it was revealed that the string quartet had won for Bartók a prize awarded by the Philadelphia Music Fund Society and shared with Casella.

> It has been such a long drawn out affair that I didn't count on winning anything, and only the day before I received the news I had sent the *Druckvorlage* to Universal Edition in order that they might get it printed. As a result, my surprise was all the greater and so much the more agreeable.

So we read in Bartók's letter to Frigyes Reiner dated October 29, the letter in which he also announced that he had finished his *String Quartet No. 4.*

The first performance of the *String Quartet No. 3* he owed to the Waldbauer–Kerpely String Quartet which introduced it in London on February 19, 1929, only two days before the première in Frankfurt given by the Kolisch Quartet. Again it was only after these performances abroad that the Waldbauers played the work in Budapest on March 4, a performance they repeated on the evening of March 20, when they also played the *String Quartet No. 4.* This was one of the increasingly rare occasions when a Budapest audience was the first to hear one of Bartók's works. Another such occasion was the première of the *Three Rondos* based on folk-songs which was heard for the first time at a recital given by the composer on November 29, 1928.

We have long since abandoned all hope of listing each one of Bartók's public appearances abroad and each occasion on which one of his works was heard for the first time in a foreign country. But we must not fail to give some account of his American tour which lasted for two months in 1927–28, partly because the tour provided him with many new experiences and partly because this was his first visit to the country which later he had to adopt as his own. It was his first opportunity to meet the people of America and learn something of their way of life as well as their music.

This was the period when European artists, one after the other, were being discovered and recognized in America. In 1925, and again in 1928, Honegger toured the United States, and Bartók's concert of January 17

242

heralded Ravel's appearance in Portland on February 15, 1928. Bartók had been planning to visit the country for many years and we know from his chance remarks when being interviewed, that many a proposed visit had been postponed. Finally he began his tour of America with a visit to New York on December 22 and 23, 1927. János Demény tells us that he then visited Philadelphia, Los Angeles, San Francisco, Seattle, Portland, Denver, Kansas City, St. Paul, Chicago, Washington D.C., New York again, Boston, Detroit, Cleveland, Cincinnati, and finally Chicago once more. He gave his final concert of the tour on February 27, and on March 6 set out for home, where scarcely two or three days after his arrival he gave a recital at the Academy of Music.

Although these cities were separated by vast distances necessitating wearisome journeys, yet some of them he visited more than once and his programmes were always both varied and significant.

Orchestral performances were followed by chamber music recitals, solo recitals by concerts with other artists and a particularly characteristic English-language lecture that Bartók himself illustrated on the piano. Here for the first time, within the space of an hour and a half, he analysed the framework of new Hungarian music, particularly his own and that of Kodály, and showed in what way this music owed its inspiration to Hungarian folk music. 'The Folk-Songs of Hungary' was the title of the lecture in which he explained the principles of his compositions. A Hungarian text of the lecture was prepared by Bence Szabolcsi and published in *Zenei Szemle* in 1928.

In the course of his American tour Bartók reviewed and strengthened his earlier friendship with Frigyes Reiner and József Szigeti. Reiner, the conductor of the Cincinnati Orchestra, was born in Hungary, and for many years had been one of Bartók's faithful admirers. It was he who had conducted the *Dance Suite* in Cincinnati at the beginning of April 1925, and in New York on January 6, 1926; and one of the first informations of Bartók's intention to visit America came from him when he was interviewed in May 1924 when he also expressed the hope that he would be able to meet Bartók personally at the music festival to be held in Prague during the summer of 1925. But there is no firm evidence that such a meeting actually took place. Their friendship, however, was greatly strengthened by the experiences they shared during the American tour.

Bartók's friendship with József Szigeti was also of some standing. The great violin virtuoso had transcribed for the violin some of the pieces of *For Children* and in one of Bartók's letters, dated October 2, 1926, there is confirmation that this was done to the composer's satisfaction. During the following spring, on April 10, 1927, they gave a joint recital in Budapest. Thereafter, Bartók's letters, which during the previous October had always begun formally with 'My dear Mr. Szigeti', were now addressed to 'Dear Colleague'. During the American tour there were several occasions on which they both took part in the same concert, once in Chicago and twice in New York. And it was in very friendly tones that Bartók wrote to Szigeti in the autumn of 1928.

> My dear Friend, I hope you'll allow me to address you in this way. When I was in America, I had already thought of suggesting it to you, but in that mad bustling country there isn't even time for a quiet talk!

As in the development of Bartók's friendship with Buşiţia, whom he first addressed in familiar fashion in a letter, so it was with Szigeti who also became a life-long friend. When he wrote to Szigeti in 1944 his letter began, 'My dear Joe'.

Letters written to his family give us brief glimpses of a man who thoroughly enjoyed travel, even the trivialities of the exhausting journeys from one place to the next as well as the brief intervals when he was allowed to take breath. Meticulously he made a note of the differences in time. 'Leaving for California on Jan. 2nd,' he wrote to his mother on a card posted from Philadelphia on December 30,

> and will be at the farthest point from you about Jan. 14th (in Los Angeles) —the time difference between you and me will then be 9 hours. When you are going to bed, I shall just be getting up!

On January 10 he wrote to Buşiţia from Los Angeles,

> Dear Friend, here I am at the end of the world, the fairy-tale sea, or rather on the shores of the Pacific Ocean . . . Now there is 10 hours difference between your time and mine.

In the letters written to his family Bartók described the American cities, the people in them and their way of life. As in the letters from Spain and Portugal he included some comments on culinary matters.

244

> I had pork chops for lunch today (in the dining-car), garnished with things that I can warmly recommend to Emil. They were quite ordinary pork chops, with mashed potatoes, hot beetroot, unpeeled apples cut in slices and *sprinkled with paprika*, and a large cup of white coffee.

(The 'recommendation' was for Emil Oláh Tóth, the husband of Elza.)

Bartók analysed American music as he experienced it for a Kolozsvár paper *Ellenzék*. He spoke about the American orchestras with unmitigated admiration.

> The best orchestras in the world, every one of them with a European conductor,

was one of his comments published on March 26, and in the same interview he said,

> Originally, jazz music was very interesting, but all kinds of pseudo-composers fell upon it and made a superficial and dull music out of it and took away its fresh and folk character . . . In the past few days, I have heard real Negro jazz in a speakeasy in Chicago. This was really good. They played from a score but many times they improvised and this was fascinating.

Finally, Bartók's conclusion was quoted verbatim.

> We have no need for jazz. We have beautiful folk music and it is superfluous to fling ourselves into the arms of jazz.

One adventure awaited Bartók which was admirably suited to his taste—a visit to the San Francisco Chinese Theatre.

> I arrived in San Francisco at 8 p.m. and went immediately to a Chinese theatre. It was strange to be wandering about alone in the Chinese quarter in the evening; everything was Chinese, all the people and the signs in the street. I found the Great China Theatre very quickly (luckily the name was written in English as well as Chinese). This is the most interesting thing I have seen in this country so far. I stayed in the theatre till midnight and would so much have liked to stay to the end, but it was not possible. Heaven knows how long a play lasts there! I was the only white man there apart from one attendant.

His description of this experience written for the benefit of his family at home, has something of the atmosphere of his own pantomime, *The Miraculous Mandarin*.

He never complained of being tired but he did write,

> . . . a person gets tired in this 'do-nothing' state. Sitting for days in a hotel,

waiting to get off a train or for a concert to begin . . . this is no atmosphere too conducive to creative work. It's all right for a couple of weeks, but after a time, you've had enough of it.

In his recollections, however, he said, 'I worked a great deal out there. . .' while in an interview given to a representative of *Délibáb* and printed on April 14 he affirmed, 'The situation in Europe is more congenial to me than that in America.'

It is difficult to appreciate the degree of resolution with which this frail man endured an inhuman burden of work and combated a succession of spiritual and physical tribulations. During these years when he was so severely tested, his sensitive constitution did not give way but became more resistant, disciplined as he was by the demands of his own impatient, creative spirit. It was as if the effort of concentration demanded of him, together with his purposeful sifting of values and search for stability, had left its mark on his outward physical appearance, etching the lines of the familiar features.

In the seventh volume of *Zenetudományi tanulmányok* (Studies in Musicology) János Demény included a portrait of the composer dating from 1916, about the time when Bartók composed *Five Songs* (op. 15), *Five Songs* (op. 16) and the *String Quartet No. 2.* He is shown with his head resting against the trunk of a tree and the lines round his mouth give an impression of gentleness and sadness. The eyes are penetrating but darkened by pain, anxiety and suspicion. The hair, already thin, was beginning to turn grey.

Photographs of the composer showing him as he was eight or ten years later, reveal an astonishing degree of change more likely to indicate the lapse of not one but two decades. The features had by now become as firm as a statue. The nose was thinner, the mouth compressed to a mere line and the hair was completely white. We see the same deep-set eyes but the expression is calmer. A sparkling intelligence is evident and there is a hint of the authority that comes from a resolved philosophy. He is shown gazing steadily at a single focal point and there is a glint in the eyes which is at once penetrating and fascinating.

This was the look remarked upon by many of his contemporaries and it is thus that he was depicted in photographs taken at that time. When Dezső Kosztolányi held his famous conversation with the composer in

1925 it was thus that he described him. We give below an extract from his introductory portrait:

'Silver head. The fine silver head of a statue which over the years has been chiselled into a masterpiece by the gentle tapping of the artist's hammer. We see a man of forty-four, the head supported by a body so slight and frail that it seems almost to disappear in a room where even during the day the lights are left burning. His gestures are few, all his energy being reserved for his art; it is in his music that he feels free to embrace the heavens and move in a dream of ecstasy. Under the youthful white brow the lower part of the face is still, only the eyes showing signs of life—dark, flashing eyes, as if the unseen brain, questing for a knowledge of the world without, had burnt in the skull two blazing apertures.'

CHAPTER X

IN THE SOVIET UNION. EUROPEAN MUSICAL FRONTS AND
BARTÓK. CHORAL WORKS. CANTATA PROFANA. 1928–1930

1 WORKS OF MORE POPULAR NATURE FOR THE PODIUM. APPEARANCE OF
THE 'VERBUNKOS' IN THE RHAPSODIES

We have already quoted the friendly form of address which Bartók used
when writing to József Szigeti. 'My dear Friend,' he had written, 'I hope
you'll allow me to address you in this way.' When Bartók wrote to the
famous violinist in the autumn of 1928 he not only used the familiar
form of address, he was also able to give his friend some good news.

> I have to tell you that I have written a minor (12-minute) composition for you
> (based on folk dances); and I want to talk to you about one or two points.

It was in this way that Bartók first made known that he had composed
the *Rhapsody No. 1*, a work specially written for József Szigeti.

Bartók's fame as a composer was by now growing so rapidly that any
new work was assured of popular success. Even in 1926 it was the necessity
to provide works for his recitals that brought to birth so many of his
piano compositions. Now the demand for his works came not only from
pianists but from string instrumentalists, orchestras and string quartets.
However, the demands of the concert platform were those of an established audience which generally preferred to listen to the easier works of
a composer whose works for the theatre and orchestral compositions
were often weighty as well as novel. Audiences especially favoured the
folk-song arrangements which they had come to know and enjoy at the
recitals given by the composer himself. It was in response to this demand
that Bartók had produced the *Three Rondos* which is very similar in
mood to folk music and which was written almost at the same time as the
Concerto No. 1 and the *String Quartet No. 3*.

Only a few years previously Zoltán Székely had transcribed for the
violin what had been known as the 'short' *Romanian Dances* and which
now became *Romanian Folk Dances*. In 1927 Szigeti had adapted for

the violin a selection of pieces from *For Children* and in 1931 Endre Gertler transcribed the *Sonatina*. The folk-song arrangements also lent themselves very readily to orchestral adaptation. In 1927 Tibor Polgár asked for and received permission to orchestrate the *Fifteen Hungarian Peasant Songs* and some selections from the *Ten Easy Pieces* (according to the music historian Ferenc Bónis, he actually completed the orchestration of the *Old Hungarian Dances*). In 1917 the composer himself transcribed the *Romanian Folk Dances* for orchestra. In 1931 his orchestrated version of the *Sonatina* appeared as *Transylvanian Dances*. During the same year he transcribed for orchestra some of his youthful piano compositions and entitled the work *Hungarian Sketches*. Two years later, he orchestrated the *Fifteen Hungarian Peasant Songs* and called the work *Hungarian Peasant Songs*. The practical reason for these transcriptions is to be found in a letter which Bartók wrote to his mother from Mondsee on August 15, 1931:

> . . . There is nothing particularly important ever since but I think it will be of special interest to you that I have orchestrated An Evening [with the Székelys], the Bear Dance, A Bit Drunk, a dirge and another short piece. This is now an orchestral suite which I put together for the sake of money. This is the sort of thing that will be performed because the music is pleasing, it is not very difficult to play, and it is by a 'known' composer. It is certain to be played a great many times, on the radio, etc. We shall see.

Bartók also made some concession to practical considerations when he composed the two *Rhapsodies* for violin. These two works, the second of which was offered to Zoltán Székely, were composed in the same year and indeed almost simultaneously. Original, and mostly Transylvanian Romanian dance melodies can be found in the two *Rhapsodies*. László Somfai identified them with certain melodies in the great collection of Romanian folk music (*Romanian Folk-Songs* by Béla Bartók, edited by Benjamin Suchoff, The Hague, 1967). Even as he wrote them down the composer had ideas for a variety of possible forms in which these works could be performed and the transcriptions for orchestra were made almost at the same time as the original pieces for violin with piano accompaniment.

> Both the 1st and the 2nd Rhapsody were originally written for violin+piano (or orchestra). The first I transcribed later for the 'cello too; or, to be more

> exact, I had always imagined it, from the very outset, as a parallel work—for violin+piano, and for 'cello+piano; but it wasn't until some time later that I transcribed it in the 'cello+piano version,

he informed László Pataki, musicologist, in a letter written at the beginning of 1921. (A journalist who interviewed Bartók at Kharkhov reported on January 12, 1929 that the composer was working on the orchestration of the *Rhapsodies* during his tour of the Soviet Union.) The performer's task was made the easier by the fact that it was possible to play the movements of the Rhapsodies as individual pieces.

The *Rhapsodies* did indeed achieve an early popularity. Zoltán Székely introduced the *Rhapsody No. 2* in Amsterdam on November 19, 1928, when he appeared together with Géza Frid. It is most likely that the second *Rhapsody* was heard in Budapest before the first, the 'cello version of which was played there on March 20, 1929, as part of a programme which also included the *String Quartet No. 4*. It seems that Szigeti first played the orchestral version during the autumn of 1929. The earliest comments on the work came from Königsberg where the orchestra was conducted by Hermann Scherchen. It was performed in Budapest on November 22, by the orchestra of the Budapest Philharmonic Society, and on November 28 Szigeti played it again, this time in London with Scherchen conducting. The violin and piano versions of the two *Rhapsodies* were heard at a concert held in the Academy of Music when Zoltán Székely and Béla Bartók were the recitalists.

In 1930 Pablo Casals included the 'cello version of *Rhapsody No. 1* in his repertoire.

> ... He plays my rhapsodies all over Europe ... probably at his concert in Pest, too,

wrote the composer in a letter written to his mother from Basle on December 10. Casals did indeed perform the work at a concert held in one of the Budapest concert halls, the Vigadó. It was reported in *Az Est* that Bartók interrupted one of his tours in order to return home especially for this concert and that, contrary to his usual practice, he travelled by night in order to arrive in good time.

Though it is true that the *Rhapsodies* were exceedingly popular, they were more significant than most pieces which are written for special occasions. This is a fact acknowledged by his contemporaries at the time. An analysis of these works reveals many interesting musical relationships.

In both *Rhapsodies* there are two consecutive dance movements, a slow movement and a fast one. Here we find an immediately recognizable kinship with the two closely related sonatas for violin and piano. Like the sonatas, the fast movements of the *Rhapsodies* are Transylvanian in character; their derivation goes back to the finale of the bagpipe dances in the early folk-song series. The 'fast' *(friss)* of the *Rhapsodies* is more closely related to the *Romanian Folk Dances* and the *Old Hungarian Dances* for it is more loosely constructed than the finale of the sonatas. This is neither a sonata nor a rondo; the structure is more like that of a movement with trio. The two movements are not interrelated; they exist in their own right, which makes the structure of the work quite unlike that of a sonata. However, the music for the violin and for the piano, separately and together, reminds us of Bartók's sonata and chamber music. The relative independence of the piano part was commented on in contemporary reviews. The sharpest differences between the two *Rhapsodies* and the two *Sonatas* is to be found in the character of the first movements of these works. In the *Sonatas* we hear an expressive 'Viennese' sound, with wide intervals, unevenly articulated time divisions; but in *lassú*, the slow movement of the *Rhapsodies*, we find taut rhythmic folk dances of *verbunkos* character.

It was long before Béla Bartók again accepted the *verbunkos* as an example of the pseudo-folk, petit-bourgeois music which was a degenerate form of nineteenth-century popular music. He turned instead to a study of genuine Hungarian folk music. For many years he rejected utterly the chauvinistic Hungarian music heard everywhere during his childhood; he felt no interest in his own youthful compositions and made use of his memories of this music only to satirize it. It was when he had become completely familiar with instrumental folk music that he was gradually drawn towards an appreciation of the Hungarian dance style which could be traced back through history and was a genuine form of folk music. In the *Dance Suite* he put the series of dances of a folk character as a ritornelle, while in the *Rhapsodies* he connected them as independent movements with the *friss*. Some ten years after composing the *Rhapsodies* Bartók again made use of this splendid heritage which from then onwards became an organic part of his continually expanding world of musical ideas. We find it in *Contrasts,* the *Divertimento* and the *Concerto No. 1.* In one manuscript version of the solo part of the great *Violin Concerto* of 1937–38 the first movement was marked 'Tempo di Verbunkos'. These words are omitted from the final version but the stately character of the *verbunkos* is retained in the intonation of the movement.

Finally, any account of the formative influences on Bartók's development as a composer must include a recognition of his close association with Kodály whose influence was particularly strong at this time. When Kodály recognized the significance of the song of Árgírus and made public his discovery, he was in fact revealing an unbelievably rich source of Hungarian folk music and a wealth of folk traditions retained by the people. With his appreciation of the organic unity that exists between folklore, the history of music and the history of literature there began a new era in the development of Hungarian musicology. This new approach even today stimulates creative research amongst Hungarian students of folklore, aesthetics and the history of music.

But the predominant influence on every aspect of Hungarian musical culture comes from the embodiment of this approach in Kodály's own compositions. This is not the place for a necessarily lengthy explanation of something to which we have already referred—the way in which the *Psalmus Hungaricus* revived and unified at various levels the Hungarian historical traditions. Year after year, Bartók had the experience of seeing and hearing works by Kodály which revived memories of historical events which had been cherished in folklore. *Háry János* was completed in the mid-twenties, in 1925–56. It was also then that Kodály began an impressive series of choral works which included *Lengyel László* and the *Tánc nóta.* The *Three Songs,* completed in 1929, was based on verses by Balassi and an unknown poet of the seventeenth century. It was then too that he began to compile the ten volumes of *Hungarian Folk Music* and to compose the *Spinning Room.* The *Dances of Marosszék,* inspired by instrumental folk dances, appeared in 1927, and even in 1930 Bartók was already including them in programmes for his own recitals. And after the première of *Rhapsody No. 1,* Aladár Tóth wrote in *Pesti Napló* on March 22, 1929, '. . . the first dance is an old Transylvanian dance melody, the style of which, in Kodály's arrangements, is reminiscent of dances from Marosszék and Kászon, so that it belongs to the kind of thematic material that Bartók now comes into contact with for the first time.'

We are well aware of Bartók's high opinion of Kodály as a creative artist. Just as Kodály's influence had been decisive in Bartók's discovery of Hungarian folk music among the peasants, so now we can be certain that it was due to Kodály that Bartók accepted the theory of the true significance and unity of the traditions that had survived throughout the history of Hungarian music. Once he had accepted this concept of the people, Bartók was no longer cut off from the historical development of his country, isolated like the Sleeping Beauty in a private dream of his own, but was gradually enabled to assume an outlook through which he was associated with the social and historical realities of his time. The introduction of a *verbunkos* character into his music is one clear indication of this transformation of his outlook.

Any assessment of the nature of this recognition of popular tradition, any evaluation of the work resulting from a renewal of the creative energies of these two composers during the late nineteen-twenties, and any conclusion as to the social timeliness of their new outlook, requires some consideration of the world situation at that time.

2 Concerts and experiences in the Soviet Union

Concert tours in the West were by this time no novelty for Béla Bartók. He had become accustomed to travelling across Europe from one great city to another, he was regularly the guest of the British Broadcasting Corporation, he often appeared in the concert halls of London, and every year he toured Germany, Italy, France, Holland, Switzerland and Czechoslovakia. And only one year after his visit to America in 1927–28, he toured the Soviet Union.

The Soviet Union at that time maintained a lively contact with progressive cultural circles throughout the world. Musical events of international significance were reported, there was an interest in new music, while in the Viennese *Anbruch* and other periodicals, there were articles about the Soviet musical life. Many famous artists were also invited to be the guests of the Soviet Union. But for understandable reasons, there was little contact between Hungary and the Soviet Union. It is true that Bence Szabolcsi and Aladár Tóth, who were at that time engaged in the task of editing the *Musical Lexicon*, invited the musicologist Viktor Belyayev, and other Soviet specialists, to be associated with the project. This, however, was merely a reflection of the attitude of our progressive intelligentsia and the friendly spirit of well-known Hungarian musicians, and was not an expression of the official attitude. It was through the medium of various international music organizations that the names of Béla Bartók and Zoltán Kodály had become known to music lovers in the Soviet Union. Bartók's works first reached the Soviet Union in 1923, at an exhibition of German books and manuscripts, and during the following year both Bartók and Kodály were discussed in an article on German music prior to that date, by Igor Glebov (Boris Asafiev). In 1925, Bartók's first two string quartets and one of his violin sonatas were played in Moscow, and *Sovremennaya Muzika*, the periodical of the Modern Music Society, published a study of the string quartets by Egon Wellesz and also the *Autobiography*.

Some of the contacts with the West mentioned earlier are worthy of further consideration. On February 13, 1928, in order to prepare the way for Bartók's tour due to begin in January 1929, the *Dance Suite* was given a première by the famous 'leaderless orchestra', the Persimfans (Pervy Simfonitchesky Ansambl). With this addition to their repertoire, Belyayev and Mosolov made known something of the artist's life, work and art. And here perhaps it is not unfitting to recall that among the enthusiastic sponsors of the Persimfans was the violinist Lev Ceytlin, whom Bartók had encountered during the Rubinstein Competition in Paris in 1905 and who had been described by Debussy in letters written from Russia in 1913 as a 'Debussyste intransigeant'.

It seems that Bartók made very careful preparations for this tour to which he looked forward with more than usual eagerness. It was to Szigeti that he turned for information, for by that time the violinist was well known in the Soviet Union.

> And then I should like you to give me some information about Russia,

he added in the letter in which he informed Szigeti that he had just completed the *Rhapsodies*.

It was arranged that he should set out at the end of the year, and he travelled by way of Warsaw to arrive in Moscow on January 2, 1929. There he waited for seven hours for a train to Kharkov. The long wait was described on a card which Bartók sent to his wife.

> ... I arrived here in real Russian weather; Moscow looks just as one knows it from pictures: the roofs loaded with snow, so that they seem ready to cave in, and little one-horse sledges tinkling everywhere. It is not so terribly cold; only about 10°C. And this cold isn't so disagreeable as that of, for instance, New York or Chicago ...

There are a few complaints about high prices and there is a postscript in which he again mentions his impression of the Russian winter:

> Maupassant is right when he says that one ought to come here in the middle of winter (just as one ought to go to Africa at the height of summer); it is then that the country is at its most characteristic.

He began his tour of the Soviet Union with a piano recital in Kharkhov on January 6. This was followed by another piano recital in Odessa on January 9, a matinée of the composer's work in Leningrad on January 16, and on January 20 he was the solo recitalist in his *Concerto No. 1* with the Leningrad State Philharmonic Orchestra. On January 24, he gave the piano recital in Moscow which brought to an end a tour which had lasted for just one month.

On his return to Budapest, Bartók was questioned by Bence Szabolcsi about his impressions of a country which until then had been quite unknown to him. Bartók's conversation with Bence Szabolcsi was published in *Zenei Szemle* in the second issue of 1929. Bartók's comments were carefully discreet.

> Alas, twenty-five or twenty-six days are scarcely sufficient for anyone to study in any depth a strange world and must be satisfied with those many suprising details which come to the surface at first glance,

he concluded. However, some of his letters and other writings give us, in his own intimate and objective style, an idea of his most important experiences during this visit.

His first impression was of the prevailing liveliness of the people and that the country was bustling with activity. Naturally, he did not fail to notice the hardships suffered by those engaged in musical activities both as regards organization of their work and from an economic point of view. The shortage of foreign currency was one of his first observations.

> ... They performed the *Dance Suite* from the pocket-edition because they hadn't enough money for the complete score published by Universal Edition (my publishers in Vienna)—not enough foreign currency (that is, the only kind they will accept in other countries). On the other hand, they can pay for copies of the score in roubles, of which they have an unlimited supply ... There are virtually no good pianos at all; the old ones have all worn out and cannot be repaired because all the materials have to be imported and, as I have already explained, this is impossible.

Behind this objective and occasionally critical tone, however, it is not difficult to hear a note indicative of sympathy and interest:

> Of the contemporary Russian musicians, Stravinsky is heard quite frequently, but I notice that the one they consider to be most truly Russian is Prokofiev and not Stravinsky. This is undoubtedly due to the attitude which Stravinsky has personally adopted. I remember that he once declared in my presence that he had no desire to return to Russia because he dissociates himself from the leaders there.

He gives a vivid description of an opera which he saw in Kharkov and found particularly interesting:

> I heard music for the stage on only one occasion, when I went to see *The Barber of Seville* at the Opera House in Kharkov. Here too there was nothing exceptional about the orchestral performance but the way in which the opera was produced, as if it were a kind of revue, was surprising in several respects. The direction was full of original ideas and on the stage there were constructivist stylized sets which during the more animated scenes (Rosina's aria in the first act for example) unexpectedly moved forward with the actors or bent together, etc. I was even more surprised when, during the intermezzo of the second act (the stage here remains empty throughout), suddenly, in a sort of improvisation, all the servants of Bartholo's household appeared (even 'players' which do not actually appear in the play at all), and sang a popular trio with great success, all the time 'acting' the part of servants having a gossip in the kitchen. It is obvious therefore that they make additions to the piece and improvise so that one can recognize the quality of intimate drama and the readiness to experiment which we have already noticed in the art of Russian directors and actors, and which is reminiscent of the old 'commedia dell'arte'.

He was particularly attracted by the folk-music research projects in Russia. He had always been interested in the wealth of ethnographic material offered by the Soviet Union. Even before the First World War he had planned to tour Russia for the purpose of collecting folk music. After the war, in 1919, he collected folk-songs in the remote high country of the Carpatho-Ukraine, and in 1928, at an international congress in Prague, he met the famous Ukrainian folklorist, Filaret Mihailovitch Kolessa, with whom he later kept in touch by correspondence. Now that he was able to see for himself what was being done in the Soviet Union he was understandably enthusiastic in his descriptions.

> The folklore collections I saw, particularly those in Petersburg, were impressive and most valuable. I found that every summer they collect folk melodies regularly, and this they will continue to do until their stock of phonograms runs out, for then they would have to import new equipment, and that is impossible. In two years they recorded 2000 cylinders in Petersburg and about 500 in Moscow. (Here, to my great surprise, I also found our latest editions of Hungarian folk-songs.)

In an article printed in *Magyar Zene* in December, 1961, the Soviet music historian, I. Nestiev, gives us more information about Bartók's visit to the Leningrad Phonogram Archives. '... In Leningrad, he was invited by Professor Asafiev to visit the State Institute of Art History of which the Professor was then the director. This invitation coincided with the opening of the ethnographic sound-recording archives, where all the material collected on ethnographic expeditions was assembled. Bartók was shown the notations by one of Asafiev's pupils, Yevgeniy Hippius, a talented Soviet folklorist. For nearly an hour the Hungarian guest listened to the recording with rapt attention. First they listened to the peasant songs about the Russian landscape in winter which were noted down on the shores of the White Sea, in the Region of Piniega. Bartók was enchanted by these ancient melodies and compared them, appropriately enough, to Bach's "hidden two-part polyphony". Next, he listened to recordings of the famous folk ensemble, the "Vladimir Hornplayers" conducted by Kondratiev. Bartók was fascinated by the originality in the playing of the orchestra composed of village shepherds, the freshness of the rhythmic irregularities and incongruities, the original treatment of polytonality, the changes in the bass and the ornamented solo in the higher register (known as "shrieking"). He followed this part of the programme with exclamations of wonder. The programme of folk music came to an end with a recording of the heroic epic song of North Osetia. The originality of these songs lies in the fact that a constantly interchanging bass is sung by five singers while the melody is sung by the solo tenor. Bartók found the melody utterly fascinating and he immediately noted that the style of the songs was rather like that of the medieval European organum. Professor Hippius tells us that Bartók listened to the recordings in the most natural manner, showing a lively interest like a great artist. From some of his observations it was obvious that as a creative artist he was moved by the aesthetic experience of listening to the music even more than he was stimulated by the strictly scientific and theoretical aspects of the material.'

Bartók also came away with a favourable impression of Soviet audiences.

> At first I had no definite impression of the concert audiences. I noticed that some pieces were received with a certain objective reserve and polite applause, but that at the end of the concerts, the audience became really enthusiastic; when this happened, the audience demanded an encore which they chose themselves, even when the artist was performing together with an orchestra. My own early experiences as a recitalist have made me familiar with this practice which, though it is now practically extinct in Europe, is still flourishing here . . . Generally speaking, it is my impression that if the programmes are to their liking, the audiences in Russia are more demonstrative than elsewhere in Europe.

These impressions of Soviet musical life were acquired during a visit which lasted for three and a half weeks. Before considering Bartók's own impact on Soviet musical circles we must mention another tour, this time of Switzerland.

Immediately after returning from his tour of the Soviet Union, Bartók gave two recitals of his own works, in Basle on January 29, and in Zurich on January 31, 1929. At these concerts he appeared together with Stefi Geyer and Ilona Durigo. These concerts are chiefly significant in that they resulted in the formation of a close friendship between Bartók and some of his admirers in Basle, among them Mrs. Müller-Widman who became a faithful correspondent. It was also as a result of these concerts that Paul Sacher, director of the Basle Chamber Orchestra, ordered larger works by Bartók which he introduced in that city, for instance the *Music for String Instruments, Percussion and Celesta*, the *Sonata for Two Pianos*, and *the Divertimento*.

3 STRENGTHENING OF BARTÓK'S CIRCLE IN HUNGARY. RECEPTION OF HIS ART IN THE SOVIET UNION AND IN THE WEST. CONFRONTATION OF BARTÓK THE 'FOLKLORIST' AND THE 'AVANT-GARDIST'. STRONGHOLDS OF INTERNATIONAL MUSICAL LIFE

In contrasting Bartók's success abroad with the antagonism he encountered at home, there is a danger of oversimplifying the situation. It would not be true to say that he gained recognition and fame in other countries while at home he met only opposition and neglect. The assessment of his position made by József Szigeti and quoted by Jenő Feiks in *Pesti Napló* on April 12, 1927, was still applicable. 'You have no idea,' Szigeti told the reporter, 'how much he and Kodály are respected abroad. Without them, modern music is inconceivable.'

Nevertheless, the situation described by Szigeti was already changing, new attitudes were being adopted, more complex international links were being forged between musicians and musical associations in different countries, and there emerged a number of focal points for these activities.

There was a gradual improvement in conditions at home. For many years it had been obvious that Bartók had the support of a strong minority of intellectuals who were associated with the progressive intelligentsia of other countries. From the mid-twenties onwards, the musical wing of this front had been greatly strengthened by yearly reinforcements of young composers graduating from the Kodály school. The ranks were led by those who are today in their sixties and were followed by the next generation over the course of twenty years. Meantime the research workers engaged in a scientific study of the new Hungarian music concentrated their activities around the production of the periodical *Zenei Szemle* and the preparation of the *Hungarian Musical Lexicon* which finally appeared towards the end of 1929. As musicologists they were inspired by the pioneering spirit of Bartók and Kodály whose work was an example to any one active in this field. Before very long, the personal enthusiasm of this devoted band, their educational programme and their propaganda began to bear fruit. In *Pesti Napló*, on March 22, 1929, Aladár Tóth was able to write of a recital of Bartók's works given on March 20, in the following terms: '...his greatest success... indeed, the first performance of the fourth string quartet with which the programme ended, brought to the composer more acclaim than he has previously been given in Hungary. No Hungarian composer has been received with such applause since the Psalmus Hungaricus...'

On the home front, therefore, there was increasing support for the new music. But while Bartók's works became every year better known and more highly regarded abroad, where he was written about with increasing frequency, his works were received in individual countries with varying degrees of approval. Conservative voices were still to be heard from time to time in one country or another, and even, as we have seen, in Cologne, on the occasion of the premiere of *The Miraculous Mandarin*. During the following years, however, the division of opinion became even greater, not only about Bartók's music but about European music in general. A very good indication of the prevailing climate of opinion is to be found in contemporary reviews and critical studies, for the critics were obliged to take a stand about such a formidable artistic form as that presented by Bartók's compositions; indeed, the very density and variety of his music was one cause of the division of opinion. In this connection, the collection of press cuttings put together by János Demény in his documented biography of the composer is particularly interesting.

Bartók's tour of the Soviet Union during January 1929 took place during the decline of RAPP, the Russian Association of Proletarian Writers. This body came into being after the civil war, at the same time as the fraternal association of artists and musicians, a group of radical artists with whom they had close ideological links. In their ideology they were very close to the bourgeois radical artists and especially the Futurists, who fought with definite revolutionary aim to destroy, in alliance with the working classes, the bourgeois social system and its ideology. We have already made reference to one of the greatest members of this group—Mayakovsky; and it was specifically in reference to Bartók's music that we commented earlier on the lively contacts between Soviet artistic circles of the twenties and the progressive, radical groups of artists in other European countries.

At the beginning, this point of view and mode of expression could not count on wide public support. In the late nineteen-twenties, a heroic period in the development of Soviet socialism, it was particularly difficult to maintain an attitude which involved criticism and even rejection of the national traditions which were the common heritage, while at the same time proclaiming exaggerated conceptions of proletarian cult. And around 1930, the national Romantic tradition developed into a stormy opposition which for a time threw the good and bad memories of the RAPP period into oblivion. It was against this background of artistic policy that we must consider the reaction of the Soviet press to Bartók's recital tour.

In one section of the press, particularly in the principal cities, Bartók was merely mentioned by name or reviewed very briefly with no special understanding of his work. But before Bartók's arrival in Leningrad, the public were provided with an introduction to his life and art by the well-known aesthetician, Mihail Drushkon, writing in *Zhizny Iskusstva*. And in a short review which appeared in Moscow, Viktor Beliaiev strongly criticized the Soviet Philharmonic Society for their failure to arrange more concerts of the composer's works and for neglecting to provide opportunities for the people to become more thoroughly acquainted with his compositions. The Ukrainian people were certainly interested in Bartók, as may be seen from the fact that he was interviewed in Kharkhov as well as in other places. We can only gain an overall impression of Soviet opinion if we put side by side all these comments, noting particularly A. Veprik's study of Bartók's music which was written specially for the occasion of his visit, and the earlier writings of Asafiev, Beliaiev, Mossolov, and others. In this way we may also learn something of the problems confronting musical circles in the Soviet Union at that time.

When the *Dance Suite* was performed during the previous year, Beliaiev had written a review which set the tone for a general assessment of Bartók. He placed him as the representative of a 'young national school,' a national Romantic developing along the same lines as the Russian 'Five'; it was this, he said, that set Bartók apart from his western colleagues who were seeking to find a new music by reviving old, bourgeois traditions. M. Grinberg, the critic who wrote for *Vetchernaya Moskva*, expressed a similar view, though in different terms. He differentiated Bartók from his western colleagues by defining the latter as 'Western, European and urbanist' in their tendencies, whereas Bartók embodied in his work the 'old traditions of folk music'. Many of the Russian critics tried to find some kinship between Bartók and the Romantic masters of the previous century, particularly with Liszt, and also, though less frequently, with Grieg. All of them, however, were chiefly concerned to note the relation between the strivings of the new music and the traditions of folk music. They also judged their Hungarian guest by how the 'ethnographic composer' dealt with musical culture.

In the periodical of the All-Union Central Reference Bureau, Anton Uglov remarks on the 'fresh' and 'refined' quality of Bartók's folk-song compositions. He attributed this quality to the fact that Bartók was 'moving in a different direction' from that taken by 'other ethnographic musicians' who 'offer nineteenth-century harmony as an accompaniment to folk melody'.

In the Soviet press as a whole there were not many critics who shared Uglov's view. The characteristic tenor of most of the articles written on this subject was their preoccupation with the problem of the division, even opposition, between folk music and musical innovation, the authors of these articles holding the view that the new elements in Bartók's art were quite separate from the folk-music elements. This was the question to which Asafiev tried to give an answer in 1924 when he wrote about Bartók's folk-song compositions, in the yearbook of *Novaya Muzika* (New Music). 'It is very difficult,' he wrote, 'to establish whether the character and form of his work is determined by folk music or whether the role of folk music is subordinated to his own method of arrangement. In Béla Bartók's art the stylist has not yet admitted defeat and as a modernist and an individualist he expresses himself with more force than as an ethnographer anxious to demonstrate the true significance of folk music and new forms of a music based on the musical traditions of folklore...' Five years later, when reviewing a concert at Kharkhov, N. Gitelis stated most emphatically that in his view there were two Bartóks. He began his article unequivocally with the statement that the composer was 'in part ethnographer... in part innovator of the new European music, who can compete with artists of the extreme left wing'. Throughout his article he continued to write of Bartók as a man with two separate roles and he concluded by deciding that Bartók was most effective in his role of ethnographer. In a more detailed study, Veprik's analysis of Bartók's dual role is even more extreme, with the result that he greatly diminishes Bartók's stature as a creative artist (*Muzika i*

Revolutzia 1929, No. 6). Indeed, he depicts a social background against which he attempts to justify this theory of Bartók's duality, saying that the composer's early work was progressive in character but that in the rest of his compositions he had retained Hungarian bourgeois traditions which were by now quite reactionary.

Towards the end of the RAPP period, those who were fanatical in their opposition to folk music and national traditions found little opportunity to express their views. A. Groman, who wrote for *Proletarskiy Muzikant,* was alone in his criticism of Bartók from this point of view. He found the folk-song compositions uninteresting and their material 'monotonous' and 'poor'. He opined that Bartók was an 'artist of purely local significance' and that he had been transformed into 'a great European figure' merely because of an interest in the creative artists of particular nations shown by European intellectuals in the changing political climate of the post-war years.

While in the Soviet Union there were fewer attempts by the bourgeois avant-garde to express opposition to the revival of folk tradition, in Germany, and particularly in the German press, such opposition was gaining strength. The first voice to be raised on behalf of the bourgeois avant-garde on this subject was that of Theodore Wiesengrund-Adorno. Thoroughly grounded as he was in musicology and philosophy, and arguing as he did from correct basic premises, he nevertheless reached the incorrect conclusion that only in the music of Schoenberg and his school was there to be found an uncompromising expression of our age and of the social crisis which he considered to be incurable. It was from this point of view that he criticized Bartók's *Concerto No. 1* after the première in Frankfurt-am-Main. '. . . Until now,' he wrote in *Die Musik* in September 1927, 'Bartók was different from other folklorists in that for him folklore was merely a starting point, something which stimulated him as a composer and permeated his subjective intentions. Today, and since writing the Dance Suite, he has retreated to a naive folklorism which in his greater works he had long since outgrown . . .'

Thus in assessing Bartók's music, Adorno too was chiefly concerned with its relation to folk music, though his point of view was quite contrary to that of the Soviet critics who used the same measuring rod. He denigrated that which the Soviet musicians recognized and listened to with pleasure. Eighteen months later, he too praised the *String Quartet No. 3* when it was performed there by the Kolisch Quartet on February 21, 1929. During the same concert there were performances of both Bartók's and Schoenberg's third string quartets, also Alban Berg's *Lyrical Suite*, also composed for string quartet. 'Then followed Bartók's new string quartet,' wrote Adorno, 'certainly not in that sphere that no one except Schoenberg would attempt, but still, an outstanding piece in its own right. It is greatly to Bartók's credit that though for a time he fell under the influence of Stravinsky's fascinating personality, he had the courage to break away and retreat to the manner of his finest works, the string quartets and the violin sonata. The discipline of form in classicist pieces indeed had a creative influence upon him... Without doubt, in his string quartet, Bartók has reached new heights as a composer.'

The Hungarian composer and critic, Sándor Jemnitz, was in spirit closer to the Viennese school than any of his compatriots. He was a former pupil of Schoenberg and a personal friend of Adorno. His reviews of Bartók's work at that time reflected Adorno's own attitude. His final conclusions about Bartók's work may well seem to us to be full of contradictions but these were nevertheless typical of the thinking of avant-garde bourgeois critics. When the *Concerto No. 1* was first performed in Budapest, he found that the third movement '... rises above Bartók's rondo forms based on folk-song traditions' (*Népszava*, March 20, 1928). And after the first performance of fifteen of the *Twenty Hungarian Folk-Songs* he wrote, '... in his new folk-song transcriptions, he came to terms with the audience and solved the problems inherent in the use of a naturally dissimilar genre ...' (*Népszava*, February 1, 1930).

Sándor Jemnitz always studied Bartók's music with care and remained his faithful admirer. His reviews were based on a real understanding of the significance of Bartók's compositions. Adorno was compelled by his own knowledge and strong convictions to write about the Hungarian master in a manner fitting to both of them. The result was that in his writings he tried to please both composer and critic. The ideological dogmatists of the bourgeois avant-garde who strongly disapproved of folk music and who were far below him, hastened to pass judgement on Bartók in a much more open and uncompromising fashion. In an article which appeared in *Die Musik* in 1927, Kurt Westphal dismissed Bartók with the impatience which was typical of this group. 'Bartók's works,' he pronounced, 'which were originally inspired by folk music, have now become second-hand creations; they may be important and of some artistic value, but they cannot be counted as original compositions.'

Opinions such as these occupied only a small proportion of the space devoted to Bartók in the European press at that time. But even at the beginning of the nineteen-thirties, Bartók himself was aware of a spreading epidemic of articles in which no respect was shown for compositions in which folk music was used as a point of departure. In his article *A népzene jelentőségéről* (On the Significance of Folk Music) he felt obliged to refute those critics who had expressed such derogatory views.

It is important that we too should be sensitively aware of these one-sided and exaggerated judgements which were expressed only tentatively at first but which later became increasingly vehement. For several decades, Hungarians were haunted by the spectre of a divided Bartók, by 'two portraits' of him—the 'ideal' and the 'distorted', an attitude which in its turn led to an unhealthy polarization of the whole concept of music.

In tracing Bartók's career we have seen how the progressive forces were compelled by the exigencies of war and the necessity to struggle against the reactionaries, to unite on a broad front in an alliance of the working-class movement and the bourgeois radical intellectuals. In the grip of historical necessity there was no time for rarefied ideological debates and it was certainly no time for discussions on aesthetics. Whatever the medium through which they expressed their views, the creative work of the avant-garde represented one aspect of the working-class struggle insofar as it attacked an obsolete framework of society and the way of life within that society.

But when the burden of the war was gradually lifted, the bonds which had united these various groups during the troubled years they had faced together, were loosened. The artists who in spite of the essentially heterogeneous nature of their views had shown a united front during the war, now began to strike out on their own, sometimes joining one or other of the various groups which were either in agreement with, or willing to acquiesce in, the prevailing structure of society and to accommodate themselves to the political situation.

The bourgeois avant-garde, with its gift for outspoken criticism, had been a valuable ally of the working class during the war years, and in some countries the struggle against reaction kept alive this alliance even in the post-war years. But events in the Soviet Union demonstrated that in the years immediately following the war, rebellious movements of a diffuse nature were inadequate as a means of satisfying the new needs that were beginning to be felt in post-war society.

A natural historical development which was to be observed during the post-war years among the Soviet people was their gradual assimilation of a musical heritage which consisted partly of traditional folk music and partly of bourgeois music. The significance of the revival of folk music, both in the Soviet Union and in Eastern Europe generally, was undoubtedly a historical reality. Tardy bourgeois revolutionaries allied themselves with the poor peasantry and drew inspiration for their art from folk traditions; their movements, defeated one after the other, were finally absorbed by the proletarian revolutionary movements through which they enriched their experience of folk art.

In traditional folk music there were revealed much older strata of musical traditions which were the common heritage of many peoples, providing sources of inspiration for many different kinds of music and at the same time facilitating the discovery of the music of the colonial peoples.

In this respect the Soviet critics were quite right to ask of Bartók that he should work in a musical tradition based on folk music. They were calling for a music in the living cultural tradition which was familiar then, as it is today, to millions of people. They forgot, however, that in their emotional response to art the people were more conservative than in their scientific and political understanding, and that recent events were still too close to make feasible a reassessment of cultural tradition so as to give it new meaning. Later attacks of the folk-music heritage were in fact based on the feelings of the masses who cherished in memory illusions of a Romantic bourgeois nationalism, those illusions which Bartók and Kodály, struggling against the popularity of the *verbunkos* and folk-art songs, had challenged in their own works.

Israel Nestiev has recorded that in those days Asafiev '. . . dreamed that modern music would return to a new kind of simplicity, to the basic wealth of primitive music which lies hidden in the folk music of many

266

countries.' A dream of some kind of folk classicism was evidently at the heart of all Soviet musical policy at that time. Yet classicism can only flourish in the soil of ideals that have become reality, and have achieved that reality through everyday personal experience. Without this, classicism is a fiction requiring to be constantly nourished by illusion.

There was a similar danger inherent in the other kind of tradition which stimulated the revival of the revolutionary era of classical bourgeois art music. We find this idea expressed by A. Veprik, in a study of Bartók written in 1929, when he writes, 'Beethoven proved to be much closer than those who stood nearer to him in time such as Schoenberg, Hindemith and Křenek, because Beethoven's art, with its dynamism, its faith in victory and its militant challenge, reflected the revolutionary bourgeois class of those times, while Schoenberg, Hindemith and Krenek, on the other hand, depict the disintegration of this class.'

We cannot even maintain that the Soviet critics failed to realize the danger of traditionalism and therefore did not try to avoid it. In 1924, Asafiev understood the 'living essence' of folk music to include 'the new forms that were based upon it'. In the article quoted above, Veprik went on to say that he could not approve of Beethoven in his entirety, and attempted to defend himself from possible accusations of having absorbed a bourgeois heritage without sifting the good from the bad. What in fact happened, however, was not dependent upon the good intentions of Soviet critics but was the result of historical necessity; thus for many years it seemed that not only had past traditions been revived but the past itself was being perpetuated, those who recalled it being hopelessly petrified in bourgeois conservatism so that they prevented the emergence of new ideas and a new way of life. The avant-garde of the bourgeoisie used the proletarian cult as a weapon to combat the ideas of such people, but in doing so they destroyed good as well as bad traditions, and in the name of artistic progress and an abstract ideal of freedom, sacrificed noble social principles while attempting to destroy a hated social system in its entirety. At the same time, musical tradition was by the same process reduced to a mere craftsmanship of form.

Two groups participated uncompromisingly in this battle. In one group were the bourgeois conservatives, convinced reactionaries who clung unquestioningly to the artistic standards of the past and dismissed the avant-garde with derision. This consistent approach became a conscious cultural political force under German fascism which adopted just such an attitude to folk tradition as well as the classical tradition. This is the origin of the fear of folk tradition experienced by the most extreme innovators who labelled as nationalist all attempts to make use of folk music.

Ranged against this group of bourgeois conservatives were those artists who were searching for a new means of expression, who were anxious to give their work a new content and whose aim was to provide in music a basis for their social ideas and socialist programme; in these attempts they tried to avoid the pitfall of an illusory and reckless classicism while at the same time refraining from innovation for its own sake. It is not probably right to include Bartók among this group of artists.

The complexity of the historical situation precludes any easy explanation of the 'leftism' of music so frequently mentioned at that time. It was a term capable of taking on different meanings according to the views of the speaker. Bourgeois critics used the word 'leftist' as a term of abuse with which to deride the views expressed by the avant-garde and to convey that these had been culled from the working class movement; they were in fact guilty of generalizing on a subject which roused their own feelings. Nevertheless, there was at that time some justification for this use of the word.

Certainly it is true that in Western and Central Europe, particularly in Germany and Austria, but for a time in the Soviet Union also, the intellectuals who were attracted by or belonged to the party of the workers, were notable for their support of the most extreme forms of artistic innovation. The gulf between these two opposite points of view was made clear on the momentous occasion of the concert held on November 6, 1927, when Anton Webern conducted the Workers Symphony Orchestra in a performance of Zoltán Kodály's *Psalmus Hungaricus* while István Stasser conducted Bartók's *Concerto No. 1* for piano with the composer as soloist. It is obvious from his comments in the *Neue Freie Presse* that the critic Julius Korngold was well aware of the objective situation and even understood its origins, but his approach was that of subjective antipathy. 'The piano becomes a machine,' he wrote, 'the orchestra a machine workshop, and all this in the service of brutal, crudely materialistic noise, and all signifying a kind of Hungarian–Russian–Bolshevik machine art.' And he went on to develop this theme saying, 'Recently one of the well-known pioneers of this trend spoke about the "party" with the loyalty and sincerity which has been accorded it for many years now. Yet in its propaganda and in its policy, in periodicals and the press generally, this party would appear to recognize and value only that which lends it support...'

This critic was wrong to identify Bartók through his music with the political left wing of the avant-garde. Such a description fails to convey the profound and organic unity of his music with the social and artistic movements of the left. In placing Bartók on the left, however, he came very close to the truth. But it would be appropriate at this point to give some details of Bartók's contacts with German intellectuals and through them, with politics. One such contact is revealed in a letter written on August 4, 1931, to Imre Weisshaus (later Pál Arma), one of his former pupils. Weisshaus had been expelled from the Academy of Music in 1925 under the pretext that he had failed to show respect towards one of the teachers there, but it was well known that the real reason for his expulsion was his connection with the left. He had emigrated to Germany where he settled in Dessau, and where it was probably at his invitation that Bartók gave a recital to left-wing intellectuals in October 1927. In the letter written in 1931, Bartók refers to this and also to the difficulty of selecting suitable works for another concert.

> ... the problem of what I should actually play. There wouldn't be much sense in playing any of my earlier works in this *fortschrittlich gesinnt* milieu ... So let us say I will play the Sonata (13 min.), improvisation (10 min.), 2 or 3 items from *Out of Doors* and a few of the *9 Little Piano Pieces* (10+8 min.); that would make 41 mins. altogether. Anything else??...

The concert did not take place but the letter and the programme remain as documents of some interest to the biographer for they show that Bartók was avoiding pieces of merely popular appeal and even when considering his folk-song compositions was careful to select the most demanding—the *Improvisations*.

In relation to politics and artistic problems of international concern, Bartók's stand was therefore quite unambiguous. The years that followed provided many painful opportunities for him to make public his beliefs.

4 Social ideals of the beginning of the century become topical again in the Hungary between the two wars. Textual and openly political works by Bartók from the end of the 1920s. Avowal of faith in the brotherhood of peoples

With the approach of the Second World War, the united front policy became even more necessary in Hungary than elsewhere in Europe. In many ways our country had scarcely advanced even so far as to achieve a bourgeois democracy and already the proletarian revolution was urging us on. The alliance of the feudal and capitalist ruling classes forced those faithful to the ideals of bourgeois and socialist progress into a continuous joint battle against the most reactionary forms of class oppression and for the most basic rights of freedom.

The policy of consolidation associated with the name of Prime Minister István Bethlen was nourished from 1925–26 by loans from the West. These had the effect of attracting foreign capital investment into the country and there followed a period of rapid industrialization. But this lasted for barely two or three years after which the world-shaking crisis of the great depression settled on an economy that was as vulnerable as it was subservient, bringing with it unparalleled misery to the poorest in the land. For even in wealthier countries the wage-earners and the small businessmen were ruined. It was the consequence of our own backwardness that it was the agricultural workers and small landowners who chiefly faced destitution in Hungary around the year 1930. The situation was very similar to that of 1905.

Rapid industrialization brought a transitory boom, and the ensuing crisis encouraged a strong tendency to revolutionary activity among the working class. More and more intellectuals found themselves without work and those in sympathy with their ideas rallied to their support. The prevailing mood of bitterness brought about the rather spontaneous demonstration of September 1, 1930. After the collapse of the Bethlen government, the fascist temper of the ruling class was revealed more openly.

Eminent literary historians maintain that with the end of the war, after the suppression of the revolution and the death of Ady, there was a break in the continuity of the period of literary militancy associated with his name. During the years of counter-revolution the literary leadership was assumed by the generation which had made its début after 1910 in the pages of *Nyugat*. Zsigmond Móricz, for instance, who was older than either Bartók or Kodály, indeed one of the oldest of Ady's contemporaries, had been unknown until his short story, 'Seven pennies', appeared in 1908.

In the history of Hungarian music, the continuous creative activity of Bartók and Kodály is seen to have spanned the forty years between the revolution of 1905 and the end of the Second World War in 1945. Their contribution to the generation of artists and writers who came to maturity in the years between the wars was formed by the spirit of Ady, and their music represents a continuous loyalty to his ideals which is not to be found in the literature of that period. It was therefore only to be expected that they should express views on social questions which they, as artists, had formulated in similar situations which had recurred time and time again.

Hungarians of Bartók's generation were faced continuously with the heavy burden of a twofold struggle, for there was an inescapable connection between the class struggle and the struggle for national liberation. In fact, Horthy transferred to his own 'court' the Viennese atmosphere of the Austro-Hungarian monarchy; he even surrounded himself with Habsburg princes. Within a short time, his alliance with German fascism further ensured the continuation of national oppression. The duality which throughout history had been the national heritage was characteristic of Hungarian culture. It was thus that Bartók and Kodály were made to feel that once again they were living in the militant atmosphere they had known as young men.

Hungarian peasant music and folk-songs, therefore, continued to have a significant role in the class struggle and the movement for national freedom; and since they could now be heard in new and modern forms, their sphere of influence was considerably extended. And as far as the future was concerned, their significance lay in their complete inseparability.

When Kodály wrote over and over again that the guardian of national culture was the Hungarian peasant tradition, he was identifying the nation with the people. This was at a time when official historians were engaged in propagating the restoration of a feudal system.

A remarkable number of vocal folk-song compositions were written by Bartók at this time. In 1929, he prepared the *Twenty Hungarian Folk-Songs* for voice and piano. (Five of these songs were transcribed for orchestra in 1933.) A year later, in 1930, the year of the *Cantata Profana*, he wrote *Four Hungarian Folk-Songs* for mixed chorus. In 1932, he wrote another choral work, the six pieces of the *Székely Songs* for male chorus. In 1935, he completed the *Twenty-Seven Choruses* for children's or women's chorus (published in 1936 by Magyar Kórus), and during the same year he completed the 3-part male chorus *From Olden Times.*

These works were undoubtedly inspired to some extent by the example of Kodály. In *Twenty Hungarian Folk-Songs* the stimulating influence of the first volumes of the 10-volume series, *Hungarian Folk Music* can be seen, while in the choral works, the effect of the Kodály choruses and the movement organized around them can be observed.

In the *Twenty Hungarian Folk-Songs* Bartók's use of folk-music material was the same as in *Improvisations* and *Village Scenes*, that is to say, he shaped, edited and harmonized the chosen folk-song until his own new version could stand in its own right. The complex and at times instrumentally difficult texture of the *Hungarian Folk-Songs* for mixed chorus shows that Bartók was attempting to deal with choral material in a similar way. After the *Székely Songs*, which were sometimes rousing in the impressive manner of choral music, Bartók arrived at the mature and individual style found in the eight volumes of choral works written for either solo voice or for children's chorus. These works are masterpieces in miniature, simple in construction, easy to sing, and containing every innovation and effect possible to instrumental art. They are closely related to the *Dialogues* written in the polyphonic spirit of 1926, the *Forty-Four Duos* for violins and the *Mikrokosmos* which Bartók was working on during this period. Listening to these compositions, we are reminded of Kodály's recollection that in his later years Bartók studied avidly the vocal contrapuntal art of Palestrina.

In drawing attention to the parallel composition of instrumental and choral works during the succeeding years, we are reminded that choral works were among the compositions produced by Bartók during the years of the First World War. But now there are other aspects of Bartók's art to be considered. The chronological sequence of the compositions mentioned above has been deliberately disregarded in order to draw attention to the new features of Bartók's attitude to folk-song. He himself said that it was simply because of its musical characteristics that he was first attracted to folk music. But it is obvious that during the late nineteen-twenties the composer paid considerable attention to the words of the songs which he chose as much for their content as for their social significance. In the *Four Slovak Folk-Songs* and in the Slovak folk-songs for male voices we see for the first time that the text has a significance of its own, and this is also true of *Village Scenes*. From the *Twenty Hungarian Folk-Songs* onwards, the idyllic atmosphere of the folk-song was clouded over with the 'shadow of blood,' to use a phrase from *Bluebeard's Castle*. More and more frequently the vocal works present us with a picture of a suffering and oppressed people. The first volume of the *Twenty Hungarian Folk-Songs* consists of sad lyrics gathered together under the title *Szomorú nóták (Sad Songs)*: 'A tömlöcben', 'Régi keserves', Bújdosó ének', 'Pásztor nóta' (In Prison, Old Lament, The Fugitive and Herdsman's Song respectively).

The *Four Hungarian Folk-Songs* for mixed chorus returns again to tales of misfortune: 'A rab' or 'A börtönben' (The Prisoner or In Prison) and 'Bújdosó' (The Rover). Finally this series reaches a climax in the text of *From Olden Times* in which the Hungarian peasant who is the hero is utterly crushed by his feudal lord.

The first part of the lyric ends with a description of the peasant's lot: 'He works all day, but only for others. They steal his crops and do not even thank him. For any offence he is thrown into a dungeon without food or water ... He is harried without mercy, by the judge for his taxes and his dues, by the shopkeeper and the innkeeper for the price of their goods. No defence avails him so long as they can scent his blood. There is no man unhappier than the peasant, his misery is greater than the ocean.

'And if finally, in the sweat of his brow, he grows the wheat and bakes the bread, what does the landlord give him in return?'
Then comes the dogged response of the chorus:
'A club, a club, a club.'
It is true that the verse ends in an apotheosis of the beauty of Nature which embraces the simple life of the peasants; but this is a vision less

representative of reality than of Bartók's own nostalgia for the country and his wish to pay homage to the final vision in the *Psalmus Hungaricus*.

Such was the living content of Bartók's and Kodály's music and ideology in the late nineteen-twenties. Kodály's historical work was synthesized from a democratic history of Hungary that was 'folk-written, folk-made, and folk-suffered'. In his works, as in Bartók's two Rhapsodies, the voices of Ady's two Kurucz characters are raised once more, and their message, moreover, is not unlike that which was cut short by Ady's death. Nor did this go unremarked by the chauvinist officials of the day. On May 1, 1929, in *Budapesti Hirlap*, Emil Haraszti violently attacked the educational programme based on folk music which was at that time only just beginning to be put into practice. He began by pouring scorn on those who, 'with pipes and drums', claim that peasant music 'replaces everything from the beginning of history to the gypsy music' and then he condemned to failure every experiment which 'puts the most loved Hungarian music on the Index and attempts to force a certain official artistic trend on the people'. He took advantage of the wildly popular success of the *palotás* in Poldini's *Farsangi lakodalmas* (Carnival Wedding), saying that 'its ideal, Hungarian gypsy style ... stands closer to the atavistic thinking of the Hungarian people than all the music of Kodály's Háry János with all its faithful folklore and artistic primitivism ...' Finally, he left his readers in no doubt as to his own position: 'We have greater need of gypsy music now than ever before, for the gypsy is Hungary's own militant irredentist, whose like as an artist cannot be found anywhere else in the world. Hungarian sighs are carried to the four corners of the world by the gypsy violin, and Hungarian hearts are heard beating in his music.' In conclusion he asks, 'Should we then, at such a time as this, deny him as a Hungarian?'

János Demény rightly saw in Haraszti's words the very spirit of István Tisza. In his comment on the article the ghost of Tisza crosses swords with the reincarnation of Ady's ideals. Haraszti was handing down the conception of that aristocratic Hungarian world with its gypsy music against which Bartók had taken up arms over twenty years previously. And we can be sure that it was no accident that the article appeared on May 1.

But those artists whose work was conceived and executed in the name of the people, were confronted by an even more dangerous enemy, a concept rooted in a distorted nationalism. Adherents of this pseudo-nationalism completely reversed the concept of a nation identified with its own people—as in Kodály's works; Haraszti spoke for them when he described pentatonic monody with its proven Asiatic origin as 'atavistic Hungarian musical thinking'. We have already seen such comments used by reviewers as terms of praise for Bartók's compositions. This concept of 'the folk,' accompanied as it was by a nationalistic peasant mythology and racist theories, was a new departure in the realms of ideology, and its attendant belief in national superiority was more dangerous than any of the theories which had preceded it. Such an ideology offered an excellent opportunity to divert the people from the tense class struggle and from the influence of the revolutionary forces and to lead them into the morass of national conflict and 'racial' hatred.

This ambiguity, caused by the very weight of historical compulsion, was to be found in Hungary between the two world wars in artistic as well as political circles. The lure of a policy offering an 'all-national' solution to the country's problems presented dangers that were by no means imaginary; this policy was unfortunately shown to be increasingly effective in the hands of those responsible for the official cultural prog-rammes. This reactionary concept of unity was in direct opposition to the views of the radical bourgeoisie and the left wing. In the sphere of music, too, it was possible to sense the danger of polarization then threatening Europe with the false conflicts pivoting around bourgeois conservatism on the one hand, and bourgeois innovation on the other. During this period, Hungary was threatened by bourgeois conservatism along three fronts: on one side were the bourgeois concert audiences who remained obstinately faithful to the classical masterpieces inherited from the past, on the other side were the supporters of a nationalistic folklorism, while on the left was the new threat inherent in the social-democratic cultural taste of the working-class movement. Among the adherents of nationalis-tic folklorism there was a right-wing element that eventually gained control of the youth organizations which, though influenced by the right, were officially sponsored; and they also penetrated the ranks of those whose aim it was to revive interest in church music in the name of the first Catholic king of Hungary, St. Stephen (1001–38). The kind of music which gained ground in the workers' choirs was choral music of a poor standard originating from the German–Austrian petit-bourgeoisie.

The complexity of the situation necessitates at this point an account of the development of Hungarian music during the succeeding years and a recognition of the part played by various progressive groups of intellectuals in sustaining revolutionary ideas among the artists of that period. There had never been the slightest doubt but that Bartók and the narrow circle of followers who really understood him, remained dedicated to the cause of social progress through unity and a rejuvenated outlook for the arts. For many reasons—his outstanding personality, his activities as an artist and as a scientist, his attitude to his fellow men, his relations to the intellectuals who were drawn to the working-class movements in both Germany and Hungary—for all these reasons, Bartók's place was unquestionably among the left-wing intellectuals of his day. Nor is there any exaggeration in our affirmation that between 1929 and 1930, in his political opinions and artistic outlook, he leaned even more strongly to the left.

We have seen from the account of his choral compositions that Bartók was very conscious of the social content of folk-song. This may be confirmed by a brief reference to his musical dramaturgy. In the summer of 1931, he adapted some of his earlier compositions to synthesize a work consisting of five movements which he entitled *Hungarian Sketches*. He attached no particular significance to this work, looking upon it only as a necessary addition to his repertoire, a work of popular appeal and therefore likely to prove financially rewarding. Yet he chose the movements with the greatest care. The central slow movement is a transcription of the second of the *Four Dirges* which we have already mentioned as a small-scale work readily recognizable as a preliminary study made before Bartók embarked upon *Bluebeard's Castle*, and incorporating the sad basic tone of *The Wooden Prince*. Here again, the slow movement is enclosed by the two Scherzos, just as the most significant part of the ballet music is found between the two dances. The first of the Scherzos is the wild *Bear Dance*, the second *A Bit Drunk* (from the *Three Burlesques*). In the ballet, the fast–slow–fast sequence of the movements appeared within the framework of a romantic, pantheistic conception of Nature, a force capable of solving men's problems;

but in the *Hungarian Sketches*, the inner movements are enclosed by two compositions based on folk-songs, indicating that the solution of men's problems must come through the organization of a society that is truly human.

Bartók now experienced a reawakening of his feeling for the Hungarian countryside, and while the number of his recitals abroad diminished, he began to give more concerts in country districts. In April 1929, when he gave a concert in Békéscsaba, he was interviewed by a representative of the Békés County publication *Közlöny*.

'He was very friendly,' wrote the reporter, 'and said that he was surprised and pleased by his reception in Kecskemét and that his visit to Szeged had been a wonderful experience. He thought that the concert audiences in country towns were very musical and progressive in their tastes, and composed of people who were gradually becoming interested in new music. He said that for him the countryside was more important than the capital. Cultural developments were more possible in the country. He spoke of the pure and unspoiled soil of the countryside, the unbiassed judgement of its people.'

It is possible that the musical understanding of concert-goers in the country districts was not quite as 'pure' and 'unspoiled' as Bartók believed to be the case. But it was true that more and more members of these country audiences were beginning to appreciate Bartók's works. In October 1929, when Bartók's works were played at a concert in Sopron, the local paper, *Nyugat-Magyarország*, printed an interesting discussion between a certain 'Alter Ego' and 'Diogenes' concerning the understanding and appreciation of modern music. And the same subject was touched upon less openly in a paper entitled *Debrecen* in a review written by Árpád Fáy on March 4, 1931.

'Many people stayed away from Béla Bartók's concert because of their unwarranted resistance to modern music. It is hard to credit that there can be so much indifference on the part of people who usually give loyal support to good music and are prepared to make sacrifices in its cause. This indifference is fostered by a prejudiced public opinion without foundation in fact which, confused and subversive in its ideology, senses something destructive in all that is new; intent upon defending its own culture, it rejects even the opportunity to be persuaded.' This critic went on to confess that he found in Bartók's playing a note of agitation, and he made other comments which show that he was trying to correlate Bartók's art with left-wing opinions. There is confirmation for this belief in the fact that during Bartók's visit to Debrecen, he was received by the Ady Society, a literary circle with a progressive outlook.

The number of occasions on which Bartók was well received in country districts, was, happily, on the increase. Perhaps we may specify one such occasion: the *Hungarian Folk-Songs* for mixed chorus were first performed in Kecskemét by Zoltán Vásárhelyi and his choir. Vásárhelyi had studied with Zoltán Kodály and is still a leading personality in the field of choral art in Hungary.

Bartók's outlook was taking on an increasingly international perspective, and it was this which separated him most surely from the narrow confines of nationalistic folklore. He had always been characterized by a breadth of outlook, even when he was only just beginning to compose and to engage in scientific activities, and this wider vision was to remain with him to the end. Now, however, he began to make speeches at international conferences at which he made particularly impassioned appeals for a joint programme of folk-song research and a mutual exchange of information. He spoke on this subject at a meeting of the Comité International de la Coopération Intellectuelle—organized by the League of Nations—in Prague, in 1928. In his capacity as a member of the Comité he made a further appeal at the beginning of July 1931, this time in the League of Nations. In the following year, in March and April 1932, we find him in Cairo at the International Congress of Arab Music.

More detailed accounts of his experiences with the League of Nations, where the proceedings at times verged on the ridiculous, make it clear that there was little hope of success for Bartók's schemes. Nevertheless, these meetings provided an opportunity which he greatly appreciated of meeting the great humanists of other countries, notably Thomas Mann and Karel Čapek. Basic to all his endeavours was the thought expressed later in the last sentence of his essay *Miért és hogyan gyűjtsünk népzenét* (Why and How To Collect Folk Music).

> If only all the money spent on armaments in one year throughout the world would be used instead for folk-music research, it would suffice to pay for a collection of all the folk music in the world.

The wide range of his interests is also illustrated by a statement made in Kharkov and quoted in *Literatura y Mistecvo* on January 12, 1929: '... He said that he was deeply interested in Ukrainian music and would like to devote more of his time to it in the future so that he could study it more thoroughly and make full use of its possibilities ... He promised to keep in close touch with Ukrainian musical circles and he also asked our own composers to write personally to him.' And here we should also mention the many articles, essays and statements—as well as the finest of his compositions which will be discussed later. Meantime we quote below from the memorable letter which Bartók wrote to the outstanding Romanian musicologist Octavian Beu, and in which the composer wrote of his work more fully than on the other rare occasions when he spoke about himself.

The letter was originally written in German on January 10, 1931, when Bartók was travelling from Berlin to Budapest, and refers to Octavian Beu's study of those works by Bartók which were inspired by Romanian folk music. Bartók's letter contains detailed comments on the study and is a valuable source of information about the composer's beliefs as a man and as an artist, and about his life and work generally.

During this period it sometimes happened, even in Slovak reviews, that Bartók was accepted as a Slovak composer because of the number of his compositions which were inspired by Slovak folk music. Beu, however, had openly written of Bartók as a *compositorul român*, that is, a Romanian composer. Bartók also comments on this in a statement which reflects all the nobility of a man who is equally conscious of a national loyalty and an international creed.

My views are as follows: I consider myself a Hungarian composer. The fact that the melodies in some of my own original compositions were inspired by or based on Romanian folk-songs is no justification for classing me as a *compositorul român;* such a label would have no more truth than the word 'Hungarian' applied to Brahms, or Schubert, and is as inappropriate as if one were to speak of Debussy as a Spanish composer because their works were inspired by themes of Hungarian or Spanish origin. In my opinion it would be better for you and other scholars to give up these labels and confine yourself to remarking that 'here and there, in this or that composition, there are themes of Romanian inspiration'. If your view were correct, I could just as easily be called a 'Slovak composer'; and then I should be a composer of three nationalities! As I'm being so frank, I should like to give you some idea of what I think about all this.

My creative work, just because it arises from 3 sources (Hungarian, Romanian, Slovakian), might be regarded as the embodiment of the very concept of integration so much emphasized in Hungary today. Of course I do not write this for you to make it public; you will yourself beware of doing so, for such ideas are not for the Romanian press. I only mention it as a possible point of view which I encountered about 10 years ago, when I was attacked in the most violent manner by our chauvinists as a musical Scotus Viator. My own idea, however—of which I have been fully conscious since I found myself as a composer—is the brotherhood of peoples, brotherhood in spite of all wars and conflicts. I try—to the best of my ability—to serve this idea in my music; therefore I don't reject any influence, be it Slovakian, Romanian, Arabic or from any other source. The source must only be clean, fresh and healthy! Owing to my—let us say geographical—position it is the Hungarian source that is nearest to me, and therefore the Hungarian influence is the strongest. Whether my style—notwithstanding its various sources—has a Hungarian character or not (and that is the point)—is for others to judge, not for me. For my own part, I certainly feel that it has. For character and milieu must somehow harmonize with each other.

It is by no means certain why Bartók abandoned the style of his two Rhapsodies and little purpose would be served by attempting to determine the cause. It is possible that he was sufficiently aware of the political situation to realize the dangers inherent in a nationalist interpretation of his music; he was aware that music based on folk dances was now being related to the historic national style of the *verbunkos;* he was possibly influenced by memories of his own early struggles against popular national music and his ingrained dislike of it; and he was also guided by the social instinct that was by now inseparable from his sensitive intuition as a musician. It is at any rate certain that it was not until ten years after the appearance of the Rhapsodies that he again employed such a national tone. His attitude to folk music was imbued with a keen sense of history, as may be seen by the fact that he recognized and represented in his art, without consideration of national differences, the common lot of peasants everywhere. This was the approach which brought him close to the revolutionary content of the European heritage of bourgeois music: the significance of his own compositions being the manner in which he achieved organic unity between the European classical heritage and the deepest levels of East European folk music. In order to achieve his own more all-embracing classicism, he set himself further aims, as Aladár Tóth noted when writing about the Hungarian première of the *String Quartet No. 4.* 'Kodály,' he wrote, 'has described the finale of Bartók's first quartet as a "return to life." 'This phrase is equally applicable to the fourth quartet too. But in contrast to the youthful spirit of the first quartet, the mood reflects the composer's maturity; it expressed the moment when, after a period of torment and tragedy, yet still sustained by his vision of the truth, Bartók returns once again to the creative activities in which he was to attain perhaps even greater heights than those he had already scaled.

It is clear from all the documentary evidence that Bartók's concept of 'integration' as quoted above bore no resemblance to the irredentist idea of integration that was so often mentioned in Hungary at that time. This letter—the mere use of the phrase 'clean source'—is a clear indication that in these anxious and troubled times we are already hearing the voice of the man who composed the *Cantata Profana.*

5 'Cantata Profana'. Influence of the kolindas. Plan for a Romanian–Slovak–Hungarian cantata triptych. The hymn of Exodus in the 'Cantata'. Musical construction of the work

The *Cantata Profana* owes its inspiration to one of Bartók's most profound experiences of folk music—his discovery of the Romanian Christmas songs known as *kolindas.* Whenever, during the course of the following years, he resumed his work on them, he was always stirred by pleasant memories of the period when he had devoted all his energies to the task of collecting folk music.

Even in 1933, in the middle of an objective scientific account of Romanian folk music written for the *Schweizerische Sängerzeitung*, there is a hint of personal enthusiasm in his references to the *kolindas.*

> ... their texts are also extraordinarily valuable and interesting both from the point of view of folklore and cultural history. These Christmas songs, however, should not be interpreted as in any way corresponding to the pious Christmas carols of Western Europe. The most important parts of the texts, perhaps one third of the whole, is in no way related to the Christian Christmas. Instead of the story of Bethlehem, they tell us how an unconquerable lion (or stag) is

miraculously slain; one of the legends is about nine brothers who went hunting in the forest until they turned into stags, and there is a marvellous story about how the sun wedded his sister the moon . . . etc. Thus, pure vestiges of pagan lyricism! . . .

In 1915, this fresh musical experience stimulated Bartók to write the two series of piano transcripts of *kolinda* melodies, *Romanian Christmas Songs*. He always enjoyed playing these at his recitals. Later he made a scientific study of his collection of *kolindas*. In 1922, he presented this collection to the Romanian government, but a project for publishing it in Romania met with constant delays and was finally abandoned. Bartók had originally prepared two copies of the manuscript, '. . .one for Bucharest,' he wrote to his mother in May 1926. 'I handed this over on Thursday at the Romanian Legation, and the other is for London . . .' In Romania, it was the Association of Composers who considered the possibility of publishing the collection, but we learn from Bartók's letters to Constantin Brăiloiu, the eminent Romanian ethnographer and musicologist, that he corresponded for a time with the Oxford University Press concerning the possibility of publishing the collection in England. Neither of these projects materialized and in 1935, the collection was published by Universal Edition. Bartók always remembered with bitterness this failure to cooperate on the part of a neighbouring country.

> There was a horrible amount of work involved, especially as regards the text. But it was just this aspect that interested me most,

he wrote to Bușiția on September 18, 1926. The English text presented even greater difficulties. During this period, he wrote irritated letters complaining that the translations of the texts were completely lacking in style. He did his best to compensate for their inadequacies in other ways. Meanwhile, as we have seen from his vocal and choral compositions based on folk-song, he became more and more interested in the texts themselves. He was haunted by the text of the *kolinda* about the old man with the nine sons who turned into stags. He translated this text for himself, working from the original Romanian text and used it as the basis of a libretto in Hungarian. And in 1930, he composed the *Cantata Profana: The Nine Enchanted Stags*, for double mixed chorus, tenor and baritone soloists, and orchestra. As was his custom he wrote the date of completion on the manuscript—September 8, 1930.

This is a strange creation which stands apart from the rest of his work, and which is, perhaps for that very reason, the most personal confession made by the composer. Its singularity is emphasized by its history. For Bartók did not intend that it should stand on its own. It was perhaps in 1933 that he wrote to Sándor Albrecht,

> . . . I am planning 3 additional pieces which will be similar in scope. I shall add them to it in such a way that they will all be linked by one idea, yet it will be possible to play all three of them separately . . .

Bartók's intention is not made clear in this letter. He may have been planning one work comprising three cantatas in which case he intended to add to the completed Romanian cantata two more, one with a Slovak theme, the other with a Hungarian theme; or he may have been planning three more works in addition to the *Cantata Profana*. The letter is ambiguous and both interpretations are equally possible. Nor is our uncertainty lessened by the undated manuscript of a draft text which has been made available by Mária Keresztury. In this text, Bartók makes use of the ancient theme of rivalry between flowers, adapting it to make a story of three contending worlds: 'Three different worlds contended with each other,/Three different worlds, three different countries.' These are the opening lines of the text. But this contest has no outcome. None can say which is the most beautiful of these worlds. The testing point was to have been revealed later. 'Better that you show me, fine and lovely countries./ Fine and lovely countries, the thing you can create./Who creates the loveliest, let her be the first,/Let her be the first and let her be my choice/ . . .' The three countries prepare for the contest but there the text comes to an end, it was never finished. In tone, the verses resemble folk lyrics and the metre is the same as that used in the text of the *Cantata Profana*. The repeated phraseology also constitutes a direct reference to the text of the *Cantata Profana*. There is every indication that this fragment is linked to the grouping of cantatas, but we are left in doubt as to whether the groups were to consist of three or four units. This text would have been equally suitable for use as one relatively independent summary of a three-part work based on Slovak, Magyar and Roma-

283

nian themes respectively, or as a third section summarizing two others. This text at any rate clarifies somewhat the significance of the proposed work: Bartók's belief in the brotherhood of all countries.

The history of the following decade shows that there was still no easy way to achieve brotherhood between the countries. Bartók's hopes remained unfulfilled. The *Cantata Profana* stood alone to remind us of his vision. The wonder is that Bartók should have ventured even to dream of completing such a work when even this one masterpiece had to wait until May 25, 1934, before being given a hearing, and then only in London. It was not heard in Hungary until November 9, 1936.

The *Cantata Profana*, therefore, was not to instigate a series of works in similar vein. And in searching for its antecedents, it is only possible to find a hint of its qualities at different levels in the earlier works. One of the most important sources was certainly the *kolinda*. Another source was the tradition which stems indirectly from Bartók's interrupted series of works for the stage. Undoubtedly, his many bitter disappointments when composing for the theatre contributed in no small measure to the development of his interest in planning large-scale choral works with epic themes. The most recent of these disillusioning episodes concerned the repeated postponement of the premiere of *The Miraculous Mandarin*.

There was a long-standing tradition for the genre in which the *Cantata Profana* was composed; Bartók was influenced by the revival of the Baroque heritage and by his own experiences during the preceding years. These factors were responsible for the title and also for many features of the work itself. The use of soloists, orchestra and chorus were indispensable properties of the genre. This is clearly illustrated by the assignment of an important dramatic function to the chorus which, like the narrator in Bach's *St. Matthew Passion*, has the role of eye-witness and commentator. The introductory passage recalls ancient mythology, evoking as it does the idea of a tale handed down through the ages from one generation to the next, a swirling sound in which we do not at first recognize a reminiscence of the opening chorus of the *St. Matthew Passion*. But this heritage is clearly revealed in the excited 'turba' scenes of the hunters' chorus and the elevated tone of the soloists with their richly ornamented style of singing.

Kodály's *Psalmus Hungaricus*, written seven years previously, was the latest work which could be looked upon as an antecedent exemplifying and encouraging a revival of the historic tradition of the genre. Bartók's *Cantata Profana* was clearly influenced by this work. Careful study reveals that even in their outward stylistic features there is a relationship between the two works. This may be seen by comparing the mystical ecstasy of the *Psalmus Hungaricus* with the mystery of the magic transformation spell in the *Cantata Profana;* or by noting the piling-up of fourth imitations of the 'true ones' in the *Psalmus Hungaricus* and the 'and their antlers' in the *Cantata Profana.* Yet in spite of such similarities, these passages, as always in Bartók's work, have a life of their own as organic parts of the masterpiece and of his own incomparable personal world. The resemblance to Kodály's work is forgotten in the magic of Bartók's personal tone. (Here the word 'magic' must be understood in its literal sense, as used by Denijs Dille when he speaks of the 'incantatorial' strength of Bartók's music which we ourselves have so often felt.) The summarizing recapitulation of the closing section, and also in places the tone, hint at an internal structure common to both works. The initial presentation of the content is also similar. In both compositions, an escape from the everyday world, and the expression of nostalgia for the world of Nature, can be heard. But this principle which underlies the opening theme and returns in the closing section, may surely be attributed to Bartók as much as to anyone else. He had recently used this method in his *String Quartet No. 4* and now in the *Cantata Profana* he was developing it according to its own inner laws. He had in the same way brought together various elements of the different sections of the *Dance Suite*, while the closing section of the *String Quartet No. 3* was openly given the title 'ricapitulazione della prima parte'.

We have now arrived at the point where we must consider the most exciting aspect of the *Cantata Profana*—the special features of its construction and dramatic content. For though we find in this work the methods of construction traditonally used by the composer, and there are many references to the principles of earlier and later compositions, the *Cantata Profana* is very different from any other work by Bartók. As in the case of the *Dance Suite*, Bartók's numbering and division of the movements does not indicate quite clearly the internal articulation.

What in other works would be a scherzo-type second movement, here appears as the wild dance of the weapons in the hunting scene. There follows the mysterious, secretive whispering of the slow movement representing the magic transformation. In the moments of climax we hear the same shuddering glissandos which breathed life into the wooden puppet. The chorus repeats: 'In the thick of the forest they were changed into stags', and softly murmurs one of Bartók's familiar centrally-pivoted whirling melodies—another variation of the theme of the fast movement in the *String Quartet No. 3* which was also to develop into the slow introduction of the *Sonata for Two Pianos and Percussion*. There is a similar relationship between the scherzo and the slow movement in the *Music for String Instruments, Percussion and Celesta*.

The dramatic dialogue between the 'most beloved stag, the dearest son' and the father going after him, is set within the cantata as a lengthy, independent unit. This tragic clash, so disproportionate in its intensity and independent in its dramatic structure, this 'combattimento' which has such a disturbing, insistently distorting effect on the whole, differentiates the *Cantata Profana* from all other works by Bartók. At the same time it is here that we find the dramatic core of his art at its most dense and where the conflict explodes in crisis. Here Bartók's tone is at its most personal and passionate. It is here that he can least tolerate the burden of calm consideration of form, for it is he personally, as represented in the figure of the stag, who is seen to be struggling to tear himself away from the paternal home.

This was not the first occasion during his artistic career that Bartók had been tempted to find in Nature—which had for so many centuries offered a seemingly ideal solution to man's problems—an escape to peace and self-justification. Around 1915, in a somewhat similar historical situation, he had developed the idea of a happy union with Nature in his work for the stage, *The Wooden Prince*. At that time he was merely expressing the romantic fantasies cherished by an admirer of Nietzsche. Now, fifteen years later, his longing to escape was the result of a much more direct social compulsion combined with greater self-awareness. He had no illusions of finding happiness in escape; he was at the mercy of the bitter conflict which was destiny.

It is true that in the article mentioned above Bartók says that the *kolindas* are related to the winter solstice and to the festivals which in pagan ritual are associated with the rebirth of Nature in the Spring. But we are well aware that it is always the crises, revolutions and social changes which are reflected in mythological and magical views of the universe. This knowledge lay at the root of Károly Kerényi's interpretation of the text of the *Cantata Profana* in an article which appeared in the *Schweizerische Musikzeitung* on September 1, 1936.

'This tale of the stags,' he wrote, 'is one of the mythological stories which are most frequently found among the peoples of Eastern Europe and Northern Asia, including the Magyars and our closest relatives, the Finno-Ugrian tribes.' This statement is also quoted by István Palkó in his article 'Őrség' (Guardian), Szombathely, 1954, in which he offers a convincing interpretation of the *Cantata Profana* as 'the Romanian people's electrifying story of their origin'.

It was again Aladár Tóth who in his review, after the première in Budapest, pointed out 'that terrible suffering caused when someone breaks away from his family and is separated permanently from the happy family circle, a suffering experienced by the one who goes just as much as by those who are left behind.' (*Pesti Napló*, November 10, 1936.) There is a heated exchange between the two sides; it is the immeasurable agony of the protagonists which causes them to make wild threats and imperious demands. The father tries to tempt his sons to return by offering them all the comforts of his home: 'The torches are lit, the table is laid'. In the music there is a reflection of Bartók's youthful idealism: the descending major form of the leitmotif evokes the desires, hopes, loves and disappointments of youth, all softened by memory. Not one of the stags, however, resembles the prodigal son of the Bible. They tasted the ecstasy of freedom and could not turn back. All the pain of separation and the intoxicating joy of freedom are compressed into the shout of the tremendous closing melismatics of the tenor solo. The chorus, on the far side of the bridge, can no longer follow him. They can only relate what is happening with all the nostalgia of a chronicler: 'and their antlers cannot enter the doorway, they enter the valleys; their slender bodies cannot wear clothes, they can only go among the boughs; their feet cannot step on the ashes of the hearth, only on soft peat; their mouths cannot drink from glasses, only from clean sources.' (In the later edition of the pocket score of the *Cantata Profana*, published by Universal Edition, the original Hungarian text is unfortunately missing. Here we give a literal translation of Bartók's original text.)

According to Aladár Tóth, this voluntary submission to sorrow and tribulation, which is also a purification ordained by a pitiless destiny, represents a declaration of war in the name of freedom. In his review he wrote of 'the wolves' song . . . this titanic music in an age of servility'. And he continued, 'But this is also the agonized message, which stirs us to the depths of our souls, the heartrending cry, of a giant among men, a poet with the soul of an eagle, who has torn himself away from our common lot to endure the solitude of eternal freedom. How came such a one to live amongst us in an age like this? But perhaps it is the very depths to which we have sunk that enables him to declare the truth now and for all time, making his epic proclamation of the truth that is hidden in the innermost recesses of our hearts. From the galleries he is acclaimed by the younger generation in a storm of applause. Who then would dare to claim that this herald of human freedom finds no response in this century?'

In his music too Bartók struggled to express this journey from the darkness of sorrow to the light of hope. The use of what is known as the 'natural' scale was also quite usual in folk music and once the sons have been transformed into stags, the introductory atmosphere, with its tonal world of contrasting elements, changes, and the magic stags are drawn into the folk-music world of open tones. In Ernő Lendvai's analytical studies, he shows us how Bartók followed this same logical path in the later works in which he passed down to us his large-scale representation of the brotherhood of the nations.

The *Cantata Profana* leaves the end of the road in shadow. It expresses only the moment when men tear themselves away from what is known and present. It may be that he was reserving the great synthesis for the last piece of the triptych. Now, however, Bartók had to overcome another temptation. Having emerged from the dark hell of solitary suffering, he had yet to resist the lure of the ecstasy of cosmic solitude, the attraction of an isolation that was as true and transparent as the world of mathematics, as icily pure as the stars and planets of the universe. This was the visionary world of Baudelaire. Such a Utopia, in which humanity could find absolution, still awaited expression in the great works to come.

CHAPTER XI

OPPRESSIVE POLITICAL ATMOSPHERE. NATIONALIST
ATTACKS AT HOME AND ABROAD. RETREAT. COLLECTING
TOUR IN TURKEY. FOLK MUSIC STUDIES AND GREAT
MUSICAL COMPOSITIONS. 1931–1936

1 ONCE AGAIN THE PLAN FOR THE PREMIERE OF 'THE MIRACULOUS
MANDARIN' IS FRUSTRATED. BARTÓK WITHDRAWS FROM BUDAPEST
CONCERT SCENE. ATTACKS IN ROMANIA. FATE OF THE SLOVAK COLLEC-
TION

'Dear Friends, the world is becoming ever more cruel, especially in the
field of the arts. And *our task* grows ever greater.' These lines were written
by Anton Webern on September 27, 1930 and addressed to Hildegard
Jone, the painter, and Josef Humplik, the sculptor. He was expressing
the growing apprehension felt by every sensitive and humane artist in
those days. There were others, gifted with still more perception, who
were increasingly depressed by the threat of war and the growing evidence
of inhumanity everywhere.

Scarcely six months after Bartók had completed the *Cantata Profana*,
Arthur Honegger's *Cris du Monde* gave to the world another expression
of anxiety and longing to escape. The composer of the agonizing ballad
of the nine miraculous stags can only have found a bitter kind of satisfaction in the fact that day after day his unquenchable desire for a better
world was all too brutally justified. His fiftieth birthday provided another
occasion to add to his many bitter experiences.

The French decoration, that of a 'Chevalier de la Légion d'Honneur',
arrived at the French Embassy in Budapest sometime in the middle of
February and according to a report in *Az Est*, it was handed over to him
only a few days later when Mihály Babits, the poet and one of the leading
literary figures of the day, was similarly honoured. Bartók was also given
the highest cultural award in Hungary, the Corvin Wreath, and this
was to have been personally presented to him and other recipients on
February 23 by Horthy himself. This occasion, however, was marked

by a brief newspaper comment by Károly Kristóf: 'Béla Bartók, who is now living abroad, did not attend.' And he added in parenthesis, 'Béla Bartók had meantime departed for London'. In fact this is the only documentary evidence of such a departure; on the contrary, there are indications in plenty to show that he remained at home from the time when he returned from his tour of Spain somewhere about February 10, until he played at a concert in Pozsony on March 4. We also find that the letter quoted earlier, in which he informed László Pataki (Polatsek) among others, of the circumstances surrounding the origin of the *Rhapsodies*, was actually dated from Budapest on the 23rd of February, the very day of the presentation. And on March 1, he gave a piano recital in Debrecen. In fact, the reasons for his failure to attend the gala festivities connected with the award were the same as those which had earlier prevented him from going to István Bethlen's garden party.

His decision was well justified. This act of official recognition served to conceal the new and pitiful tragicomedy that was being enacted around the proposed Budapest première of *The Miraculous Mandarin*. This was the situation which represented the real relationship between Bartók and those responsible for the cultural policies of Hungary. And as the discussions between the composer and the authorities at the Opera House became more and more contentious, it was Károly Kristóf who again informed readers of *Az Est* about each stage of the argument. It would be difficult now, after such a lapse of time, for anyone to recall from memory the exact course of events. It is at any rate certain that at the Opera House everything was done to destroy the *Mandarin* conceived by Bartók; and the reason for this was in part due to the fact that no one there was capable of producing it as the composer intended. ' . . .The director and the ballet master were adamant in their view that no one could dance to such music and that it was therefore necessary to coach the dancers for a freely-interpreted pantomime . . . The director based his instructions on *The Veil of Pierette*,' recalls Gyula Harangozó, the outstanding character-dancer, and later ballet-master of the Opera House, and, among others, the choreographer of *The Miraculous Mandarin*. He was referring to the ballet by Dohnányi and his wife, Elsa Galafrés, and he added, 'What was easily solved in that work and others like it, with their light, melodic music, spelled disaster in the case of the modern and more exacting music of the *Mandarin*.'

Problems of choreography, however, were less important to the management than their concern to ensure that the production would in no way reveal the true significance of this shocking human drama. They made every conceivable effort to change the meaning of the play, even seeking assistance from the author of the libretto, Menyhért Lengyel. A new version was concocted and the director, László Márkus, gave a statement to *Az Est* in which he attempted to explain its meaning, a statement, however, which shows only that this main intention was to deprive the play of its original meaning: 'The action does not now take place in a room as in the original, but out of doors. The atmosphere is that of a suburban slum in a great city. The emphasis is on the Girl's passion and her unwillingness to take part in the robberies... In Lengyel's new version, *The Miraculous Mandarin* has become somewhat of a Grand Guignol play. This effect is intensified by the fantasy of the setting so that the whole episode may be regarded as a dream.'

Instead of social truth, a Grand Guignol nightmare: thus, by substituting dream for reality, the Opera House management hoped to make the pantomime acceptable to the authorities. But the première was postponed only a few days before it was due to take place on the pretext that Karola Szalay, who was to play the leading role, had fallen ill and had been ordered to rest for four weeks. One announcement succeeded another, while the Opera House continued to maintain the legend of Karola Szalay's illness. Their next move was to declare that Bartók wished to adapt the music to suit the new text. (The closing scene in its final shortened version was probably written during these months of rehearsal in 1931.) The public was therefore asked to wait 'until after Easter...' The true circumstances of the postponement may be found in Gyula Harangozó's recollections from which we have quoted above. 'After so much preliminary fuss,' he wrote, 'we felt quite nervous and very curious to know what Bartók thought of the production. Bartók was no expert in choreography but he had enough insight as an artist to realize that what he had seen bore very little relation to his music. He questioned the experts on various points of detail but received only a confused explanation, and after listening for some time he said, "I am afraid it is because you do not understand my music that you have misinterpreted me." Thereupon he left the Opera House and did not attend any more rehearsals.' (*Táncművészet*, February, 1955.) By now there had even been references in *Az Est* to the fact that this falsification of his work had not been effected with the approval of the composer, and his displeasure was an open secret in Budapest. This intervention on the part of the composer was welcomed at the Opera as another excuse for delay, for there were rumours that the reactionary, right-wing opponents of the *Mandarin* were preparing to hold a demonstration. Whatever the final reason for the decision, the fact remains that the Hungarian première of *The Miraculous Mandarin* was again abandoned, and between the two world wars there was no further serious attempt to produce it.

The premiere of the pantomime would have provided a suitable opportunity to honour Bartók on the occasion of his fiftieth birthday. But no such honour was accorded him. His finest anniversary tribute came from the pen of Aladár Tóth and was published in *Pesti Napló*: 'In Hungary today one showy celebration succeeds another,' he wrote. 'In such a country, who would want to honour Bartók in the same way? This spiritual giant is a solitary hermit among us. We must respect his seclusion and remain silent. And if we are permitted to say a few words we must not squander them in some anniversary greeting but rather try to interpret the significance of the silence which surrounds the fifty-year-old Bartók. That silence seems to tell us that it is not for us to honour an artist who achieved an honourable position without any assistance from us; that it is not for us to hasten with gifts to an artist when we made no haste to accept the gifts he had to offer; that it is not for us to disturb the privacy of an artist whom we ourselves would have none of. We have no right to feel proud of an artist who was born among us and lived for us, but whom we did not accept as one of ourselves. The time is not yet ripe for a Bartók celebration in Hungary. First we must work for this genius, then we can honour him. The bronze for his statue in the public square can be moulded only by the fire of our own devotion and understanding. If during his remarkable career as an artist we have allowed him to reach the age of fifty without fostering such feelings in our hearts, then let us set to work and in the next ten years repair all our omissions.

Until then every celebration is an act of hypocrisy. That is the significance of this silence . . .' (*Pesti Napló*, March 29, 1931).

But during the ten succeeding years there was little reparation for the neglect which had been his lot. Bartók remained silent and, as once before during the second decade of the century, he made no appearances on the concert platforms of Budapest. On the few occasions when he consented to broadcast, he gave talks on folk music or gave recitals of piano music selected from the piano literature of the past. Sometimes he would accept an invitation to appear at an orchestral concert as soloist in one of the great classical concertos. One such occasion provided a unique experience when he gave an outstanding performance of the *Danse Macabre* which demonstrated his own profound relation to Liszt (February 3, 18, 1936). Sometimes he played arrangements for two pianos with either Edwin Fischer or Ernő Dohnányi, and together they played Bach's triple concertos on May 4, 1937. He was always especially pleased to play sonatas or to act as accompanist. He consented to give a sonata recital on January 12, 1934 when he played with Imre Waldbauer who had always been one of his favourite partners. Just one month later, he was accompanist at a concert, one of a series of concerts arranged by the Collegium Musicum. On April 18 of the same year he appeared with Zathureczky at a concert specially arranged by the Academy of Music. A year later, on March 30, 1935, he played with Feuermann, and later that year, on October 20, 1935, he played with Szigeti. These were all interesting and even notable occasions in the musical life of Budapest but they did not arouse the eager anticipation experienced before the great piano recitals at which he had introduced his own latest compositions. For a long time the master did not play his own works for the audiences of Budapest. Even when his *Concerto No. 2* for piano was given a first performance in Budapest on January 2, 1933, he entrusted the solo part to Lajos Kentner. Nor did he take part in the Bartók evening organized by UMZE on January 3, 1934. Throughout this period he played his own works only in the provinces—in Debrecen, Békéscsaba, Szombathely, Szeged and Pápa. At one of the concerts in Békéscsaba, Mária Basilides sang some of his songs, and in Pápa, he played sonatas with André Gertler as his partner.

He continued to make tours abroad: the thirties provide us with a long record of his success as a concert artist and recitalist. But the map of his tours was being transformed by the spread of fascism. It was not long after Bartók's fiftieth birthday that the scandalous treatment of Toscanini in Bologna aroused the indignation of all those who believed in freedom. On May 15, 1931, the great conductor had refused to conduct the orchestra when called upon to play the Italian fascist anthem, the 'Giovinezza'. By way of reprisal, he was attacked and beaten in the street, and finally driven from his native land. Bartók himself drafted the statement by ISCM protesting against such condemnation 'on any other grounds than the artistic,' deploring such increasingly frequent 'interference and use of violence' and demanding from ISCM the formation of 'a suitable world organization for safeguarding the freedom of artists'.

Alfred Einstein was still in Berlin to publish in the *Berliner Tagblatt* a greeting to Bartók on his fiftieth birthday. Schoenberg, Hindemith and Klemperer were still active in the German capital. And during the early thirties Berlin was still the first stopping place for many Hungarian emigrants, including the young Ferenc Szabó. But it was only two years later after the notorious Nazi 'coup' that they were forced to move on yet again, in the company of many outstanding writers and scientists, including Thomas Mann. After a brief stay in France, Schoenberg emigrated to America in 1934. This was the year in which Goebbels banned the works of Hindemith who shortly afterwards followed his distinguished compatriots into exile. For some time he was active in Turkey, but the outbreak of war in 1939 drove him too to seek a home in the United States. Otto Klemperer was already an exile when he conducted the première of Bartók's *Concerto No. 2* for piano in Budapest, and it was as an exile that he was received in Austria.

It was natural that Nazi Germany should have no welcome for either Bartók or his music. Nor did Bartók seek friendship from that quarter. When the Spanish Civil War came to its tragic end he also ceased to visit Spain, a country which had provided him with many memories of tours undertaken in his early youth. The great Spanish musicians, De Falla and Casals, also found it impossible to stay in their own country.

It was thus that Bartók developed closer links with the few Western countries still unaffected by Nazism. He continued to make regular guest appearances in England and with the assistance of Zoltán Székely and Géza Frid he became more well known in Holland and Belgium. André

Gertler, who had been one of Hubay's most gifted pupils, was active in Belgium at that time and it was there too that Denijs Dille made the decision to devote himself to the study of Bartók's art which later brought him fame. And for as long as he remained in Europe Bartók continued to enjoy the friendship and cooperation of the Basle Orchestra, its conductor and the circle of friends who supported it.

The deterioration of relations between Hungary and her neighbours was even more distressing to Bartók than events in Western Europe. We have to remember that as far back as in 1910 he had shown his own eagerness to cooperate by offering his collection of folk-songs to the Turócszentmárton Publishing Company. He had not spared himself in the task of collecting Slovak folk music and owed much of his inspiration to Slovak folk-songs. As soon as the cessation of hostilities made it possible, in 1920, his first gesture was an attempt to re-establish mutual cooperation, and he began to send the first part of his collection to the Slovenská Matica. By 1928 he had handed over the entire collection. The correspondence which followed, from which we may learn the story of endless procrastination connected with the publishing project, makes ignoble reading. These documents comprise no small part of János Demény's third volume of the collected letters and we shall therefore spare our readers as well as ourselves yet another account of this sorry affair. For it is more important to remember the inspiration that Bartók found in Slovak culture. Though after 1938 any hope of the collection being published in Slovakia seemed forlorn indeed, yet post-war friendship between the two countries made the publication possible. The first volume was published by the Slovak Academy of Sciences in 1959.

In Czechoslovakia between the two world wars the same struggle as elsewhere in Central Europe was being enacted between the forces of progress and reaction. Meantime in Romania as in Hungary the nationalists continued to inject their own special poison into the political atmosphere. Bartók's fiftieth birthday provided them with an opportunity to combine forces with the Hungarian reactionaries. The Romanians were proposing to put up a memorial plaque on the house where Bartók was born in Nagyszentmiklós. Bartók was invited to attend the ceremony and also three concerts were being arranged for mid-January 1931. In an unpublished letter dated February 22 and addressed to Constantin

Brăiloiu, Bartók explained that he had refused the invitation and had expressed a wish that the inscription should be in both Romanian and Hungarian. When this was reported in the *Budapesti Hirlap* on March 20, Bartók's wish had been distorted into a demand that the inscription should be in the Hungarian language only. By manipulating the facts in this way the party which was opposed to the idea of friendship between Romania and Hungary, succeeded in preventing the plaque from being erected.

In 1934, there was another incident in connection with the proposed memorial plaque. Bartók was planning to visit Bucharest where he had been asked to lecture in the Academy on February 18, on the subject of East European folk music, and to attend, on February 19, a concert of Baroque music when the programme would also include some of his own works and those of Kodály. On February 21, he was to play for the Bucharest Radio. These plans stimulated his admirers in Temesvár to revive the idea of a memorial plaque. They again organized the ceremony which was by now three years overdue. Their intention was that it should take place after Bartók's stay in Bucharest so that it would coincide with the twenty-fifth anniversary of the date when Bartók first began to collect Romanian folk-songs. Hearing of these plans, Tiberiu Brediceanu, a bank manager in Brassó and an amateur composer, informed the Bucharest government that the Hungarian master (and incidentally member of the Romanian Academy) was politically dangerous. The Romanian government therefore held up Bartók's entry permit for some days. Meantime the Romanian Composers' Association under the directorship of George Enescu and Constantin Brăiloiu, did everything possible to counter this attack by the nationalists. In this they were greatly assisted by an article in the Romanian paper *Universul* in which Bartók was accorded the highest praise. He was allowed to enter the country and Brediceanu was summoned to appear before the Association. His confused story of letters from Máramaros showing that Bartók had launched an unworthy attack on Romanian folk music, was exposed as both false and ridiculous. Nevertheless, the unveiling of the memorial plaque was postponed yet again; nor was the composer able to revisit the place of his birth. Radu Urleţianu, the conductor who had first conceived the idea of a memorial plaque and who had organized the ceremony, was so hounded by rampant chauvinism that he was driven to commit suicide.

The concert in Temesvár did in fact take place. On May 2, 1936, Bartók gave a joint sonata recital with Ede Zathureczky. It was Bartók's last performance in Romania. His visit was made in the emotional atmosphere of intense nationalism which had previously been aroused by his activities in the field of folk music. In February, in the *Gând Românesc*, a university teacher, Coriolan Petranu, published an attack on Bartók in which he severely criticized his research in connection with his collection of Romanian folk music. His most serious accusation was that although Bartók 'in 1913, with the publication of his Bihar collection, had been acknowledged as an impartial research worker in the field of Romanian folk music', he had nevertheless, in 1920, shown his bias in the study entitled *The Romanian Folk-Music Dialect of Hunyad* which appeared in the *Zeitschrift für Musikwissenshaft*. Petranu claimed that Bartók had deliberately established a Székely influence in the Romanian music of the Mező region and of Nagyküküllő and Kisküküllő, and that he had done so in order to support the revisionist demands of Horthy's Hungary. Shortly before the Bartóks arrived in Romania these accusations were repeated in the pages of the periodical *Fruncea*.

Bartók gave no detailed reply to these accusations until 1937 when his comments were published in *Szép Szó*. But he reacted to it immediately by giving a statement to the *Temesvári Hirlap*. He revealed that the original text of the study in question had been written in 1914 and for this reason alone could not be considered as revisionist. (It is characteristic of the strange atmosphere of 1920 that he was attacked by Hungarian chauvinists on the grounds that in that very same study he had shown bias in favour of the Romanian people.) He also repudiated very briefly some of the accusations made by Petranu, using the arguments which he elaborated later for his article in *Szép Szó*.

We are not in a position to substantiate with scientific evidence the claims made by either side at that time. These claims involved factual details about East European folk music which are still by no means certain. Even on the basis of our present knowledge it is not possible to make definitive judgements on questions of originality and spheres of influence.

With regard to the political, scientific and ethical aspects of the controversy, we can only follow the example of the contemporary journalists, recording, like them, our regret that men engaged in a scientific study of folk music should have been involved in such undignified disputes because of the poisonous atmosphere of nationalist prejudice. However, Bartók's whole career, his outlook and personal bearing, leave us in no doubt as to his own good faith and honourable intentions. It is rather in the statements made by his opponents that we can find evidence of an attempt to aggravate nationalist feelings. In fact, because of the tense atmosphere prevailing at the time of Bartók's visit, and because it was said that a demonstration was being planned against the guest artists, the composer and his companions cut short their tour and returned straight home from Temesvár.

It was as a result of these experiences that Bartók in 1937 concluded bitterly that,

> though musical folklore owed a great deal to nationalism, today it is so harmed by ultra-nationalism that the damage now exceeds the former benefits.

Népdalkutatás és nacionalizmus (Folk-Song Research and Nationalism).

In 1951, in a changed and healthier political atmosphere, the memorial plaque was finally erected. In accordance with his wish, the inscription which denotes his birthplace is in two languages, Romanian as well as Hungarian.

Now, as so often before, he found solace in the 'clean sources' of folk music. As he became more and more cut off from the outside world by a wall of hatred, his own inner world expanded to ever greater dimensions. This was a world dominated by memories of his early collecting tours and his peaceful sojourns among the peasants; a world irradiated by an idealized vision of country life, a world in which there were no national frontiers nor barriers of human prejudice. In this inner world he could freely contribute to the brotherhood of the nations. In 1943 he wrote in an article (entitled: 'Diversity of Material yielded up in profusion in European melting-pot') in *Musical America*,

> There is peace among the peasants; hatred against their brothers is fostered only by the higher circles.

This time Bartók's withdrawal was complete; not only mental and symbolic, but physical too. When the Academy of Sciences commissioned him to classify the folk-music material he had collected, he left the Academy of Music and in September 1934 he moved into a small room on the first floor of the Academy. This became his workshop and today it is marked by a memorial plaque. Here he worked untiringly, examining his notes over and over again, listening to the phonograph recordings and studying the many thousands of songs now so familiar to him, assessing them in the light of each new theory. Members of the Folk-Music Research Group of the Hungarian Academy of Sciences, whose daily task it is to handle Bartók's handwritten notes, can bear witness to the energy and attention to accurate detail which enabled him to make his notations perfect.

He had at that time already completed the first basic phase in the task of classifying. In the case of the Magyar–Slovak–Romanian monographs, he had reached the second and more difficult phase of summarization. Now he had to work out and describe the methods of working on the living material and elucidate the problems of comparison. It was round about this time that he wrote his two most significant studies laying down the two basic principles of summarization.

One of these studies, on the subject of methodology, appeared as the sixth issue of *Popular Folk-Music Notebooks*, in 1936, edited by Antal Molnár, and was entitled 'Why and How To Collect Folk Music'. It is a comprehensive guide to the theory and practice of folk-music collection. It is the work of an expert who has had thirty years' experience as a folklorist and who brings to his task not only a scientific training but also the deep understanding of a man for whom folk-songs breathe the very spirit of life itself. It is also a work born out of his daily contact with living people, the experiences he shared with them, their cares and their joys. In this work there is not even the memory of the romantic young musician who had first been attracted to folk music 'only' because of his interest 'in music'. This book passes on the wisdom of a scientist and educationalist who had experienced for himself the many difficulties connected with all attempts to collect folk music and who knew that a collector must be gifted with both love and tact in order to be successful in collecting the songs of a peasant living a life quite different from his own.

Nor did Bartók's study consist of mere abstract theories; he wrote it for a specific practical purpose. At that time village life was becoming a favourite subject for sociological studies and there was a spreading fashion for collecting folk music. In addition to the small group of experts who had been trained by Zoltán Kodály, others began to invade the villages—young composers and hordes of dilettantes who collected folk music as a hobby. The encouragement and the warnings in Bartók's study were intended for them too. They were reminded that the collection of folk-songs was not merely a pleasant way of passing the time but a serious occupation to be undertaken with a sense of responsibility. A fund of professional knowledge was needed and it was essential to be in close contact with the people; for many details of a living performance could be retained only in the human memory, as for example the manner of singing and the niceties of vocal colour. He gives a long list of the various points on which would-be collectors must be well informed, and defines the qualities of a good collector. He wrote in conclusion,

> A collector such as I have described, with all this ability, knowledge and experience, does not to my knowledge exist, nor will such a one ever be found. From our present understanding of what is involved it seems that no one man can possess all the qualities necessary for collecting folk music satisfactorily. Perhaps by a division of labour it would be possible to achieve results approaching more nearly to perfection.

Here Bartók first expressed an idea which was far from being generally accepted at that time, the idea of a truly modern method of collective research which has been so fruitful in practice.

There was also a far-reaching purpose in his study entitled *Népzenénk és a szomszéd népek népzenéje* (Our Folk Music and the Folk Music of Neighbouring Peoples). This also appeared in the *Népszerű zenefüzetek* in 1934. And here again the message was a timely one, for the study was a documented statement of the common and inseparable destiny of the Danubian peoples who had been roused one against the other. In some of his conclusions he was ahead of current knowledge and established fact. Today our attitude to some of the questions he raised is rather different: for example, we take a different view of the musical relations between neighbouring peoples, the formation of the style of new Hungarian folk music, its origin and dissemination, the origin of the *verbunkos* style and the distribution in Eastern Europe of melodic types with Arabic embellishments. But in addition to this comparative account of the Danubian peoples and their music, Bartók's study ranged widely over the whole field of research into historical processes which were at the root of the phenomenon of folk music; and his conception of a historical atlas showing the folk music of all the peoples of East Europe remains as fascinating and impressive today as it was in 1934.

> ... We have arrived at the most exciting chapter in the history of folk-song research, the chapter which I would call 'casual detection in musical folklore'... The ancient cultural relations of peoples who have been scattered far and wide, could and should be discovered. There is much to be revealed about ancient settlements and the as yet unsolved problems of history. It is now possible to discover what contact there was between neighbouring peoples, in what way they were linked, or perhaps separated, by spiritual beliefs.

Though this quotation is taken from Bartók's later study, 'Why and How To Collect Folk Music', it does in fact summarize the basic theme of the earlier comparative study.

As a young man he had undertaken long journeys on which he had attempted to trace folk music with a possible relationship to Hungarian folk music or that of neighbouring peoples. During the hottest weeks of the African summer he searched for variants of a melodic type that he had discovered in 1912 among the Romanians of Máramaros and in 1913 in Biskra. He would have liked to continue the search for our kin in Russia. But between the two world wars, he was prevented from making excursions to collect folk music, on the one hand by his own many commitments and on the other by the unfavourable political conditions then prevailing in East Europe. However, we can see from the volume and nature of his correspondence during these years that he did not abandon his original aims but sought new ways by which to achieve them. Filaret Kolessa sent him collections of Romanian folk music, and later, in 1939, Dezső Zádor sent him recordings of Ruthenian folk music. Letters from Brăiloiu supplemented his knowledge of Romanian folk music, and he studied Croatian and Bulgarian folk music with the help of Vinko Žganec and Raïna Katzarova respectively.

As his knowledge of the subject increased and the songs with which he had some acquaintance swelled in number, he found it more and more painful to be obliged to recognize the existence of sources still unknown to him. He was keenly aware that his survey, meticulous though it was, could never be a substitute for first-hand research in the places where the songs were still sung by the people.

> ... We are thoroughly familiar with only about half of the territories inhabited by Romanians, those regions, that is to say, which once formed part of the old Hungary. If only we had been able to do research work not only in the Transylvanian areas but also in the Moldavian regions bordering on the Székely regions, it would have been possible to see all these complex problems much more clearly,

he exclaimed in 1934 in the comparative study. In this lament we can sense with what bitterness he had resigned himself to the loss of twenty years of research: he was remembering that in 1914 he had been on the point of departure for Moldavia, a tour which, like so many others, fell victim to the war. From the tone of his exclamation, it would seem that he recognized that there was indeed a gap in his experience, for which he was later reproached by Petranu, who said that he was familiar with only a fraction of the Romanian folk-music region. And in his own summary of methodology in 1936, Bartók wrote,

> ... Important areas from the point of view of folk music, such as Greece, Turkey, all of Central Asia, are completely unknown. If there is anywhere a burning need to stimulate 'intellectual cooperation' between nations, then it is here in the field of folk music. Yet in this field as in all others, this so-called 'cooperation', which has already become notorious, has failed utterly.

He never quite gave up the hope of one day resuming his collecting tours. On March 2, 1934, a conversation with Bartók was printed in *Brassói Lapok*. 'And now,' said Bartók,

> I should like to become familiar with the folk music of the former regions of Romania—of Bukovina and Bessarabia. I am very grateful to the Romanian Composers' Association for putting at my disposal an enormous quantity of material recorded on hundreds of cylinders ... When I have made a thorough study of the subject on the basis of these recordings, then I shall return to old

Romania with my wanderer's staff in hand and continue my researches in the places where this music may still be heard.

As we have seen, Bartók was not allowed to make his proposed tour. But, at the age of fifty-five, the scientist-composer did take his 'wanderer's staff in hand' when he made what proved to be his last tour—to Anatolia in Turkey. He has himself given us the clearest available account of the scientific purpose and practical achievements of this expedition.

> At that time, when we set to work, we increasingly had the impression that . . . the origin of the pentatonic style is Asiatic, and points toward the Northern Turks. On the other hand, we had no proof with which to substantiate our conviction. But during the course of the last ten years, these proofs have turned up in the shape of Cheremis melodies . . . Besides those Magyar songs which were variants of Cheremis songs, we also found Magyar songs which were variations of melodies found in the neighbourhood of Kazan. Not long ago, I received Mahmud Ragib Kösemihal's book published this year, 'The Tonal Characteristics of Turkish Folk Music', and I found some of these types of melodies there too . . . It is obvious that every melody of this kind originates from a common source, and it seems that this source is to be found in ancient Northern Turkish musical culture . . .

In these words Bartók informed his Turkish audience of the hypothesis which had prompted him to make this tour to collect folk music (*A Nép-zene*, 1936). Later, in an interview given in America in 1941, he confirmed that his Tuskish tour was an organic part of the scientific programme which he had been following for several decades, that it was a logical stage in the development of the theories which had prompted him to plan a tour of Russia before the First World War. He said to the representative of *The Etude*, an American periodical which published the statement in February 1941,

> I first traced Finno-Ugrian–Turkish resemblances to the people of the Volga region, and from there finally to Turkey.

In 1937, Bartók's account of his tour was published in *Nyugat*. He also gives his readers some idea of the circumstances in which the tour was proposed:

> About two years ago, Turkish official circles began with the help and direction of Hindemith to organize municipal education on European lines. But they had no adviser as to how a Turkish national music should be developed from

Turkish folk music. They had no one who could have given instructions for the actual collection of the folk-songs.

It was therefore decided that the Ankara branch of the Halkevi, the only Turkish political party, should invite me.

Such were the circumstances which led to my trip to Asia Minor ... I was invited to Ankara to give three lectures on musical folklore and to participate in an orchestral concert of Hungarian music. In addition I was promised two trips to enable me to make records of Anatolian Turkish folk music for the Hungarian Academy of Sciences. Needless to say, I accepted this invitation with the greatest of pleasure.

It was László Rásonyi, a Hungarian teacher at Ankara University, who first conceived the idea of inviting Bartók to visit the country. Details of the advance preparations for the trip are to be found in the letters which he and Bartók wrote to each other prior to the visit. It is clear that Bartók made the same careful preparations as when he visited Máramaros and the Transylvanian regions. He knew the importance of some degree of familiarity with the Turkish language and we may read in one of his letters dated

August 21, 1936
I have struggled through the grammar; it's more difficult than I thought at first.

He was away in Turkey for about three weeks, from November 5 until the end of the month. He was therefore not at home for the Budapest première of the *Cantata Profana*. His engagements in Ankara, including the lectures and the concert, were successfully fulfilled, but he had to abandon the first of the two collecting tours which had been arranged because of a slight indisposition. He published a brief account of the second tour, which lasted for six days, in *Nyugat*. He tells his story with his customary humour, revealing an unabated pleasure in both collecting and travelling; there is true literary merit in the style.

He was accompanied during the expedition by a young Turkish composer who was also a student of folklore, Achmed Adnan Saygun. The friendly relations which developed between him and Bartók proved to be of an enduring nature.

Because of the particular circumstances in which he made the tour and also because of certain local customs, Bartók did not manage to accomplish all that he had hoped. But the tour was by no means un-successful. In the course of only six days, he recorded in the Asia Minor territories a total of ninety melodies of which twenty showed a relationship with the group of descending pentatonic Magyar melodies, thus proving that his original hypothesis was not without basis.

He returned home from this final collecting tour with the memory of many new and interesting experiences and a monograph of melodic material collected from a small selected area. This collection remains unpublished to this day.

3 GREAT COMPOSITION FOR CHILDREN: '44 VIOLIN DUOS' AND 'MIKRO-KOSMOS'. 'PIANO CONCERTO NO. 2', 'STRING QUARTET NO. 5', 'MUSIC FOR STRING INSTRUMENTS, PERCUSSION AND CELESTA', AND 'SONATA FOR TWO PIANOS AND PERCUSSION'

Besides seeking relief from the horror of the world situation in his study of folk music, Bartók also turned, like so many musicians before him, to the familiar world of children, in which he found a refreshing inno-cence and honesty. He had already made the very natural gesture of offering the newly-discovered wealth of folk music in the earlier four notebooks *For Children*. His intention is made clear even in the titles, and in *Ten Easy Pieces* and *Bagatelles* he spoke to the children in every line as well. In the first tender developments of his new period of com-position there are also unmistakable references to the world of children. We know from a later statement by the composer that the *Nine Little Piano Pieces* were originally planned as a series of ten pieces like the *Ten Easy Pieces*. The tenth piece which was omitted was later developed into a work which anticipated the *Mikrokosmos*.

His arrangements of folk-songs collected under the title *For Children* created their own descendants, even if in this case they were not for the piano but for the violin—the four volumes of the *Forty-Four Duos*. Eight of these latter pieces were given a first hearing at a concert held on January 20, 1932, in the Academy of Music, under the auspices of ISCM, when Imre Waldbauer and György Hanover were the artists. Bartók wrote for the première:

When writing the Forty-Four Duos, some of which will be performed at the ISCM concert today, I had in mind the same purpose as that which caused me to write the series entitled *For Children:* to provide works suitable for performance by students during the first few years of study, works in which a natural simplicity is combined with the melodic and rhythmic characteristics of folk music.

On this occasion too it was Aladár Tóth who immediately realized where the *Duos* belonged: 'In Bartók's violin duos, there is a happy union—and perhaps on a higher level than in the earlier volumes of piano pieces entitled *For Children*—between the child, the genius and the common folk,' he wrote in his review. And in the preface to this work, Bartók explained,

> In all these duos, with the exception of two, a peasant melody serves as the principal theme.

These violin pieces also resemble the earlier *For Children* in that here too Bartók adhered faithfully to the original melodies. But in the *Forty-Four Duos* Bartók develops still further the third basic idea of the series *For Children*, an idea greatly cherished in the meantime so that it had by now become a major theme, the ideal of brotherhood. In the earlier work he had made use of only Slovak and Magyar melodies. Since then Bartók had travelled in many lands and had become acquainted with many kinds of folk music. The violin duos bring messages from far and near through the use of Romanian, Southern Slav, Ruthenian and Arab songs, dances associated with folk customs; thus the eyes, ears and mind of the child who studies this music, are opened to the wide range of the world's beauty. The eight pieces of the fourth volume form a particularly brilliant framework for various folk dances, a kind of 'round dance of the peoples' as in the closing movement of Bartók's *Dance Suite*. The series ends with a Transylvanian dance, the Ardeleana, because in Bartók's system of values, Transylvania is an example of a country in which there is a long history of coexistence among its peoples.

In some of the pieces, however, the method of arrangement is different from that in the volumes of *For Children*. The discipline of a strict polyphonic construction as well as an infinite abundance of ideas, are as much of the essence of the violin rendering as they are essentially a part of the precise and detailed method of composition which Bartók had pursued since 1926. He was not himself responsible for the choice of instrument but was commissioned to write for two violins. The work originated from the circumstance that Erich Doflein, a teacher at the Freyburg (Breisgau) High School for Music, had devised a violin method and had edited a collection of pieces suitable for performance in connection with this method. Such prominent composers as Hindemith and Orff were associated with his work. He asked Béla Bartók to permit a violin transcription of some of the pieces of *For Children,* or alternatively to transcribe them himself. Bartók preferred to write new pieces, however, and it was thus that, in 1931, he wrote the *Forty-Four Duos.*

Throughout the period when he was engaged in the composition of these pieces he was also conducting a lengthy correspondence to ensure that the work would comply with the technical requirements. He wrote the last pieces first and only then went on to write the easier pieces.

'In this work, he found that ideal state of which the onlooker may ask whether it is the composition which defines the method, or the method the composition . . . The repetition of melodies a fifth higher or lower, which plays such an important role in the Hungarian melodic world, is again a bridge between the method and "real" music. Bartók gives this transposition stylistic value by carrying the pentatony as a song-verse variation to the other strings . . . style and method are fused once more . . .' This quotation from Professor Doflein's recollections (published in *Musik im Unterricht* in October and December 1955) gives us a new and profound insight into Bartók's composing methods. He makes a valuable contribution to our understanding of instrumental performance and the use of stylistic features which are technically appropriate to the instrument, thus helping us to understand why it was always through the medium of the short piano piece that Bartók worked out his new discoveries—discoveries of method and of musical types—which then became an integral part of his art. Professor Doflein's article also enables us to understand how it was that Bartók, who did not play a string instrument, was nevertheless the creator of the greatest string quartets of the twentieth century, one outstanding violin concerto, the fascinating solo sonata for violin and a master of percussion colour.

From all these comments, as well as from Bartók's own letters, a picture of the great composer begins to emerge. And now, with the help of Frank Whitaker, we take another look at Bartók as he was to be discovered sometime during the mid-twenties, when he was at work on his *Concerto No. 1.*

'I remember calling on him one hot afternoon in his flat in Budapest and finding him with a side-drum on his knees and a rapt look on his face. In one hand he had a drumstick: with the other he was fiddling with the snares or catgut strings, that are stretched across a side-drum to make it rattle. A pair of cymbals lay at his feet. I wish I remembered exactly what he was doing with them all, but I don't. However, the point is that he had discovered a new effect, and for the next five minutes or so, having motioned me to a chair, he alternately thwacked the drum with startling vigour and listened to the echoes wide-eyed and still, like a thrush that hears a footstep on the lawn.

'The same afternoon a question arose about the practicability of a passage in his Second Violin Sonata. In a flash the thrush became a hawk, and the hawk had run out of the room and fetched the queerest-looking fiddle I ever saw. Perhaps some peasant had made it, for the flat was full of rustic handiwork . . . But it served its purpose. Bartók proved his point and honour was satisfied.'

(Radio Times, February 26, 1932)

The account by Whitaker may also be supplemented by some interesting sections of Bartók's letters written during the thirties at the time of the Basle compositions. On August 31, 1936, for instance, he wrote to the secretary of the Basle Chamber Orchestra about the technical problems involved in the performance of the *Music for String Instruments, Percussion and Celesta.* He listed the particular methods of playing the strings that the work demanded, adding,

> . . . but these methods are not at all difficult (I myself, although I do not play the violin, can produce them very nicely), only somewhat unusual.

When he first began to think about the composition of the *Sonata for Two Pianos and Percussion,* Bartók was uncertain whether two percussion players would be adequate for rendering the part or whether it would be necessary to add a third. (It was because of this uncertainty that he did not venture to call the work a quartet.) His final decision on this point was conveyed to the Basle group in a letter dated November 11, 1937:

Not long ago, I had the chance to thoroughly observe a percussion ensemble: I realize that the work can be performed quite adequately by two percussion players, just as I originally intended.

There comes to mind, as we read these lines, the picture, taken long ago, of Bartók playing the *tekerő lant* (hurdy-gurdy) at the time when he was so engrossed in the task of collecting folk music. And we may also recall a still earlier memory, of a small boy sitting beside his mother as she plays the piano and silently following the beat and rhythm changes on his toy drum. Scarcely six months before, at the age of two and a half, he had only just begun to talk, but very soon afterwards he could pick out a melody on the piano keys.

All through his life, Béla Bartók retained the memory of that small boy who did not like to talk or sing but who found excitement and happiness in exploring the wonders of music through manual technical experiences. He made music, experimented, made discoveries and 'played' in the truest sense of that word. On a variety of instruments and particularly, of course, on his piano, he produced at once, miraculously, out of the foundations of a tangible tonal realm that was both sensual and exciting in its reality, an evocation of the whole colourful world. His instruments are touched with the magic of those mythological musicians at whose command all things sprang to life: in his music we sense the whole universe. It is remarkable how frequently Bartók's friends tried to convey his sensitiveness by comparing him to a musical instrument: Kosztolányi, for instance, writing of a conversation with the composer in 1925, referred to Bartók as a 'well-proportioned, sonorous string instrument', and Menuhin spoke of 'a shaman's drum'.

This is the Bartók who holds the key to an understanding of the *Mikrokosmos*. In the case of this work too Bartók had in mind a practical purpose when he was writing it. A few days before leaving for his final tour of the United States, Bartók described the development of this work and explained how it had originated to Miklós Szentjóbi. We have already quoted extracts from the letter reproduced here.

One of the pieces in the Mikrokosmos is the same age as the Nine Little Piano Pieces which appeared in 1926 ... At that time, I was already considering the idea of writing some extremely easy piano music suitable for beginners. I only really set to work, however, in the summer of 1932; in that year I prepared about 40 pieces, in 1933–4 another 40, and another 20 or so in the years that followed. Finally, by 1938, I had put together rather more than one hundred pieces. But there were still some things lacking. During this last year I repaired these omissions, and the first half of the 1st volume was completely finished. There had arisen in my own home a most appropriate opportunity to try out the material. In 1933, my little son, Péter, begged us to teach him to play the piano. I thought about it for a long time and finally, greatly daring, set to work on what was for me an unusual task. Apart from vocal and technical exercises, the only music given to the child was taken from the Mikrokosmos; I hope this was good for him, but I must confess that I too learned a great deal from the experiment . . .

Thus, the composition of the one hundred and fifty-three numbered pieces of the *Mikrokosmos* and the thirty-three related finger exercises occupied Bartók over a span of fourteen years, the years of the final creative period in Europe when he composed his greatest works. Technically and aesthetically, these miniature masterpieces disclose every detail of that incredibly complex process of assimilation by which, from 1926 onwards, the composer consciously reorganized his whole system of musical expression. He organized the twelve tones, now freed from earlier restrictions, into a much broader, more complex system than anything previously employed. In this system he united, in accordance with their common principles, the stylistic elements of art music and of the folk music of Europe and beyond, adding to the significance of each, and progressing logically towards a new stage in the history of music. Thus he came closer to a vision of the whole world than ever before. Yet this vision of Bartók, overwhelming in its grandeur (the inner musical secrets of which have been explored with great care and in great detail by Ernő Lendvai), is brought within our human grasp in the *Mikrokosmos*. As in some magic transformation in a fairy tale, so in this music, the awe-inspiring stars of the universe gently reveal to us their secrets. We are shown the very principles of creation, as known to science.

The phenomenon of physical sound is revealed in all its wonder. At the heart of each piece there is a wealth of sequence simultaneity, registers, colouring, and dynamics. But in the overtone playing of the 102nd piece, this assumes a direct role. The various intervals are arranged, as found earlier in the piano études of Debussy, to show their character and function in Bartók's world. The 'Thirds' (71) and 'Fourths' (131),

'Major Seconds Broken and Together' (132), 'Minor Seconds and Major Sevenths' (144) and 'Minor Sixths in Parallel Motion' (62) are virtually preliminary studies for the dancing interval mixtures of the second movement of the *Concerto*.

The sound system comes into being and finds its conclusion in a variety of ways. Sometimes it widens and narrows from a central point in interval steps; this was one of Bartók's oldest ideas and one which he had already tried out in the *Bagatelle No. 2,* since when he had on innumerable occasions shown how he could develop in an astounding way the mere germ of a melody. Such a melody or theme that develops out of a central point is governed by its own internal principle, as for example the theme of the second movement of the *String Quartet No. 3*, the theme of the magic spell when the stags are transformed in the *Cantata Profana* or the beginning of the introduction of the *Sonata for Two Pianos*. This type originated far back among the early works and is repeated again in many of the pieces of the *Mikrokosmos*. The broadening in both directions, which is implicit in its realization, contains within it the principle of mirror movement found in classical polyphony; this is also true of the two pieces of 'Line and Point' (64A, B1), and the 'Dragon's Dance' (72). His nearest recent approach to this system was the bitonal division of complementary tonal groups as in the 'Two Major Pentachords' (86), 'Diminished Fifths' (101), 'Playsong' (105), and 'From the Island of Bali' (109). In the last of these, the idea of bitonality, which came from the *Bagatelles* and which had been so often used since, is paired with the principle of contrary motions. Often the central tone is missing from the system and the widening starts out from the virtual central point.

János Kárpáti holds the view that through this whole or partial twelve-tone system built on a complementary principle and these methods of structural tone groups, tonal cells, and interval outlines, Bartók's method of tonal order is related to that used by his surrealist contemporaries in Vienna. (There is a convincing example in the first movement of the *String Quartet No. 3*.)

Already in 1926 Bartók had within his grasp the basic principles of polyphonic contruction which would enable him to bring forth his *Mikrokosmos*. In the succeeding years he remained faithful to these principles, and as a continuation of the *Dialogues* in the *Nine Little Piano Pieces*, he composed short pieces in which he used all the methods of classical polyphony. A consciously and logically developed polyphony is consistently found in such pieces as 'Reflection' (12), 'Imitation and Counterpoint' (22), 'Imitation and Inversion' (23–25), 'Canon at the Octave' (28), 'Imitation Reflected' (29), 'Canon at the Lower Fifth' (30), 'Little Dance in Canon Form' (31), 'Free Canon' (36) or 'Chromatic Invention' (91–92). Even when the titles do not specifically suggest the fact, we are always aware that this music has come from the workshop which later produced *Music for String Instruments, Percussion and Celesta*.

In the gradual realization of the tonal system through the building up of different principles, the student becomes familiar with virtually every scale known to the history of music; in the arrangement of the twelve-tone scale, even the more exotic scales are to be found. Besides pentatony, all the modal scales make their appearance; in one piece, 'In Oriental Style' (58), we find the Arabic scale of augmented seconds, while the scale of 'From the Island of Bali' reminds us of the tonal world of gamelan music.

A variety of rhythms, forte passages, and different methods of performance all have their part in a successful rendering of the *Mikrokosmos*. The pianist who penetrates to the heart of the music becomes accustomed to surprises and difficulties, so various are the types of beats, the changes in rhythm and the elision of beat divisions. In many of the pieces, including the six splendid dances that bring the series to an end, a new and interesting feature is apparent—a typically Bulgarian rhythm, which Bartók used as a medium through which he could achieve a faithful expression of his own fantastic rhythmic imagination. Other principles of form used by Bartók may be found condensed in these little pieces. Here, in Ernő Lendvai's words, the traditional fifth relations of tonality meet, as in the great works, a construction based on polarity and axes of thirds. Besides the three-part form and simple, basic construction that is so familiar from folk music, complex bridge forms appear among these pieces, as in the 'Minor Seconds, Major Sevenths' (144). There are a striking number of variations, a favourite method used by Bartók and inherited from folk music. Motival variation, constant inner development, transformation and unfolding are all features of other genres too. For it is surely true to say that the polyphonic genres represent a particular use of variation technique not only in the history of music but also in the technique of serial.

Many of the pieces were written with the deliberate intention of introducing various techniques of piano playing. There is no mistaking the purpose of the pieces entitled 'With Alternate Hands' (10), 'Thumb Under' (98), 'Crossed Hands' (99), and others. Like the piano music of Couperin, some of the pieces provide an opportunity for using two pianos or may be used as an accompaniment to songs. But certainly in most of the pieces, the ideal unity, mentioned by Doflein, is realized: the internal order of the music, the craftsmanship of the composition and the techniques of piano playing are indivisible.

In achieving the *Mikrokosmos*, Bartók was indebted to two masters and his work is a tribute to all that he learned from them. In the piece 79 he pays homage to Johann Sebastian Bach, and in number 80, to Robert Schumann. Bach guides him through the labyrinth of strict counterpoint, shows him by example how to achieve the clear, geometric structure of these miniature masterpieces and provides a model for their inner unity between the techniques of composition and performance. The spirit of Robert Schumann may be felt in the many character pieces in which Bartók evokes, from the unique formations of piano music, his own colourful world, his visions of 'far-away peoples and distant landscapes', for this is what Schumann did in the first *Kinderszenen*; for such evocations do not merely provide a basis for a tonal order, but are examples of real music which reflects the living voice of a people, as heard in the Magyar folk-songs or in Russian, Yugoslavian, Transylvanian or Bali-Island pieces. Here is the very genre of historic dances such as the Bourrée or the Minuetto. But some of the sketches are more freely drawn. Interval steps, whimsical, wild or fearsome, become a 'Dragon's Dance'. A 'rustling' tone, and the movements of 'rocking' or 'boating', are introduced into the music. The piano imitates the sound of folk instruments such as the bagpipes and the whistle (88 and 138). The lilting 6/8 movement develops into a 'Notturno' (97), while a strange restless piece with changing tonalities is given the title 'Wandering' (18) like one of the *Twenty-Seven Choruses* (No. 12). We are invited to share the 'Village Joke' (130) or we find ourselves at the 'Big Fair'

(47) and in another piece an incessant buzzing and momentary hiss is explained by the title 'From the Diary of a Fly' (142).

It is even more interesting to trace the characters and types of the small world of the *Mikrokosmos* to their origin or developments in the large works. In 'Melody in the Mist' (107), he worked out the method of a unison melody which disappears from time to time in tone patches, like the murmuring of the chorus in the background in *The Miraculous Mandarin*, or parts of the slow movement of the *Dance Suite* or the 'Night Music'. The two variations of the 'Line and Point', like the first and second scherzos of the *String Quartet No. 4*, illustrate the duality of diatonic and chromatic as well as that of widening and narrowing. 'Village Joke' repeats one of the initial ideas of the second movement of *Music for String Instruments, Percussion and Celesta*, but the largo of 'In Four Parts' (89), on the other hand, anticipates the spiritual chorale tone of the *Concerto No. 3*. Finally, the minor third signal of the last Bulgarian dance is one of the later descendants of the Arab dances and appears many times in Bartók's great works, from the ostinato of the second movement of the *Sonata for Two Pianos* to the close of the *Concerto*. It is scarcely necessary to dwell on any particular aspect of the tonal system, the principles of construction or the manner in which the artistic outlook of the composer is so profoundly identified with the music of the *Mikrokosmos*.

These little piano pieces with their homely atmosphere constitute a microcosm in the true sense of that word, reflecting the creative moments and inner life of a solitary person who has withdrawn into the family circle. All the great works composed during the same period, each one a masterpiece of the twentieth century, speak to the world at large. This also applies to the *Concerto No. 2* for piano on which Bartók commenced work in October 1930, immediately after finishing the *Cantata Profana*. It was finished sometime in September or October 1931.

From the date of the first performance onwards, the *Concerto No. 1* for piano provoked the most varied opinions all over the world. Nor should this occasion bring any surprise. For it received its first public performance at a critical time, and we also have to remember that this was a work of daring innovation in which the composer tentatively introduced the germ of ideas which were developed only later in the great works. A knowledge of these works enables us to look back with greater understanding than would be possible from an analysis of the work and its antecedents. Fascinating and full of grandeur as it is, the *Concerto No. 2* for piano provides at one and the same time a medium for superior composing techniques and opportunities for performance inherent in the difficult but rich and impressive solo part. As in the case of its predecessor, the première again took place in Frankfurt with Bartók as soloist, this time on January 23, 1933, with Hans Rosbaud conducting. During the following six years it was performed twice in London, probably twice in Warsaw, and once in Vienna, Winterthur, Zurich, Stockholm, Prague, Rotterdam, Basle, Schaffhausen, Utrecht, Birmingham, Brussels and Luxembourg. All these performances were by famous orchestras, with Bartók as the soloist, but audiences in Budapest had to wait until March 22, 1938, to hear it performed by the composer with Ernest Ansermet conducting. At all these performances the work, unlike the first concerto, was most warmly received.

Yet in many respects the second piano concerto was very similar to the first. It was similarly constructed, with three movements, the core of the work being the central slow movement which is balanced on either side by symmetrical bridge structures. But in the later work the construction is more clearly defined and is given weight by the insertion of a contrasting Scherzo played at an alarming speed in the middle of the slow movement. The slow movement before and after the Scherzo is easier to understand than the slow movement of the first concerto. The percussion signals in the first concerto are replaced in the second by a suppressed lamenting and mysterious melody heard in a veiled chorus of strings. These sounds recall the ghostly tone of the *String Quartet No. 2*, the *Dance Suite*, and later, the slow movement of the *Divertimento*. The piano continues the sharp and passionate dialogue with the strings, in which we can see Bartók's indebtedness to Baroque music, and which is also a feature of the second movement of Beethoven's Piano Concerto in G Major. In a succession of rising and falling movements, the first and last, Baroque in quality, the piano assumes the dominant role before launching into the concentrated brilliance of the solo part. It is the piano solo which then illuminates and defines every architectural elaboration of the whole vast structure.

If we compare the *String Quartet No. 5* also written at this time with the *String Quartet No. 4* written in 1928, we find that in these works too there are certain similarities. The *String Quartet No. 5* was completed between August 6 and September 6, 1934. It had been commissioned by the Library of Congress, Washington, D.C., and it was there that it was heard for the first time, on April 8, 1935, when it was performed by the Kolisch Quartet. In both works there is the same symmetrical bridge structure, but in the *String Quartet No. 5* there are seven sections whereas in the earlier work there are only five. The structural axis of the earlier work is the slow movement placed between two Scherzos, while the *String Quartet No. 5* resembles the *Concerto No. 2* for piano in that a Scherzo movement with a Bulgarian rhythm is inserted between the two inner slow movements. The seven-part structure is based on the three-part system of the Scherzo itself. Other typical features are the use of a single theme in the symmetrically paired movements and the way in which the second half of the work throws off the tense mood created by the narrow intervals with which it begins and allows a diatonic development into a much lighter atmosphere.

However, in spite of these numerous internal similarities—perhaps even because of them—we are immediately struck by the difference in tone between the two string quartets, as was the case with the two piano concertos. This was also remarked upon by Bartók's contemporaries. Antal Molnár, writing in *A ma zenéje*, said of the *String Quartet No. 5* that 'we not only find the spherical geometry of the fourth string quartet but also a heavenly confidence in the mode of expression . . .' Comments made by Sándor Jemnitz in his review after the première on March 3, 1936 in Budapest, included the remark that here the composer was 'speaking in a mature and masculine idiom, purged of all emotion, with the calm wisdom of the classical masters'. These critics had heard aright. The creative process that had begun in 1926 or even earlier had now reached the moment of fulfilment. We have seen that already in the great works written before 1930 there was a hidden promise of new structural forms, and that at every level of his stylistic communications there had been a wealth of material from which he had now conceived and fashioned the awe-inspiring structures of the *Concerto No. 1* and the *String Quartets Nos. 4* and *5*. The instrumental style of a whole era matured as a conscious system from the date of the *Nine Little Piano Pieces*, the *Forty-Four Duos* and the miniature masterpieces of the *Mikrokosmos*.

The works after 1930 are made almost eloquent by an attempt to incorporate the flood of thoughts which had been waiting for realization and which had now found their way into the open. Unlike Kodály's songs and choral works, Bartók's vocal works are not the direct expression of a delight in singing. His music is based on an instrumental concept. Like Beethoven, Bartók was driven to verbal communication by an inner compulsion; he forced himself to speak and to prophesy because he was living at a time when it was unthinkable not to do so.

In Bartók's earlier works, human lament and protest in times of crisis had found expression in the sighing sounds of the castle in *Bluebeard's Castle*, the murmuring of the chorus in the background of *The Miraculous Mandarin* and the yearning note of the 'Night's Music'. But in the later choruses these feelings also found eloquent expression in words. These were inspired by the lyrics of folk-songs; in the case of the *Cantata Profana* Bartók conceived the words and music almost simultaneously. The stubborn tone of choral declamation in the *Cantata Profana* and later in the *From Olden Times* spilled over into the instrumental music of the period. For instance, the broken choral recitation in 'the largest stag, the favourite son' section of the *Cantata Profana* is echoed in the hard, repetitive notes heard in unison at the beginning of the *String Quartet No. 5* and again even more strongly in the declamatory tone of the returning main subject of the first movement after this has been sundered by an outburst of chords. What was formerly expressed as a minor third ostinato now becomes an exclamation, either heard as the obvious complaining of the piano parlando of the slow movement in the *Concerto No. 2* or expressing effort and struggle as at the beginning of the *String Quartet No. 5*. The tense whispering sounds which expressed the Mandarin's determined resistance and will to live now become the ostinatos of the slow movement of the *Sonata for Two Pianos*, continuing yet again the tone of resistance expressed in the 'but they will not go' section of the *Cantata Profana* and the cry of victory heard in the *Mikrokosmos* and at the end of the *Concerto:* in every one of these compositions we are hearing the unyielding cries of men who are prepared to die for the cause of freedom.

The instrumental and choral works mutually influence each other. Within the purified atmosphere of the children's choruses, the human voices reflect the cleansed, lucid structure of the *Mikrokosmos* and the *Forty-Four Duos* with their ethereal instrumental effects. Later these same choruses were to lend charming, playful ideas to the composer, enriching his instrumental inventiveness. Ten years later, the play of interchanging voices in major thirds at the end of 'Breadbaking', is used to bring to its close the first movement of the *Concerto No. 3*.

Though one might well have thought it impossible for Bartók to maintain such perfection, that 'heavenly confidence' and 'calm wisdom of the classical masters' which had amazed his contemporaries, it in fact represented for him merely an intermediary stage at which he did not even pause before advancing to yet greater heights. The struggle had not ended. Indeed, it was only now that it had begun in earnest. Again and again, every new creation demanded of him a new solution, gained only by incessant effort; each problem had to be solved in a different way and each solution brought him nearer perfection. In each new work the intellectual battleground covered a broader segment of human affairs. In every new creation, over and over again, he had to breathe new life into the styles that had been fashioned previously, to make them capable of conveying, arranging and emphasizing a much richer and more aspiring content. During the years following the composition of the *String Quartet No. 5*, Bartók composed two incomparable masterpieces of the twentieth century, *Music for String Instruments, Percussion and Celesta* and the *Sonata for Two Pianos*, the first of these being commissioned by his friends in Basle.

Bartók had first come in contact with the Basle Chamber Orchestra and its director, Paul Sacher, in 1929. In the summer of 1936, they requested him to compose a work for string orchestra possibly supplemented by a few other intruments. When, on June 27, Bartók wrote to accept the commission, he already had a complete plan in mind.

> I am thinking of a work for strings and percussion (thus, besides the strings, there would be piano, celesta, harp, xylophone and percussion instruments).

Writing again on August 31, he added that sixty-six pages of the score were already complete, 'about four still missing'. He gave it a temporary title in French, *Musique pour instruments à cordes, batterie et célesta en quatre mouvements*, with some idea of renaming it later. The work, however, became known by this title: *Music for String Instruments, Percussion and Celesta*. Bartók was present when the work was given its première in Basle on January 21, 1937. At the first performance in Budapest on February 14, 1938, Ernő Dohnányi was the conductor.

Ernő Lendvai, who has been responsible for some of the most painstaking analyses of Bartók's compositions, is of the opinion that Bartók's intention in writing the *Sonata for Two Pianos* was to create 'a kind of macrocosm', which would set a seal upon all that he had achieved in the *Mikrokosmos*. The list of instruments which Bartók planned to use, and the fact that the character of both works is that of chamber music, confirm this view. On the other hand, the concept of a 'macrocosm', or universe, is realized on a grander scale in the *Music for String Instruments, Percussion and Celesta*.

For thirty years, Bartók had been trying to resolve the problem of the relationship between man and nature, man and the universe, man and freedom. Ever since he had first become aware of the questions raised in *Zarathustra* by Nietzsche and in the music of Strauss, he had attempted in every one of his compositions to penetrate to the heart of these problems, approaching them in many different ways. But never before had he considered at such a high philosophical level the problem of human existence in relation to the universe: the identity, in the words of Kant, between the inner moral laws and the starry sky. Now he was asking whether there could be any direct link between the individual personal existence of a human being and the impersonal, objective world of nature outside himself. Was it possible to find in the unfeeling majesty of a precisely ordered universe an answer to the problem of human existence? Was this the way to bring to an end the manifold worries and uncertainties which trouble mankind?

Bartók's attraction to the idea of a mathematically ordered nature, to the intellectual beauty of the cosmic structure, and his illusion of a transcendental solution, were never stronger than at the time when he was composing the *Music for String Instruments, Percussion and Ce-*

lesta. Like so many of his contemporaries he too might have succumbed to the temptation to search for artistic truth in the enticing combinations of abstract forms, he too might have found some easy path from the laws of morality to the numerical mysticism of the starry sky. The way would have been easy for him, gifted as he was with constructive genius and endowed with all the refinements of knowledge acquired during the previous ten years.

But he rejected any such easy solution. He rejected it in the first movement of the *Music for String Instruments, Percussion and Celesta*, this marvellous creation of the twentieth century with its brilliant strictly defined arrangement of form.

From the central A, the theme, which coils upwards from compressed melodic rings of narrow intervals, soars into a masterly fugue. It soars heavenwards in both directions, ever deeper and higher at one and the same time. Finally, upon reaching the contrasting polarity of the E flat, the swirling of the congested theme turns away as from a taboo, returning to its starting point, and like a genie released only temporarily from its flask, melts into the initial A.

The approach is solitary and speculative and indicates no solution: the circle closes just as it did in the opera, *Bluebeard's Castle*. There the enchanted ring spread from F sharp to C, while here it goes from A to E flat. We sense the torment and doubt with which Bartók approaches the twin pillars of Kant's ethics, so absolute in their duality.

If the fugue is counted as a first movement, the *Music for String Instruments, Percussion and Celesta* becomes a four-movement work. It is a comparatively rare form among the structures used by Bartók. He uses music which is similar in tone from which to fashion the introduction linked to the fast movement in the *Sonata for Two Pianos* and also as a framing ritornelle in the *String Quartet No. 6*, the two works that followed. Bartók had last used this tone some thirty years previously in the *String Quartet No. 1* when he had employed it as a loosely constructed independent movement ending with a firm reflection of the profound philosophical problems of the first movement.

The theme of the fugue permeates the entire work with all the stubborn persistence of a Berlioz '*idée fixe*'. In the second movement, the material of the fugue is used to form a scherzo in which the later developments of the rustic, barbaric, measured dance and ecstatic waltz of *The Miraculous Mandarin* are fused in a kaleidoscope of brilliant, sometimes almost macabre, variations. The closed bridge symmetry of the third movement reiterates the temptation of the 'starry skies' solution, expressed here as a solitary night vision. Fragments of the basic theme weave together and frame the various parts, foreshadowing the ritornelle construction of the *String Quartet No. 6*.

In the fourth movement, these rigidly enclosed forms are replaced by a garland of free, jubilant folk dances and the anxious basic theme with its short intervals widens into diatony and swells into a broad hymn. Here we find the only true solution to our universal dilemma: a noble unity between man and nature can only be realized in conditions which ensure social coexistence. This idea of the brotherhood of man, which was the basic theme of the work, was at the same time a political theme of topical significance, offering to the world of the mid-thirties a practical programme for the realization of men's hopes.

This work provides a superb example of human achievement in the field of music in the twentieth century; it reveals an astonishing wealth of musical genres, types and characters, all of which play their part in the logical development of the thought and contribute to solutions based on common principles. Every now and then, some surprising idea illuminates the dance rhythms and tone typical of the period. Bence Szabolcsi, in his biography of Bartók, characterized the piece as 'one of the most grandiose works by the composer . . . revealing possibilities of a new tone which are unique in their time; and above all this, there is a tremendous range of musical content which, from the initial fugue through the abandoned dance phantasy and night monologue, arches to a hymnic dithyramb, exemplifying within itself the inferno of our present age and the way forward to Paradise.'

After the première of this work, Bartók's friends in Basle did not give him much time to rest before presenting him with a further request, in May 1937. This time he was asked to provide a chamber work for the Basle section of the International Society for Contemporary Music. Already in June, while taking a summer holiday in Carinthia, Bartók had drawn up certain proposals, and in a letter dated September 2, he announced that he had completed the first two movements and half of the third movement of his new work. On January 16, 1938, almost exactly one year after the première of *Music for String Instruments, Percussion and Celesta*, Béla Bartók together with his wife, Ditta Pásztory, played the piano parts at the première of the *Sonata for Two Pianos and Percussion*. The percussion instruments were played by Fritz Schiesser and Philipp Rühlig of Basle. These names should be recorded for Bartók, in his letters, always wrote appreciatively of their participation.

Bartók wrote this work because he was attracted by the technical problems and possibilities of their solution inherent in a composition for piano and percussions instruments. Writing on this subject in the Basle *National Zeitung*, he said,

> Slowly . . . the conviction grew within me that a single piano and the frequently very sharp tones of the percussion are not well balanced. For this reason, I modified my conception, and used with the percussion not one piano but two.

Stimulated by the challenge of this technical problem, Bartók produced a brilliant, vivid and colourful chamber work with a variety of interesting sound effects. The starting point for the content, however, is once again the disturbing question which Bartók felt compelled to resolve in ever newer ways—the problem of human freedom and social harmony. In this work we sense Bartók's driving urge to escape not into the uncertainties of abstract idealistic philosophy as in the *Music for String Instruments, Percussion and Celesta*, but by making a direct personal attack as in the *Cantata Profana*. The *Sonata for Two Pianos* travels headlong down the path taken by the hunter's sons who were miraculously transformed into stags, but here the flight is more disturbing and merciless. The slow introduction, expressive of emergence from the twilight of historical non-existence, is followed by a wild chase in which the hunter's cries rouse the forest, but no force in nature can now constitute an obstacle capable of halting the flight of the creature driven by fanatic longing to seek his freedom. In the fearsome depths of the forest at night, 'nel mezzo del cammin di nostra vita', the miracle takes place once again. But this time we do not have to stay with the father as he gazes after his sons, watching the stags disappear into the distance where they find their freedom. This time we too can travel the path to freedom, as in the *Music for String Instruments, Percussion and Celesta*, the *Mikrokosmos* and the string quartets. We too can share the joy liberated in the finale, the joy of release, at once playful and piercing.

The tone of the last movement is less elevated, closer to the earth than the hymn expressive of fulfilment at the end of the *Music for String Instruments, Percussion and Celesta*. Here Bartók repeats, even more openly than in the second movement of the *Music*, his references to popular genres, street songs and dances. These references to everyday genres were to be made in all the works to follow, mostly in the last movements of his compositions where they would be found as frivolous or grotesque distortions of a serious thought.

The numerically perfect geometric order of Bartók's musical constructions was first demonstrated by Ernő Lendvai in his analysis of the *Sonata for Two Pianos*. It is undoubtedly true that on the basis of the magnificent internal order of his forms, Bartók must be ranked equal to the greatest masters of musical construction in all the history of music— Bach and Beethoven. But his greatness as a composer and as an artist lies in the fact that the perfection of his works and the fascinating novelty of his world of sounds was based on a use of forms suited to an exemplary and strict exposition of his ideals which thus made a convincing appeal to the emotions and the intellect.

4 INAUGURAL ADDRESS AT THE ACADEMY OF SCIENCES. REVIVÁL OF BARTÓK'S WORKS IN THE OPERA HOUSE, BARTÓK COMPOSITIONS IN THE STRENGTHENING CHORAL MOVEMENT. BARTÓK AND THE PROGRESSIVE HUNGARIAN INTELLIGENTSIA

On February 3, 1936, Béla Bartók spoke at the inauguration ceremony in which he was formally awarded a chair in the Hungarian Academy of Sciences. At last the Academy had recognized the scientific value of his research work in the field of folk music in which he had now been engaged for more than thirty years. He gave his address in the small chamber of the Academy immediately next to the room in which he worked on his study of folk music.

On this occasion, however, he did not choose to speak about folk music, but about Ferenc Liszt. It was just at the time when the whole nation was commemorating the fiftieth anniversary of the composer's death. This fact provided an obvious motive for the choice of subject. But the real reason why Bartók chose to speak about Liszt was his own great interest in the master with whom, from early youth, he had felt a bond of creative sympathy. He began his lecture by recalling the article which he had written a quarter of a century before on the occasion of the centenary of Liszt's birth.

At this ceremony a man who was himself a master of composition was enabled to speak about the significance of Liszt in the history of music: a master, moreover, with a real understanding of Liszt's music and one who had assimilated into his own compositions Liszt's most far-reaching innovations. Nor were these confined to such open references as the reminiscence of the *La Leggierezza* which occurs in the introductory theme of the *Sonata for Two Pianos* (Bartók himself once playfully drew the attention of Aladár Tóth to this similarity); for Liszt also exerted a profound and lasting influence on the structure of Bartók's tonal system, his method of construction and his artistic outlook. Those who had the opportunity, that very evening or two weeks later on February 18, of listening to Bartók's authentic interpretation of Liszt's *Danse Macabre*, were able to appreciate for themselves how near in spirit these two masters were.

Though Bartók spoke on what appeared to be a historical subject, there were both political and personal implications in what he said. He began his speech, just as he had done many years before, with a reference to the appreciation and recognition of Liszt's work by the public, but his comments show that he was also thinking about the fate of his own works. When he came to consider the relation between Liszt and Hungarian folk music, he found an opportunity to deplore his own recent experience of uncomprehending attitudes to folk music. Concerning a collection in Borsod County, he said that in 1933 ' . . .the coldness and apathy of the official circles frustrated everything . . .' And he added,

> Finally, I would again mention the controversy of the last few years, to some extent deliberately fostered in the columns of the press, in which the dilettante protagonists of popular art music—who are unfortunately in the majority among the upper classes—do their best to disparage the music of the peasants.

He cited as an example an article which had appeared on June 9, 1933, in the popular *Rádió Újság*, in which he was attacked because of his interest in folk music, and the Radio criticized for lending him support. It would have been possible to find many such examples in the pages of the contemporary press.

In his closing remarks dealing with the question of Liszt's claim to Hungarian nationality, he spoke about the composer's life and quoted Liszt's own statements on the subject, and it is not difficult to hear in Bartók's emotional tone an echo of his own bitter struggle to win recognition as a Hungarian, both at home and abroad, as well as the painful memory of all his sufferings which call to mind the query of a wounded Ady, 'Am I not a Hungarian?'

His fierce indignation against those 'who prevent us, as much as they can, from following the tradition of Liszt,' was fostered by a very real sense of grievance. Only recently, in December 1935, the Kisfaludy Society has scarcely concealed their scorn for him by awarding him the Greguss Medal, one of their prizes for practising artists, not for his most recent work but for the *Suite No. 1* which he had written thirty years previously. It was scarcely possible to demonstrate more clearly their antagonism to the Bartók who had created the string quartets, the piano concertos and the neglected stage works. The 'upper classes' mentioned in Bartók's speech at the Academy could scarcely have declared themselves more openly.

Bartók wrote angrily to reject the insulting award. He brought his letter to a close with the firm determination to have nothing to do with it.

> ... I do not wish to accept the Greguss Medal, neither now, nor in the future, nor during my lifetime, nor after my death,

he wrote, much to the discomfiture of the members of the society. The isolated position in which he now found himself was the logical outcoms of the attitude he had maintained for many years, exemplified in hie rejection of the Corvin Wreath and his refusal to attend government receptions. It was just after the scandalous incident of the Greguss Medal and while he was preparing to set out on his tour of Turkey that he wrote to László Rásonyi,

There is one thing that I absolutely don't want in this matter, and that is the financial assistance of the Hungarian Ministry of Culture. I have my pressing reason for this.
(December 18, 1935)

To dwell on such incidents, however, would be to distort and oversimplify the situation in which Bartók found himself at that time. In fact, never before had the great composer, whose own works were of a crystal-like purity, been so encompassed about with confused intellectualism and contradictory cultural movements. In the words of István Péterfi, it was a 'sly' situation. It was also an increasingly complex situation, for those who opposed the official cultural policy were growing in number, their rank swelled by a younger generation who sought to resolve the political crisis through cultural activities.

At all events, it was now that the Opera House again scheduled two of Bartók's stage works for performance—*The Wooden Prince* for January 30, 1935 and *Bluebeard's Castle* for October 29, 1936. These two revivals in two successive years met with the same kind of public response as when they were first performed in 1917 and 1918. And once again, the performances heralded a growing interest in the music of Bartók. It was the younger generation of artists at the Opera House who finally fulfilled the hopes of István Péterfi, Antal Molnár, Aladár Tóth and Sándor Jemnitz, who for decades had been pressing for performances worthy of the works themselves. The ballet was conducted by János Ferencsik, while the opera was conducted not by Egisto Tango again, but by Sergio Failoni. Jan Cieplinsky was the choreographer, Gusztáv Oláh and Zoltán Fülöp the scenic designers and Kálmán Nádasdy was the director. The ballet dancers who received special mention from the critics included Karola Szalay, Bella Bordy, Gyula Harangozó and László Csányi. Ella Némethy and Mihály Székely appeared for the first time in the two roles of *Bluebeard's Castle*.

The revival of *Bluebeard's Castle* was followed on November 9 by the Budapest première of the *Cantata Profana*, a somewhat belated occasion, coming as it did six years after the work was completed and two and a half years after the first performance in London. The occasion of the première was a concert of the Philharmonic Society when the orchestra was conducted by Ernő Dohnányi and the solo parts were

326

sung by two outstanding artists from the Opera, Endre Rösler and Imre Palló. Its true success, however, came only after the second performance one month later. This was on December 10, during a Bartók programme at the Vigadó Concert Hall arranged by the Budapest Education Committee. The work was conducted by Viktor Vaszy, the young conductor of the Palestrina Chorus, and the evening developed into nothing less than one long tribute to the composer. This reception caused the critic Gyula Fodor to conclude as follows: 'It is now clear that Bartók's work arouses so much interest that there is no difficulty in filling every seat in the Vigadó.' The warmth and enthusiasm of the lively young audience even resulted in some relaxation of the composer's reserve which had by now become habitual. This was the first occasion after an interval of many years when he played one of his own works, the *Rhapsody* op. 1, on a concert platform in the capital city.

His art always sprang from the life he shared with others. He breathed in unison with the people, drew strength from the common lot, and even when living a hermit-like existence in his own home, or making the wearying journeys incumbent upon a performing artist who had to appear on the concert platforms of the world, he always addressed himself to the people. For a long time there was only the stimulus of an occasional concert in the provinces to nourish the personal relations of composer and audience. But Bartók never ceased to feel the need for such communion. In his choral works, too, he was looking for the comradeship of other artists who could work with him actively and share his destiny. He was impelled by a great need to reach an understanding with his people and he felt that he had an important message for them. They listened and understood. On May 11, 1936, some of his *Hungarian Folk-Songs* for mixed chorus (Nos. 2, 3, 4) were heard for the first time in Kecskemét, where they were sung by Zoltán Vásárhelyi's choir. The programme also included Kodály's choral work *Molnár Anna*, and a choral composition by Kodály which had had a previous hearing, *Jesus and the Traders*. All these pieces were exceptionally difficult to perform. The programme was repeated in Budapest on May 14 at the Academy of Music by the *Városi Dalárda* (City Choral Society) of Kecskemét.

One of Bartók's earlier choral works, *Four Old Hungarian Folk-Songs*, written in 1912, was selected as one of the compulsory pieces for the national choral festival held in Szombathely in June 1936. This evoked a comment from Ferenc Jankovich, a poet who was also a musician, that those of Bartók's works which had previously been considered too difficult for performance were given 'a rendering by village choirs that could serve as an example to the whole nation'.

When a concert was planned to take place in Kecskemét on April 18, 1937, the occasion became an event of national importance. Here, for the first time, it would be possible to hear *From Olden Times*, Bartók's astonishing series for male chorus. And at a choral concert given by the youth choirs in the Budapest Academy of Music on May 7, the people of Budapest also heard this immense new choral work as well as eighteen new choral works for children. Bartók himself played a number of pieces selected from his *Mikrokosmos*.

In one of his letters dated May 24, he describes this concert for the benefit of the wife of Professor Müller in Basle. His comments on the choral works for children are given below:

> It was a great experience for me when—at the rehearsal—I heard for the first time my little choruses coming from the lips of these children. I shall never forget this impression of the freshness and gaiety of the little ones' voices. There is something in the natural way these children from the suburban schools produce their voices, that reminds one of the unspoilt sound of peasant singing.

Here he was referring to the László Perényi-Preisinger's Children's Choir, the Liget Street Boys' Choir of Kőbánya. And his comments in this letter are a reflection of that quality which so much impressed Aladár Tóth when listening to the *Violin Duos* and which impelled him to say that for Bartók nature and the world of children were one and the same thing, and that both symbolized a society that was very close to nature.

Kodály greeted the publication of the choruses for women and children with these words.: 'Hungarian children do not yet realize that at Christmas, 1936, they received a gift that will last a lifetime. Only those know it who would like to give to Hungarian children in the future a world in which the air is purer, the sky bluer and the sun gives more warmth ... Only those who long cherished desire to have Bartók in their company now see their hopes fulfilled.' We also realize from this message why it was that in a letter which Bartók wrote some six months later he laid particular emphasis on the quality of the suburban children's singing. Kodály goes on to explain that in these choruses, Bartók is not speaking to the well-to-do city child who has been taught to play some instrument like generations of children before him, but rather to that 'mass of orphan children' for whom 'all the treasure concealed in instrumental literature is unattainable'. Nor was he offering them folk music such as he created for instrumental players but was speaking to them 'in his own individual language'. As Kodály puts it, 'there is none of the "pedagogical" self-importance, nor the gurgling of an adult trying to imitate children. He does not "stoop" to their level but considers them as human companions. It was an attitude that may only be adopted by comeone who, in spite of his gray hairs, has remained young in heart. Someone who feels an adult responsibility for what he says to children but who says something that adults too can appreciate. This is an art of great value to adults too.'

Bartók's interest in the art of choral compositions was comparatively recent and since he was following so closely in the footsteps of Kodály, the latter was able to greet him in the familiar manner of one who had already made the same journey. It was Kodály's educational programme, put into practice on a large scale all over the country over a period of ten years, as well as his example as a composer, that was responsible for the development and greatly improved standard of the national choral movement based on folk music. It was his pupils who organized and taught choirs similar to that of Kecskemét. It was not for the first time that we attempted to apply the lessons so bitterly learnt in past ages, hoping to safeguard social progress and the ideals of national independence by fostering cultural and intellectual movements. Abortive hopes of a great revolutionary era were transformed, because of political compulsion, into a nation-wide programme for education, one result of this being, as we have seen, the extension of the choral movement organized on the basis of Kodály's teachings. Undoubtedly, the movement was both far-reaching and effective, and united under its banner numbers of people with widely differing aspirations and interpretations of national unity; in general it might be said to have symbolized a united national resistance to German pressure. However, because of their lack of political sophistication, the great masses who took part in the movement willingly simplified the danger of fascism which they thought of as merely representing a threat to the nation and the national culture. Thus, with all the enthusiasm shown in the movements for national independence in the nineteenth century, they countered nationalism with nationalism.

At first, the movement quite rightly took advantage of all the opportunities offered as a result of the short-sightedness of official cultural policy. A number of splendid pioneering cultural projects were officially accepted because their true intention was hidden beneath an outward show of blatant nationalism. But the nationalist spirit grew in strength, and like the sorcerer's apprentice, began to take charge where once it had been subservient. Gradually, the idealists were unable to withstand the pressure of dishonest intruders, and indeed, after some time became the tools of the officials; the latter, profiting from this experience, began to use the youth movement also as a medium through which to convey their own creed.

Understandably, then, organized labour showed little interest in a musical movement which had nevertheless been initiated on the basis of correct artistic aims. And it is true that deep within the movement the flames of a continuous revolutionary tradition were never extinguished. This fire sprang to life in the symbolic language of Kodály's gigantic choral work *Jesus and the Traders*. And Bartók's *From Olden Times* did not even make use of symbolism. Every word and every tone in this work was an undisguised political appeal. Writing after the Budapest première, Aladár Tóth commented that the work 'had a topicality rarely heard in Hungarian music... Never before has a Hungarian shown such determination in naming that curse against which we must fight and that great treasure for which we must struggle in our battle for the Hungarian people.'

The most gifted members of our intelligentsia saw clearly enough, even at that time, both the progressive and retrograde aspects of the folk-song choral movement. They remained faithful to the basic revolutionary ideals of the movement and watched with anxiety the danger inherent in their distortion. Young members of the labour movement who had been trained in music, Sándor Vándor for instance, or Sándor Kuti, the younger, set themselves the task of giving to the labour movement a progressive musical culture of a high standard which would truly serve the people and speak for them.

The progressive members of the intelligentsia of those days formed a loosely knit group which it would be difficult to describe in general terms. The analysis of their activities, mode of life and historical role is a task for future historians, though the material for such a study survives in personal memories rather than in written sources. They were neither united nor organized. The historical function of these intellectuals whose views and interests were common to both socialists and members of the bourgeoisie, was to provide a rather homogeneous, active and absorbent medium around the core of party intellectuals. They met in private houses, studios and coffee houses; there they argued, formulated, passed on and exchanged their life-giving ideas. They acted as a medium for and created a living current between the working class, the illegal party and many outstanding intellectuals who otherwise had no personal connections with the Communists. They were to be found actively at work among the personal friends and pupils of both Bartók and Kodály; they helped to swell the audiences for the work of the two composers, propagated their ideals and fostered a climate of opinion in which the new music was more readily accepted by the broad mass of the people.

It is not necessary to delve beneath the surface of the age to discover the cultural realities and revolutionary traditions that still persisted. The official cultural policy was never strong enough to choke the living culture and conscience of the nation.

However, one indication of the power of officialdom is the fact that the Opera House was only allowed to revive *The Wooden Prince* and *Bluebeard's Castle* on condition that the name of Béla Balázs would not appear on the posters. Balázs was living abroad as an émigré, but Bartók fought to secure royalties for him, and when these were finally granted, Bartók personally forwarded the money to him. Nor were the authorities successful in their attempt to prevent István Péterfi from referring to Balázs in his review of the ballet. In fact Péterfi actually began his review with a quotation from the review of *Bluebeard's Castle* written at the time of the opera's first performance by Béla Reinitz, head of the Music

Committee of the Republic of Councils. The fact that he was able to do this becomes all the more interesting when we realize that Reinitz, to whom Bartók had dedicated his *Five Songs* based on poems by Ady, was at that time still living in Budapest. His former colleagues saw him frequently, either in his own home or in his favourite coffee house. Many of those former colleagues were in official positions in 1936, and Reinitz did not conceal his opinion of the contemporary government leaders.

The confusion of the period may be summed up, more clearly than by further analysis, in one of István Péterfi's reminiscences. In June, 1936, the permanent Committee for Literature and Art of the League of Nations met in Budapest. Thomas Mann was a member of this committee and took part in the session. István Péterfi quotes the description of this occasion given by the great German author himself in his reminiscences entitled *Sechzehn Jahre:* ' . . .it was in the Hungarian capital that I made an impromptu speech against the murderers of freedom, explained the necessity for a militant democracy; this statement, almost wholly lacking in tact, offended the character of the whole meeting which consisted of purely academic exchange and which because of the presence of fascist representatives, was of a deceptive nature. The Hungarian audience, on the other hand, responded with a demonstration of their approval that lasted for minutes . . ."

On June 8, a government reception was held in the Gerbeaud Pavilion in the City Park. István Péterfi tells us that Thomas Mann and his party 'had no wish to sit at the same table as the Minister of Culture, Bálint Hóman'. The great author pleaded 'indisposition' and refused the invitation. Lajos Hatvany, at one time also a friend of Ady, and now host to Thomas Mann and his family, gladly seized this opportunity to organize a gathering in his own home. It seems that Bartók was also suffering from the same kind of 'indisposition'. He accepted Hatvany's invitation with pleasure and arrived at the house together with Béla Reinitz. Thus the annals of history include an account of the 'private' meeting between the great author and the great composer, but there is no record of the official government reception.

This episode, perhaps more than any other single event of those days, demonstrates the living reality of the revolutionary spirit bequeathed by Ady. There were living in our midst men who had been the personal friends of Ady, men who had witnessed the dawn of hope at the time of the Republic of Councils and who had worked to make that hope a reality. They taught in obscure secondary schools and technical colleges, passing on to another generation what they had themselves inherited. Again and again, the forces of reaction had to combat the living spirit of Ady. When Kodály composed *The Peacock*, in which he set to music some of Ady's verses, this work symbolized the beginnings of a fusion between our great new choral art and the labour movement. In our account of the years before the First World War, we were constantly aware of the manner in which Ady's work as a pioneer affected the art of Bartók. During the years at present under consideration, we see how Bartók, among others, now passed on the Ady heritage to a younger generation of artists and poets, notably Attila József.

It is probable that the two men met only once, when Bence Szabolcsi was also present. Bartók had just given a lecture on mechanical music in the smaller chamber of the Academy of Music when Attila József, editor of the magazine *Szép Szó*, asked if he could have the text of the lecture for his paper, a request which was granted. '. . .and he spoke to Bartók not as a pupil but with the respect and devotion of a son,' said Bence Szabolcsi.

Not long before his death, Attila József drafted the outline of a study of Bartók, but this was never written. His famous poem, *Bear Dance*, was inspired by Bartók's music. Nevertheless, in its rhythm and tone, the poem recalls the last memorable piece of the *Ten Easy Piano Pieces*, and has also certain other common scherzo intonations such as may be found, for example, in the dance of the wooden puppet. When he came to examine the similarities between the Bear Dance and 'night poetry' of the two artists, as well as those features which are in general characteristic of their respective work, Bence Szabolcsi established that it was in their night poetry that 'the two poets of the dark era were closest to each other'.

An attempt to discover the wider significance of the artistic approach behind the principles of their works, leads us to many ideas held in common by these two men. Much interesting deliberation would be aroused by an analysis of the continuous line of thought from the village peasant content of Bartók's music to Attila József's poetry of urban poverty. Certainly the cosmic nature pictures of Bartók's night poetry may be placed side by side with the *Bear Dance* and József's scenes from city life. It was only after the death of Attila József that Bartók's *Bear Dances* took on a new form and broadened their content in the Burletta of the *String Quartet No. 6,* in *Contrasts* and in the *Concerto* with its grotesque world of the urban dance of death.

Different aspects of the common content of their work are emphasized by Ady, Bartók and József, but their poetic relationship is assured by the ideal which they held in common, that of the brotherhood of people.

CHAPTER XII

LAST YEARS AND WORKS IN EUROPE. 1937–1940

1 Campaign of slander against Bartók and Kodály in the clerical
press. Struggle with fascism, anxiety for Hungary and Europe.
Rescue of manuscripts

The atmosphere in which Béla Bartók spent his last years at home in his
native country was made even more unbearable by the increasing menace
of fascism and the threat of a war which was soon to become a reality.

The press campaign which developed around the educational influence
of the music of Bartók and Kodály was a clear sign of the increasing
pressure of German policy in Hungary and the imminent military action
associated with it.

The alarm was sounded at the beginning of July in the columns of
Magyar Kultúra, a paper owned by Béla Bangha, an extreme and impatient Jesuit preacher, and a man with very considerable influence. It was
obvious that his attack had been provoked by the rapid development of
the Youth Choirs movement and the increasing popularity of the music
of Bartók and Kodály. An unsigned column headed 'Penpoint' began the
attack: 'Anyone who cannot see that in Hungary today there is more and
more official support for the Bartók and Kodály cult, must be blind.
In our papers, discussion of art is confined to exaggerated praise for the
genius of Bartók and Kodály; and what is more shocking, the children's
choirs in the schools of Budapest, directed by ambitious teachers, both
men and women, appear before the public with nothing to offer except
choral works by Bartók and Kodály.' The writer goes on to say that he
does not wish to disparage the 'talent, or if you like, the genius' of the
two masters, but he feels that their music, like the poetry of Ady, represents the victory of a 'bleak, destructive soul'. This criticism was, he felt,
especially true of Bartók's music. Nevertheless, he believed that adults
should listen to their music if they wished to do so, and might even take
pleasure in it—a critical pleasure, of course; but it was his opinion that
young people, who 'have not developed a critical faculty', should not be

compelled to study it in what was 'virtually an official organization. And still less should the carols of the church be led in this direction'.

The anonymous author of the article noted the rapidly growing popularity of this new kind of music among young people, and the possible ways in which the authorities through their educational policies could make use of this popularity, either deliberately or without being fully conscious of their intentions.

The writer, in describing what he thought of as a 'danger' in the movement, was more clear-sighted and possessed a greater political acumen than many of the numerous leaders of the Youth Choirs, who were often well-intentioned but politically naive, or the liberal, or pseudo-liberal workers within the educational organization. He saw clearly enough that at the very heart of the movement there was a progressive humanistic content which, in his article, he had called 'destruction'. The writer felt he had a responsibility towards young Catholics, he feared the confused ideas which might cause them to compromise their ideals, he wished to protect them from exposure to such disturbing influences and from the danger of pollution by the politically mature progressive members of the intelligentsia and the basically humanistic ideals of the movement.

This article aroused a storm of opposition, and the author of the article could not have imagined the flood of letters, unanimous in their protest, which were in fact sent to the editors of *Magyar Kultúra*. Even the editors of the *Magyarság*, who were well known as supporters of the government, did not allow such a slander against the intellectual riches of the country to pass unnoticed. Letters appeared in the press by, among others, Antal Molnár, Aladár Tóth and Kodály himself. Nor did Aladár Tóth and Sándor Jemnitz make any secret of the fact that in Bartók's music they heard a cry for freedom and human dignity. Now the *Népszava* took up the challenge and stated in an article that music had to be considered as a matter of ideology. 'And let us admit,' continued the writer, 'that it is in the field of music that we have most to lose. Poetry, which responds most directly to the spirit of the age, has burned itself out . . . Painting and sculpture are also slowly surrendering to the pitiless spirit and conscious purpose of the times . . . Only music has so far shown resistance. Béla Bangha touched on the very heart of the matter when he protested against the pieces from the Bartók–Kodály folk-music collections being sung by children's choirs. This old champion of the extreme right is quite correct in thinking that all the activities growing out of Bartók's music, whether consciously or unconsciously fostered, have their influence on the souls of children. The difference between us lies in the fact that we consider this influence to be not only desirable but necessary. Yet, it is necessary that in this age, with its general lack of education, its dilettantism, pseudo-Hungarianism, racism, and every kind of blatant propaganda, at least in the field of music, the truth of art should be allowed to remain triumphantly victorious.'

In August a reply came from Bangha and his associates. 'Penpoint' now directed his scathing words not so much against the composers as against the author of the article in which they had been defended. This time 'Penpoint' came right out into the open, thereby justifiying all that had been said about him in *Népszava*. 'That art,' he declared, 'which is not intended for the nation as a whole and which contributes nothing to the culture and communal life of our times, but which is the willing servant of a group of proletarians and hyper-intellectuals who are totally isolated from the body of the nation and quite without thought of nationalism, that art, I say, is completely destructive . . . Let them attempt to offer a choice. I dare say that, given that choice, the child of today would decide with flushed face in favour of the military march, the *Giovinezza*, or the *Horst Wessel*. Whether this is a matter about which one should be glad or sorry, whether this is a desirable or an accursed state of affairs, that is another question . . .' The article was again unsigned. Music had also become a battlefield in the war of political ideas, and the two opposing forces were taking up their positions.

When Bartók returned home after his summer vacation, he maintained an attitude to the press campaign that was both wise and composed.

> When a person is in the public eye, anything can be said about him . . . What is destructive about my music? Even the writer of the article could not say. I cannot even try to improve my work since I do not know what they are complaining about. I consider the whole matter beneath my attention,

he wrote to the folklorist, János Manga, according to a report which appeared in the *Prágai Magyar Hirlap* in November.

The storm aroused by the article in Bangha's paper had scarcely abated when the press found another opportunity to launch a personal attack on Bartók. It was just at that time that he refused to give permission to the Hungarian Radio to permit the transmission of his piano recitals over the German and Italian broadcasting systems. 'The reason for my decision,' he told a reporter from the *Pesti Napló*,

> is simply that I have never performed either for the Italian Radio or for that of the Third Reich, and indeed, I have never been directly invited to do so by either of these two companies. In the circumstances, I do not consider it right that they should be allowed to transmit performances I gave for the Budapest Radio, just like that, as a free gift . . .

(October 10, 1937)

Endre Hlatky, at that time the director of the Budapest Radio, made a statement to the same effect. But all his attempts to show that the ban had no political implications were in vain. The excuse may well have had some validity, but everyone was perfectly aware of the greater truth that lay behind the decision. For some years now, Bartók's letters had revealed his increasing anxiety about the trend of events in Europe. Nor did he conceal in these letters what he felt about the fascist countries, especially Hitler's Germany. Already in May 1937, he was confessing to Mrs. Müller-Widman that the reason why he and his family did not go to the Italian Dolomites for their holiday was because his hatred of Italy had grown to 'unnatural proportions'. On January 31, on his way home from the first performance abroad of the *Sonata for Two Pianos*, he wrote from Germany to Sándor Albrecht in Bratislava, and instead of putting at the head of his letter the name of the country from which he was writing, he drew the heavy outline of a swastika.

After Hitler's occupation of Austria on March 11, 1938, Hungary too was in imminent danger of occupation by the fascists. In Austria, internal preparations for transforming the country into a fascist state had been set in motion long before the actual 'coup'. As Bartók wrote to Mrs. Müller-Widman in May 1937, in the letter quoted above,

> Actually, they say that Austria has also been infected with the Nazi poison, only it is not so obvious there.

338

All hopes and illusions were shattered by the Anschluss that took place ten months later.

Bartók saw quite clearly in which direction the Germans were most likely to move next. He was acutely aware of the approaching threat to his immediate material position and also the danger of reducing still further the already limited sphere of his artistic activities.

> That is the imminent danger that Hungary will surrender to this regime of thieves and murderers,

he wrote on April 13, 1938. And he continued:

> In our country, unfortunately, nearly all of our 'educated' Christians are adherents of the Nazi regime; I feel quite ashamed of coming from this class.

This line of thought led him to conclude that in his opinion, after the fall of Hungary and Czechoslovakia, Switzerland and even Belgium would be the next victims, countries which were equally important to him, both because of his own personal feeling towards them, and also because his own career was linked with their fate.

It was not long before history proved Bartók's premonitions to have been correct. The occupation of Austria was followed by one political crisis after another. At the talks held in Munich, only six months after the 'coup', Hitler succeeded in overruling the leaders of the Western Allies. He occupied the major part of Czechoslovakia and returned to Hungary some of the territories that had been hers before 1920. A wave of irredentism swept the country when the gift of this 'mess of pottage' was made known.

> You can't imagine to what extent this has strengthened his (Hitler's) following in this country,

was Bartók's bitter comment made in another letter dated October 9, 1938.

He could measure the strength of nationalism in Czechoslovakia by the degree to which his own career was affected. In the letter mentioned above, which was written to Mrs. Müller in Basle, Bartók complained that,

> throughout these last 4 or 5 years, *I have not had permission* to appear publicly in Slovakia . . .

And we find him writing to Sándor Albrecht whit the query,

> I would like to know which Society it was that would have liked Ede Zathureczky and me to take part in a concert in Pozsony last year. And who was responsible for not giving us permission to appear?

After the occupation of Austria, it was not difficult to foresee that Czechoslovakia would be the target of the next German onslaught.

Even at the time of the Anschluss, it was already apparent that his work and his rights as a composer were under threat. Like Kodály and other Hungarian composers, Bartók was a member of the Austrian Composers' Copyright Association. The office of the Association was taken over by the Nazi-German STAGMA and within a few weeks the Hungarian members received a questionnaire on the subject of their 'Aryan' origin. Immediately after the Anschluss, Bartók wrote to his friends in Basle,

> Naturally, neither I nor Kodály will fill in the form: our opinion is that such questions are unlawful and illegal.

Together with Kodály and many other Hungarian composers and writers, Bartók made a public statement denouncing these proceedings. And he immediately forbade the performance of some of his folk-music compositions at the music festival held in Baden-Baden.

At the same time it was necessary to make some provision for the protection of his works and composing rights. On April 4, he wrote to Géza Frid in Holland, asking if he could be accepted as a member of the composers' association there. Finally, however, both he and Kodály became members of an association in England. And it was to an English firm that he entrusted the publishing rights for his compositions.

> I have signed the contract with Boosey and Hawkes, and from now on they will publish my works. U.E. (Universal Edition), Vienna, persist in retaining their rights in connection with the compositions already published,

he wrote to Sándor Veress on June 3, 1939.

Directly after the occupation of Austria by Nazi Germany, Bartók began to send his manuscripts abroad for safe keeping. He first asked his friends in Basle to keep them for him. On April 13, 1938, he wrote a long letter in which he said,

As far back as Nov. I noticed that Hungarian policy was being diverted from the right track; I then conceived the idea of putting at least the original manuscripts of my musical compositions in some safe place.

Then he continued with his request,

Well, now I ask you both, would you be so kind as to give shelter to my manuscripts? With no obligation to be responsible for them, of course: I would bear all the risk.

But soon he began to feel that the manuscripts would not be safe even in Basle and he sent them still further away. Czechoslovakia was occupied on March 15, 1939, and on April 8, 1939, he wrote from Venice to the wife of Professor Müller,

I find the latest events (you know what I am thinking of) so alarming and dangerous that I must come to a decision, though with a heavy heart, to take various precautionary measures. I would like to ask you to send my manuscripts together with the lists, to my publisher, Boosey and Hawkes, 295 Regent Street, London ... After all, London is further away from the land of the monsters.

During this period, we find in his letters from time to time complaints about the pressure of work under which he was labouring. He wrote to Basle on January 3, 1938,

The fact that I am so overburdened with work has never before tortured me so much.

And to Endre Gertler on January 25, 1938, he wrote,

I am leading an unimaginably hectic life in Budapest.

Already on May 24, 1937, during the previous year, he had told Mrs. Müller that his correspondence was a burden to him. He was plagued by letters that were merely sent to annoy him, and he had so much trouble with publishers and concert agencies that he postponed the torment of writing to them from one day to another, in fact 'for as long as possible'. When he was able to write a purely personal letter to a friend, without reference to business affairs, he explained,

... here there are other obstacles: first, lack of time in general, together with incredible arrears of work (for instance, part of my Arab collection of cylinders, which I made in 1913!!, I have still not written down) ...

He needed a secretary with a good knowledge and understanding of several languages and with the ability to conduct his correspondence independently. 'Unfortunately, I cannot afford such an assistant even if one were to be found.'

It was primarily because of his concert engagements abroad that his work at home accumulated in this way. In a letter written from Amsterdam, Bartók informed Endre Gertler that after the première of the *Sonata for Two Pianos* in Basle, he and his wife would be travelling in Holland, Belgium and giving concerts in London and Luxembourg until the end of January. It was just at this time that his glorious composition, *Music for String Instruments, Percussion and Celesta* was achieving a success unknown in the case of his other works. In the space of less than two years after the first performance in Basle, it was played sixteen times in various cities. In Paris, it was played twice in one season. In Holland at least Bartók was able to be present on some of the occasions which heralded the success of this work, though it is true that his first experience of the rehearsals was not very encouraging. This was at The Hague, where, however, the actual performance was more successful than might have been anticipated from the rehearsals. And this occasion was followed by six performances in one month in various cities in Holland, undertaken by the Concertgebouw Orchestra conducted by Edward van Beinum. The critics gave an ecstatic reception to both the work and Bartók's own appearances. During his last years in Europe, he was invited to return to Holland over and over again.

In the summer of that year, Bartók and his wife set out to give a series of joint concerts. In June, they played the *Sonata for Two Pianos* for the Luxembourg Radio and again in London when Hermann Scherchen was the conductor. In November they toured Belgium and Holland as guest artists and once again played the *Sonata* in Amsterdam and Brussels. During this tour, there were first performances of the *Music for String Instruments, Percussion and Celesta* in both Brussels and Antwerp. Two and a half months later, in the middle of February 1939, they set out again, this time playing the *Sonata for Two Pianos* once in Zurich and twice in Paris. They then visited Switzerland where they played the *Concerto No. 2* for piano in Lausanne and also in a radio programme given by the Suisse Romande Orchestra conducted by Ernest Ansermet.

The coaching and rehearsals preceding any performance of the *Sonata for Two Pianos* was always an occasion of some considerable excitement. Either the tympanists were not adequate to the part, or the pianos were unsuitable, or something else would invariably go wrong. In Venice, for example, at the first performance in April 1939, only one piano was a full concert grand, while the other was what Bartók described as

> . . . quite short! (they claim that in Venice there are no other large ones to be found); there are no *timbales mécaniques;* and instead of two tympanists, there are six! . . . one worse than the other. I shall never play in this country again.

On this occasion, he had been on a tour with Ede Zathureczky on which he set out on March 30, and they had appeared in Parma, Milan, Florence and Rome. When, in December, he again went to Italy to give concerts together with his wife, this was certainly contrary to his original intentions.

2 'CONSTRASTS', 'VIOLIN CONCERTO', 'DIVERTIMENTO' AND 'STRING QUARTET NO. 6'

It is almost inconceivable that during this period there was any time left for composition. Antal Molnár noted that Bartók composed in the same way as Mozart—preparing his material, mentally, that is, and then writing it down during his short summer vacations.

During his summer vacation in Braunwald, Switzerland, in 1936, he wrote almost the whole of the *Music for String Instruments, Percussion and Celesta.* The following year, the Bartóks spent their summer holidays in Heiligenblut, Carinthia, and it was there that he composed the *Sonata for Two Pianos.* Then in 1938 they returned once more to Braunwald. The weather was not very good, but the composer, who had always loved nature, was able to enjoy two fine days. ' . . .We have made good use of this day,' he wrote.

> From 9 till 4 1/2 we were up in the mountains. We climbed up to the snow level, about 1900 metres, we saw a mountain daw and picked 3 different kinds of gentians . . .

This letter was written round about July 4 and addressed to Mrs. Müller, but it was not until October 9 that he wrote to his friends in Basle to tell them what he had been composing during the summer:

> ... I have been working hard this summer. I have finished the violin concerto and two pieces (commissioned) for Szigeti and the American jazz clarinetist Benny Goodman (3 pieces, to be exact, 16 minutes altogether).

These two pieces, to which Bartók refers in his letter as '3, to be exact' were in fact the movements of *Contrasts*.

József Szigeti's reminiscences provide a solution to the puzzling question of the number of movements in this work. It was at the suggestion of Szigeti that Benny Goodman, the world-famous clarinet player, had commissioned the work from Bartók. He asked for a slow–fast, double dance like that of the *Rhapsodies* written ten years previously. The intention was to allow the complete work to be recorded on one disc which, in those days, was played at normal speed.

It was for this reason that at the first public performance of the work at the Carnegie Hall on January 9, 1939, *Contrasts* was performed as a composition in two movements. The players were József Szigeti, Benny Goodman and Endre Petri. The title first given to this work was *Rhapsody* for clarinet and violin, *Two Dances*: a) *Verbunkos*, b) *Sebes*.

József Szigeti, with great kindness, put at my disposal that part of an unpublished letter that Bartók had addressed to him in which additional information is given about the title and the further course of the work.

> ... Well, yes, I do not like the title Rhapsody very much. (I wrote about this in my letter.)

This letter was lost, according to József Szigeti.

> ... I would prefer the title Two Dances! If you possibly can, change this in the programme.—As far as the orchestration is concerned, I looked and looked at the thing, and it could be done in some way. Indeed, in September, I wrote a central (3.) movement, (Lento 4' 13" in length) with the title Pihenő. I could do it in January, and you could get the score around the end of February.

(December 1st, 1938.)

It was at Bartók's request, therefore, that on the programme of the first performance, the title *Rhapsody* was supplemented with the subtitle

Two Dances. But in the account given in the letter written to Mrs. Müller-Widman in October, it becomes clear that the composer did not consider even the two-movement form as final. In the supplement to the fourth edition of his book *With Strings Attached*, József Szigeti attributes this to Bartók's 'unfailing sense of form, of equilibrium, call this sense as you will, that compelled him to add this—as it turned out—so necessary Nightpiece, with its wonderful repose and out-door feeling.' (József Szigeti was also kind enough to send me the manuscript of the supplement.) Finally, Szigeti, Goodman, and Bartók recorded the three-movement work in its complete form for the Columbia Recording Company in April 1940. This was the time when it was finally entitled *Contrasts*, after many hours of deliberation in Szigeti's Park-Avenue apartment in New York.

The orchestral version mentioned in the unpublished letter, however, remained only a plan.

At the same time, Bartók was under pressure to complete the *Violin Concerto*. This was a large work in three movements, with a playing length of more than half an hour, and though Bartók had begun working on it during the previous summer when he was composing the *Sonata for Two Pianos*, he was still working on it through the late autumn. It is true that in one of his letters written at the beginning of October Bartók mentions that he has finished the work, but he can only have been referring to the piano abstract: the score is dated December 31, 1938, clearly the date when he completed the orchestration.

The *Violin Concerto* was dedicated 'to my dear friend, Zoltán Székely'. Zoltán Székely was the soloist at the first performance given by the Concertgebouw Orchestra conducted by Willem Mengelberg in Amsterdam on March 29, 1939. It seems likely that the date of the première had been fixed well in advance, for Bartók sent the score to Holland at the beginning of January in batches as these were completed. He wrote to Mrs. Zoltán Székely on January 10, informing her that on the previous day he had posted the first eighty pages and that in two days' time, on January 12, he was planning to send the last sixteen pages together with the piano abstract. The only occasion on which it would be possible for the composer to discuss the work with the violinist, he added, was sometime during his stay in Paris between March 4 and March 7. Bartók was not present at the première.

The *Violin Concerto* was still not quite complete when Bartók received another commission, again from his friends in Basle. At the end of November 1938, Paul Sacher asked for a string composition for the Basle Chamber Orchestra and Bartók accepted the commission. When he and his wife were travelling home from Paris at the beginning of March 1939, they broke their journey at Basle where they stayed with Sacher. Evidently they seized this opportunity to discuss the proposed work, for Bartók wrote to Sacher on July 1,

> ... As I told you in March, I cannot begin work until August; I will be able to tell you something definite at the end of August when the work has begun to take shape. As you see, my work schedule is the same every year. Apart from this, I am thinking of some kind of Concerto grosso interchanged with a concertino ...

The Bartók family spent July in Surlej, Switzerland. Stefi Geyer, who lived in Switzerland, was also there and she and the Bartóks visited each other on several occasions. Bartók himself had arrived direct from Scheveningen in Holland, where on June 30, he had played his *Concerto No. 2* for piano. After the family holiday, Bartók remained alone in Switzerland, travelling on from Surlej to Saanen where he stayed until the end of August in an isolated wooden chalet in the mountains so that he could work on his new composition without interruptions.

> ... Somehow I feel like a musician of olden times—the invited guest of a patron of the arts,

he wrote on August 18, in a letter to greet his eldest son Béla on his birthday,

> for here I am, as you know, entirely the guest of the Sachers; they see to everything—from a distance. In a word, I am living alone—in an ethnographic object: a genuine peasant cottage. The furnishings are not in character, but so much the better, because they are the last word in comfort. They even had a piano brought from Berne for me. I had been notified that it would arrive on August 2nd at 10 o'clock, and, just imagine, it did not arrive at noon or sometime in the afternoon (as usually happens at home) but was actually here at 9.45. The janitor's wife cooks and cleans; she is a very nice and honest woman, and my wish is her command. Recently, even the weather has been favouring

me—this is the 9th day that we've had beautifully clear skies, and not a drop of rain has fallen since the 9th. However, I can't take advantage of the weather to make excursions: I have to work. And for Sacher himself—on a commission (something for a string orchestra); in this respect also my position is like that of the old-time musician. Luckily the work went well, and I finished it in 15 days (a piece of about 25 minutes), I just finished it yesterday. Now I have another commission to fulfil, this time a string quartet for Z. Székely (i.e. for the 'New Hungarian Quartet'). Since 1934 virtually everything I have done has been commissioned.

This latest commission 'something for string orchestra,' was responsible for the creation of the *Divertimento*, a work in three movements, which was completed within the incredibly short space of two weeks. Then, before leaving Saanen, Bartók began work on the last of his great European works, the *String Quartet No. 6*. He finished the work at home, the date of completion written on the score being November 1939. It was the outbreak of war that put an end to his peaceful stay in Saanen. Even in Scheveningen, he had been surrounded by preparations for war; and even more so in Switzerland:

... they have taken defence measures on the more important passes, etc.—military preparedness. I saw this for myself on the Julier Pass; for example, boulders have been made into road-blocks against tanks, and such like attractions ...

Bartók had enjoyed scarcely three weeks of peace in Saanen before he had to make all haste for home. September 1, 1939, saw the outbreak of the Second World War.

Some of Bartók's biographers and a number of musicologists consider that in certain respects the *Violin Concerto* marks the beginning of a new period in the classification of Bartók's works; they believe that in this work we are already in a world that is separate from that of the last great work, the *Sonata for Two Pianos*. Bence Szabolcsi, for instance, looks upon this phase as the 'fifth stylistic period'. Even if we do not share his view as to the sharpness of the dividing line between the *Sonata for Two Pianos* and the *Violin Concerto*, still we cannot but notice that there are some striking features of the last European compositions which link them to the succeeding works composed after Bartók had emigrated to America, and at the same time distiguish them from their immediate predecessors.

A first glance reveals one obvious feature—the return, in a variety of forms, of the *verbunkos* dance character. We have already mentioned that the manuscript copy of the orchestral part of the *Violin Concerto* carried the instruction 'tempo di Verbunkos'. It was only in the final version that this was altered to the version generally used, 'allegro non troppo'. In the first movement of *Contrasts*, there is, as it were, a quotation from the *Rhapsody No. 1*. And in the *Divertimento*, as in the *Violin Concerto*, the character of the first movement is that of the folk *verbunkos*, though it is also marked 'allegro non troppo'.

The distinguishing feature of these works lies in the fact that here, more than in the *Rhapsodies* and other works of that period, this historical dance type with its national tone, provided material that was readily incorporated into Bartók's compositions, at many levels of both style and content, so that it became an organic part of the new creation. It is not merely a quotation but develops rich inner characteristics of its own. In the *Violin Concerto* it becomes a broad sphere of melody inspired by folk music. With its noble sweep and richly shaded inner content, it provides many examples which serve to illustrate Bence Szabolcsi's description of the whole period as 'warmly melodious'. In the first movement of *Contrasts*, the dance type becomes tense and has something of the character of a march; the rhythm is gallant and proud and there is a faint reference to the elegant opening gesture of Stravinsky's *Apollo Musagetes*. We meet it again in the Marcia of the *String Quartet No. 6*. In the first movement of the *Divertimento*, it appears as a playful, teasing, quite charming variant of the melody.

From time to time, as the reference to Stravinsky demonstrates, it turns to Baroque music. For instance, in the *Violin Concerto* and even earlier in the *Concerto No. 2* for piano, the same theme is used in the first and third movements; in the first movement in an even form, in the third movement in an uneven form; this is similar to the Baroque custom of linking the main dance to the associated 'proportions' of the identical themes, such as the dance pairs found in some of Vivaldi's violin concertos. In the tone of the last movement of *Divertimento* there is also a link between folk dance music and Baroque concert music.

It is for this reason that the *Divertimento* can bear material of much more weight than can be found in the *Rhapsodies*. Its tone constantly becomes more and more serious, and from the syncopated exclamations, the crossbars of the vertical cords in the first movement of the *Divertimento* become wholly tragic in colour. There is a threatening flash of diabolic light when the dance music which evokes the idea of a great city finds its pair and becomes united with jazz music in both style and tone. In the last movement of *Contrasts*, this same tone becomes quite wild and terrifying, lending a ghostly colour to the cackling of the clarinet and a note of unchecked glee to the mistuned violin. Another variation of this device is to be found in the Burletta of the *String Quartet No. 6*. Here we have all the wildness of the *Bear Dance* united with the grotesque quality of *A Bit Drunk;* we are reminded of the Old Gentleman in *The Miraculous Mandarin* and the menacing shadow of the Wooden Puppet in *The Wooden Prince*. It is here that Bartók's idea of the bear dance comes closest to that of Attila József: it expresses all the composer's defiance of the terrible mechanism of civilization and the inhumanity of the twentieth century.

These works are seething with memories and equally full of experiment. They recall the pieces composed during the years of the First World War. Bence Szabolcsi sees a vision of war in the second movement of the *Divertimento*. And it is true that in the dark course of the funeral march there is a reminiscence of the last movement of the *String Quartet No. 2*, its outbursts of complaint and spasmodic jerkiness remind us of the last of the *Four Orchestral Pieces*, while in its unrestrained sobbing we hear again the weeping tone of the castle in *Bluebeard's Castle*. But the world of the *String Quartet No. 2* is also brought to life in the *String Quartet No. 6*. Certainly it is true that in its construction the last string quartet summarizes a mastery of structure acquired over a whole career. The introductory ritornelle, which between the various movements is always sounded in different initial notes and in ever greater proportions, widens out into the slow closing movement. The basic material of which it is composed, and the broading, twining triola motion, may be traced backwards from the *Sonata for Two Pianos*, through the *Music for String Instruments, Percussion and Celesta*, the *Sonata for Violin and Piano No. 1*, as far as the *String Quartet No. 2* and indeed the first piece of the *Two Portraits* or the first movement of the *String Quartet No. 1*. Its relation to this latter work lies not in the triola motion, but in the further development of the intertwining character of the melodic structure.

In this resurrection of old memories and the new synthesis on a higher plane, the renewed influence of Beethoven is clearly visible. Although this was always present in the disciplined construction, especially in the string quartets (this is pointed out in the study by János Kárpáti), it now comes very close to being a quotation. The fast theme in the first movement of the *String Quartet No. 6* bears a close relation to the Great Fugue in Beethoven's String Quartet op. 133. The treading rhythm of the Marcia movement, in which we have just recognized a turn from Stravinsky, taken as a whole, is more closely related to the Great Fugue and by the same token to the second movement of Beethoven's Piano Sonata op. 101.

Around this period, Bartók's tone became much more relayed, melodious and intimate. The melodic and harmonic realm became diatonic and there was a return to his earlier affinities with folk music. 'It is as if, only now, in the midst of these dark years, he found his faith, confidence and optimism. He had never previously written so melodiously and comprehensibly as he did at that time, and at no other time was he able to summarize and synthesise, as he did then, all the achievements of his life,' wrote Bence Szabolcsi in his biography of Bartók. After the première of the *Violin Concerto*, one of the critics drew attention to this change of tone in which he saw a loss of the hard core at the centre of the earlier works and therefore a 'loosening of concentrated critical strength'. Ever since there has been, among those who believe in extreme innovations of idiom and technique, a group of critics who hold that in his later period, Bartók yielded to the taste of the audience.

We do not share this view; like Bence Szabolcsi, we believe that the tone of reconciliation found in the composer's later work is the result of the clarification and summarization which he was already approaching 'in the piano music, and especially in the Mikrokosmos (1926–37)'. Now he had reached a higher rung of the 'spiral path', to which the composer himself likened his development, when talking to Bence Szabolcsi.

There were many reasons why it was precisely at this time and in this manner that Bartók now reached such a synthesis. No adequate explanation is to be found in the four pieces which immediately preceded this flowering, three of them being examples of popular genres—a virtuoso concerto, a rhapsody-like concert piece and a divertimento. Yet now he found it possible to create in the *Divertimento* a more profoundly tragic tone, and in the *String Quartet No. 6* a tone that was more relayed than that of its predecessors. In seeking the cause of this new tone we must consider the historical situation and social stimulus of the period when Bartók was driven to write his choral works. It was more important at that time to unite the masses, in their thoughts and feelings, through the humanizing medium of music, rather than to search for a philosophy which would provide an answer to individual problems. Now once again, partly because of external pressure, partly because within the country there were stronger and more wholesome attitudes, the political climate favoured the development of a united front between all progressives anxious to save humanity from a new and deadly menace.

Throughout his life, Bartók had always identified the concepts of humanism, humaneness and freedom, with nature, the peoples of the world and their folk music. As we know, his principal occupation when at home was the sorting and revision of his folk-music collections. In one of his letter to Mrs. Müller, he told her that he spent ten hours every day working on his folk-music collection in the room provided for him in the Academy of Sciences. He lived almost like an exile in his own country, lost in happy memories of his youthful collecting tours. This absorption in folk music and the happy mood of those distant journeys are alike reflected in his music. The folk-like turns in some of the later works, the sighs which remind us of Kodály's music, the painfully beautiful vision of the second movement of the *Violin Concerto*, the sudden halt in the *Divertimento* with the pizzicato quotation from the 'Girl' motif, the sad ending of the *String Quartet No. 6*, all bear witness to the fact that during his last years at home, Bartók was already an émigré in spirit, living under the burden of unremitting homesickness. For a long time now, his message had been intended not for those immediately around him but for a much wider community.

3 Plans for emigration. Concert tour in the United States. Farewell to Europe

During the last creative years spent in his native country, he was beset with cares and burdened with anxiety. When the situation was at its most difficult, he was quite unable to work.

> My own position has been made so difficult as a result of this damned German advance, that for weeks I have had to give all my thoughts and energies to solving the various problems that have arisen,

he wrote to László Rásonyi on April 28, 1938. From the time of the occupation of Austria onwards, the thought of emigration never ceased to trouble his mind, and each succeeding political event strengthened his desire to escape. The letter written to Mrs. Müller on April 13, 1938, shows that he was fully aware of the danger.

> That is an imminent danger that Hungary will surrender to this regime of thieves and murderers. The only question is—when and how? And how I can then go on living in such a country or—which means the same thing—working, I simply cannot conceive. As a matter of fact, I would feel it my duty to emigrate, so long as that were possible.

In a letter written to Zoltán Székely and his family on October 24, he exclaimed,

> One ought to get away from here, from the neighbourhood of that pestilential country, far, far away, but where: to Greenland, Cape Colony, the Tierra del Fuego, the Fiji Islands, or somewhere even the Almighty has not heard of!

The instinct to escape was held in check by more sober considerations, such as those of emigration after the First World War. Soon after he had first thought of emigrating, we find him expressing his doubts in a letter written on April 13 to his friends in Basle:

> But—even in the most favourable circumstances—to have to earn my living in some foreign country (to start toiling at the age of 58, to begin, say, teaching, and to be wholly dependent on it) would be immensely difficult and would cause me such distress of mind that I can hardly bear to think of it. In that event I could achieve nothing, and in such conditions I could not do my proper and most important work anywhere else either. Consequently, it is exactly the same for me whether I go or stay.—And then I have my mother here: shall I abandon her altogether in her last years? No, I cannot do that!

A year later, he was still no nearer to a decision. On June 3, 1939, he wrote to Sándor Veress in London, saying,

> Your information that I plan to leave Hungary is wrong. This news has been spread about for some time and many people have spoken to me about it.

He went on,

> As to whether I ought to emigrate (if that were possible), that is another question There are several ways of looking at it. Anyone able to leave who nevertheless stays, may be said to give tacit consent to everything that is going on here. One cannot make a public statement to say that that is not the case because nothing but trouble would come of it and then it would be pointless to stay. On the other hand, it might be said that no matter how far the country sinks into the mire, everyone has a duty to stay and help to the best of his ability. The only question then would be whether, within the foreseeable future, such help would bear fruit? Hindemith tried to do this for five years in Germany, but it seems he has lost confidence. For my part, and this is entirely a personal feeling, I have no confidence. On the other hand, there is a certain kind of work which I can only do here (for another year at least) because it is dependent on access to material in the museums. And then again, I am not attracted to any particular country as a place worth going to, that is, if I want to do more than merely exist. To put it another way, for the time being I am at a loss what to do, although it is my feeling that anyone who is able to leave should do so . . .

When he wrote of 'a certain kind of work' that was dependent on access to museums, Bartók was referring to the preparatory work in connection with the publication of his folk-music collections; on September 14, 1937, Bartók had handed in to Géza Voinovich, Secretary General of the Academy of Sciences, a written report of his work in which he stated that he planned to finish it within three years.

Writing to Mrs. Müller of October 9, 1938, he said sadly,

> I am leading an even more retired life here, if that is possible; I do not feel like meeting people, everyone is suspected of Nazism. I work nearly 10 hours a day, exclusively on folk-music material; but I would have to work 20 hours to make real progress. A distressing situation—I would so very much like to finish this work before we are involved in the next world catastrophe that's hanging in the air. And at this rate it will take a few more years!

In the course of the following year, however, he had to come to terms with the fact that it would after all not be possible for him to complete the work. In the letter to Sándor Veress from which we have already quoted he wrote,

> Kodály has no intention of leaving, so that if the worst comes to the worst, he would continue the work on the folk-music publication.

Only a few months later, in December 1939, Bartók suffered the loss of his mother to whom, from early childhood, he had been so deeply attached. It is probable that he never quite recovered from this blow. He spoke of his feelings in a letter to Mrs. Müller dated April 2, 1940,

> Three and a half months have passed since I lost my mother, and I still feel as if it had just happened yesterday. It is difficult to describe my state of mind which, in any case, it might be perhaps difficult for others to understand.
>
> However, it is the self-reproaches that are most difficult to endure—all the many things I should have done differently to make my mother's life easier and to comfort her in her last years. It's too late now, nothing can be repaired or set right again—nothing, never. Of course, it was all so confused and complicated; I was under pressure from so many contradictory motives at one and the same time. Last summer, for instance, I went to Saanen to be totally undisturbed, so that I could write 2 works as quickly as possible; I spent 3 1/2 weeks there, the works got done, wholly or in part, and those 3 1/2 weeks I took away from my mother. I can never make amends for this. I should not have done it—and there were many similar things in the past—and none of this can be helped now.

This letter was written from Naples. The following day he embarked on a boat bound for the United States and remained away from Europe, counting travelling time, for a period of two months. Together with József Szigeti, he gave concerts in Washington, at Columbia University in New York and in two other cities. This tour served to prepare the way for his eventual emigration. In July, he wrote to Gyula Kertész, the publisher of his choral works,

> I have to go to America once again (if it's possible). My wife will be going with me, and we shall be staying for a longer period.

The death of his mother severed the last of the ties that held him to Hungary. Those who, like Bence Szabolcsi, were still able to talk with him during that last summer, record his growing irritation, his longing and determination to escape. He saw only a dark future for his native country and he lived by the thought, 'I must get away from here'.

During his last few months in Hungary, he did not compose at all. In the letter to Gyula Kertész he wrote,

> Owing to recent developments, I find it impossible to write more choruses, indeed anything at all—and this is probably how it will be for the rest of the year. What the future will bring—only Wotan (and his earthly deputy) knows.

And when Sacher asked him to write the customary programme notes for the first performance of the *Divertimento* he failed to respond, nor did he attend the premiere at Basle on June 11. It is most probable that the *String Quartet No. 6*, completed in 1939, was the last work he composed in his own country. It is conceivable that he did in fact add one or two more pieces to the *Mikrokosmos* at the very end of 1939. It is possible that it was at this time that he added the sixth and final dance to the Bulgarian dance series; certainly only five of these were included in the programme of a recital he gave on December 12, 1939, in Rome. All six dances were first included in his recital given on May 1, 1940 in New York. Very possibly, on this occasion he also played the 'Peasant Dance', the 'Change of Time' and the 'Harmonics'. At his farewell concert in Budapest on October 8, the programme included, in addition to the other pieces, that entitled 'Subject and Reflection'. During the last years, he gave fewer and fewer recitals. There are records of a few concerts, held in Budapest and various country districts, at which he played together with either Ditta Pásztory or Ede Zathurecky. Already in 1940, Bartók and his wife were giving most of their time and attention to the preparations for their journey.

Bence Szabolcsi tells us that this prolonged period of leave-taking was painful for everyone; for those who were to be left behind, it was painful to hear the Bartóks play for the last time, on October 8, in the great hall of the Academy of Music; and for those who were leaving, it was painful to realize that only three or four days remained before their departure.

Just before they left, a concert tour lasting for three months was announced in *Magyarország*, but Bartók already suspected that this journey would be of much longer duration. Before he left, he made a will dated October 4, in which he made a number of provisions and left instructions that as long as the former Oktogon Square and Köröd bear the names of the two men after whom they are now named, and further, as long as there shall be any squares or streets in Hungary named after these two men, no square, street or public building shall be named after me in this country; and until then no memorial plaque for me shall be put in any public place.

These 'two men' were Hitler and Mussolini.

Because of the war, their journey was both complicated and dangerous. In making the necessary preparations, Bartók was assisted by friends in Switzerland. He and his wife travelled to Switzerland by way of Italy and spent October 13, 14 in Geneva. It was probably there that Bartók said good-bye to his Swiss friends and wrote his last letter from Europe. Writing to Mrs. Müller, he spoke of a farewell 'for who knows how long—perhaps for ever!' And to Paul Sacher, in a hasty letter of farewell written on a sheet of paper with the letter-head of the Geneva Cornavin Hotel, he wrote:

Perhaps we are facing uncertainty, but I have no choice. I wonder for how long. God knows!

After many trials and tribulations as they journeyed through France, they reached Lisbon, where he had played so often as a young man, and on October 20, they boarded a ship for the United States.

CHAPTER XIII

IN EMIGRATION. THE END OF LIFE AND CREATIVITY
1940–1945

1 ADVENTUROUS JOURNEY. SETTLING DOWN AND HOUSING PROBLEMS. FOLK-MUSIC ACTIVITY AT COLUMBIA UNIVERSITY. THE SERBO-CROATIAN COLLECTION

Seen from a distance of over three thousand miles, Béla Bartók in America becomes for Europeans a distant figure much more vague and indistinct than when he was at home. We cannot follow the details of his daily life, and we have no first-hand knowledge of the environment in which he found himself, the places in which he worked and made his home. Though there are periods of his life in Hungary of which we know very little, the European period generally has a certain visible unity and continuity of development. The reverse is true of the years spent in the United States. These five years glide past like a shadow, relieved by occasional flashes of light in which we glimpse the composer momentarily or during some particular episode of his life. What he thought and felt at this time, and what he was actually seen to be doing, may be pieced together from his published letters, statements made either privately to friends or for publication, a few newspaper articles, photographs and amateur films.

The story that emerges is sad and moving in the extreme. The facial lines which began to be visible in the portraits taken during the last years in Europe, now become permanent and more deeply etched. The eyes, so frequently mentioned because of their penetrating glance, gaze at us from beneath a high, lined forehead; the soft white hair is sparse, the delicate skin yellow like parchment. Nor is his gaze directed towards us. There is an inward concentration in his eyes which provides the most striking feature of the photograph. The glance, formerly so alert and questioning, no longer seems to fix itself on the immediate surroundings or the person to whom he is speaking, but is focussed on some distant point.

The worries of his life at home were still with him and new ones were added to increase his burden. It seemed that his foreboding was justified and all that he had feared before setting out had now become a reality. He had indeed taken the path to an uncertain existence and now spent day after day in a state of physical and mental inactivity. The journey itself had not been lacking in unpleasant incidents. The Bartóks arrived in New York on October 30, 1940, only to find that their baggage was not on the boat: it was still at the Spanish border, held up because of difficulties with the customs authorities.

> So that we arrived in New York almost without a change of clothes, without either a tuxedo or evening dress. It should be here within 1 week or 2, if it arrives at all,

he wrote to his son, Béla, in Budapest soon after their arrival. But the '1 week or 2' became three and a half months, and their baggage did not reach them at their apartment in New York until February 11, 1941.

For a considerable time, Bartók had to devote much of his attention to settling his affairs at home. Before leaving Hungary, he had applied for a pension and he was now involved in a good deal of correspondence on this subject: he also had to write numbers of business letters in connection with his passport, copyright taxes, and the question of foreign currency. His younger son, Péter, had stayed behind to complete his studies at college in Sárospatak after which it was intended that he should join his parents in America.

But the first essential was for Bartók to find some means of earning a living in the United States. During the first few weeks after their arrival, Bartók and his wife lived in a hotel, meantime searching, with the help of friends and acquaintances, for a more permanent home. It was not just a flat for which they were looking. Bartók needed a quiet place where it would be possible for him to work, and for both of them it was essential that they should have a home in which they could practise and rehearse on two pianos. It was for this reason that when they were still in Hungary, they had retreated to an ever greater distance from the centre of Budapest: first, in 1928, they had moved to Kavics utca, then in 1932 to Csalán út. Accommodation such as they had enjoyed in Hungary was not easily found in New York, and for Bartók, with his refined hearing, the problem was acute. His over-sensitive ears had become a legend; it was said that he could hear a whisper through closed doors, and amazing evidence of his phenomenal hearing is offered by those who knew him well.

In one of his stories, Chekhov tells of a peasant boy whose vision was much sharper than that of ordinary mortals. The boy could see life and motion in the world about him that was invisible to others. Beyond the world of everyday realities, the boy's acute vision enabled him to see a distant world of his own, unattainable by others, infinitely beautiful and alluring ... Thus Bartók's acute hearing enabled him to create a special world of his own, the world of his 'night music'.

In New York, however, this gift of acute hearing must have been more of a burden than an asset. There he was surrounded not by the nature music of the night, but rather the street noises of the introductory passages in *The Miraculous Mandarin*. Even at home in the quiet flat in Csalán út in Buda, he had worn ear-plugs when he was working; the noisy flat in Queens on 73rd Road would have been unendurable for any prolonged period. 'You ask why we had to move from Forest Hills,' he wrote to his son on May 7, 1941, the day they moved.

> Well, because the place was unsuitable in every way. It was a large apartment house, and we were piano-played and radio-blasted from right and left; a lot of noise came in from the street night and day; every 5 minutes we heard the rumble of the subway which made the very walls shake. Lastly, it took more than an hour to get from there to Columbia. We were lucky in that the very first place we looked at in this part of the city proved to be perfectly suitable for us. This is a 3-apartment family house; we are in the middle; and the people above and below are quiet. It is a garden-city district, peaceful, near a most lovely park with rocks, trees and lawns (rather like the Hill of Roses in Budapest).

The new flat was in The Bronx, in Cambridge Avenue. They lived there for about two years.

This flat was nearer Columbia University, Bartók's sole source of a relatively stable income from employment in America. For, strange as it may seem, Béla Bartók, one of the foremost composers in the world and a famous pianist, was faced during the last years of his life with oppressive financial trouble.

Many of his friends in the United States, particularly those of his own nationality, believe that his lot as an émigré was not as hard as one might deduce from what he himself wrote and said. Once, when visiting his native country, Ernő Balogh, a former pupil who gave real assistance to Bartók during a period of great difficulty, said that the maestro was not an easy man to help. He was quite wearingly puritanical about money matters and was suspicious of any assistance, financial or otherwise, that was not offered as a direct return for a particular commission. (It was with the greatest difficulty that he was prevailed upon to accept an advance payment from Koussevitzky for the *Concerto*.) But even if we accept that to some extent he was obstinately resigned to his straitened circumstances as an outward sign by which he could justify his despair as an exile, nevertheless his reception in the United States and the conditions in which he had to live were hardly worthy of a man of his stature. His letters leave us in no doubt about this.

Before he arrived in New York, a number of concerts had been arranged for him, but by the end of the season, in mid-April, he had fulfilled all these engagements and he had received very few invitations for the following season. On October 17, 1941, he wrote to Wilhelmine Creel, one of his pupils in Budapest during the nineteen-thirties and now living in Seattle,

> If I tell you that we have for this season one orchestra-engagement, three two-piano recitals, four minor engagements (piano solo or lecture) and that is all, then you easily see how precarious our situation is.

Three days later, writing to his son, 'in a very depressed mood', he described their situation even more tersely:

> Concerts are too few and far between; if we had to live on the proceeds, I am sure that we might well go hungry.

When he wrote again to Wilhelmine Creel in March 1942, his prospects seemed to be even more bleak.

> Our situation is getting daily worse and worse. All I can say is that never in my life since I earn my livelihood (that is from my 20th year) have I been in such a dreadful situation as I will be probably very soon.

This letter is dated March 2, the very day on which he received notice from the Baldwin Company, which until then had put two pianos at their disposal, that one of the pianos must be returned. Also, in spite of many wearisome inquiries, much form-filling and the support of his guarantors, Bartók and his wife had still only been given permission to stay temporarily in the country. They were still classed as 'visitors' and they had not even managed to secure visas as immigrants. Meantime, Péter's arrival was now imminent.

> I am rather pessimistic, I lost all confidence in people, in countries, in everything,

continued Bartók, summing up his view of the situation with some bitterness.

For certainly the musical world of the United States seemed to be unaware of Béla Bartók's significance and, especially during the first months of his stay, failed to take advantage of his presence in their country. One of Bartók's American friends, Tibor Serly, the composer and conductor, has said that the reception given to Bartók on arrival was much more modest than that given to other famous composers who had emigrated earlier, Schoenberg, Stravinsky and Hindemith for instance. Only a few personal friends were on the pier to greet the Bartóks. Serly's account is confirmed by Bartók's letter written on his sixtieth birthday, March 25, 1941, and addressed to his son,

> ... apart from 5 people who cabled greetings, nobody cared a red cent about March 25.

János Demény quotes a remark made by H.H. Stuckenschmidt in his *Urbanität und Volksliedgeist. Über Béla Bartók* published in *Der Monat* in August 1953: '...At any rate, the marvellous synthesis of urbanism and folk-song spirit embodied by him did not cultivate the adulation and propagation of a clique; and because of his shy and retiring disposition, he was not the sort of person about whom legends were likely to circulate. He did not proclaim any particular trend, he did not utter atelier slogans, nor chimed in with the *dernier cri*, so he remained in the eye of the masses aesthetically what he was (considered to be) geographically—an outsider, the inhabitant of a culturally peripherial country.' The solitary life into which he had latterly withdrawn before leaving Europe was now forced upon him for a time in the new world.

In these circumstances an invitation to do research work on certain aspects of folk music at Columbia University was not only welcome from a financial point of view, it was an act of encouragement badly needed by the composer at the time. Soon after his arrival in the United States, on November 25, Columbia University had conferred on him an honorary doctor's degree and during the second half of the school year of 1940–1 has asked him to take charge of the Parry collection of folk music. Milman Parry was a professor of classical philology at Harvard University who, working on the assumption that in the folklore of the Balkan peninsula he might come upon traces or fragments of Homeric epics, had gone to Yugoslavia in 1933 and 1934 where he had made two thousand six hundred recordings; when he died suddenly in 1935, he had not arranged this material.

Bartók set to work in rare spirits, writing to his son on June 20, 1941,

> The reason for inviting me here (apart from the fact that it would help me personally) was so that I could accomplish certain research work, that is, to study and transcribe this incomparable material on Yugoslav folk music. It is, in fact, this work which brought me here (as far as work is concerned, without taking into consideration my own feelings): material such as this can be found nowhere else in the world, and (apart from some Bulgarian material) this is what was so badly lacking to me over in Europe.

His work in this new field of research brought him a fund of information and he discovered new links between material coming from different sources, so that he acquired a more complete view of Central and Eastern European folk music as a whole. He prefaced the collection with a study of methodology in which we find a mature summary of the principles of sorting and arranging which he applied to the collection and which he had arrived at after a lifetime of scientific study; the preface synthesizes, on a higher plane, the results of the two earlier studies, 'Our Folk Music and the Folk Music of the Neighbouring Peoples' and 'Why and How To Collect Folk Music'.

The collection, entitled *Serbo-Croatian Folk-Songs*, was not published until after Bartók's death. The first half of the volume is the work of Bartók; the second half was completed by Albert B. Lord.

Even this work was by no means assured, and every six months Bartók was faced with uncertainty as to whether his contract would be renewed for the following semester. There was always a fear that he would have to leave the work unfinished. The contract was in fact regularly renewed until 1943, but this scarcely ensured financial security for Bartók, since the fee of two thousand dollars every six months was only sufficient to provide a bare existence. There was, however, a constantly repeated offer of work from Washington University in Seattle where Mrs. Creel was living. But Seattle was far away, on the West Coast. Bartók thought of it as 'really the end of the world', and if he had been obliged to move there he would have felt an exile indeed. The continuity of his studies at Columbia University provided him with a more living connection with musical folklore, and indeed, a sense of his own continuous link with the folk music of his native country and South-Eastern Europe in which he found great personal satisfaction. He was able to create the mood and atmosphere without which, even when he was at home, he had been unable to exist; this atmosphere was all the more necessary now that he no longer had the stimulus of collecting from the people. And it was in order to preserve this atmosphere that he had brought with him his enormous Romanian collection. When he was unable to go to the University to continue his work there, it was this collection that he continued to sort and arrange for publication.

We have seen how the spread of inhumanity in Europe had gradually narrowed the sphere of Bartók's activities in that continent and particularly in his own country; and how he had been forced to retreat into an inner world of ideas in which humanism and the ideals of law and freedom were identified with nature and the peasant way of life. There were, however, many aspects of his home life which had remained unchanged for many decades; he enjoyed the continuity of the familiar scene about him. The well-known scenes of town and country, his home and place of work, familiar household objects, his family and small circle of friends, his native language and the appreciative Hungarian audiences, constituted a buffer state in which he could live poised between the free world of ideas and the practical realities of life. This state dissolved about him in his new and unfamiliar surroundings. Bartók's withdrawal from the practical world of affairs was now virtually complete; he lived only in the realm of the intellect. He could find a world of his own and feel a relation to society, only in memory.

His questing eyes, whether focussed on the far distance or turned in upon himself, sought to find in his present surroundings some trace or symbol of a departed world. A friend of the Bartóks in New York, Ágota Illés, in whose country home they spent a considerable part of the summer of 1941, has published under the pseudonym of Agatha Fassett her recollections of their years in America. Her account offers evidence of Bartók's withdrawal into himself; she tells us that it was only possible to attract his attention by speaking of something that roused memories of his youth, his early experience of the countryside and the villages where he collected folk-songs from the peasants.

There was a certain romanticism in this attitude just as there were certain romantic features in his art; but there was also a core of reality, not in the vague sense of a general human understanding, but the living reality of personal friends, villages that really existed, cities where he knew individual people whose fate in the war was a subject of constant anxiety; he relived in his own mind all that was happening to them in Europe. He brooded over their misfortunes as he worked on the folk-music material, and it was with them in mind that he set out his belief in humanism in his later writings; he thought of them when his feeling of homesickness was most acute.

The dreary circumstances in which they tried to make a new home for themselves, while waiting for their son Péter to join them, gave rise occasionally to the thought of returning home; Bartók mentions this possibility in his letters as a last resort. But Péter, after a journey which lasted for four months, arrived in New York in April 1942, and the family reunion to some extent confirmed their resolve to stay.

2 GRAVE ILLNESS, INABILITY TO WORK. HELP FROM FRIENDS, SUPPORT FROM ASCAP. COMMISSION BY KOUSSEVITZKY: 'CONCERTO FOR ORCHESTRA'. WORLD-WIDE SUCCESS OF THE 'VIOLIN CONCERTO'. VACATION IN ASHEVILLE, 'SONATA FOR SOLO VIOLIN'

By this time, Bartók was already seriously ill. He had never been possessed of much physical stamina, and his constitution had been permanently affected by the prolonged illnesses of his childhood and the tuberculosis from which he had suffered as a young student. Later, short periods of feverish illness sometimes offered him an 'escape' from the ruthless pressure of his work. A brief period of ill health was often the aftermath of too much exertion on a collecting tour, sudden change of climate and foreign tours. This may be verified in newspaper reports and recollections by his contemporaries.

During the summer before their departure, he had complained of rheumatic pains:

> . . . Both my shoulders are now completely affected by the arthritis which has been coming on for years. For a while, I could not raise my right arm at all, to say nothing of not being able to play the piano!

he wrote to Mrs. Müller on September 6, 1940. In August 1941, the pains returned.

> . . . now, for a change, in my left shoulder. For ten days, I could hardly move my left arm, and the condition was almost worse than when I had it in my right arm last year. This Riverton is a God-forsaken place; there is neither a doctor nor a pharmacy . . .

He was writing from Agatha Fassett's country house in Riverton where the Bartóks spent the vacation of 1941; by a strange coincidence the date of this letter written to his son Béla is the same as that written about his attack the previous year.

His condition improved during the autumn. He was given X-ray treatment for his shoulders, and though this did not cure the condition, it at least enabled him to play the piano again in October. Apart from the interest of his work on the South Slav folk-music collection, the winter was a period of gloom and despair, as we have already seen from the letters quoted above. In April he became ill again, this time more seriously. Only a month after writing his disconsolate letter to Wilhelmina Creel in March 1942, at the time when one of the loaned pianos had been taken away from him, he suffered a feverish attack in which his temperature averaged 100.4 °F and sometimes rose much higher. His summer vacation by the sea in Massachusetts was followed by only a short period of apparent improvement, but in fact he was losing strength and his temperature rose again. When he appeared in his shirtsleeves at a concert rehearsal in New York in January 1943, Agatha Fassett, who was present, tells us that members of the orchestra were shocked to see how thin he had become. The occasion was the rehearsal for the concert held on January 21, at which the Bartóks introduced the orchestral version of the *Sonata for Two Pianos and Percussion*, with Frigyes Reiner conducting. The adaptation had already been completed in 1940, probably in the hope that the orchestral accompaniment would facilitate the sale of the composition. But this is not the way things have turned out. The paler orchestral version is slowly fading into oblivion, lacking as it does the originality and peculiar tonal magic of the first composition.

Bartók had been invited to give a series of lectures at Harvard University during the following semester, but when the time came he was again in a feverish condition, his temperature sometimes as high as 104 °F, and his weight had fallen to, as he himself said, 'the ridiculous weight of 87 pounds.' In February, his strength had failed to such an extent that he collapsed while giving a lecture at Harvard and he had to be taken to hospital.

His friends were deeply shocked by this sad turn of events. Now they rallied to help him, though virtually at the last moment. Harvard University offered to pay for all immediate hospital expenses, and when Ernő Balogh turned to ASCAP for help in connection with further medical treatment, this organization without any hesitation offered most generously to pay for all future hospital care; and this was done in spite of the fact that Bartók was not a member of the organization.

Meantime, Bartók's old friend, József Szigeti, helped in another way. He approached the world-famous conductor of the Boston Symphony Orchestra, Serge Koussevitzky, and the latter then commissioned Bartók to write an orchestral work for the foundation he had established in memory of his wife, Natalie. In May, he visited Bartók in the sanatorium to which he had been moved, discussed the proposed work, and in spite of the composer's protests, handed him a cheque for five hundred dollars, half the fee for the composition. It was because of all the help received from ASCAP that Bartók's health began to show signs of improvement; the treatment provided helped to prolong his life. And the commission from Koussevitzky restored his desire to work. He broke his silence as a composer and gave us the last flowering of his creative genius. It is true that his last years were dogged by the twin stars of illness and despair and it is difficult to decide which brought him the most suffering. Writing to Wilhelmine Creel on the previous New Year's Eve, he was already painting a dark picture of the future,

> ... my career as a composer is as much as finished; the quasi boycott of my works by the leading orchestras continues, no performances either of old work[s] or new ones. It is a shame—not for me, of course,

Now, on May 23, after Koussevitzky's visit, Ditta Pásztory wrote thankfully to József Szigeti, 'I am so glad that plans, musical ambitions, compositions are stirring in Béla's mind—a new hope, discovered in this way quite by chance, as it were incidentally. One thing is sure: Béla's "under no circumstances will I ever write any new work"– – –attitude has gone. It's more than three years now– – –'

For the time being there could be no thought of serious work. After further examinations, the doctors told him that he was suffering from 'polycithemia' but in fact they had diagnosed leukaemia. Still, thanks to the careful treatment he was receiving, his condition eased somewhat. During April and May he managed to put on some weight and gradually his temperature was reduced. At the beginning of July he went on holiday to Saranac Lake where he stayed until October, all his expenses being paid for by ASCAP. Towards the end of August there was a marked improvement in his health, he began to work again and when he returned to New York in October, he took with him the completed score of the new work written for the Koussevitzky Foundation, the *Concerto for Orchestra*, which he later described to Wilhelmine Creel as

> ... a rather long work of about 40 min. in 5 movements. All September I was very busy with this, without any detriment to my health.

He added the date of completion, October 8, 1943, at the end of the score which was acknowledged by Koussevitzky in a letter dated November 11.

Although this work bears the Baroque title *Concerto*, as did so many of Bartók's works, and though indeed the term was widely used in the musical literature of the period, it is in fact a symphony in five movements. As was his custom, Bartók wrote a short analysis of the work for the première on December 1, 1944. Here he speaks at some length of the title, describing the work as 'symphonic-like' and accounting for his choice of title by pointing out that the instrumental parts demanded a soloistic, virtuoso technique. He conceded that his intention in writing the work was to provide the Boston Symphony Orchestra, for whom the work had been commissioned, with a composition which they could render effectively and impressively, the kind of work in which they could display their own artistry.

The *Concerto for Orchestra* was not heard in Europe until after the war when it was on the whole well received by the public; this work and the *Concerto No. 3* for piano remain even today two of the composer's most popular works. Professional musicians, on the other hand, found it shocking and expressed the belief that Bartók, in his last years, had been obliged to make concessions to American taste and had betrayed his earlier ideals as conveyed through the string quartets and the *Music for String Instruments, Percussion and Celesta*.

But if we consider the composer's works as a whole, we realize that though the *Concerto for Orchestra* is more popular in tone than the rest of the works, it is organically linked to its predecessors. Like so many of the great masters throughout the history of music, Bartók communicated his ideas in a variety of genres, sometimes in concentrated form and at other times 'diluted'. He had no wish to be praised as a 'misunderstood' composer and therefore assessed realistically the demand for his music which he satisfied with an appropriate arrangement in genre and form which entailed no intellectual compromise. Even as a performing artist, he selected and arranged different programmes for different audiences and occasions. After his sorry experience with the *Concerto No. 1* for piano, he realized that in a concerto a brilliant instrumental performance and a more relaxed tone in the form of communication were not concessions but characteristics of the genre itself. This recognition has ensured the success of the *Concerto No. 2* for piano and the *Violin Concerto*. Nor is it surprising that when composing the *Concerto for Orchestra* his first concern should have been for the success of the performing artists; this was also natural in the case of the *Concerto No. 3* which he intended for his wife and the *Viola Concerto* which was personally commissioned by William Primrose. But it was also natural that in the string quartets, which were intended for an intimate audience, and in the Basle composition (*Music for String Instruments, Percussion and Celesta* and the *Sonata for Two Pianos*), he should have 'condensed to the limit' as he himself described his method to Denijs Dille in 1937. Equally, the diluted genre of the *Concerto for Orchestra* in no way disrupts the homogeneous nature of Bartók's music.

The source of the fascinating wealth of ideas in the *Concerto*, however, lies not only in the nature of the genre itself and the possibilities it offers but also in the composer's own mood at that time. In the five movements of the work Bartók found a medium through which he could express everything that he had perforce repressed during his years of silence. The richness of his *Concerto* has been demonstrated in one small section of the composition orchestrated, recorded on tape and presented by Tibor Serly, at the Bartók Archives in Budapest, on September 12, 1963. From the tone of this section and especially from the ostinato rhythm of the kettledrums it seems highly probably that this is a transcription of the middle part of the second movement of the *Concerto* which had been left out of the final version. Indeed, the work is broadly constructed, divided in various ways and is given content by the communicativeness of the artist.

The division of the work into five movements revives Bartók's early type of symmetrical bridge structure in which the slow middle section is enclosed between two scherzos. In this work, however, the internal division of the single movements is also quite detailed. A slow introductory section which in itself exists at many levels, leads into the first movement and later provides the musical idea for the development of the third movement. The first movement is stern, while the fifth movement is loosely constructed in a garland sonata form with an independent series of variations in the development section. The two scherzos are disposed between the structural pillars of the first, third and fifth movements, the second movement being a trio structure of considerable dimensions, the fourth a combination of the rondo and a bridge construction.

Apart from the *Concerto* there is scarcely any other work by Bartók which is so openly programmatic and which might almost be said to have a plot worked out from its inception to the final conclusion. It is true that in his symphonies there is always a reminder that his work may be traced back through that of Richard Strauss, Liszt and Berlioz to the great dramatic constructions of Beethoven. In the anxious slow movement of the *Divertimento* for example, there is a reference to the threat of war and the destitution that would be the inevitable outcome of war. The *Concerto*, however, is a more open expression of the composer's thoughts. There are occasional moments, it is true, when the composer allows us to hear briefly the internal monologue of *Bluebeard's Castle* or the solitary 'music of the night': these moments occur at the most profound level of the work, forming as they do the core of the third movement—which is also the central point of the construction. This central and inner core consists of a heartrending song of lament (as Bartók himself describes it in his own brief analysis). For the main part, however, it is played on an 'open stage' and ever since the first performance has excited the imagination of directors and choreographers because of its visual, almost cinematographic scherzo movements.

This was probably the first time since the *Kossuth Symphony* that Bartók himself mentioned in his explanatory notes the programmatic nature of one of his works. He began the notes with the following sentence:

> The general mood of the work represents, apart from the jesting second movement, a gradual transition from the sternness of the first movement and the lugubrious death-song of the third, to the life-assertion of the last one . . .

It is a comment that might equally well be made in connection with most of Bartók's works, at least those written during the second half of his career. Just what the composer meant by the word 'sternness' is brought out clearly enough in the musical plot of the *Concerto*. Our own view that when composing this work the thoughts of the composer were centred on the fate of Hungary in the face of German invasion, is confirmed by Ferenc Fricsay who quotes remarks made to this effect by Bartók when talking to the pianist György Sándor. And in this work too the solution he offers is the idea of the 'brotherhood of the peoples' as depicted in the great dance tableau of the last movement and in the variations of the middle section with its international connotations.

The full significance of the remarks made by Bartók and quoted by Fricsay may be seen if we refer to the fourth movement where the *Concerto* is especially illustrative in character. The title of the movement is 'Intermezzo interrotto'. A young man confesses his love and serenades his beloved only to be interrupted by a band of rowdy drunkards whistling a couplet. The musical idea of the interrupted serenade and the rondo-like division of conflicting musical characters may have its origin in the first book of Debussy's Preludes (Sérénade interrompue). Bartók's individual technique in the use of quotation, however, gives it an entirely new content. In the tones of the serenade, we can recognize a song that was extremely popular in the period between the two world wars, 'Szép vagy, gyönyörű vagy, Magyarország' (Hungary, gracious and beautiful). The trivial fun-fair music that interrupts the serenade is reminiscent of a frivolous couplet from Lehár's *The Merry Widow*. It is of course possible that the popular refrain from this operetta was still in Bartók's mind when he wrote this work. The gay hero of the operetta pours out his admiration for the girls of easy virtue. It is at any rate certain that in one of his early letters the young Bartók had cited *The Merry Widow* as an example of foreign-influenced shallow musical taste.

Bartók's quotation of the serenade, with its serious lyrical tone, clearly indicates the symbolic reference to Hungary in this movement. The melody of the brutal night attack is also a quotation, this time from a polka variation in one of the symphonies by Shostakovitch, the Soviet composer, where this theme also characterized the tone of foreign intruders. It is in fact possible to recognize the inversions of two melodies.

It is especially interesting, however, to note the manner in which the composer adds weight and significance to the melodies quoted in the *Concerto*. It was thus that the *verbunkos* melodies, which had meantime acquired a much greater significance, were introduced into the works Bartók composed during his last European period: these *verbunkos* melodies represented an idea of absolute patriotism which had developed from the nationalist sentiment of the *Kossuth Symphony* and the *Suite No. 1* and which had now matured to become the loftier vision of this later period. In the *Concerto* we find once again the folk art-song, but now it is given a new content, and its tone has an important role in the composition. But as well as this song, a whole series of popular styles of varying degrees of merit is worked into the dramatic whole. When we hear the choral trio of the second movement and the American dance-music tone of the last movement, we are stirred by a faint memory of Mozart's *Magic Flute* in which the master made use of the most popular street songs together with the rich traditions of Baroque genres, in order to people a world in which all humanity had its rightful place.

So rich is the total effect of this great work that we are scarcely aware that in it Bartók remains faithful to the principles contained in, for example, his string quartets, that he conjures up this variegated world of the *Concerto* from a strict thematic unity, and that virtually all the important themes of the work spring from one musical cell.

It was not possible to stay at Saranac Lake later than October and Bartók therefore hurried back to New York where at last, four and a half years after the première, he had an opportunity of hearing the orchestral version of his *Violin Concerto*. He had been unable to take part in the first performance when this was given by the Amsterdam Concertgebouw Orchestra and the only way he had been able to contribute to that occasion had been to rehearse it with Zoltán Székely in Paris. Now that the violinist, Tossy Spivakovsky, had included it in the programme of a concert to be given in the Carnegie Hall, the composer awaited his first hearing of the work with understandable excitement. What he heard relieved his anxiety and fully satisfied him.

> The performance was excellent: soloist, conductor, orchestra were first rate (and the composer too!),

he wrote jestingly to Wilhelmine Creel on December 17.

> The orchestration proved to have no mistakes.

During this period, the *Violin Concerto* was being performed in various parts of the United States and it was invariably well received. Soon after the performance at the Carnegie Hall, Yehudi Menuhin played it in Minneapolis with Mitropoulos and his orchestra. At the end of November, when Menuhin was appearing in New York and had played not only the *Violin Concerto* but also the *Sonata No. 1,* an opportunity arose for a meeting between these two great musicians of our age. Bartók continued the letter quoted above with a description of this meeting and some rare words of praise for the famous violinist.

> It was on this occasion that I met him the first time ... he is really a great artist; he played at the same concert Bach's C major sonata in a grand, classical style. My sonata, too, was excellently done. When there is a real great artist, then the composer's advice and help is not necessary, the performer finds his way quite well, alone. It is altogether a happy thing that a young artist is interested in contemporary works which draw no public, and likes them, and—performs them *comme il faut*.

As a result of the meeting, Menuhin commissioned Bartók to compose a sonata for solo violin.

An approaching vacation afforded a splendid opportunity for Bartók to write the sonata. His health continued to improve and by November he felt that he had regained all his former strength. 'However, matters are not as simple as this,' he wrote at this time to Professor Wood in Seattle.

> The doctors say I am now in a state of reconvalescence, and must be extremely careful during this winter in order to avoid a relapse which would be disastrous.

During the second half of December, in order to escape the hard New York winter, he travelled to Asheville, North Carolina, where the climate was much milder. He stayed there until the end of April. But before he left New York, Columbia University again renewed his contract for the first half of the coming year. He could not know that the funds of the foundation from which the University had so far paid his grant were now exhausted, and the fee for a further period of six months consisted of contributions from various public bodies and organizations which had responded to appeals from Bartók's personal friends. All that Bartók knew was that he could leave New York secure in the knowledge that his family was provided for at least until his return.

Spring in Asheville revived memories of other summers spent in work. Full of the confidence that had returned with the improvement in his health, alone with nature once again, the composer of the *Music for String Instruments, Percussion and Celesta* faced the stimulating task of writing a solo violin sonata.

> At present I feel quite well, I have no temperature, my strength has returned, and I am able to take nice walks in the mountain forests—yes, I climb mountains (only very cautiously, of course). In March my weight was 87 lbs., now it is 105 lbs.,

he wrote on January 30, 1944, to József Szigeti. For a brief interval he was imbued with the spirit of his own youthful aspirations and the daring achievements of his maturity. He felt strong enough to express in a disciplined manner the feelings which had found no outlet during his illness and he felt cleansed in heart and mind, ready for new and inspiring spiritual experiences. And he could count on the support of his new friend, the young violinist.

In its outward form, the violin sonata may be described as Baroque. But within this Baroque framework we find monologues which are the concentrated distillations of Bartók's thoughts. The first movement, 'Tempo di ciaccona', is a traditional structure with variations and motives through which we hear the folk-song tone of the slow three-quarter beat of a *chaconne*. The second movement is marked 'Fuga' and is related in theme to the fugue of the *Music for String Instruments, Percussion and Celesta* and also to the beginning of the *String Quartet No. 5*. The third movement, 'Melodia,' at times approaches the idyllic tone of the slow movement of the *Violin Concerto*, but in the turns of the melody with its small intervals, there is also a reminiscence of the slow movement of the *Sonata* for violin and piano No. 1. On the other hand, when we consider the headlong phantom galloping of the presto section of the fourth movement, which is almost alarming in its speed, then it becomes clear that the solo sonata in fact represents Bartók's advance along the path taken seventeen years previously in the *String Quartet No. 3*. In this breathtaking finale there is no break: the music surges forwards, ever forwards. There is none of that classical fulfilment found in the works with a closed symmetry and folk-dance tableaux. Here rather we find the demons of the diabolic scherzos, formerly enclosed in the central sections of Bartók's compositions, but now unleashed at last and set free. There is probably some justification for the theory put forward by certain students of Bartók's work that here in the solo sonata was the germ of a new creative period, a new vision, a new beginning such as occurred several times before in the course of his development.

3 Première and success of the 'Concerto'. Hopes of recuperation. The Romanian folk-music collection. News from home at the end of the war. Anxiety and homesickness

In the longer letters which Bartók wrote to his friends, he sometimes classified the events of his life as either 'good' or 'bad'. One of the events which naturally came under the heading 'good' was the fact of his growing success. During the early part of the summer, Menuhin added fingering

374

and bowing instructions to the manuscript of the solo sonata. When he played it at his concert in New York on November 26, he gave what was, in Bartók's opinion, '... a wonderful performance'.

Five days later, on December 1 and 2, Koussevitzky introduced the *Concerto* for orchestra in Boston.

> We went there for the rehearsals and performances—after having obtained the grudgingly granted permission of my doctor for this trip,

he wrote to Mrs. Creel on December 17, 1944.

> It was worth while (!), the performance was excellent. Koussevitzky is very enthusiastic about the piece, and says it is 'the best orchestra piece of the last 25 years' (including the works of his idol Shostakovich!).

According to the account that Bartók gave to Tibor Serly, Koussevitzky spoke about the last twenty years during rehearsals, but in the enthusiastic mood engendered by the performance, Bartók added another five years in his letter to Mrs. Creel.

The *Concerto* was given further performances in Boston on December 29 and 30, and Koussevitzky planned to play the work in New York in January. Menuhin, in the meantime, was touring the cities of the old and new world with the *Violin Concerto*. The composer also announced performances

> ... this year in Washington, Baltimore, in Pittsburgh, and (in Sept.) in London (B.B.C.) twice! Next season he is going to play it in Philadelphia and probably in Boston.

Another item of 'good' news was the continued improvement in the composer's health, although he himself was constantly aware of the precarious nature of the improvement. In the letter to Mrs. Creel written on December 17, 1944, and quoted above, he gives a more precise account of his condition:

> you said in one of your letters that my recovering was a miracle. This is true only with some reservations: it was only a hemisemidemimiracle. Of course, that lung-infection disappeared as mysteriously as it came—this you know from my last letter. There are, however—and almost continuously—some minor troubles which probably never can be completely cured and make a regular job or concertizing etc. impossible for me ... Surely, I do not feel as agile and lively as 4 years ago, and must take great care of myself, especially in un-

But the 'minor troubles' were in fact rather serious. After his return from Asheville, his spleen was affected and he had to undergo X-ray treatment. In March 1945, he fell a victim to acute pneumonia, which was fortunately cured very quickly by means of the newly-discovered antibiotic, penicillin.

Also to be counted among the items of 'good' news was the improvement in his financial circumstances at this time. During the period when he has been confined to hospital, the problem of finding a permanent home had been temporarily shelved. The Bartók family gave up the apartment in Riverdale and took rooms in the Hotel Woodrow. Then, while Bartók was in Asheville, his wife rented a two-room apartment on the West Side, 57th Street. This became the family home during 1944–45, during the periods when they were in New York. Bartók described the apartment as being

> . . . of course, too small for both of us. We very often hamper each other in our activities, but we must be glad to have got such an apartment, at least.

As for his financial circumstances, he was able to write to Mrs. Creel before Christmas, 1944, that ' . . .this is now fairly well settled.' He had a regular income from his compositions and could say with some certainty,

> So, for the next three years, a modest living is secured for us. (Doctors' expenses for me, if necessary, are still paid by Ascap.)

But the 'bad' news was by no means lacking. In sorting the Romanian material he had brought with him, and in preparing for publication the South Slav folk-songs on which he had been working at Columbia University, he experienced as much anxiety as joy. The summer months at Saranac Lake in 1944 were overshadowed by the task of mastering the linguistic difficulties and correcting the proofs of the introduction to the Serbo-Croatian Folk-Songs; the hope that this would appear in the autumn of that year had to be abandoned. The situation in regard to the Romanian and Turkish collection was even more desperate.

Before leaving for Asheville, he wrote irritably to Wilhelmine Creel about

... the impossibility of publishing my scientific works (Romanian, Turkish folk music material) ... Now I deposited the whole Mss. at Columb. Univ. Library—there they are available to those few persons (very few indeed) who may be interested in them.

(December 17, 1943.)

Though Bartók writes of the 'whole Mss.,' only two volumes of the Romanian collection could have been given to the Library at that time: the third volume, a collection of lyrics, was deposited later. But we are moving ahead of events; let us return to the description of his work sent to Mrs. Creel one year after the date of the letter quoted above.

I spent all my time—except those few weeks needed for the solo-violin sonata—to do some special scientific work. Perhaps you know that [I] gave the final shape to the musical part of the Romanian Folk Music collection during my illness. These consist of two volumes: I: instrumental, II: vocal melodies. Now, this year I worked on and almost finished the IIIrd volume, comprising all the texts ...

The Turkish collection is still unpublished. The Romanian collection was published by Benjamin Suchoff in 1967, in three large volumes, with 2555 melodies and their texts. They illustrate not only the incredible labour and touching care which Bartók devoted to this enormous task, but also the special attention he paid to the texts in his collections of folk-songs, bearing out previous remarks about his increasing interest towards lyrics. The refinement and enrichment of his attitude as a scientist, as shown in the systematic arrangement and cataloguing of his material, are proof of the experience and profound study gained from his contact with modern scientific methods during his period of activity at Columbia University.

The subjects which caused Bartók to express himself in the most depressing terms were, however, the war situation and the fate of Europe, especially the fate of the Hungarian people. Sometimes he touched on these subjects very briefly, but this was merely a sign that he found it painful to write at any length. In his thoughts, his own destiny was linked with that of Hungary: he felt himself to be Hungarian, his own career bound up with Hungarian culture. His great hope was that the war would soon come to an end so that he could bring his period of exile to an end and find peace in his own country. This idea is constantly reflected in all his writings. ' . . .But what most worries me,' he wrote to Mrs. Creel on December 17, 1943,

> is this lagging and slow procedure of the 'battlefields'. There is no end in sight —and the destroying of Europe (people and works of art) continues without respite and mercy. Personally, I do not know, how long I can endure the insecurity of this gipsy life . . .

He expected that following United States intervention the war would come to a speedy end, and when his son Péter joined the Navy in February 1944, there was a degree of comfort in the thought that his son was with the Allies, actively engaged in the fight against fascism. Péter, however, was not sent to the front. First, he had to complete an army course in electrical engineering, then, from September, he was stationed in Panama where he remained until his demobilization in the summer of 1945.

The impatience with which Bartók awaited a successful outcome of the war is best illustrated by his reaction to news of advances being made by the Allied Forces on all fronts.

> I would feel happy about what there is to feel happy about if I didn't have the permanent feeling that all this comes too late. Too late perhaps for me, too, but how much more so for those who are being killed off in the meantime,

he wrote to his friends, Pál Kecskeméti and his wife, Erzsébet Láng, on August 22, 1944. Every setback filled him with despair and his feeling that success would come too late for him personally is expressed once more in a casual phrase written in September 1944,

> . . . the standstill in both East and West, the Arnhem adventure, Warsaw, Hungary—well, let's drop the subject!

As the war neared its end during the summer of 1945, the tone of his letters became even more impatient and irritable. The news from home which came to him through a variety of different channels was sometimes good and sometimes bad, nearly always incomplete and left him in agonizing suspense as to the true state of affairs. He succeeded in finding out that his closest friends and relatives, among them Kodály and his family, were alive and well. He also learnt that the folk-music collection had been saved.

'Both copies of the notation of the 13,000 songs are intact and carefully hidden,' he wrote to the Kecskeméti family on July 21. 'From whom did we still have to hide it even on June 25?' he queried bitterly and suspiciously. By this time, Bartók was gravely ill, waiting daily to hear that it would be possible to go home. It was in disheartened tones that he wrote to the composer Jenő Zádor, on July 1:

> We have been receiving some extremely depressing news from Hungary: appalling devastations, terrible misery, chaos threatening (a great number of Hungarian newspapers from Budapest are finding their way—presumably through the Russian Embassy—to a Hungarian Communist newspaper here, which reproduces them in facsimile; also a few people have received news through private channels). As I see it, for the time being one cannot even think of returning to Hungary. Nor is there any means of doing so—neither— transport nor (Russian) permit. But even if there were means, in my opinion it would be better to await developments. Heaven knows how many years it will be before Hungary can pull herself together in some measure (if at all). And yet I, too, would like to return, for good . . .

The Parliament, which at this time reassembled once again in Budapest, elected Bartók as a member, but they awaited his return in vain. There is no reason why we should make any attempt to conceal his disheartened remarks. The creative spirit of the great artist and composer was still fresh and he looked ahead to new achievements. As once before in his early years, his enquiring mind was leading him towards new paths of development; once again, during the years of exile, at the end of his life, we find in his music ever more ambitious attempts to express the aspirations of the human soul. At the same time, the frail human being who had been so much persecuted was ill, weary, longing for rest and only too willing to retreat within the enclosed circle of the daily round amidst a few cherished possessions where he was solaced by memories of the past. He could not risk the shock of seeing the changed face of the home he had left so long ago; he preferred to see it through the glow of memory and retain the picture which had sustained him during the years of exile. It was for these reasons that his last letters were so nostalgic in tone.

Meantime a happy experience was planned for the summer of 1945. Menuhin invited Bartók to stay with him in California. On April 5, Bartók replied that he had completed plans for the trip:

> my doctor is quite enthusiastic about California as a summer place for me, and so am I. Therefore, we are very happy to be able to accepte [*sic*] your kind invitation. We will go there for about 3 months and will leave New York about June 15. We will send you news about our arrival in San Francisco in time . .

But it was not the time of his arrival he in fact wrote. On June 6, he had to refuse the invitation because of a deterioration in his health.

> I do not feel quite well, and for variety's sake—now Mrs. Bartók was ill for several weeks and does not yet feel quite well. We simply are scared to try such a long journey, connected, especially now, with all kind of annoyances . . . I had so many musical plans connected with my stay there . . .

And so Bartók and his wife returned for the summer to Saranac Lake, though this time their quarters were less comfortable than during the previous summer. Then too, at the beginning of July, Bartók had to 'emigrate' to Canada so that he could apply for an 'immigration' permit from the nearest United States consulate. This was the only way in which it was possible for him to extend his stay. The whole excursion lasted no more than three days, but in the heat of summer this was no light undertaking for a sick man, especially as he had to spend one whole day merely waiting for the permit. On July 7, he wrote to friends in New York,

> From 9 in the morning until 6.30 in the evening (with only a break for lunch) I loafed, loitered and sat around in that Consulate, consumed with anger and anxiety.

The rest of the summer was relatively uneventful and peaceful. He found time to do some composing: he completed a piano concerto which he had begun earlier. He worked on it in secret, planning it as a surprise for his wife.

The *Concerto No. 3* for piano was the last work that Bartók completed. It is of course true that during the course of the year Bartók also completed an outline of the *Viola Concerto* intended for William Primrose in sufficient detail to enable Tibor Serly to reconstruct and orchestrate it; this necessitated much hard work on the part of Serly, but the result of his efforts has been to give us a *Viola Concerto* which is still played today as a work by Bartók. For this, we owe a debt of gratitude to Tibor Serly, which should never be forgotten in the history of music. Only because of his work have we been given a conception of the *Viola Concerto*. The present form of the work gives us the impression that the concerto is not related to the *Sonata for Solo Violin* but rather to the family of compositions which are more popular in tone and more 'warmly melodic'. It is scarcely possible, however, to imagine what the final form would have been like if Bartók had been able to complete it.

Among Bartók's compositions, we can find numerous illustrations of the fact that he did not consider these to be necessarily in their final form even after publication. He revised the piano accompaniment for each new edition of *Twenty Folk-Songs* (1906) and *For Children;* and other pieces, for instance *The Miraculous Mandarin*, were modified many times. We are not familiar with the original piano version of the *Four Orchestral Pieces,* but it is clear that this must have been very different from the orchestral work which appeared ten years later and which contains features related to another new work of that period, *The Miraculous Mandarin*. We have at hand the complete piano outline of the *Viola Concerto* and it is therefore possible to compare this with the orchestrated version.

It is immediately obvious, even to the layman, that Bartók's first conception of the work underwent important changes while he was engaged in the task of orchestration. The *Sonata for Solo Violin* is another example of a work which Bartók modified at a later stage. It was a long time after Menuhin had first introduced the work that Bartók wrote to him on June 6, 1945, saying that

> somewhere we must try to settle the final form of the solo sonata next winter.

His method of working is very well described by the famous remark made by Racine: 'My work is complete. All I have to do is to write it!' The score of the *Viola Concerto* as we know it today probably represents a later, but not the final form.

He did not live to complete all the commissions he had received. In 1945, the Hungarian composer, Jenő Zádor, who lived in California, passed on to him a request from a certain Hollywood conductor named Schildkret, who had made the same request some years previously, to compose an introductory movement for a cycle entitled *Genesis*. He did not accept the commission. And he wrote only a few notes of a seventh string quartet which he had discussed with Ralph Hawkes, the head of the New York branch of Boosey and Hawkes.

The *Concerto No. 3* for piano and orchestra, however, is entirely Bartók's own work apart from the orchestration of the last seventeen bars. The composer was working on the last page of the score when Tibor Serly came to see him. The very next day he was taken to hospital and Serly had said that he felt his visit had prevented Bartók from completing the score. It was for this reason that he felt a sense of obligation to finish the orchestration.

The character of this work derives from its intimate tone and radiant harmony in which we sense the composer's reconciliation with the world. Here we find none of the searching and struggling that was an essential part of the *Concerto for Orchestra* and many of the earlier works. In the first movement, the sunny and romantic nature scenes in E major recall the playful, dancing tone of the *Divertimento;* and though the dance becomes progressively wilder and ends with all the turbulence of the *Allegro Barbaro*, there is no sense of destructiveness and even in its tension preserves its playfulness. It moves forward in a spirit of bravado rather than true anger.

It is in the second movement that the inner programme and train of thought is fully revealed. Running through the pious chorale melody are the descending waves in the clear major of the strings. It is not difficult to pick out an almost exact quotation from one of the movements of Beethoven's late string quartets, the third movement of the String Quartet in A minor, op. 132. In Beethoven's work the movement has the lengthy title of 'Heiliger Dankgesang eines Genesenen an die Gottheit, in der lydischen Tonart'. It is the movement which is discussed at such length in Thomas Mann's *Magic Mountain*. The middle section of the movement depicts in musical terms the loud and cheerful sounds of the dawn chorus followed by a return of the chorale melody in the wind instruments. The solo piano part consists of counterpoint variations.

In the middle movements of Bartók's earlier works we have already heard the music of the dawn. But in each case this music was of a soothing nature, intended to signify the end of night, as for instance in the *String Quartet No. 5* or when the song of the nightingale is heard in the slow movement of the *Concerto*. Here, however, the birdlike sounds persist throughout the middle section, sounds that are joyfully repeated on the piano, thus clearly identifying the idea of recovery and relaxation in nature. At the same time, this movement demonstrates the extent to which Bartók has been influenced by his greatest masters, Beethoven and Bach. The chorale variation recalls the spirit of Bach. It is also to Tibor Serly that we owe the information that during his last years, Bach's organ preludes and Beethoven's string quartets were constantly in Bartók's hands.

When Péter was demobilized in August, his parents were still at Saranac Lake and it was there that he joined them. But toward the end of August and at the beginning of September, Bartók's condition suddenly deteriorated. His temperature rose each evening and the family hurriedly returned to New York. For a time he was treated at home and for a week or two he worked on the score of the *Concerto No. 3* for piano. On September 21, his temperature dropped suddenly. The Hungarian doctor who was treating him, Dr. Rappaport, considered this to be an ominous sign, and arranged for him to be taken to the West Side Hospital nearby. There he was given blood transfusion, fed on dextrose and with the aid of oxygen, kept alive for a few more days. He died on September 26, 1945.

Only a few friends attended his funeral. He was buried in Ferncliff Cemetery in Hartsdale, Westchester. In 1950 a bronze tablet was placed on his grave by American admirers of his work, no other memorial being permitted by the regulations of the cemetery. But barely twenty years after Bartók's death, his life work has taken its place among the precious cultural treasures which are our human heritage.

APPENDICES

CHRONOLOGICAL SURVEY OF THE MAJOR EVENTS IN THE LIFE OF BÉLA BARTÓK

1881. March 25. Birth at Nagyszentmiklós (Sînnicolaul Mare, Romania since 1920), in what was at that time Torontál County. First child of Béla Bartók, headmaster of the school of agriculture, and Paula, *née* Voit.

1887. January 16. Formation of the Nagyszentmiklós Music League of which Béla Bartók sr. was elected chairman. His son, Béla, who had already shown a remarkable interest in music, was further inspired by the concerts given by members of the society. About this time, Béla was given his first piano lessons by his mother.

1888. August 4. Death of the composer's father. Responsibility for the family now rested on the mother who first gave piano lessons, then, from 1889, taught in schools, so that she could support her two children, Béla and Elza, four years younger.

1892. May 1. Bartók's first public recital, given at Nagyszöllős where his mother had been working as a school teacher since 1889. The programme included his own composition, *The Flow of the Danube*. It was on this occasion that the boy's remarkable gifts were first noticed, by Keresztély Altdörfer, an organist from Sopron.

In the autumn of this year, Mrs. Béla Bartók was granted a year's leave of absence, which she spent with her family in Pozsony (now Bratislava), where Béla began to study regularly under László Erkel.

1894. For eight months, Mrs. Bartók taught at Beszterce (now Bistriţa). She was then transferred to Pozsony where she was able to settle with her family. In the favourable atmosphere of this town which had many historic links with famous musicians, and where he was now taught by both László Erkel and Anton Hyrtl, Bartók's talent unfolded. During his last years at the secondary school, he composed songs and chamber work.

1899. January. He was interviewed at the Budapest Academy of Music by István Thomán who accepted him as a student for the autumn term. In February, he suffered from inflammation of the lungs but nevertheless succeeded in passing his matriculation examination. In September, he enrolled at the Budapest Academy of Music where he studied the piano under István Thomán and composition with Hans Koessler. Both teachers accepted him for the second year of the course.

1900. During his first year at the Academy, he made progress particularly in the technique of piano playing and in the study of music literature—especially the works of Wagner. He passed his examinations with high honours. In August, he again suffered from lung trouble and it seemed for a time that he would have to abandon altogether the study and practice of music as a career.

1901. After treatment in Meran, he recovered, and in March was able to practise the piano again with renewed energy. However, he had missed the second year of the course at the Academy, and when he returned there in September, he had to repeat it.

1902. February 12. Bartók was decisively influenced by the experience of hearing *Thus Spake Zarathustra* by Richard Strauss. He began to compose once more, now a confirmed disciple of Strauss.

In the autumn, his virtuoso piano performance of the score of Strauss's *Ein Heldenleben* made a profound impression on musical circles in Budapest. It was at this period that he became acquainted with the group of artists who met at the home of Mrs. Gruber, *née* Emma Sándor, later the wife of Zoltán Kodály.

1903. January 26. Bartók played *Ein Heldenleben* in the Tonkünstlerverein, Vienna. He was not required to sit for the examinations at the end of the school year. He finished his studies with flying colours. On July 2, in *Zenevilág*, Pongrác Kacsóh wrote the first notice of any length to appear about him. In the spring of this year, political unrest and the stir of patriotic movements throughout the country confirmed Bartók in his determination to use his musical talent for the benefit of the national culture. In this spirit he composed his *Kossuth Symphony*, by now a follower of Liszt as much as of Strauss.

1903–4. He spent much of the winter season in Berlin, but as his career as a concert pianist began to develop, he visited many other cities too.

1904. January 13. Première of the *Kossuth Symphony* in Budapest. February 18, première in Manchester, with Hans Richter conducting.

He spent the summer in Gerlicepuszta where he formed a friendship with Kálmán Harsányi, later a noted poet, some of whose poems he set to music. At this time he planned to arrange and popularize the best of the known art songs which were most truly akin to Hungarian folk music. In November, he finished the first version of his *Rhapsody* for piano, marked op. 1, a work definitely in the spirit of Liszt.

1905. In the spring, in Vienna, he composed his *Suite No. 1* and began work on the *Suite No. 2*. During the summer he became increasingly aware of the significance of peasant folk music and started to collect folk-songs in Békés County. In August, he competed unsuccessfully in the international Rubinstein competition, both as a composer and as a pianist. However, his whole life was enriched by his experience of Paris.

1906. March–April. With Ferenc Vecsey as his partner, Bartók gave recitals in Spain and Portugal. He returned home by way of North Africa, his first important visit to that continent, and also visited France and Italy. By the summer of this year, he had already begun a systematic collection of Hungarian folk music, and during the autumn he began to collect Slovak melodies too. In December, *Hungarian Folk-Songs*, prepared jointly with Kodály, was published. Due to lack of demand, however, the series was discontinued.

1907. January. Bartók succeeded István Thomán, who retired at this time, as professor at the Academy of Music. During the summer he travelled extensively in Transylvania where he first encountered the oldest strata of Hungarian folk music. He also became acquainted with the music of Debussy which was brought to his attention by Kodály who had just visited Paris. In the autumn, Bartók passed through one of the most serious crises of his life, both personal and ideological. He completed the *Suite No. 2* which he had begun earlier, and which already showed signs of the style which he was just beginning to develop under the influence of his knowledge of folk music.

1908. This year saw the first expression in a mature individual style of the synthesis of his dual experience of classical and folk music. He also composed a noteworthy work, the *String Quartet No. 1.*

1909. Summer. Bartók began to collect Romanian folk music and formed a lasting friendship with János Buşiţia, a teacher at Belényes.
   In the autumn, he married Márta Ziegler.

1910. March 17 and March 19. The works of Zoltán Kodály and Béla Bartók were introduced at two composer's recitals, which have become memorable in the history of modern Hungarian music; the occasion was also noteworthy on account of the first appearance of the Waldbauer–Kerpely String Quartet which later achieved world fame. During this year, too, Bartók made his first overtures to the appropriate authorities in Slovakia and Romania in an attempt to secure their collaboration in his project for a scientific study of folk music. In August his first son, Béla, was born.

1911. Bartók completed *Bluebeard's Castle*, and presented it, unsuccessfully, in the competition organized by the Lipótvárosi Kaszinó. Some of the younger musicians, among them Bartók, formed the New Hungarian Music Association (UMZE), its main purpose being to encourage an appreciation of orchestral composition and to promote performances of a high standard of new Hungarian works. In honour of the one hundredth anniversary of Liszt's birth Bartók wrote an analysis of the significance of his art.

1912. Because of the evident failure of UMZE, and lack of understanding on the part of critics and audiences, Bartók withdrew from public musical life. During the following years, he devoted much of his energy to folk-music research and teaching, the former with the help of his wife. During this period he composed the first piano version of *Four Orchestral Pieces*.

1913. June. Visit to Biskra, North Africa, where he collected Arabic folk music. Bartók and Kodály submitted jointly a project for folk-music research to the Kisfaludy Society from which, however, they received no response. Bartók's Bihar collection was published by the Romanian Academy of Sciences.

1914–6. Plans to collect folk music in Russia were frustrated by the outbreak of war and further tours of Transylvania were prevented by Romania's entry into the war in 1916. Anxieties due to the hardships of war and also his wife's illness arose. Yet Bartók composed a number of works during the war years, *String*

Quartet No. 2, the *Suite* for piano, two cycles of songs and a few significant series of folk-song compositions; all these works represent a striving for a new style of expression.

1917. May 12. Première of *The Wooden Prince* at the Opera House, with Egisto Tango as the inspiring conductor of the orchestra. The considerable success of this work marked a change of mood in the public attitude to Bartók's work.

1918. January 12. Concert of soldiers' songs of the Monarchy organized by the Defence Ministry in Vienna. In the programme notes for this concert Bartók first outlined his evaluation of the various types of Hungarian folk music. May 24. Première of *Bluebeard's Castle* and *The Wooden Prince*, performed in one programme at the Opera House. In October, Bartók began working on *The Miraculous Mandarin*.

1919. Spring. Completion of *The Miraculous Mandarin*. During the period of the Republic of Councils, Bartók, like Kodály and Dohnányi, was an advisory member of the Music Committee headed by Béla Reinitz. The counter-revolutionary regime suspended Dohnányi, Director of the Academy of Music at the time of the revolution, and also his deputy, Kodály. The teachers who demonstrated their support were brought under disciplinary action. On November 25, Jenő Hubay was appointed Director of the Academy.
Bartók considered the idea of settling abroad.

1920. On January 10, disciplinary action was instituted against Kodály because of his membership of the Music Committee of the Republic of Councils. Dohnányi and Bartók protested that Kodály was not alone in this.
From the end of February, Bartók spent two months in Berlin where he gave recitals and discussed his works. He was requested by Reinhardt to write the music for *Lysistrata*, and it was reported in Hungary that he would not return home. At the end of May, extreme right-wing circles initiated a violent press campaign against him, accusing him of being unpatriotic.

1921. The European musical world celebrated his 40th birthday. In March, the *Anbruch* of Vienna celebrated his anniversary with a special issue. In March, together with Kodály, he completed a joint collection of folk-songs, entitled *Erdélyi Magyarság* (Transylvanian Folk-Songs).
In October, Bartók completed his scientific study, *The Hungarian Folk-Song*.

1922. In February, he gave concerts in Transylvania, and in March and April, in England and France. London and Paris premières of his *Sonata for Violin and Piano No. 1* with Jelly Arányi. This concert tour established his international reputation. From that time on, most of his time was taken up with annual concert tours abroad. In the summer, the International Society for New Music of which Bartók always remained an active member was founded. In October, he again gave concerts in Transylvania.

1923. In the spring, he took his *Sonata for Violin and Piano No. 2* with him on his concert tour of England and Holland. After decades of delay, his Máramaros collection of Romanian folk music was published in a German edition.

At the end of August, he married Ditta Pásztory, later to be his partner at the piano.

On 19th November, the *Dance Suite* was heard for the first time, together with Kodály's *Psalmus Hungaricus*.

1924. The extreme right wing in Hungary continued its attacks and urged disciplinary action against Bartók because of his Transylvanian concert tour. In October, he was fêted in Bucharest. The Romanian king bestowed the Bene Merenti medal (1st class) upon him, Bartók composed the cycle *Village Scenes*. By the autumn, he had virtually completed the orchestration of the score for *The Miraculous Mandarin*.

1925. Bartók gave recitals in Italy in the spring and autumn. In the May music festival of the International Society for Contemporary Music in Prague, Talich presented the *Dance Suite* with great success. The *Dance Suite* was repeated upon the occasion of the guest appearance of the Prague Philharmonic Orchestra in Budapest.

Bartók discussed the publication of his Romanian *kolinda* collection with English and Romanian publishers but to no effect. The scheduled performance of *The Miraculous Mandarin* in Budapest was postponed.

1926. At the beginning of the year, renewed proposals to produce the pantomime in Budapest were made, but the performance was again postponed.

On 27th November, Jenő Szenkár introduced it in Cologne, where it was denounced in clerical circles, thereby creating a scandal.

In the course of this year, with his series of piano works (*Sonata, Concerto No. 1* for piano, etc.), Bartók introduced compositions of a new order to the public, in a different tone, in which there was a synthesis of his earlier achievements and all that he had learned from Baroque models.

1927. February 19. *The Miraculous Mandarin* was presented in Prague with great success.

In September, the *String Quartet No. 3* was completed. In December, Bartók set out for his first concert tour of the United States.

1928. He spent the first two months of the year in the United States. In September, he completed the *String Quartet No. 4*.

In October, his *String Quartet No. 3* was awarded first prize in the Philadelphia Musical Fund competition. He took part in the International Folk Music Congress in Prague.

At the end of December, he set out for the Soviet Union on his only guest tour there.

1929. He spent the greater part of January in the Soviet Union. At the end of the month, he made guest appearances in Switzerland, in Basle and Zurich. It was at this time that he became acquainted with Paul Sacher and the Basle Chamber Orchestra. His new folk-song compositions gave proof of his growing interest in the texts.

1930. The *Cantata Profana* was composed. This period marked the beginning of another withdrawal by the composer. For six years, he did not play his own works in Budapest.

1931. In a letter written at the beginning of the year, he set down his ideal of the brotherhood of peoples. On his 50th birthday, he was made Chevalier of the Legion of Honour. He was also awarded the Hungarian Corvin Wreath but did not attend the presentation ceremony. In March, the reactionary domestic climate again prevented the Budapest première of *The Miraculous Mandarin*. Chauvinistic Romanian circles prevented a memorial plaque from being set up to mark his place of birth. In July, he took part in a session of the League of Nations Committee for Intellectual Cooperation in Geneva.

In this year, he completed the *Concerto No. 2* for piano and composed the *Violin Duos*.

1932. In April and May, he took part in the International Congress of Arab Folk Music in Cairo.

1934. In February, during a tour of Romania, he studied Romanian folk music in the Bucharest Phonogramme Archives. Members of the Composers' Association, notably Constantin Brăiloiu, defended him against the false accusations made by Romanian chauvinists.

In September, he retired from teaching, and at the request of the Hungarian Academy of Sciences, began work on the publication of the Hungarian folk-music collection. During the course of this year he wrote his study, 'Our Folk Music and the Folk Music of Neighbouring Peoples', and composed the *String Quartet No. 5*.

1935. On January 30, the Budapest Opera House revived *The Wooden Prince*.

1936. On February 3, Bartók was made a member of the Academy of Sciences and read a paper entitled 'Liszt Problems'. The Liszt concerts, given during the Liszt Centenary celebrations, were made memorable by his performance of Liszt's *Danse Macabre*. In this year, he wrote his study, 'Why and How Do We Collect Folk Music'.

In the summer, commissioned by Paul Sacher and the Basle Chamber Orchestra, he composed the *Music for String Instruments, Percussion and Celesta*.

In October, the Opera House revived *Bluebeard's Castle;* in November, the Hungarian première of the *Cantata Profana* was held. In November he visited Turkey where for the last time he collected folk music.

1937. In May, at the festival of his choral works at the Academy of Music, he played a series of pieces from *Mikrokosmos*. His work for male chorus *From Olden Times* was presented at this concert. In the summer, he composed the *Sonata for Two Pianos and Percussion*. The reactionary journal of Béla Bangha and his associates, *Magyar Kultúra*, embarked on an open attack against the choral works and educational aims of Bartók and Kodály.

In October, Bartók refused to allow the radio networks of fascist Italy and Nazi Germany to perform his works.

1938. On March 11, after Hitler's occupation of Austria, Bartók began to safeguard his works by sending them away first to Switzerland and then later to England. With many other Hungarian composers, he protested against the racist regulations of the German Copyright Association, and together with Kodály, transferred to the English association. In the summer, he completed his *Violin Concerto*, and composed the trio, *Contrasts*.

1939. The German occupation of Czechoslovakia in March again aroused thoughts of emigration. In Switzerland in August, during the last weeks before the outbreak of war, he completed his *Divertimento*, and later, his last composition to be written in Europe, the *String Quartet No. 6*. December, death of Bartók's mother.

1940. His mother's death strengthened his resolve to leave Europe. In April and May, he again toured the United States.

Together with his wife, he gave a farewell concert to the Budapest public on October 8th. On October 20th, they embarked for America. They arrived in New York at the end of October. They fulfilled the concert engagements to which they were already committed, although oppressed by the necessity of finding somewhere to live and to earn a living.

1941. It became obvious that concert engagements decreasing in number no longer offered a means of making a livelihood. A commission from Columbia University ameliorated his ever increasing financial distress. The commission provided work for six months during four consecutive years—the notation and preparation for publication of the Parry Yugoslav collection of folk music. At the end of the summer, there was a recurrence of his illness, apparently arthritic in nature.

1942. Another year clouded by deteriorating health and material difficulties. In April, after an adventurous journey, his son, Péter, who had remained in Hungary, joined his parents. A seaside vacation was temporarily beneficial to his health but afterwards the fever returned and he began to lose hope.

1943. On 21st January, the Bartóks introduced the version of the *Sonata for Two Pianos*, with orchestral accompaniment, with Frigyes Reiner conducting, in New York. This was Bartók's last public appearance.

In February, while lecturing at Harvard University, Bartók became so ill that he had to be taken to hospital. His illness was diagnosed as leukaemia, and friends arranged for ASCAP to pay his medical expenses.

In May, Koussevitzky commissioned him to write an orchestral piece, the *Concerto for Orchestra*. The Bartóks spent the summer at Saranac Lake. By the autumn, his condition was noticeably improved and in September, he wrote the score of the *Concerto*.

In November he met for the first time Yehudi Menuhin who commissioned a solo sonata for violin.

In December, he travelled south to Asheville for another rest.

1944. In Asheville, he enjoyed a period of renewed strength. The fever departed and he was able to go for walks. He composed the *Sonata for Solo Violin* for

Menuhin and continued working on the collection of Romanian folk music that he had taken with him.

In January, Péter was called up for service with the US Marines.

The Bartóks again spent the summer at Saranac Lake where it seemed that Bartók was maintaining his progress physically. On December 1st, he took part in the highly successful première of the *Concerto* in Boston.

1945. In February, Bartók contracted pneumonia but recovered quickly.

He planned to spend the summer in Alma, California where he and his wife had been invited to stay by Yehudi Menuhin, but his physical condition prevented him from going. His health deteriorated. They again spent their holidays at Saranac Lake, where he finished his last composition, the *Concerto No. 3*. His *Viola Concerto* was completed only in a piano version. Péter was discharged from the army and joined his parents at Saranac Lake. Early in September, Bartók's condition began to deteriorate rapidly. They returned hurriedly to New York. He was taken to the West Side Hospital where he died on 26 September.

WORKS BY BÉLA BARTÓK
1. EARLY COMPOSITIONS

The following list of Béla Bartók's compositions written during his youth is taken from the one that Denijs Dille so kindly put at my disposal. It does not contain school exercises or fragments. The works marked by * cannot be found either in manuscript, copy or printed form. Where the original title of the works that have come down to us is unknown, I have given the posthumous one with a || || symbol. According to information given by Denijs Dille, Bartók himself was the source for the titles of unknown works.

1890

1 WALCZER op. 1 for piano — unpublished
2 VÁLTOZÓ DARAB [Changing Piece] op. 2 for piano — unpublished
3 MAZURKA op. 3 for piano — unpublished
4 A BUDAPESTI TORNAVERSENY [Budapest Athletic Competition] op. 4 for piano — unpublished
5 SONATINA No. 1, op. 5 for piano — unpublished
6 OLÁH DARAB [Romanian Piece] op. 6 (according to another copy: OLÁHOS [Romanian-like]) for piano — unpublished

1891

7 GYORSPOLKA [Fast Polka] op. 7 for piano — unpublished
8 'BÉLA' POLKA op. 8 for piano — unpublished
9 'KATINKA' POLKA op. 9 for piano — unpublished
10 TAVASZI HANGOK [Voices of Spring] op. 10 for piano — unpublished
11 'JOLÁN' POLKA op. 11 for piano — unpublished
12 'GABI' POLKA op. 12 for piano — unpublished
13 NEFELEJTS [Forget-me-not] op. 13 for piano — unpublished
14 LÄNDLER No. 1, op. 14 for piano — unpublished
15 'IRMA' POLKA op. 15 for piano — unpublished
16 RADEGUNDI VISSZHANG [Radegund Echo] op. 16 for piano — unpublished
17 INDULÓ [March] op. 17 for piano — unpublished
18 LÄNDLER No. 2, op. 18 for piano — unpublished
19 CIRKUSZ POLKA [Circus Polka] op. 19 for piano — unpublished
20 A DUNA FOLYÁSA [The Flow of the Danube] op. 20 for piano (1890–4) — unpublished
20a A DUNA FOLYÁSA [The Flow of the Danube] violin part (1890–4) — unpublished
21 SONATINE No. 2, op. 21 for piano — unpublished

1892

22* LÄNDLER No. 3, op. 22
23 TAVASZI DAL [Spring Song] op. 23 for piano — unpublished
24* SZÖLLŐSI DARAB [Szöllős Piece] op. 24

1893

25 'MARGIT' POLKA op. 25 for piano — unpublished
26 'ILONA' MAZURKA op. 26 for piano — unpublished
27 'LOLI' MAZURKA op. 27 for piano — unpublished
28 'LAJOS' VALCZER [Lajos Waltz] op. 28 for piano — unpublished

1894

29 'ELZA' POLKA op. 29 for piano — unpublished
30 ANDANTE CON VARIAZIONI op. 30 for piano — unpublished
31* X. Y. op. 31
32 SONATA ||No. 1|| IN G MINOR op. 1 for piano — unpublished
33 SCHERZO for piano — unpublished

1895

34 FANTASIA IN A MINOR op. 2 for piano — unpublished
35 ||SONATA No. 2 IN F MAJOR op. 3|| [untitled, D. Dille's reconstruction] for piano — unpublished
36 CAPRICCIO (in B Minor) op. 4 for piano — unpublished
37 SONATA FOR PIANO AND VIOLIN op. 5 — unpublished
38* SONATA No. 3 IN C MAJOR op. 6
39* PIECES FOR VIOLIN op. 7

1896

40* FANTASIA FOR VIOLIN op. 8
41* FANTASIA FOR VIOLIN op. 9
42* QUARTET No. 1 IN B MAJOR op. 10
43* QUARTET No. 2 IN C MINOR op. 11

1897

44* ANDANTE, SCHERZO, FIN[ale] op. 12 for piano
45 DREI KLAVIERSTÜCKE op. 13
  Publication: 1st piece: *Der junge Bartók II. Klavierstücke* (D. Dille). B. Schott's Söhne Mainz—Editio Musica Budapest, 1965, pp. 1–3.
46* PIANO QUINTET IN C MAJOR op. 14
47* TWO PIECES op. 15 for piano (?)
48* GREAT FANTASY op. 16 for piano (?)

396

49 SONATE FÜR VIOLINE UND PIANOFORTE op. 17 — unpublished
50 SCHERZO ODER FANTASIE FÜR DAS PIANOFORTE op. 18
      Publication: *Der junge Bartók II. Klavierstücke* (D. Dille). B. Schott's Söhne
      Mainz—Editio Musica Budapest, 1965, pp. 4–14.

1898

51* SONATA op. 19 for piano — unpublished
52 QUARTETT FÜR PIANOFORTE, VIOLINE, VIOLA UND VIOLONCELLO
    op. 20 — unpublished
53 DREI KLAVIERSTÜCKE ||op. 21||
      Publication: 1st and 2nd pieces: *Der junge Bartók II. Klavierstücke* (D. Dille).
             B. Schott's Söhne Mainz–Editio Musica Budapest, 1965, pp. 15–17.
54 DREI LIEDER FÜR EINE SINGSTIMME MIT PIANOFORTE-
    BEGLEITUNG
      1. 'Im wunderschönen Monat Mai' (Heine)
      2. 'Nacht am Rheine' (Karl Siebel)
      3. 'Die Gletscher leuchten in Mondenlicht'
      Publication: 1st song: *Bartók Béla. Levelek, fényképek, kéziratok, kották*
             [Béla Bartók. Letters, Photographs, Manuscripts, Scores].
             Collected and edited by János Demény. Magyar Művészeti Tanács,
             Budapest, 1948, pp. 204–205, facsimile
55 SCHERZO IN B MINOR [for piano] — unpublished
56 QUARTETT IN F DUR — unpublished

1899

57 TIEFBLAUE VEILCHEN (Schoenreich-Carolath) ... für Sopran Solo mit
    Orchester-Begleitung — unpublished

1900

58 SCHERZO (SZONÁTAFORMÁBAN) [Scherzo (in sonata form)] for piano
    (1900?) — unpublished
59 SCHERZO ||in B minor, for piano|| — unpublished
60 ||HAT TÁNC|| [Six Dances] for piano ? — unpublished
60a VALCER ||for orchestra = 1st and 2nd dance|| — unpublished
61 ||Három vegyeskar|| [Three Mixed Choruses] — unpublished
      1. 'Der Tod das ist die kühle Nacht' (Heine)
      2. 'Was streift vorbei im Dämmerlicht'
      3. 'Suchst du mir denn immer nach'
      Transcription: No. 2, for male chorus
62 LIEBESLIEDER FÜR DAS PIANOFORTE UND EINE SINGSTIMME
      1. 'Du meine Liebe [!] du mein Herz' (Rückert)
      2. 'Diese Rose pflück' ich hier' (Lenau)

3. 'Du geleitest mich zum Grabe'
4. 'Ich fühle deinen Odem' (Lenau)
5. 'Wie herrlich leuchtet' (Goethe)
6. 'Herr, der du alles wohl gemacht'
Publication: 2nd and 4th songs: *Der junge Bartók I. Ausgewählte Lieder*
(D. Dille). B. Schott's Söhne Mainz—Editio Musica Budapest,
1963, pp. 8 and 12.
63 SCHERZO ||for piano|| — unpublished
64 VARIATIONS (original title: VÁLTOZATOK F. F. EGY TÉMÁJA FÖLÖTT
[Variations on a Theme by F. F.]) for piano — unpublished

1901

65 SCHERZO ||IN B-FLAT MAJOR, for orchestra|| [the orchestration of the Trio
is missing but the draft is extant] [1901?] — unpublished
66 TEMPO DI MINUETTO ||for piano|| — unpublished

1902

67 NÉGY DAL ÉNEKKARRA ÉS ZONGORÁRA [Four Songs for Voice and
Piano] (Lajos Pósa)
1. 'Őszi szellő' [Autumn breeze]
2. 'Még azt vetik a szememre' [They are accusing me of]
3. 'Nincs olyan bú' [There is no greater sorrow]
4. 'Ejnye, ejnye' [Oh dear, Oh dear]
Publication: Bárd Ferenc és fia Budapest, 1904.
68 ||SYMPHONY IN E-FLAT MAJOR|| (in piano extract; orchestration of the
Scherzo movement was also completed) — unpublished
69 ||DUO FOR TWO VIOLINS|| — unpublished
70 ||ALBUMBLATT A DUR, for violin and piano|| — unpublished

1903

71 NÉGY ZONGORADARAB [Four Piano Pieces]
1. TANULMÁNY BALKÉZRE [Study for the Left Hand]
2. I Ábránd [Fantasy No. 1]
3. II Ábránd [Fantasy No. 2]
4. Scherzo
Publication: Bárd Ferenc és fia Budapest, 1904 (all four pieces separately);
Zeneműkiadó Vállalat Budapest, 1956 [in one volume].
72 SONATA FOR PIANO AND VIOLIN
Allegro moderato [molto rubato]
Andante
Vivace
Publication: Documenta Bartókiana (D. Dille), Akadémiai Kiadó Budapest.

1st and 2nd movement: at the end of vol. No. 1 (1964) (Musikbeilagen, without page numbering); 3rd movement: at the end of
Vol. No. 2 (1965) (Notenbeilage), pp. 175–200.

73 EST [Evening], (Kálmán Harsányi), for voice with piano accompaniment
Publication: *Der junge Bartók I. Ausgewählte Lieder* (D. Dille). Schott's Söhne
Mainz—Editio Musica Budapest, 1963. p. 16.

74 EST [Evening], (Kálmán Harsányi), for male chorus
Publication: Documenta Bartókiana (D. Dille). Akadémiai Kiadó Budapest,
at the end of Vol. No. 1 (Musikbeilagen), without page numbering

75 'KOSSUTH' Symphonic Poem for full orchestra
Publication: Zeneműkiadó Vállalat Budapest, 1963.

75a GYÁSZINDULÓ [Funeral March] 9th and 10th points of the 'Kossuth' Sym-
phonic Poem, piano, for two hands
Publication: Kunossy Szilágyi és Társa [in trust]. By the composer; Charles
Rozsnyay, Budapest

76 ||FOUR SONGS||

1903—1904

77 PIANO QUINTET
Publication: Zeneműkiadó Vállalat, Budapest, 1970.

2. MATURE COMPOSITIONS
GENERAL REMARKS

The following list of Bartók's mature compositions is taken—with few corrections—from the second edition of the collection entitled *Bartók—Sa vie et son œuvre* (edited by Bence Szabolcsi. Corvina, Budapest, 1968, pp. 283–313). We did not wish to alter the generally known and quoted numbering in this list for the sake of changed numbering of the list of the early compositions given before.

With musical works the following data are indicated: 1. the English title printed in upper case. In those works which did not have an original English title, or one that is generally known from existing publications, we have used English titles as they appear in the list of works in: *The Life and Music of Béla Bartók*, by Halsey Stevens, Oxford University Press, New York, 2/1964. If the original title is Hungarian, it is printed in parentheses after the English title in upper case italics. 2. The title is followed by the name of the instrument or ensemble the piece was written for, except in cases when it is evident from the title. 3. The year of composition is in parentheses; italicized if it appears on the published copy, and in Roman type if it is established from Bartók's correspondence or other documents. 4. After the title and other data of composition the list of the individual parts is indicated: by Arabic numerals if the parts are independent and by Roman numerals if they are movements. Separate titles of parts are italicized; in Roman type in they are translations of the original Hungarian titles. The original Hungarian (or Romanian or Slovakian) titles are italicized and in parentheses following the English translation. The untitled parts and movements are marked by the tempo. 5. Insofar as the publication refers to folk-songs which often serve as the basis of a composition, the title or the first line of the song is given in parentheses in its original language (unless it is, at the same time, the title of a piece or of a part). 6. As for dedications, we have indicated only the name of the person concerned, thus departing from the text found in the original publication; where the dedication refers to the first name only, we list the family name in parentheses. 7. Concerning publishing data, the abbreviation of the publisher is followed by the year of the edition or copyright—inasmuch we have succeeded in finding them—and the number of the record, in parentheses. If the information is missing after the name of the publisher, it indicates that we took it from other lists and had no opportunity to check them. 8. Arrangements made by the composer are included in the list as separate works, with the exception of arrangements for piano and ballet suites. Transcriptions made by others are not mentioned in the list.

Abbreviations of music publishers:

B	Bárd Ferenc és Fia Budapest
BH	Boosey and Hawkes Ltd. London
MK	Magyar Kórus Budapest
R	Rozsnyai Károly Budapest
Rv	Rózsavölgyi és Társa Budapest

UE   Universal Edition Wien Leipzig New York
WPhV Wiener Philharmonischer Verlag A.G. Wien
Zk   Zeneműkiadó Budapest

COMPOSITIONS

26 — RHAPSODY for piano op. 1 *(November 1904)*
dedicated: to Emma Gruber
editions: Rv 1909 (3199) (in this edition only the first part of this work—Adagio mesto—is published), 1923 (3199), Zk 1955 (1971) (these two editions of the complete work indicate: 'première version')
transcription: for piano and orchestra (see No. 27)

27 — RHAPSODY for piano and orchestra (1904?) transcription of No. 26 (this version, referred to as 'Concertstück' in Bartók's letters of 1905, and as 'Hungarian Rhapsody' by certain contemporary critics, completes the version for piano solo with a 39-bar introduction)
editions: Rv 1910 (with the indication 'deuxième version'), UE, Zk 1963 (1023)
transcription: for two pianos, four hands, 1905
editions: Rv 1910 (3337), 1919 (second, revised edition) (3337), UE (6858)

28 — SCHERZO for piano and orchestra op. 2 (1904) (mentioned also as BURLESQUE)
editions: Zk 1961 (3556), Schott 1962 (5023)

29 — HUNGARIAN FOLK-SONGS *(MAGYAR NÉPDALOK)* I. for voice and piano (end 1904 or early 1905)
   1. They mowed the pasture already *(Lekaszálták már a rétet)*
   2. Kiss me for I have to leave *(Add reám csókodat, el kell mennem)*
   3. Fehér László stole a horse *(Fehér László lovat lopott)*
   4. The horses of Eger are all grey *(Az egri ménes mind szürke)*
editions: No. 1 Zk 1963 (4219), Schott 1963 (5390) (Der Junge Bartók I); No. 4 Documenta Bartókiana IV (edited by D. Dille, Budapest—Mainz, 1970), facsimile

30 — UNPUBLISHED SZÉKELY FOLK-SONG *(SZÉKELY NÉPDAL)*
'Piros alma leesett a sárba' (The red apple has fallen in the mud) for voice and piano (1905)
edition: published in a supplement to the magazine *Magyar Lant* (1905)

31 — SUITE No. 1 for orchestra op. 3 *(Vienna, 1905)* (revised *c.* in 1920)
editions: Rv 1912 (3513), Zk 1956, 1961 (1022)

32 — TO THE LITTLE 'TÓT' *(A KICSI 'TÓT'-NAK)* five songs for voice and piano *(Vienna, 20th December 1905)*
   1. I am sleepy my dear mother (Álmos vagyok édes anyám lelkem)
   2. Oh, oh, look here (Ejnye, ejnye, nézz csak ide)

3. The little bird has soft and warm feathers (Puha meleg tolla van a kis madárnak)
(István Havas)
4. Bim, bam, bim, bam, rings the bell (Bim bam bim bam zúg a harang)
5. The rain is falling on the dry trees (Esik eső esdegél száraz fákra)
dedicated: [to Béla Oláh Tóth] 'the little tót' (the name of the dedicatee is phonetically and etymologically identical to the common Hungarian name 'tót,' which means 'Slovak'; hence the Hungarian title)
Unpublished. The third song is reproduced in facsimile in: Bartók Béla. Levelek, fényképek, kéziratok, kották (Béla Bartók. Letters, Photographs, Manuscripts, Scores). Collected and edited by János Demény. Magyar Művészeti Tanács, Budapest, 1948, pp. 206–7. No. 1 entitled Evening Song (*Esti dal*— Bartók) in Ödön Geszler: Gyakorlati és elméleti énekiskola a polgári fiú- (leány-) iskolák számára [Practical and Theoretical Textbook of Singing for Upper Primary Boys- (Girls-) Schools]. R 2/1928–1929, I 56 (p. 82) and I 74 (p. 100), respectively I 67 (p. 85) and I 81 (p. 99), only the voice parts, in altered versions, No. 1 with changed text (by Sándor Peres).

32a — CHIME *(HARANGSZÓ)* for two voices a cappella (after 1905); text by Béla Sztankó
edition: Ödön Geszler: Gyakorlati és elméleti énekiskola a polgári fiú- (leány-) iskolák számára [Practical and Theoretical Textbook for Upper Primary Boys- (Girls-) Schools]. R 2/1928–1929, II 32 (p. 44), respectively II 36 (p. 45).

33 — HUNGARIAN FOLK-SONGS *(MAGYAR NÉPDALOK)* for voice and piano *(December 1906)*. In collaboration with Zoltán Kodály. (Nos. 1–10 were arranged by Bartók. Before emigrating to the United States, in 1938 he revised these pieces.)

1. I left my fair homeland (Elindultam szép hazámbul)
2. I would cross the Tisza in a boat (Által mennék én a Tiszán ladikon)
3a Popular ballad (Fehér László)
3b Popular ballad (Fehér László)
4a Behind the garden of Gyula (A gyulai kert alatt)
4b Behind the garden of Kertmeg (A kertmegi kert alatt)
5. The street is on fire (Ucca, ucca, ég az ucca)
6. In my window shone the moonlight (Ablakomba, ablakomba)
7. From the withered branch no rose blooms (Száraz ágtól messze virít a rózsa)
8. I walked to the end of the great street in Tárkány (Végigmentem a tárkányi)
9. Not far from here is Kis Margitta (Nem messze van ide Kis Margitta)
10. My sweetheart is plowing (Szánt a babám)

editions: R (without number, indicating B.K.), Rv 1938 (second edition revised; the melismata which had been left out in the first edition were added to the melodies; No. 5 omitted and replaced by No. 4b) (1584). Zk 1953 (reprint of the 1938 edition) (1175)

33a — HUNGARIAN FOLK-SONGS for voice and piano (December 1906)
1. On this side of the Tisza, on that side of the Danube (Tiszán innen Dunán túl)
2. Woods, valleys, narrow parks (Erdők, völgyek, szűk ligetek)
3. The snow is melting (Olvad a hó)
4. Down at the tavern (Ha bemegyek a csárdába)
5. Fehér László stole a horse (Fehér László lovat lopott)
6. My glass is empty (Megittam a piros bort)
7. This maiden threading beads of glass (Ez a kislány gyöngyöt fűz)
8. The young soldier (Sej, mikor engem katonának visznek)
9. And they still say, Oh, Ah (Még azt mondják sej, haj)
10. My dear daughter (Kis kece lányom)

(These songs, like the series No. 33, are adaptations of a series of folk-songs planned in collaboration with Kodály, but which were not published in Bartók's lifetime. Nos. 5 and 10 now appear, for piano solo, in the volume *For Children* (No. 42) (numbered I. 28 and I. 17)

editions: Nos. 3, 4, 6, 7, 8 Zk 1963 (4219), Schott 1963 (5390) (Der junge Bartók I)

33b — TWO HUNGARIAN FOLK-SONGS for voice and piano (1906?)
1. My mother's rose tree *(Édesanyám rózsafája)*
2. My sweetheart, you are beyond the Málnás woods *(Túl vagy rózsám, túl vagy a Málnás erdején)*

editions: No. 1 Zk 1963 (4219), Schott 1963 (5390), (Der Junge Bartók); No. 2 Documenta Bartókiana IV (edited by D. Dille, Budapest—Mainz, 1970)

34 — SUITE No. 2, for orchestra op. 4. (movements I–III *Vienna, 1905*, and IV *Rákospalota, 1907*) (Revised in 1920 and 1943)
I. Comodo
II. Allegro scherzando
III. Andante
IV. Comodo

editions: Owned by the composer (1907) (B.B.) First revision: UE 1921 (6986), Hawkes & Son 1939. Second revision: BH 1948 (16160)

transcription: for two pianos (see No. 115a)

35 — DE GYERGYÓ. 3 HUNGARIAN FOLK-SONGS *(GYERGYÓBÓL. HÁROM CSÍK MEGYEI NÉPDAL)* for 'tilinkó' and piano (1907)
1. Rubato
2. L'istesso tempo
3. Poco vivo

editions: Zk 1961 (3744), Schott (entitled: Aus Gyergyó) (5329)
transcription: for piano (see No. 35a)

35a — THREE HUNGARIAN FOLK-SONGS *(HÁROM CSÍK MEGYEI NÉPDAL)*
for piano (1907) (transcription of No. 35)
1. Rubato
2. L'istesso tempo
3. Poco vivo
editions: R (419. 1580), Zk 1954 (1764)
35b — FOUR SLOVAKIAN FOLK-SONGS for voice and piano *(c.* 1907)
1. Roses in the fields (V tej bystrickej bráne)
2. Pod lipko nad lipko
3. Dirge (Pohrební písen)
4. The message (Priletel pták)
editions: Nos. 1, 3, 4; Zk 1963 (4219), Schott 1963 (5390) (Der junge Bartók I)
36 — CONCERTO for violin and orchestra *(Jászberény, 1st July 1907—Budapest,*
5th February 1908). For the first movement, see 'Two Portraits', No. 37
dedicated to Stefi Geyer
edition: BH 1969 (18502)
transcription: The second movement for violin and piano
unpublished
37 — TWO PORTRAITS *(KÉT PORTRÉ)* for orchestra op. 5 (1907–16)
1. One Ideal *(Egy ideális)*
2. One Grotesque *(Egy torz)*
The first portrait is identical to the first movement of the violin concerto
No. 36, the second movement is the 14th Bagatelle (see No. 38) orchestrated.
editions: R (767) Zk 1953 (1002) and 1954 (1673), BH
38 — FOURTEEN BAGATELLES *(TIZENNÉGY ZONGORADARAB)* for piano
op. 6 *(Budapest, May 1908)*
1. Molto sostenuto
2. Allegro giocoso
3. Andante
4. Grave (Mikor gulyásbojtár voltam)
5. Vivo (Ej' po pred naš, po pred naš)
6. Lento
7. Allegretto molto capriccioso
8. Andante sostenuto
9. Allegretto grazioso
10. Allegro
11. Allegretto molto rubato
12. Rubato
13. *(Elle est morte . . .)* Lento funebre
14. *Valse (Ma mie qui danse . . .)* Presto
editions: R (338), UE (6844), Zk 1953 (943), Suvini Zerboni (4814)
transcription: No. 14 for orchestra is identical to No. 2 of the Two Portraits,
No. 37 (orchestrated between 1911 and 1916)

39 — TEN EASY PIECES *(TÍZ KÖNNYŰ ZONGORADARAB)* *(Budapest, June 1908)*

Dedication *(Ajánlás)*

1. Peasant's song *(Paraszti nóta)*
2. Painful wrestling *(Lassú vergődés)*
3. Slovak peasants' dance *(Tóth legények tánca)*
4. *Sostenuto*
5. An evening at the village *(Este a székelyeknél)*
6. Hungarian folk-song *(Gödöllei piactéren leesett a hó)*
7. Aurora *(Hajnal)*
8. Hungarian folk-song *(Azt mondják, nem adnak)*
9. Finger exercise *(Ujjgyakorlat)*
10. Bear dance *(Medvetánc)*

editions: R 1908 (293), UE (6841), Zk 1951 (300), Schott (4396), Suvini Zerboni (4657)

transcriptions: Nos. 5 and 10 for orchestra 1931; identical to Nos. 1 and 2 of the Hungarian Sketches (see No. 97)

40 — STRING QUARTET No. 1, op. 7 *(1908)*

I. Lento

II. Allegretto

(Introduzione)

III. Allegro vivace

editions: Rv 1911 (3287), Zk 1956 (1585) Suvini Zerboni (5064) (the edition gives the incorrect indication: op. 8a)

41 — TWO ELEGIES *(KÉT ELÉGIA)* for piano op. 8b (1. *February 1908*, 2. *December 1909*)

editions: R 1910 (478), UE (6845)

1. Grave
2. Molto adagio, sempre rubato

42 — FOR CHILDREN *(GYERMEKEKNEK)* for piano (1908-9) 85 folk-songs, in four volumes, arranged for beginners. The first two volumes (I: Nos. 1–21, II: Nos. 22–42) contain Hungarian folk-songs, and the two others (III: Nos. 1–22, IV: 23–42) Slovakian folk-songs. The collection was revised in January 1945. The revised work contains 79 pieces and was published in two volumes, with the Hungarian folk-songs in the first and the Slovakian in the second volume. The pieces Nos. II. 25, II. 29, IV. 27, IV. 33 and IV. 34 of the original version were omitted in the revised version. Nos. IV. 33 and IV. 34 were composed by Emma S. Kodály. The Slovakian texts were translated into Hungarian by Béla Balázs, and into German by Emma S. Kodály. (The numbers in parentheses are taken from the new edition.)

Volumes I and II

1. Allegro *(Children at Play)* (Süssünk, süssünk valamit) (I.1)
2. Andante *(Children's Song)* (Süss fel nap) (I.2)

3. Andante (Elvesztettem páromat) (I.3)
4. Allegro *(Pillow Dance)* (Elvesztettem zsebkendőmet) (I.4)
5. Poco allegretto *(Play)* (Cickom, cickom) (I.5)
6. Allegro *(Study for the Left Hand)* (Hej, tulipán, tulipán) (I.6)
7. Andante grazioso *(Play Song)* (Keresd meg a tűt) (I.7)
8. Allegretto *(Children's Game)* (Ej görbénye, görbénye) (I.8)
9. Molto adagio *(Song)* (Fehér liliomszál) (I.9)
10. Allegro molto *(Children's Dance)* (Az oláhok, az oláhok facipőbe járnak) (I.10)
11. Molto sostenuto (Elvesztettem páromat) (I.11)
12. Allegro (Lánc, lánc, este, lánc) (I. 12)
13. Andante *(Ballad)* (Megöltek egy legényt) (I. 13)
14. Allegretto (A csanádi legények) (I. 14)
15. Allegro (Icike, picike az istvándi ucca) (I. 15)
16. Andante rubato *(Old Hungarian Tune)* (Nem loptam én életembe) (I.16)
17. Adagio *(Round Dance)* (Kis kece lányom) (I. 17)
18. Andante non molto *(Soldier's Song)* (Nagyváradi kikötőbe) (I. 18)
19. Allegretto (Ha bemegyek, ha bemegyek, ha bemegyek a dobozi csárdába) (I. 19)
20. Poco Allegro *(Drinking Song)* (I. 20)
21. Allegro robusto (I. 21)
22. Allegretto (Debrecenbe kéne menni) (I. 22)
23. Allegro grazioso *(Dance Song)* (Így kell járni, úgy kell járni) (I. 23)
24. Andante sostenuto (Víz, víz, víz) (I. 24)
25. Allegro (Három alma meg egy fél) (–)
26. Andante (Kerülj rózsám, kerülj) (I. 26)
27. Allegramente *(Fast)* (I. 27)
28. Parlando (Fehér László lovat lopott) (I. 25)
29. Allegro (Ej, haj, micsoda) (–)
30. Andante *(Choral)* (Felhozták a kakast) (I. 28)
31. Allegro scherzando *(Pentatonic Tune)* (Anyám édesanyám (I. 29)
32. Allegro ironico *(Jeering Song)* (Besüt a nap a templomba) (I. 30)
33. Andante sostenuto (Csillagok, csillagok, szépen ragyogjatok) (I. 31)
34. Andante (Fehér fuszujkavirág) (I. 32)
35. Allegro non troppo (Kertbe virágot szedtem) (I. 33)
36. Allegretto (Nem messzi van ide Margitta) (I. 34)
37. Poco vivace (Ha felmegyek a budai nagy hegyre) (I. 35)
38. (no tempo indication) *Drunkard's Song* (Tíz litero bennem van) (I. 36)
39. Allegro. *Swine-Herd's Song* (Házasodik a trücsök, szúnyog lányát kéri) (I. 37)
40. Molto vivace. *Winter Solstice Song* (Adjon az úr isten) (I. 38)
41. Allegro moderato ('Elmész ruzsám?' 'El bíz én') (I. 39)
42. Allegro vivace. *Swine-Herd's Dance* (Házasodik a trücsök) (I. 40)

Volumes III and IV:

1. Allegro (Keby boly čerešne, čerešne, višne, višne) (II. 1)
2. Andante (Kalina, malina) (II. 2)
3. Allegretto (Pod lipko, na lipko edná mala dve) (II. 3)
4. *Wedding Song (Lakodalmas)* (Ej, Lado, Lado) (II. 4)
5. *Variations (Változatok)* (Lecela pava, lecela) (II. 5)
6. *Rondo I (Round Dance I)* (Stará baba zlá) (II. 6)
7. *Sorrow (Betyárnóta)* (II. 7)
8. *Dance (Táncdal)* (Hej na prešovskej tudni dva holubky šedza) (II. 8)
9. *Round Dance II (Gyermekdal)* (Zabelej sa, zabelej, zabelej) (II. 9)
10. *Funeral song (Temetésre szól az ének)* (V mikuklášskej kompanii) (II. 10)
11. Lento (V tej bystrickej bráne) (II. 11)
12. Poco andante (Suhajova mati) (II. 12)
13. Allegro (Anička mlynárova) (II. 13)
14. Moderato (Ore, ore šest volov) (II. 14)
15. *Bagpipe* (I) *(Dudanóta)* (Tancuj, dievča, tancuj) (II. 15)
16. *Lament (Panasz)* Lento (II. 16)
17. Andante (Sluzilo dievča na fare) (II. 17)
18. *Teasing song* (Gúnydal) Sostenuto — Allegro vivace (Mau som ta dievča) (II. 18)
19. *Romance (Románc)* Assai lento (Daľel na dube, žalostne dube) (II. 19)
20. *Game of tag (Kergetőző)* Prestissimo (Nechocže ty, Hanulienka z rana do trňa) (II. 20)
21. *Pleasantry (Tréfa)* Allegro moderato (Sadla dola, plakala) (II. 21)
22. *Revelry (Duhajkodó)* Molto allegro (Hnali švarni šuhji kozy do dúbravy) (II. 22)
23. Molto rubato, non troppo lento (Ja som bača velmi stary) (–)
24. Poco andante (Koj som išol cez horu) (II. 23)
25. Andante (Daľel na dube, žalostne dube) (II. 24)
26. *Scherzando* Allegretto (II. 25)
27. Teasing song *(Csúfolódás)* Allegro (–)
28. *Peasant's flute (Furulyaszó)* Andante molto rubato (II. 26)
29. *Pleasantry* (II) *(Még egy tréfa)* Allegro (II. 27)
30. Andante molto rubato (Dosti som sa nachodil) (II. 28)
31. *Canon (Kánon)* Poco vivace (II. 29)
32. *Bagpipe* (II) *(Szól a duda)* Vivace (Zahradka, zahradka) (II. 30)
33. The orphan *(Árvagyerek)* Poco andante (Ej, hory, hory, zelené hory) (–)
34. Romance *(Románc)* Poco allegretto (Viem ja jeden hájiček) (–)
35. *The highway robber (Nóta egy másik betyárról)* Allegro (Bol by ten Jánošik) (II. 31)
36. Largo (Kebych ja vedela) (II. 32)
37. Molto tranquillo (Pri Prešporku, pri čichom Dunajku) (II. 33)

38. *Farewell (Búcsú)* Adagio (Ešťa sa raz obzrieť mám) (II. 34)

39. *Ballad (Ballada)* (Pásol Janko dva voly) (II. 35)

40–41. *Rhapsody (Rapszódia)* Parlando molto rubato — Allegro moderato (Hej! pofukuj povievaj; Hej! ten stoličny dom) (II. 36–37)

42. *Dirge (Sirató ének)* Lento (II. 38)

43. *Mourning song (Halotti ének)* Lento (Dolu dolinami) (II. 39)

editions: R I (376, 378), II (377, 378), III (634), IV (728), UE I–IV (6842–6843, 6872–6873), Zk 1950 I–IV (1–4) Version revised in 1945: BH 1947 (15936–15937)

transcriptions:

1. Volume II, No. 42 for orchestra. Identical to No. 5 of the Hungarian Sketches (see No. 97)

2. Volume I, No. 16 for voice and piano (see No. 109)

3. Pieces selected for violin and piano by Tivadar Országh, with corrections by Bartók entitled: *Magyar népdalok* [Hungarian Folk-Songs] (1934)

editions: R 1934 (1699), Zk 1954 (1527)

43 — TWO ROMANIAN DANCES *(KÉT ROMÁN TÁNC)* for piano op. 8a (2: March 1910)

editions: Rv 1910 (3333) (in two versions), UE (6857), Zk 1951 (60)

transcription: No. 1 for orchestra (see No. 47a)

44 — SEVEN SKETCHES *(VÁZLATOK)* for piano op. 9b (the edition gives the incorrect indication: op. 9) (1: *1908*, 3: *August 1910*)

1. Portrait of a young girl *(Leányi arckép)* Andante (con moto)

2. *See-saw, dickory-daw (Hinta palinta)* Comodo

3. Lento

4. Non troppo lento

5. Romanian folk-song *(Román népdal)* Andante

6. In Romanian style *(Oláhos)* Allegretto

7. Poco lento

dedications: 1: to Márta [Ziegler–Bartók], 3: to Emma [Sándor–Kodály] and Zoltán [Kodály]

editions: R (769), UE (6840), Zk 1594 (1762)

45 — FOUR DIRGES *(NÉGY SIRATÓÉNEK)* for piano op. 9a (the edition gives the incorrect indication: op. 8b or gives no opus number) (4: *Budapest 1910*)

1. Adagio

2. Andante

3. Poco lento

4. Assai andante

editions: Rv (3438), UE (6658), Zk 1955 (1765)

transcription: No. 2 for orchestra 1931. Identical to No. 3 of the Hungarian Sketches (see No. 97)

46 — TWO PICTURES *(KÉT KÉP)* for orchestra op. 10 *(Budapest, August 1910)*

1. *In full flower (Virágzás)*

2. *Village dance (A falu tánca)*
editions: Rv 1912, 1921 (3557), Zk 1953 (1003), 1954 (1765)
transcription: for piano solo
editions: Rv 1921 (3558), UE (6850), Zk 1953 (867)

47 — THREE BURLESQUES *(HÁROM BURLESZK)* for piano op. 8c
(1: *November 1908*, 2: *May 1911*, 3: *1910*)
    1. *Quarrel (Perpatvar)*
    2. *A bit tipsy (Kicsit ázottan)*
    3. Molto vivo capriccioso
dedication: 1: to Márta [Ziegler–Bartók]
editions: Rv 1912 (3437), UE (6659), Zk 1954 (1763)
transcription: No. 2 for orchestra, 1931. Identical to No. 4 of the Hungarian
Sketches (see No. 97)

47a — ROMANIAN DANCE for orchestra (1911) transcription of No. 1 of the Two
Romanian Dances for piano (see No. 43)
edition: Zk 1965 (4692)

48 — BLUEBEARD'S CASTLE *(A KÉKSZAKÁLLÚ HERCEG VÁRA)* Opera in
one act, libretto by Béla Balázs *(Rákoskeresztúr, September 1911)*, op. 11.
Published in Hungarian, German, English and French; German translation
by Wilhelm Ziegler and Füssl-Wagner (1963), English translation by Chris-
topher Hassall.
dedication: to Márta [Ziegler–Bartók]
editions: UE 1922 (7028), 1963 (13641)
transcription: for voice and piano
editions: UE 1922 (in German and Hungarian), (7030) (in German and French)

49 — ALLEGRO BARBARO for piano (1911)
editions: UE 1918 (5904), K.M.P., Kiev 1927 (135)

50 — FOUR OLD HUNGARIAN FOLK-SONGS *(NÉGY RÉGI MAGYAR NÉP-
DAL)* for 4-part male chorus, a cappella (1910) (texts in Hungarian and
German)
    1. Long ago I told you *(Rég megmondtam bús gerlice)*
    2. Oh God, for whom am I waiting? *(Jaj istenem, kire várok)*
    3. In my sister-in-law's garden *(Ángyomasszony kertje)*
    4. Jóska Geszte saddles his velvety horse *(Geszte Jóska bársony lovát
nyergeli)*
edition: UE 1928 (8891); modificated version, with altered harmonies;
No. entitled: Farmboy, load the cart well *(Béreslegény, jól megrakd
a szekeret)*

51 — FOUR PIECES *(NÉGY ZENEKARI DARAB)* op. 12 for orchestra (1912)
(orchestrated in 1921)
    1. *Preludio*
    2. *Scherzo*
    3. *Intermezzo*

4. *Marcia funebre*
editions: UE 1923 (7270), BH
52 — PIANO METHOD *(ZONGORAISKOLA)* (1913) in collaboration with Sándor
Reschofsky (see No. 53)
editions: Rv 1913 (3635), Zk 1954 (without number)
53 — THE FIRST TERM AT THE PIANO *(KEZDŐK ZONGORAMUZSIKÁJA)*
pieces for the 'Piano Method' of Bartók–Reschofsky (No. 52); (the numbers
in parentheses are those of the piano method)
1. Moderato (21)
2. Moderato (22)
3. Dialogue *(Párbeszéd)* (24)
4. Dialogue *(Párbeszéd)* (26)
5. Moderato (36)
6. Moderato (40)
7. Folk-song *(Népdal)* (44)
8. Andante (51)
9. Andante (59)
10. Folk-song *(Népdal)* (68)
11. Minuet *(Menüett)* (89)
12. Swineherd's dance *(Kanásztánc)* (77)
13. Folk-song — Where have you been little lamb? *(Hol voltál báránykám?)*
(95)
14. Andante (105)
15. Wedding dance *(Lakodalmas)* (116)
16. Peasant dance *(Paraszttánc)* (115)
17. Allegro deciso (118)
18. Waltz *(Keringő)* (119)
editions: Rv 1929 (4936), Zk 1952 (986), 1955 (989), Schott (4335)
54 — (Composition prior to op. 1)
55 — SONATINA for piano (1915)
I. Bagpipers *(Dudások)*
II. Bear Dance *(Medvetánc)*
III. *Finale*
editions: Rv 1919 (3929), (3953), UE 1920 (6508), Zk 1951 (117), Schott (4399),
Mouzghis (Moscow) 1933
transcription: for orchestra (1931) (probably from a transcription for violin
and piano by André Gertler). Identical to the Transylvanian Dances (see
No. 96)
56 — ROMANIAN FOLK DANCES *(ROMÁN NÉPI TÁNCOK)* for piano (1915)
1. Stick dance *(Jocul cu bâtă)*
2. Sash dance *(Brâul)*
3. In one spot *(Pe loc)*
4. Horn dance *(Buciumeana)*

410

5. Romanian Polka *(Poarga românească)*
6. Fast dance *(Măruntelul)*

dedicated: to Professor Ion Bușiția

edition: UE 1918 (5802)

transcription: for orchestra, 1917. Identical to the Romanian Folk Dances (see No. 68)

57 — ROMANIAN CHRISTMAS CAROLS *(ROMÁN KOLINDA-DALLAMOK)*
for piano (1915) in two series

1st series

1. Allegro (Pă cel plai de munte)
2. Allegro (Intreabă și'intreabă)
3. Allegro (D-oi roagă sa roagă)
4. Andante (Ciucur verde de mătasă)
5. Allegro moderato (Coborât-o coborât-o)
6. Andante (In patru cornuți de lume)
7. Andante (La lină fântână)
8. Allegretto (Noi umblăm d-a corindare)
9. Allegro (Noi acum ortacilor)
10. Più allegro (Tri crai dela răsăritu)

2nd series

1. Molto moderato (Colo'n jos la munte'n josu)
2. Moderato (Deasupra pa răsăritu)
3. Andante (Crește-mi Doamne creștiu)
4. Andante (Sculați, sculați boieri mari)
5. Moderato (Ai, Colo'n josu mai din josu)
6. Andante (Si-o luat, luată)
7. Variante della precedente (Colo sus, mai susu)
8. Allegro (Colo sus pă după lună)
9. Allegretto (De ce-i domnul bunu)
10. Allegro (Hai cu toții să suimu)

editions: UE 1918 (5890), BH (modifications, made for concert performance, are not included in the first edition and in that of BH)

58 — TWO ROMANIAN FOLK-SONGS for 4-part female chorus a cappella (1915) unpublished

59 — NINE ROMANIAN SONGS for voice and piano (1915) unpublished

60 — THE WOODEN PRINCE *(A FÁBÓL FARAGOTT KIRÁLYFI)* choreographic poem in one act, libretto by Béla Balázs *(Rákoskeresztúr, 1914–16)*, op. 13. Published with texts in Hungarian, English and German

dedicated: to Egisto Tango

edition: UE 1924 (6638)

transcriptions: 1: for piano solo

edition: UE 1921 (6635)

2: Orchestral Suite

edition: UE

61 — FIVE SONGS *(ÖT DAL)* for voice and piano op. 15 (1915–16) [2: *5th February (1916)*, 3: *Rákoskeresztúr 27th August 1916*, 4: *6th February* (1916)] poems by unknown authors
1. My love *(Az én szerelmem)*
2. Summer *(Nyár)*
3. Night of desire *(A vágyak éjjele)*
4. In vivid dreams *(Színes álomban)*
5. Here, in the valley *(Itt lent a völgyben)*
   edition: UE 1961 and 1966 (13150L)

62 — SUITE for piano op. 14 *(Rákoskeresztúr, February 1916)*
1. Allegretto
2. Scherzo
3. Allegro molto
4. Sostenuto
   There was originally an Andante between the first and second movements, which was later withdrawn by Bartók. The Andante was published in Új Zenei Szemle 1955, No. 10, pp. 3–4.
   edition: UE 1918 (5891)

63 — FIVE SONGS *(ÖT DAL)* for voice and piano op. 16 *(Rákoskeresztúr, February–April 1916)*, poems by Endre Ady. Published with texts in Hungarian and German (UE), German and English (BH). The German text was translated by R. St. Hoffmann
1. Three autumn tears *(Három őszi könnycsepp)*
2. Sounds of autumn *(Az őszi lárma)*
3. My bed calls me *(Az ágyam hívogat)*
4. Alone with the sea *(Egyedül a tengerrel)*
5. I cannot come to you *(Nem mehetek hozzád)*
   dedicated: to Béla Reinitz 1920
   editions: No. 2: supplement to No. 5 of the 'Musikblätter des Anbruch' of 1921. The complete series: UE 1923 (6934), BH 1939 (17598)

63a — SLOVAKIAN FOLK-SONG (Kruti tono vretana) for voice and piano (1916)
   editions: Zk 1963 (4219), Schott 1963 (5390) (Der junge Bartók)

64 — EIGHT HUNGARIAN FOLK-SONGS *(NYOLC MAGYAR NÉPDAL)* for voice and piano (1907–17). Published with texts in Hungarian, German and English. The English text was translated by Nancy Bush
1. Black is the earth *(Fekete főd, fehér az én zsebkendőm)*
2. My God, my God, make the river swell *(Istenem, Istenem, áraszd meg a vizet)*
3. Wives, let me be one of your company *(Asszonyok, asszonyok, had' legyek társatok)*
4. So much sorrow lies on my heart *(Annyi bánat a szívemen)*
5. If I climb yonder hill *(Ha kimegyek arr' a magas tetőre)*
6. They are mending the great forest highway *(Töltik a nagyerdő útját)*

7. Up to now my work was plowing in the springtime *(Eddig való dolgom a tavaszi szántás)*

8. The snow is melting *(Olvad a hó, csárdás kis angyalom)*

   editions: UE 1922 (7191), Hawkes & Son 1939, BH 1955 (18065)

65 — HUNGARIAN FOLK-SONG *(LESZÁLLOTT A PÁVA)* for piano (1914–17? 1923?) (originally one of the pieces from the fifteen Hungarian Peasant Songs (?) (see No. 71)

   Later, it appeared in revised form with the pieces published in the album 'Homage to Paderewsky' (see No. 66)

   editions: facsimile in the June–July 1925 issue of the revue Periszkóp and in the supplement to Új Zenei Szemle 1954, March issue

66 — THREE HUNGARIAN FOLK TUNES for piano (1914–17). These were originally part of the Fifteen Hungarian Peasant Songs (see No. 71)

   1. The peacock *(Leszállott a páva)*
   2. At the Jánoshida fair-ground *(Jánoshídi vásártéren)*
   3. White lily *(Fehér liliomszál)*

   editions: in the Album 'Homage to Paderewsky' BH 1942, BH 1942 (17679)

67 — STRING QUARTET No. 2, op. 17 *(Rákoskeresztúr, 1915–17)*

   I. Moderato
   II. Allegro molto capriccioso
   III. Lento

   Between August 1935 and 1936 Bartók changed the tempi but the editions disregard it

   dedication: to the Hungarian Quartet; Waldbauer, Temesváry, Kornstein, Kerpely

   editions: UE 1920 (6371), WPhV (202)

68 — ROMANIAN FOLK DANCES *(ROMÁN NÉPI TÁNCOK)* for orchestra (1917). Transcription of the dances for piano solo of 1915 (No. 56)

   editions: Rv, UE 1922 (6545)

69 — FIVE SLOVAK FOLK-SONGS *(TÓTH NÉPDALOK)* for 4-part male chorus, a cappella (1917). Published with the Slovakian text and translations into English, Hungarian and German. German translation: Mirko Jelusich; Hungarian Translation: Wanda Gleimann; English translation: Nancy Bush

   1. Ah, listen now my comrades *(Ej, posluchajte málo)*
   2. Back to fight *(Ked'ja smutny podjem)*
   3. War is in our land *(Kamarádi moj)*
   4. Ah, if I fall in Battle *(Ej, a ked'mna zabiju)*
   5. Time went on *(Ked's om siou na vojnu)*

   editions: UE 1918 (6101), BH 1939 (17682)

70 — FOUR SLOVAK FOLK-SONGS *(NÉGY SZLOVÁK NÉPDAL)* for 4-part mixed chorus and piano (1917), published with texts in German, English, Hungarian and Slovakian

   1. *Wedding Song from Poniky (Lakodalmas) (Zadala mamka)*

2. *Song of the Hay-harvesters from Hiadel* *(Szénagyűjtéskor énekelt dal)* *(Na holi, na holi)*

3. *Dancing Song from Medzibrod* *(Rada pila, rada jedla)*

4. *Dancing Song from Poniky* *(Táncdal)* *(Gajdujte, gajdence)*

editions: UE 1924 (7595) BH 1939 (17658), Zk 1950 (24)

71 — FIFTEEN HUNGARIAN PEASANT SONGS *(TIZENÖT MAGYAR PA-RASZTDAL)* for piano (1914–18)

1–4. Four old laments *(Négy régi keserves ének)*

1. Rubato (Megkötöm lovamat)

2. Andante (Kit virágot rózsám adott)

3. Poco rubato (Aj, meg kell a búzának érni)

4. Andante (Kék nefelejts ráhajlik a vállamra)

5. *Scherzo* (Feleségem olyan tiszta)

6. *Ballade (Tema con variazioni)* (Angoli Borbála)

7–15. Old Dance Tunes *(Régi táncdalok)*

7. Allegro (Arra gyere, a mőrre én)

8. Allegretto (Fölmentem a szilvafára)

9. Allegretto (Erre kakas, erre tyúk)

10. L'istesso tempo (Zöld erdőben a prücsök)

11. Assai moderato (Nem vagy legény, nem vagy)

12. Allegretto (Beteg asszony, fáradt legény)

13. Poco più vivo — allegretto (Sári lovam, a fakó)

14. Allegro (Ésszegyűltek, ësszegyűltek az izsapi lányok)

15. Allegro (Bagpipe air without words)

editions: UE 1920 (6370), Mouzghis (Moscow) 1933 (13790g), BH 1948

transcriptions: Nos. 6–12, 14–15 for orchestra, 1933, entitled: Hungarian Peasant Songs (Magyar parasztdalok) (see No. 100)

72 — STUDIES for piano op. 18/3: *Rákoskeresztúr, 1918)*

1. Allegro molto

2. Andante sostenuto

3. Rubato; Tempo giusto, capriccioso

editions: UE 1920 (6498), BH 1939 (15828), Mouzghis 1957 (26254g)

73 — THE MIRACULOUS MANDARIN *(A CSODÁLATOS MANDARIN)* op. 19

Pantomime in one act, libretto by Menyhért Lengyel *(Rákoskeresztúr, October 1918–May 1919)*

editions: UE 1927 (8909), WPhV 1958 (304)

transcriptions: 1. for piano duet (Hungarian and German texts)

edition: UE 1925 (7706) (in two versions) 2. Orchestral Suite from the music of the pantomime *(Rákoskeresztúr, 1919)*

edition: UE 1927 (8909)

74 — EIGHT IMPROVISATIONS ON HUNGARIAN PEASANT SONGS for piano op. 20 *(Budapest, 1920)*

I. Molto moderato (Sütött ángyom rétest)

II. Molto capriccioso

III. Lento rubato (Imhol kerekedik)

IV. Allegretto scherzando (Kályha vállán az ice)

V. Allegro molto

VI. Allegro moderato, molto capriccioso (Jaj istenem, ezt a vént)

VII. Sostenuto, rubato (Beli fiam, beli)

VIII. Allegro (Télen nem jó szántani)

dedication: No. VII to the memory of Claude Debussy

editions: No. VII: published in the "Tombeau de Claude Debussy", 1920; No. IV: Musical supplement to the issue of 1st March 1921 of the Revue Musicale; The complete work: UE 1922 (7079), BH

75 — SONATA No. 1 for violin and piano *(Budapest, October–December 1921)* (On concert programmes of the period: op. 21; the opus number does not appear on the printed scores)

I. Allegro appassionato

II. Adagio

III. Allegro

dedicated: to Miss Jelly Arányi

editions: UE 1923 (7247), BH 1939 (15983)

76 — SONATA No. 2 for violin and piano *(Budapest, July–November 1922)*

I. Molto moderato

II. Allegretto

dedicated: to Miss Jelly Arányi

edition: UE 1923 (7259)

77 — DANCE SUITE *(TÁNC SUITE)* for orchestra *(Radvány, August 1923)*

I. Moderato

II. Allegro molto

III. Allegro vivace

IV. Molto tranquillo

V. Comodo

[VI.] Finale

editions: UE 1924 (7545), WPhV 1925 (200)

transcription: for piano solo, 1925

edition: UE 1925 (8397)

78 — VILLAGE SCENES *(FALUN)* Slovak folk-songs for female voice and piano *(Budapest, December 1924)* published with German (Bence Szabolcsi), Hungarian (Viktor Lányi), Slovakian and English (Martin Lindsay) texts.

1. *Hay-making (Szénagyűjtéskor)*

2. *At the Bride's (A menyasszonynál)*

3. *Wedding (Lakodalom)*

4. *Lullaby (Bölcsődal)*

5. *Lads' Dance (Legénytánc)*

dedicated: to Ditta [Pásztory–Bartók]

editions: UE 1927 (8712), BH 1954

transcription: Nos. 3–4–5 for 4 or 8 female voices and chamber orchestra, 1926 (see No. 79)

79 — THREE VILLAGE SCENES *(FALUN)* for 4 or 8 female voices and chamber orchestra *(Budapest, May 1926)* (Transcription of three pieces from No. 78)

    1. *Wedding (Lakodalom)*

    2. *Lullaby (Bölcsődal)*

    3. *Lads' Dance (Legénytánc)*

edition: UE 1927 (8714)

transcription: for four or eight female voices and piano

edition: UE 1927 (8713)

80 — SONATA for piano *(Budapest, June 1926)*

    I. Allegro moderato

    II. Sostenuto e pesante

    III. Allegro molto

dedicated: to Ditta [Pásztory–Bartók]

edition: UE 1927 (8772)

81 — OUT [OF] DOORS *(SZABADBAN)* for piano *(Budapest, June–August 1926)*

    1. *With Drums and Pipes (Sippal, dobbal)*

    2. *Barcarolla*

    3. *Musettes*

    4. *The Night's Music (Az éjszaka zenéje)*

    5. *The Chase (Hajsza)*

dedicated: to Ditta (Pásztory–Bartók)

edition: UE 1927 (8892), separately: UE (8893), (8894), (8895), (8896), (8897); in two books (1–3, 4–5) (8892 a–b)

82 — NINE SMALL [LITTLE] PIANO PIECES *(KILENC KIS ZONGORA-DARAB)* (1926)

Book I: *Four Dialogues (Négy párbeszéd)*

    1. Moderato

    2. Andante

    3. Lento

    4. Allegro vivace

Book II:

    5. *Menuetto*

    6. *Air (Dal)*

    7. *Marcia delle bestie*

    8. *Tambourine (Csörgő-Tánc)*

Book III:

    9. Preludio—All'ungherese

dedications: (Nos. 1 and 9) to 31st October 1926

editions: UE 1927 (8920), (8921), (8922), BH 1939 (15829)

83 — CONCERTO No. 1 for piano and orchestra *(Budapest, August–November 1926)*
    I. Allegro
    II. Andante
    III. Allegro
  editions: UE 1927 and 1928 (8777), (12674)
  transcription: for two pianos, four hands
  edition: UE 1927 (8779)

84 — THREE RONDOS ON FOLK TUNES *(HÁROM RONDO NÉPI DALLA-MOKKAL)* for piano (1: 1916, 2–3: 1927)
  1. Andante
  2. Vivacissimo
  3. Allegro molto
  editions: UE 1930 (9508) (a passage from No. 1 appeared in facsimile, entitled: Slovak Folk-Song *(Tót népdal)*, in the January–February issue 1928 of Zenei Szemle)

85 — STRING QUARTET No. 3 *(Budapest, September 1927)*
  Prima parte. Moderato
  Seconda parte. Allegro
  Ricapitulazione della prima parte. Moderato
  Coda. Allegro molto
  dedicated: to the Musical Fund Society of Philadelphia
  editions: UE 1929 (9597), WPhV 1929 (169)

86 — RHAPSODY No. 1 for violin and piano (1928)
    I. Moderato *(Lassú)*
    II. Allegretto moderato *(Friss)*
  dedicated: to József Szigeti
  editions: UE 1929 (9865), BH (17491) in two versions, Part I published separately: UE (9935); Part II: UE (9936)
  transcriptions:
  1. for violin and orchestra (see No. 87)
  2. for violoncello and piano (see No. 88)

87 — RHAPSODY No. 1 for violin and orchestra (1926)
  (transcription of No. 86)
    I. Moderato *(Lassú)*
    II. Allegretto moderato *(Friss)*
  dedicated to József Szigeti
  editions: UE (9858), BH 1939 (16229)

88 — RHAPSODY for violoncello and piano (1926)
  (transcription of No. 86)
    I. Moderato *(Lassú)*
    II. Allegretto moderato *(Friss)*
  edition: UE 1930 (9866), BH (17763)

89 — RHAPSODY No. 2 for violin and piano (1928) (revised in 1945)
    I. Moderato *(Lassú)*
    II. Allegro moderato *(Friss)*
  dedicated: to Zoltán Székely
  editions: UE 1929 (9891), BH 1939 (15890), Part I published separately: UE (9925); part II: UE (9926)
  transcription: for violin and orchestra (see No. 90)

90 — RHAPSODY No. 2 for violin and orchestra (1928) (transcription of No. 89) (revised in 1944)
    I. Moderato *(Lassú)*
    II. Allegro moderato *(Friss)*
  editions: UE 1929 (9867), revised edition: BH 1949 (16230)

91 — STRING QUARTET No. 4 *(Budapest, July–September 1928)*
    I. Allegro
    II. Prestissimo, con sordino
    III. Non troppo lento
    IV. Allegretto pizzicato
    V. Allegro molto
  dedicated: to the Pro Arte Quartet
  editions: UE 1929 (9788), WPhV (166)

92 — TWENTY HUNGARIAN FOLK-SONGS *(HÚSZ MAGYAR NÉPDAL)* for voice and piano (1929), texts in Hungarian and German. The texts of the first volume were translated into German by Bence Szabolcsi and R. St. Hoffmann, and the second, third and fourth volumes by R. St. Hoffmann.
  Volume I: Sad Songs *(Szomorú nóták)*
    1. In Prison *(A tömlöcben)*
    2. Old lament *(Régi keserves)*
    3. The fugitive *(Bujdosó ének)*
    4. Herdsman's song *(Pásztornóta)*
  Volume II: Dancing Songs *(Táncdalok)*
    5. Slow dance *(Székely lassú)*
    6. Fast dance *(Székely friss)*
    7. Swineherd's dance *(Kanásztánc)*
    8. Six-florin dance *(Hatforintos nóta)*
  Volume III: Diverse Songs *(Vegyes dalok)*
    9. The shepherd *(Juhászcsúfoló)*
    10. Joking song *(Tréfás nóta)*
    11. Nuptial serenade *(Párosító I)*
    12. Humorous song *(Párosító II)*
    13. Dialogue song *(Pár ének)*
    14. Complaint *(Panasz)*
    15. Drinking song *(Bordal)*
  Volume IV: New Style Songs *(Új dalok)*

16. I Allegro (Oh, my dear Mother) *(Hej, édesanyám)*

17. II Più allegro (Ripening cherries) *(Érik a ropogós cseresznye)*

18. III Moderato (Long ago at Doboz fell the snow) *(Már Dobozon régen leesett a hó)*

19. IV Allegretto (Yellow cornstalk) *(Sárga kukoricaszál)*

20. V. Allegro non troppo (Wheat, wheat) *(Búza, búza, búza)*

editions: UE 1932 (1521), (1522), (1523), (1524), BH 1939 (17651), (17652), (17653), (17654)

transcriptions: Nos. 1, 2, 11, 14 and 12 for voice and orchestra (1933), Five Hungarian Folk-songs (see No. 101)

93 — FOUR HUNGARIAN FOLK-SONGS *(MAGYAR NÉPDALOK)* for mixed chorus, a cappella *(Budapest, May 1930)*. Published with texts in Hungarian, German and English; German translation by R. St. Hoffmann and Bence Szabolcsi. English translation by M. W. Pursey and Nancy Bush (BH)

1. The Prisoner *(A rab)*

2. The Rover *(A bujdosó)*

3. The Marriageable Girl *(Az eladó lány)*

4. Song *(Dal)*

editions: UE 1932 (10371), BH 1939 (18007), (18008), (18009), (18010)

94 — CANTATA PROFANA *(THE GIANT STAGS) (A KILENC CSODA-SZARVAS)* for double mixed chorus, tenor and baritone soloist and orchestra. *(Budapest, 8th September 1930.)* From the texts of Romanian folk-songs, translated into Hungarian by Bartók. Published with texts in Hungarian, German and English. German translation by Bence Szabolcsi (1934); English translation by Bartók, M. D. Calvocoressi (1951); new English translation by Robert Shaw (1955)

I. Molto moderato (attacca)

II. Andante (attacca)

III. Moderato

editions: UE 1934 (10613) (facsimile of Bartók's manuscript), 1957 (12760), 1961 (10613)

transcription: for double mixed chorus, tenor and baritone soloists and piano

editions: UE 1934 (10614) (facsimile of Bartók's manuscript), UE 1951 (10614)

95 — CONCERTO No. 2 for piano and orchestra *(Budapest, October 1930–September–October 1931)*

I. Allegro

II. Adagio–Presto–Adagio

III. Allegro molto

editions: UE 1932 (10442) (facsimile of Bartók's manuscript), 1955 (10442), (12193)

transcription: for two pianos, four hands

edition: UE 1941 (10995)

96 — TRANSYLVANIAN DANCES *(ERDÉLYI TÁNCOK)* for orchestra (1931).
Transcription of the Sonatina No. 55 (probably from the version for violin
and piano by André Gertler)
   I. Bagpipers *(Dudások)*
   II. Bear Dance *(Medvetánc)*
   III. *Finale*
editions: Rv 1932 (5440), Zk 1955 (1021)
97 — HUNGARIAN SKETCHES *(MAGYAR KÉPEK)* for orchestra *(Mondsee,
August 1931)*. Transcriptions of Nos. 5 and 10 of the Ten Easy Pieces
(No. 39); No. 2 of the Four Dirges (No. 45); No. 2 of the Three Burlesques
(No. 47), and No. 42 of Vol. II of For Children (No. 42) (No. 40 of Vol. I
of the 1945 version)
   1. An evening at the village *(Este a székelyeknél)*; in the Zk edition: An
   evening with the Székelys
   2. Bear Dance *(Medvetánc)*; in the Zk edition: Bears Dance
   3. Air *(Melódia)*
   4. A bit tipsy *(Kicsit ázottan)*
   5. Dance of the Ürög swineherds *(Ürögi kanásztánc)*
editions: R. Rv, Zk 1953 (1001) and 1954 (1674)
98 — FORTY-FOUR DUOS for violins (1931)
Volume I:
   1. *Teasing Song (Párosító)*
   2. *Dance (Kalamajkó)*
   3. *Menuetto*
   4. *Midsummer Night Song (Szentivánéji)*
   5. *Slovak Song (1) (Tót nóta) (1)*
   6. *Hungarian Song (1) (Magyar nóta) (1)*
   7. *Rumanian Song (Oláh nóta)*
   8. *Slovak Song (2) (Tót nóta) (2)*
   9. *Play (Játék)*
   10. *Ruthenian Song (Rutén nóta)*
   11. *Lullaby (Gyermekrengetéskor)*
   12. *Hay-harvesting Song (Szénagyűjtéskor)*
   13. *Wedding Song (Lakodalmas)*
   14. *Cushion Dance (Párnás-tánc)*
Volume II:
   15. *Soldier's Song (Katonanóta)*
   16. *Burlesque (Burleszk)*
   17. *Marching Song (1) (Menetelő nóta) (1)*
   18. *Marching Song (2) (Menetelő nóta) (2)*
   19. *Fairy tale (Mese)*
   20. *Song (Dal)*
   21. *New Year's Greeting (1) (Újévköszöntő) (1)*

22. *Mosquito Dance (Szúnyogtánc)*
23. *Wedding Song (Menyasszony-búcsúztató)*
24. *Gay Song (Tréfás nóta)*
25. *Hungarian Song (2) Magyar nóta) (2)*
Volume III:
26. *Teasing Song ('Ugyan édes komámasszony')*
27. *Limping Dance (Sántatánc)*
28. *Sorrow (Bánkódás)*
29. *New Year's Greeting (2) (Újévköszöntő) (2)*
30. *New Year's Greeting (3) (Újévköszöntő) (3)*
31. *New Year's Greeting (4) (Újévköszöntő) (4)*
32. *Dance from Máramaros (Máramarosi tánc)*
33. *Harvest Song (Aratáskor)*
34. *Counting Song (Számláló nóta)*
35. *Ruthenian 'kolomejka' (Rutén kolomejka)*
36. *Bagpipes (Szól a duda)*
    Variant of No. 36
Volume IV:
37. *Prelude and Canon (Preludium és kánon)*
38. *Rumanian Whirling Dance (Invărtita bâtrănilor) (Forgatós)*
39. *Serbian Dance (zaplet) (Szerb tánc)*
40. *Rumanian Dance (Oláh tánc)*
41. *Scherzo*
42. *Arabian Song (Arab dal)*
43. *Pizzicato*
44. *Transylvanian Dance (Ardeleana) ('Erdélyi' tánc)*
editions: Nos. 31, 37, 34, 32, 40, 44, 41: Spielmusik für Violine Heft 4. Schott
   1932 (33107). Complete edition: UE 1933 I. (10391), II. (10392), III. (10393),
   IV. (10394), in two books (10452 a–b) the four volumes in one book (10452)
transcriptions: 1: Nos. 28, 38, 43, 16 and 36 for piano, 1936 (see No. 105),
   Petite Suite. 2: No. 32 for piano
unpublished
99 — SZÉKELY SONGS *(SZÉKELY DALOK)* for 6-part male chorus a cappella
   (Budapest, November 1932)
   1. How often I've grieved for you *(Hej, de sokszor megbántottál)*
   2. My God, my life *(Istenem, életem)*
   3. Slender thread, hard seed *(Vékony cérna, kemény mag)*
   4. In Kilyénfalva girls are gathering *(Kilyénfalvi közeptizbe)*
   5. Slender thread, hard seed *(Vékony cérna, kemény mag)*
   6. Do a dance, priest *(Járjad pap a táncot)*
editions: MK 1938, 1–2 (418 I.), 3–6 (418 II.), Zk 1955 1–2 (1972)

100 — HUNGARIAN PEASANT SONGS (MAGYAR PARASZTDALOK) for orchestra (1933), transcriptions of Nos. 6–12, 14 and 15 of the Fifteen Hungarian Peasant Songs for piano (see No. 71)

    I. *Ballade (Tema con variazioni)*

    II. Old dance tunes *(Régi táncdalok)*

editions: UE 1933 (10573) (facsimile of Bartók's manuscript), BH 1939 (16167)

101 — HUNGARIAN FOLK-SONGS *(MAGYAR NÉPDALOK)* for voice and orchestra (1933), transcription of Nos. 1, 2, 11, 14 and 12 of the Twenty Hungarian Folk-songs (see No. 92)

    1. In prison *(Tömlöcben)*

    2. Old lament *(Régi keserves)*

    3. Nuptial serenade *(Párosító I)*

    4. Complaint *(Panasz)*

    5. Humorous song *(Párosító II)*

unpublished; copyright by UE 1933 (7270)

102 — STRING QUARTET No. 5 *(Budapest, 6th August–6th September 1934)*

    I. Allegro

    II. Adagio molto

    III. Scherzo

    IV. Andante

    V. Finale

dedicated: to Mrs. [Elisabeth] Sprague-Coolidge

editions: UE 1936 (10736), WPhV (167)

103 — TWO AND THREE-PART CHORUSES for choir and school orchestra a cappella (Volumes I–IV); for female chorus a cappella (Volumes VII and VIII) (1935)

Volume I:

    1. *Spring (Tavasz)*

    2. *Only tell me (Ne hagyj itt)*

    3. *Enchanting song (Jószág-igéző)*

Volume II:

    1. Letter to those at home *(Levél az otthoniakhoz)*

    2. Play song *(Játék)*

    3. Courting *(Leánynéző)*

    4. Alas, Alas *(Héjja, héjja, karahéjja)*

Volume III:

    1. Don't leave me *(Ne menj el)*

    2. I have a ring *(Van egy gyűrűm)*

    3. I've no-one in the world *(Senkim a világon)*

    4. Bread-baking *(Cipósütés)*

Volume IV:

    1. Hussar *(Huszárnóta)*

    2. Loafer's song *(Resteknek nótája)*

3. Wandering *(Bolyongás)*

4. Girls' teasing song *(Leánycsúfoló)*

Volume V:

1. Mocking of youth *(Legénycsúfoló)*

2. Michaelmas greeting *(Mihálynapi köszöntő)*

3. The wooing of a girl *(Leánykérő)* (numbered incorrectly: Volume V, No. 1)

Volume VI:

1. Lament *(Keserves)*

2. Bird song *(Madárdal)*

3. Jeering *(Csujogató)*

Volume VII:

1. Regret *(Bánat)*

2. Had I not seen you *(Ne láttalak volna)*

3. The little bird flew away *(Elment a madárka)*

Volume VIII:

1. Pillow dance *(Párnás táncdal)* (numbered incorrectly: Volume VIII, No. 3)

2. Canon *(Kánon)*

3. God Be with You *(Isten veled)*

dedication: (Volume IV, No. 4) on 31st October 1935

editions: MK 1937 (the volumes and the choruses published separately under Nos. 3351–3377), later (1938) collected into one volume, in the above order entitled: Bartók Béla kórusművei [The choruses of Béla Bartók]; enlarged with the chorus for male voices (From Olden Times) (see No. 104). New edition of the choruses (separately and in one volume) (excluding No. 104) in revised order: MK. Reprint of this last edition (separately and in one volume) in the Zk edition of 1953 (1103). The choruses I. 1, 2, 3 III. 1, 4, IV. 1, 2, V. 1, 3 published by BH, with texts in English, translated by Nancy Bush, and in German, translated by Ernst Roth 1955 (17721), (17725), (17722), (17728), (17726), (17727), (17729), (17724), (17723), except I. 1, 3 and V. 3 with a piano reduction of the orchestral accompaniment. I. 4, II. 3, IV. 3, VI. 3, III. 4

Chinese edition, 1960

transcriptions: IV. 3, III. 4, IV. 1, III. 1, IV. 2, I. 2 and V. 1 for school choir and orchestra, 1937

editions: (the first five) MK 1937 (5551), (5553), (5555), (5556), (5559), (the same in one volume) Zk 1962 (4168), III. 1: Zk 1959 (2889), III. 4: Zk 1958 (2867), IV. 3: Zk 1959 (2866)

104 — FROM OLDEN TIMES *(ELMÚLT IDŐKBŐL)* for 3-part male chorus a cappella (1935). (From revised texts of folk-songs and other old songs)

1. No-one's more unhappy than the peasant *(Nincs boldogtalanabb)*

2. One, two, three, four *(Egy, kettő, három, négy)*

3. No-one is happier than the peasant *(Nincsen szerencsésebb)*
edition: MK 1937 (321)

105 — PETITE SUITE for piano (1936) transcription of Nos. 28, 38, 43, 16 and 36 of
the Forty-Four Duos for two violins (see No. 98)
1. *Slow tune (Lassú)*
2. *Whirling Dance (Forgatós)*
3. *Quasi pizzicato (Pengetős)*
4. *Ruthenian Dance (Oroszos)*
5. *Bagpipes (Dudás)*
edition: UE 1938 (10987)

106 — MUSIC FOR STRING INSTRUMENTS, PERCUSSION AND CELESTA
(Budapest, 7th September 1936)
I. Andante tranquillo
II. Allegro
III. Adagio
IV. Allegro molto
dedicated: to the Basle Chamber Orchestra and its conductor Paul Sacher
editions: UE 1937 (10815) and (10888), WPhV (201), Mouzghis (Leningrad)
1963 (2326)

107 — MIKROKOSMOS progressive piano pieces (1926–39)
1st Volume
1–6. *Six Unison Melodies (Hat unisono dallam)*
7. *Dotted Notes (Kóta ponttal)*
8. *Repetition (Hangismétlés)*
9. *Syncopation (Szinkópák)*
10. *With Alternate Hands (Két kézzel felváltva)*
11. *Parallel Motion (Párhuzamos mozgás)*
12. *Reflection (Tükörkép)*
13. *Change of Position (Fekvésváltozás)*
14. *Question and Answer (Kérdés és felelet)*
15. *Village Song (Falusi dal)*
16. *Parallel Motion and Change of Position (Párhuzamos mozgás helyzetvál-*
tozással)
17. *Contrary Motion (Ellenmozgás)*
18–21. *Four Unison Melodies (Négy unisono dallam)*
22. *Imitation and Counterpoint (Imitáció és ellenpont)*
23. *Imitation and Inversion (Imitáció és fordítása)*
24. *Pastorale*
25. *Imitation and Inversion (Imitáció és fordítása)*
26. *Repetition (Hangismétlés)*
27. *Syncopation (Szinkópák)*
28. *Canon at the Octava (Kánon oktávban)*
29. *Imitation Reflected (Imitáció tükörképben)*

3rd Volume:

426

143. *Divided Arpeggios (Tört hangzatok váltakozva)*

144. *Minor Seconds, Major Sevenths (Kis másod- és nagy hetedhangközök)*

145. a), b) *Chromatic Invention (Kromatikus invenció)*

146. *Ostinato*

147. *March (Induló)*

148–153. *Six Dances in Bulgarian Rhythm (Hat tánc bolgár ritmusban)*

dedications: 1–66 to Péter [Bartók], 148–153 to Miss Harriet Cohen

editions: BH 1940 (15196), (15197), (15192), (15191), (15189), (15187), Zk 1951 (125), (126), (127), (128), (129), (130), No. 142 BH (16534)

transcriptions: Nos. 113, 69, 135, 123, 127, 145 and 146 for two pianos, four hands, entitled: Seven Pieces from Mikrokosmos (see No. 108)

108 — SEVEN PIECES FROM MIKROKOSMOS for two pianos, four hands Nos. 113, 69, 135, 123, 127, 145 and 146 from Mikrokosmos (see No. 107)

1. *Bulgarian Rhythm*

2. *Chord Study*

3. *Perpetuum Mobile*

4. *Canon and Inversion*

5. *New Hungarian Folk-Song*

6. *Chromatic Invention*

7. *Ostinato*

edition: BH 1947 (15856)

109 — HUNGARIAN FOLK-SONG *(DEBRECENNEK VAN EGY VIZE)* for voice and piano (1936) (?) No. 16, Volume I from 'For Children' (No. 42), arrangement for voice and piano

edition: in the collection Gyöngyösbokréta [Crown of Pearls] by Béla Paulini (Vajna és Bokor, Budapest, 1937) p. 10

110 — SONATA FOR TWO PIANOS AND PERCUSSION *(Budapest, July–August 1937)*

I. Assai lento — Allegro molto

II. Lento ma non troppo

III. Allegro non troppo

edition: BH 1942 (8675)

transcription: for two pianos and orchestra, 1940, entitled: Concerto for two pianos and orchestra (see No. 115)

111 — CONTRASTS for violin, clarinet and piano *(Budapest, 24th September 1938)*

I. *Recruiting Dance (Verbunkos)*

II. *Relaxation (Pihenő)*

III. *Fast Dance (Sebes)*

dedicated: to Benny Goodman and József Szigeti

editions: BH 1942 (B. Ens 49–73), (18756)

112 — VIOLIN CONCERTO *(Budapest, August 1937–31st December 1938)*

I. Allegro non troppo

II. Andante tranquillo

III. Allegro molto
dedicated: to Zoltán Székely
edition: BH 1946 (9003)
transcription: for violin and piano
editions: BH 1941 (8296), Mouzghis (Moscow) 1964 (767)

113 — DIVERTIMENTO for string orchestra *(Saanen, 2nd–17th August 1939)*
    I. Allegro non troppo
    II. Molto adagio
    III. Allegro assai
dedicated: to the Basle Chamber Orchestra
editions: BH 1940 (8716), (8326)

114 — STRING QUARTET No. 6 *(Saanen—Budapest, August–November 1939)*
    I. Mesto — Più mosso, pesante — Vivace
    II. Mesto — Marcia
    III. Mesto — Burletta
    IV. Mesto
dedicated: to the Kolisch Quartet
edition: BH 1941 (8437)

115 — CONCERTO for two pianos and orchestra *(December 1940)* transcription of the Sonata for two pianos and percussion (see No. 110)
edition: BH

115a — SUITE FOR TWO PIANOS op. 4/b (1941) (free transcription of No. 34)
    I. *Serenata*
    II. *Allegro diabolico*
    III. *Scena della puszta*
    IV. *Per finire*
edition: BH 1958 (18574)

116 — CONCERTO FOR ORCHESTRA *(Saranac Lake, 15th August–8th October 1943)*
    I. *Introduzione*
    II. *Giuoco delle coppie*
    III. *Elegia*
    IV. *Intermezzo interrotto*
    V. *Finale*
dedicated: to the Koussevitzky Music Foundation in memory of Natalie Koussevitzky
edition: BH 1946 (9009)
transcription: for piano solo (2 or 4 hands) or two pianos (27 January 1944)
unpublished

117 — SONATA FOR SOLO VIOLIN (Asheville, *14th March 1944*)
    I. *Tempo di ciaccona*
    II. *Fuga*

III. *Melodia*

IV. *Presto*

edition: BH 1947 (15896) (edited by Yehudi Menuhin). The version of the last movement, including quarter-tones, is unpublished

118 — UKRANIAN FOLK-SONG *(A FÉRJ KESERVE)* for voice and piano (New York, February 1945)

dedicated: to Pál Kecskeméti

edition: in facsimile, in: Bartók Béla levelei — Az utolsó két év gyűjtése. [Béla Bartók's Letters — Collection of the Last Two Years.] Collected and edited by János Demény. Művelt Nép, Budapest, 1951, pp. XIV–XV.

119 — CONCERTO No. 3 for piano and orchestra (1945). The last 17 bars were orchestrated by Tibor Serly

    I. Allegretto

    II. Adagio religioso—poco più mosso—tempo I

    III. Allegro vivace

editions: BH 1946 and 1947 (9122)

120 — CONCERTO for viola and orchestra (1945), unfinished. Arranged and orchestrated from Bartók's notes, by Tibor Serly

    I. Moderato (attacca)

    II. Adagio religioso-allegretto (attacca)

    III. Allegro vivace

edition: BH 1950 (16953)

121 — CADENZAS FOR THE CONCERTO FOR TWO PIANOS AND OR-CHESTRA IN E-FLAT MAJOR BY MOZART (K 365) (1940?)

Unpublished

EDITIONS OF SELECTED WORKS

(published either during Bartók's lifetime, or with his approval)

YOUNG PEOPLE AT THE PIANO *(ZONGORÁZÓ IFJÚSÁG)* (1938) (two albums containing the following pieces: For Children (No. 42) (I: Nos. 1–4, 6, 10, 15, II: Nos. 22, 26, III: Nos. 6, 7, 8, 14, 18, IV: Nos. 24, 28, 32); Ten Easy Pieces for Piano (No. 39): Nos. 1, 2, 3, 8.

editions: R and Rv (joint publication) 1938 (6171) and (6172), Zk 1952 (987) and (988)

ALBUM OF BARTÓK'S WORKS *(BARTÓK-ALBUM)* composer's selection (1939) with the following pieces: Fourteen Bagatelles (No. 38): Nos. 1, 2, 3, 4, 10; Three Burlesques (No. 47): Nos. 1, 2; Two Romanian Dances (No. 43): No. 1; Seven Sketches (No. 44): Nos. 1, 2, 5, 6; Ten Easy Pieces for Piano (No. 39): Nos. 5 and 10

editions: Rv 1946 (7045), Zk

3. BOOKS, STUDIES, ARTICLES

Compiled by András Szőllősy

The list of Bartók's writings is up to the time of his death. Except for the first posthumous publications, it does not include the translations published since. During Bartók's lifetime some of his writings were published in different languages at different intervals with minor or major changes in the text. This bibliography is merely chronological: does not indicate repetition or variation. As to the critical comparison of the different works, we consider the notes to Volume I of *Bartók összegyűjtött írásai I* [Collected Writings of Bartók I] (edited by András Szőllősy. Zk, Budapest, 1967, third edition) to be decisive.

I am grateful to László Somfai for his kind and valuable assistance in compiling this bibliography.

András Szőllősy

Kossuth. Szimfóniai költemény. Írta Bartók Béla [Kossuth. Symphonic Poem. By Béla Bartók]. *Zeneközlöny*, No. 6, 1904, pp. 82–86.

Symphonic poem—'Kossuth'—Béla Bartók (1881). Programme of the 1903–4 concert season of the Hallé Concert Society, pp. 506–511. (Concert on February 18, 1904, Manchester Free Trade Hall.)

Strauss: Sinfonia Domestica (op. 53). *Zeneközlöny*, No. 10, 1905, pp. 137–143.

Székely balladák [Székely Ballads]. *Ethnographia*, No. 1, 1908, pp. 43–52 and No. 2, pp. 105–115.

Dunántúli balladák [Transdanubian Ballads]. *Ethnographia*, No. 5, 1909, pp. 301–305.

Elektra. Strauss Richárd operája. Bemutató előadás a m. kir. operaházban 1910. március 11-én [Elektra. Opera of Richard Strauss. Première at the Hungarian Royal Opera House on March 11, 1910]. *A Zene*, No. 4, 1910, pp. 57–58.

Rhapsodie für Klavier und Orchester (op. 1) von Béla Bartók. *Die Musik*, No. 16, 1909–1910, pp. 226–228.

Rhapsodie für Klavier und Orchester op. 1. *Festheft zum 46. Tonkünstler-Fest des Allgemeinen Deutschen Musikvereins, 27–31. Mai in Zürich*, Gebrüder Hug and Co. Zurich, 1910, pp. 184–185.

Rhapsodie für Klavier und Orchester op. 1. *Schweizerische Musikzeitung und Sängerblatt*, No. 17, 1910, pp. 184–185.

Bartók Béla. *Budapesti Újságírók Egyesülete Almanachja*, Budapest, 1911, p. 292.

A hangszeres zene folkloreja Magyarországon [The Folklore of Instrumental Music in Hungary]. *Zeneközlöny*, No. 5, 1911, pp. 141–148; No. 7, pp. 207–213; No. 10, pp. 309–312; and No. 19, 1912, pp. 601–604.

A magyar nép hangszerei. I. A kanásztülök [Hungarian Folk Instruments. I. The Swineherd's Horn]. *Ethnographia*, No. 5, 1911, pp. 305–310.

A magyar zenéről [On Hungarian Music]. *Auróra*, No. 3, 1911, pp. 126–128.

Delius-bemutató Bécsben [A Delius-premiere in Vienna]. *Zeneközlöny*, No. 11, 1911, pp. 340–342.

Liszt zenéje és a mai közönség [The Music of Liszt and Today's Public]. *Népművelés*, No. 17–18, 1911, pp. 359–362.

Liszt zenéje és a mai közönség [The Music of Liszt and Today's Public]. *Zeneközlöny*, No. 18, 1911, pp. 556–560.

Az összehasonlító zenefolklore [Comparative Music-Folklore]. *Új Élet–Népművelés*, No. 1–2, 1912, pp. 109–114.

A clavecinre írt művek előadása [The Performance of Works Written for the Clavecin]. *Zeneközlöny*, No. 7, 1912, pp. 226–227.

A magyar nép hangszerei. II. A duda [Hungarian Folk Instruments. II. The Bagpipe]. *Ethnographia*, No. 2, 1912, pp. 110–114.

Cântece poporale românești din comitatul Bihor (Ungaria); Chansons populaires roumaines du département Bihar (Hongrie). Academia Română Librăriile Socec & Comp și C. Sfetea. Bucharest, 1913 (371 tunes).

A hunyadi román nép zenedialektusa [The Romanian Folk-Music Dialect of Hunyad]. *Ethnographia*, No. 2, 1914, pp. 108–115.

Observări despre muzica poporala românească (Observations on Romanian Folk Music). *Convorbiri Literare*, No. 7–8, 1913, pp. 703–709.

Ueber die magyarische Musik. *Der Merkur*, No. 21, 1916, pp. 757–758.

'A fából faragott királyfi'—A M. Kir. Operaház bemutatójához—II. A zeneszerző a darabjáról ['The Wooden Prince'—About the Premiere at the Hungarian Royal Opera House—II. The Composer on His Work]. *Magyar Színpad*, No. 105, 1917, p. 2.

A Biskra-vidéki arabok népzenéje [The Folk Music of the Arabs of Biskra and Environs]. *Szimfónia*, No. 12–13, 1917, pp. 308–323. (With 43 handwritten notes of Bartók in facsimile.)

Primitív népi hangszerek Magyarországon [Primitive Folk Instruments of Hungary]. *Zenei Szemle*, No. 9 and No. 10, 1917, pp. 273–275; pp. 311–315.

Die Melodien der madjarischen Soldatenlieder. K.u.K. Kriegsministerium, Musikhistorische Zentrale, Historisches Konzert am 12. Jänner 1918. (Program) Vienna, Universal Edition A.G., pp. 36–42.

'A kékszakállú herceg vára' Az Operaház újdonsága. I. Szerzők a darabjukról ['Bluebeard's Castle' A Novelty of the Opera House. I. The Authors Speak of Their Work]. *Magyar Színpad*, No. 143, 1918, p. 1.

Béla Bartók (Selbstbiographie). *Musikpädagogische Zeitschrift*, No. 11–12, 1918, pp. 97–99.

Béla Bartók Selbstbiographie. *Rheinische Musik- und Theaterzeitung (Allgemeine Zeitschrift für Musik)*, No. 5–6, 1919, pp. 1–2.

Musikfolklore. *Musikblätter des Anbruch*, No. 3–4, 1919, pp. 102–106.

Der Musikdialekt der Rumänen von Hunyad. *Zeitschrift für Musikwissenschaft*, No. 6, 1920, pp. 352–360.

Das Problem der neuen Musik. *Melos*, No. 5, 1920, pp. 107–110.

Hungary in the Throes of Reaction. *Musical Courier*, Vol. LXXX, No. 18 (2090), (1920), pp. 42–43.

Bartók válasza Hubay Jenőnek [Bartók's Answer to Jenő Hubay]. *Szózat*, No. 125, 1920, p. 2.

Ungarische Bauernmusik. *Musikblätter des Anbruch*, No. 11–12, 1920, pp. 422–424.
Die Volksmusik der Araber von Biskra und Umgebung. *Zeitschrift für Musikwissenschaft*, No. 9, 1920, pp. 489–522. Off-print: Druck und Verlag von Breitkopf & Härtel, Leipzig, 1920.

Kodály's New Trio, a Sensation Abroad. *Musical Courier*, Vol. LXXXI, No. 8 (2106) (1920), pp. 5 and 19.

Der Einfluss der Volksmusik auf die heutige Kunstmusik. *Melos*, No. 17, 1920, pp. 384–386.

Arnold Schönbergs Musik in Ungarn. *Musikblätter des Anbruch*, No. 20, 1920, pp. 647–648.

To Celebrate the Birth of the Great Bonn Composer, Dohnányi Gives Ten Beethoven Recitals in Budapest. *Musical Courier*, No. 23, 1920, p. 7.

Kodály Zoltán [Zoltán Kodály]. *Nyugat*, No. 3, 1921, pp. 235–236.

Aki nem tud arabusul . . . [Asinus ad lyram]. *Szózat*, No. 32, 1921, p. 4.

Schönberg and Stravinsky Enter 'Christian-National' Budapest Without Bloodshed. *Musical Courier*, No. 24, 1921, pp. 7 and 51.

Selbstbiographie. *Musikblätter des Anbruch*, No. 5, 1921, pp. 87–90.

New Kodály Work Raises Storm of Critical Protest. *Musical Courier*, issue of March 31, 1921, pp. 6 and 12.

Önéletrajzom [My Autobiography]. *Magyar Írás*, No. 2, 1921, pp. 33–36.

Lettera di Budapest. *Il Pianoforte*, No. 5, 1921, pp. 153–154.

Budapest Sorely Wishes Dohnányi's Return. *Musical Courier*, issue of July 14, 1921, p. 37.

The Relation of Folksong to the Development of the Art Music of Our Time. (Transl. Brian Lunn.) *The Sackbut*, No. 1, 1921, pp. 5–11.

Della musica moderna in Ungheria. *Il Pianoforte*, No. 7, 1921, pp. 193–197.

Lettera di Budapest. *Il Pianoforte*, No. 9, 1921, pp. 277–278.

Two Unpublished Liszt Letters to Mosonyi. (Transl. Frederick H. Martens.) *The Musical Quarterly*, No. 4, 1921, pp. 520–526.

La musique populaire hongroise. *La Revue Musicale*, No. 1, 1921, pp. 8–22.

The Development of Art Music in Hungary. *The Chesterian*, No. 20, 1922, pp. 101–107.

Bartók Béla (Önéletrajz) [Béla Bartók (Autobiography)]. *Az Est Hármaskönyve, lexikon az újságolvasó számára*, Budapest, 1923, columns 77–84. (With a facsimile of the first fourteen bars of the Sonata No. 2 for Violin and Piano.)

Volksmusik der Rumänen von Maramureş. *Sammelbände für vergleichende Musikwissenschaft*, Vol. IV. Drei Masken Verlag, Munich, 1923 (339 tunes).

Ábrányi, Emil; Arányi, Jelly; Buttykay, Ákos; Demény, Dezső; Durigó, Ilona (Kasics); Erkel, Franz; Földesi, Arnold; Geyer, Stefi (Schultess); Haselbeck, Olga; Hauser, Emil; Horváth, Attila; Hubay, Eugen (Jenő); Hungarian Opera, Pantomime and Ballet; Jacobi, Viktor; Jankó, Paul; Jemnitz, Alexander; Juhász, Aladár; Kabos, Ilona (Zsigmondi); Kacsóh, Pongrác; Kálmán, Emmerich; Keéri-Szántó, Imre; Kerner, Stephan; Kerpely, Eugen (Jenő); Kodály, Zoltán; Kornstein, Egon; Környey, Béla; Kósa, Georg; Kovács, Sándor; Lajtha, László; Lehner, Eugen (Jenő); Lendvai, Ervin; Lichtenberg, Emil; Marschalkó, Rózsi (Székelyhidy); Mihalovics, Ödön; Molnár, Anton; Nyiregyházi, Erwin; Pártos, Stephan; Popper, David; Radnai, Miklós; Radó, Aladár; Reiner, Fritz; Rózsa, Ludwig; Rubinstein, Erna; Rumanian Folk-Music; Sándor, Erzsi (Bosnyák); Siklós, Albert; Slovak Folk-Music; Szabados, Béla; Székelyhidy, Franz; Szendy, Árpád; Szirmai, Albert; Takács, Mihály; Tarnay, Alajos; Telmányi, Emil; Temesváry, János; Thomán, Stephan; Várkonyi, Béla; Vecsey, Ferenc; Waldbauer, Emmerich; Weiner, Leo; Zágon, Géza Vilmos; Zsolt Nándor; and also the passages relating to Hungary in the articles Academies, Chamber-music players, Opera houses, Orchestras, Publishers and, finally, a contribution, not to be measured precisely to the article Harmony. *A Dictionary of Modern Music and Musicians*, J.M. Dent and Sons, London, 1924.

A magyar népdal [The Hungarian Folk-Song]. Rózsavölgyi és Társa, Budapest, 1924 (320 tunes),

U zródel muzyki ludowej [At the Sources of Folk Music]. *Muzyka*, No. 6, 1925, pp. 230–233.

Бела Барток, Автобиография [Béla Bartók, Autobiography]. *Современная музыка*, No. 7, 1925, pp. 1–6.

Das ungarische Volkslied, Versuch einer Systematisierung der ungarischen Bauernmelodien. *Ungarische Bibliothek für das Ungarische Institut an der Universität Berlin* (edited by Robert Gragger), first series, No. 11. Walter de Gruyter & Co., Berlin–Leipzig 1925 (320 tunes).

Ábrányi, Emil; d'Arányi, Jelly; Demény, Desiderius (Dezső); Durigó, Ilona; Erkel, Franz; Földesi, Arnold; Geyer, Stefi; Haselbeck, Olga; Hauser, Emil; Horváth, Attila; Hubay, Jenő (Eugen Huber); Jacobi, Viktor; Jankó, Paul von; Jemnitz, Alexander; Juhász, Aladár; Kabos, Ilona (Zsigmondi); Kacsóh, Pongrácz; Kálmán, Emmerich; Keéri-Szántó, Imre; Kerner, Stephan; Kerpely, Eugen (Jenő); Kodály, Zoltán; Kornstein, Egon; Környey, Béla; Kósa, Georg; Kovács, Sándor; Lajtha, László; Lehner, Eugen (Jenő); Lendvai, Ervin; Lichtenberg, Emil; Marschalkó, Rózsi (Székelyhidy); Mihalovich, Edmund von; Molnár, Anton; Nyiregyházy, Erwin; Pártos, Stephan; Popper, David; Radnai, Miklós; Radó, Aladár; Reiner, Fritz; Rózsa, Ludwig; Rubinstein, Erna; Rumänische Volksmusik; Sándor, Erzsi (Bosnyák); Siklós, Albert; Slowakische Volksmusik; Szabados, Béla; Székelyhidy, Franz; Szendy, Árpád; Szirmai, Albert; Takács, Mihály; Tarnay, Alajos; Telmányi, Emil; Temesváry, János; Thomán, Stephan; Ungarische Oper, Pantomime u. ungar. Ballett; Várkonyi, Béla; Vecsey, Ferenc; Waldbauer, Emmerich; Weiner, Leo; Zágon, Géza Vilmos; Zsolt, Nándor; and also the passages related to Hungary in the articles Kammermusik-Vereinigungen, Konservatorien, Opernhäuser, Orchester, Verleger. *Das Neue Musiklexikon*, Max Hess Verlag, Berlin, 1926.

Zum Problem 'Klavier', Rundfragebeantwortungen. (Common title, together with the articles of other authors.) *Musikblätter des Anbruch*, No. 8–9, 1927, p. 390.

O wpływie muzyki wiejskiej na twórczość artystyczna [The Influence of the Peasant Music on Artistic Creation]. *Muzyka*, No. 6, 1927, pp. 256–259.

Küzdelmes út a harcoktól az elismerésig [A Hard Way from the Fights to Recognition]. *Színházi Élet*, No. 51, 1927, pp. 49–51.

The Folk-Song of Hungary. *Pro Musica*, 1928, pp. 28–35.

Magyar népzene és új magyar zene (Hungarian Folk Music and New Hungarian Music). *Zenei Szemle*, No. 3–4, 1928, pp. 55–58.

The National Temperament in Music. *The Musical Times*, No. 1030, 1928, p. 1079.

Zenefolklore-kutatások Magyarországon [Music-Folklore Research in Hungary]. *Zenei Szemle*, No. 1, 1929, pp. 13–15.

Magyarországi népzenei kutatások [Music-Folklore Research in Hungary]. *Az 1928. évi prágai nemzetközi népművészeti kongresszuson benyújtott jelentések a magyar népművészetről*, Hungarian Academy of Sciences, Budapest, 1929, pp. 44–51.

Węgierska muzyka ludowa [Hungarian Folk Music]. *Muzyka*, No. 4, 1929, pp. 201–202.

(The Analysis of the *String Quartet No. 4*). Without title, in German, French and English in the pocket partitions of the Universal: 9788 and Wiener Philharmonia: 166. (Only in the impressions after 1930.)

Der Einfluss der Volksmusik auf die heutige Kunstmusik. *Melos*, No. 2, 1930, pp. 66–67.

Cigányzene? Magyar zene? Magyar népdalok a német zeneműpiacon [Gypsy Music? Hungarian Music? Hungarian Folk-Songs on the German Music Market]. *Ethno-*

graphia, No. 2, 1931, pp. 49–62. The music examples are facsimiles of Bartók's handwriting. Off-print: Rózsavölgyi és Társa, Budapest, 1931.

Mi a népzene? [What is Folk Music?]. *Új Idők*, No. 20, 1931, pp. 626–627.

A parasztzene hatása az újabb műzenére [The Influence of Folk Music on the More Recent Art Music]. *Új Idők*, No. 23, 1931, pp. 718–719.

A népzene jelentőségéről [On the Importance of Folk Music]. *Új Idők*, No. 26, 1931, pp. 818–819.

Über die Herausgabe ungarischer Volkslieder. *Ungarische Jahrbücher*, No. 3, 1931, pp. 191–205. The music examples are facsimiles of Bartók's handwriting. Off-print: *Ungarische Bibliothek* (editor Gyula Farkas), Walter de Gruyter, Berlin–Leipzig, 1931.

Möller, Heinrich: Ungarische Volkslieder (Das Lied der Völker, Bd. 12. Mainz, B. Schott's Söhne). *Zeitschrift für Musikwissenschaft*, No. 11–12, 1931, pp. 580–582.

The Peasant Music of Hungary. *Musical Courier*, Vol. CIII, No. 11 (2683), (1931), pp. 6 and 22.

Slovakian Peasant Music. *Musical Courier*, Vol. CIII, No. 13 (2685), (1931), p. 6.

Mi a népzene? [What Is Folk Music?]. *Magyar Minerva*, No. 7, 1931, pp. 193–195.

A parasztzene hatása az újabb műzenére [The Influence of Peasant Music on the More Recent Art Music]. *Magyar Minerva*, No. 8, 1931, pp. 225–228.

A népzene jelentőségéről [On the Importance of Folk Music]. *Magyar Minerva*, No. 9, 1931, pp. 257–259.

Nochmals: Über die Herausgabe ungarischer Volkslieder. *Zeitschrift für Musikwissenschaft*, No. 3, 1931, p. 179.

Les recherches sur le folklore musical en Hongrie. *Art Populaire (Congrès International des Arts Populaires à Prague, 1928, Résumés)*, Vol. II, 1931, pp. 127–128.

Magyar népi hangszerek [Hungarian Folk Instruments]. *Zenei Lexikon*, Vol. II (edited by Bence Szabolcsi and Aladár Tóth). Andor Győző, Budapest, 1931, pp. 58–63.

Román népzene [Romanian Folk Music]. *Zenei Lexikon*, Vol. II (edited by Bence Szabolcsi and Aladár Tóth). Andor Győző, Budapest, 1931, pp. 419–420.

Szlovák népzene (Slovak Folk Music). *Zenei Lexikon*, Vol. II (edited by Bence Szabolcsi and Aladár Tóth). Andor Győző, Budapest, 1931, pp. 571–572.

Hungarian Folk Music. (Transl. M. D. Calvocoressi.) Oxford University Press, London; Humphrey Milford, 1931 (320 tunes),

(On the *Violin Duos*.) Without title, facsimile of Bartók's handwriting; annex of the programme of the first concert of UMZE (New Hungarian Musical Association), January 20, 1932.

Neue Ergebnisse der Volksliederforschung in Ungarn. *Anbruch*, No. 2–3, 1932, pp. 37–42.

Volksmusik und ihre Bedeutung für die neuzeitliche Komposition. *Mitteilungen der Österr[eichischen] Musiklehrerschaft*, No. 2, 1932, and No. 3, pp. 6–10; pp. 5–10.

Gegenantwort an Heinrich Möller. *Ungarische Jahrbücher*, No. 1–2, 1932, pp. 130–131.

Proposition de M. Béla Bartók concernant les éditions des textes authentiques (Urtextausgaben) des œuvres musicales et des éditions en fac-similé des manuscrits d'œuvres musicales (In German too). *Société des Nations. Commission de coopération intellectuelle, sous-commission arts et lettres, 1931–1938 (procès verbaux)*. Comité permanent des lettres et des arts, 2e session, convoquée à Francfort du 12 au 14 mai 1932.

Ungarische Volksmusik. *Schweizerische Sängerzeitung*, No. 2, No. 3, and No. 4, 1933, pp. 13–14; pp. 21–22; pp. 31–32. Off-print: Bern, 1933, Unionsdruckerei.

'Zum Kongress für arabische Musik—Kairo 1932.' (Common title, together with the articles of other authors.) *Zeitschrift für Vergleichende Musikwissenschaft*, No. 2, 1933, pp. 46–48.

Hungarian Peasant Music. (Transl. Theodor Baker.) *Musical Quarterly*, No. 3, 1933, pp. 267–287.

Rumänische Volksmusik. *Schweizerische Sängerzeitung*, No. 17, No. 18, and No. 20, 1933, pp. 141–142; pp. 148–149; pp. 168–169. Off-print: Bern, 1933, Unionsdruckerei.

Bela Bartók Replies to Percy Grainger. *The Music News*, issue of January 19, 1934, p. 9.

Muzica populară si insemnătatea ei pentru compozitia modernă [Folk Music and Its Importance for Modern Composition]. *Revista Fundatiilor Regale*, No. 6, 1934, pp. 111–121.

Népzenénk és a szomszéd népek népzenéje [Our Folk Music and the Folk Music of Neighbouring Peoples]. *Népszerű zenefüzetek*, (edited by Antal Molnár, No. 3, n.d. [1934]). The musical examples are facsimiles of Bartók's handwriting.

Miért gyűjtünk népzenét? [Why Do We Collect Folk Music?].

Az Országos Magyar Királyi Liszt Ferenc Zeneművészeti Főiskola Évkönyve az 1934/35-iki tanévről (edited by Kálmán Isoz). Hungarian National Royal Liszt Ferenc Conservatory, Budapest, 1935, pp. 3–7; and off-print.

Miért gyűjtünk népzenét? [Why To Collect Folk Music?]. *Válasz*, No. 7–8, 1935, pp. 397–400.

Die Volksmusik der Magyaren und der benachbarten Völker. *Ungarische Jahrbücher*, No. 2–3, 1935, pp. 194–258. The musical examples are facsimiles of Bartók's handwriting. Off-print: *Ungarische Bibliothek* (edited by Gyula Farkas). First series; No. 20, Walter de Gruyter & Co., Berlin–Leipzig, 1935.

'Magyar népzene' ['Hungarian Folk Music']. *Révai Nagy Lexikona*, Vol. XXI, Appendix A–Z. Révai Testvérek Irodalmi Intézet Részvénytársaság, Budapest, 1935, pp. 571–572.

Román népzene [Romanian Folk Music]. *Révai Nagy Lexikona*, Vol. XXI, Appendix A–Z. Révai Testvérek Irodalmi Intézet Részvénytársaság, Budapest, 1935, pp. 725–726.

Szlovák népzene [Slovak Folk Music]. *Révai Nagy Lexikona*, Vol. XXI, Appendix A–Z. Révai Testvérek Irodalmi Intézet Részvénytársaság, Budapest, 1935, pp. 776–777.

[Preface] Without title, with a facsimile of Bartók's signature. *Búzavirág. Magyar férfikórusgyűjtemény Bartók Béla előszavával.* (Edited by Sándor Arany.) Co-operative 'Kazinczy', Tornalja, 1935, p. 5.

Melodien der rumänischen Colinde (Weihnachtslieder). Universal Edition A.G., Vienna, 1935 (484 tunes). The musical examples are facsimiles of Bartók's handwriting.

A népzenéről [On Folk Music]. *Népszava Naptár*, Budapest, 1936, edition the bookshop 'Népszava', pp. 51–54.

Nachwort zu der 'Volksmusik der Magyaren und der benachbarten Völker' — Antwort auf einen rumänischen Angriff. *Ungarische Jahrbücher*, No. 2–3, 1936, pp. 276–284; also off-print.

Dialectul muzical al românilor din Hunedoara [The Musical Dialect of the Romanians in the County of Hunedoara]. *Muzica si Poezie*, No. 4, 1936, pp. 6–14.

Miért gyűjtünk népzenét? [Why To Collect Folk Music?]. *Magyar Dal*, No. 2, 1936, pp. 2–4.

Muzica populară românească [Romanian Folk Music]. *Muzica si Poezie*, No. 5, 1936, pp. 18–22.

Liszt Ferenc. *Nyugat*, No. 3, 1936, pp. 171–179.

Muzica populară românească [Romanian Folk Music]. *Muzica si Poezie*, No. 6, 1936, pp. 21–24.

Muzica populară românească [Romanian Folk Music]. *Muzica si Poezie*, No. 6, 1936, p. 24. (This article is the translation of the article Romanian Folk Music in: *A Dictionary of Modern Music and Musicians*, J.M. Dent and Sons Ltd., London, 1924, pp. 426–427.)

Népzenegyűjtés [Collecting Folk Music]. *Apollo*, No. IV, 1936, pp. 31–39.

Bartók Béla székfoglalójának kivonata. Liszt Ferenc [Summary of the Inaugural Lecture of Béla Bartók. Ferenc Liszt]. *Akadémiai Értesítő*, No. 462, 1936, pp. 29–34.

A propos du Jubilé Liszt. *La Revue Musicale*, No. 167, 1936, pp. 1–4 (137–140).

Muzica populară maghiară si cea românească [The Hungarian Folk Music and that of the Romanians]. *Muzica si Poezie*, No. 9–10, 1936, pp. 18–44.

Cercetările de folklore muzical in Ungaria [Hungarian Musical Folklore Researches]. *Muzica si Poezie*, No. 12, 1936, pp. 18–19.

Despre muzica populară românească [On the Romanian Folk Music]. *Muzica si Poezie*, No. 12, 1936, pp. 19–23.

Liszt-problémák. Székfoglaló előadás a Magyar Tudományos Akadémián 1936 február 3-án [Liszt Problems. Inaugural Lecture at the Hungarian Academy of Sciences on February 3, 1936]. In: *Liszt a mienk*. Dante, Budapest, 1936, pp. 53–67. The same volume has been published under the title *Liszt Ferenc*, Dante, Budapest, n.d. [1936]. Off-print: Printing House V. Hornyánszky, Budapest, 1936.

La Musique populaire des Hongrois et des peuples voisins. *Archivum Europae Centro-Orientalis*, 1936, No. 4, pp. 197–232 and I–XXXII. The musical examples are facsimiles of Bartók's handwriting. Off-print (bound together with the 'Réponse à une attaque roumaine'): *Études sur l'Europe Centre-Orientale*, Budapest, No. 5, 1937, pp. 1–36 and I–XXXII.

Réponse à une attaque roumaine. *Archivum Europae Centro-Orientalis*, Vol. II (1936), No. 3–4, pp. 233–244. Off-print (bound together with 'La Musique populaire des Hongrois et des peuples voisins'): *Études sur l'Europe Centre-Orientale*, Budapest, No. 5, 1937, pp. 37–48.

Musique et chansons populaires. *Acta Musicologica*, No. 3–4, 1936, pp. 97–101.

Népzene és népdalok [Folk Music and Folk-Songs]. *Szép Szó*, No. 10, 1936, pp. 274–278.

Miért és hogyan gyűjtsünk népzenét? A zenei folklore törvénykönyve [Why and How To Collect Folk Music? The Code of Musical Folklore]. *Népszerű zenefüzetek*, B. Somló, No. 5, Budapest, 1936.

Halk müziği Hakkinda [On Folk Music]. Ankara, 1936, Printing House of Raceb Ulusoglu. Ankara, *Halkevi Nesriyati Büyük Boy*, No. 8.

A gépzene [Machine Music]. *Szép Szó*, No. 11, 1937, pp. 1–11.

Népdalgyűjtés Törökországban [Folk-Song Collecting in Turkey). *Nyugat*, No. 3, 1937, pp. 178–181.

Népdalkutatás és nacionalizmus [Folk-Song Research and Nationalism]. *Tükör*, No. 3, 1937, pp. 166–168.

Válasz Petranuék támadására [Answer to the Attack of Petranu and His Friends]. *Szép Szó*, No. 13, 1937, pp. 263–272. Also off-print.

Aufbau der 'Musik für Saiteninstrumente'—Structure of 'Music for String Instruments'—Plan de 'Musique pour instruments à cordes'. In the partition of the work published by Universal Edition (UE. 10.888).

Collecting Folk-Songs in Anatolia. *Hungarian Quarterly*, No. 2, 1937, pp. 337–346.

Badání o lidových písních a nacionalismus [Folk-Song Research and Nationalism]. *Rytmus*, No. 9–10, 1937, pp. 95–96.

Scrieri mărunte despre muzica populară românească [Short Articles on Romanian Folk Music]. Collected and translated by Constantin Brăiloiu. Bucharest, 1937.

Az úgynevezett bolgár ritmus [The So-Called Bulgarian Rhythm]. *Énekszó*, No. 6, 1937–1938, pp. 537–541.

Béla Bartók über sein neuestes Werk. *Nationalzeitung* [Basel], issue of January 13, 1938.

Opinions sur l'orientation technique, esthétique et spirituelle de la musique contemporaine. Opinion de M. Bela Bartok (Varsovie) [*sic*], *La Revue Internationale de Musique*, No. 3, 1938, pp. 452–453.

Du Lied Populaire au Nationalisme. *La Revue Internationale de Musique*, No. 4, 1938, pp. 609–615.

[On Ravel.] Without title. *La Revue Musicale*, No. 187, 1938, p. 436 (244).

Bela Bartok à l'orchestre de la Suisse Romande. Analyse du 'Deuxième Concerto' pour piano et orchestre de Bela Bartok, par son auteur. *La Radio* [Lausanne], issue of February 17, 1939, pp. 280 and 282. The musical examples and the signature are facsimiles of Bartók's handwriting.

Bartók Béla: Az én oldalam [Béla Bartók: My Page]. *Film, Színház, Irodalom*, No. 14, 1941.

Race Purity in Music. *Modern Music*, 1942, pp. 153–155.

Parry Collection of Yugoslav Folk Music. *The New York Times*, issue of June 28, 1942.

Diversity of Material Yielded up in Profusion in European Meltingpot. *Musical America*, No. 1, 1943, p. 27.

A régi magyar népzenéről [On Ancient Hungarian Folk Music]. *Emlékkönyv Kodály Zoltán hatvanadik születésnapjára*. Magyar Néprajzi Társaság, Budapest, 1943, pp. 5–8.

Szabolcsi, Bence (Benedict): *The Universal Jewish Encyclopedia*. New York, Vol. X (1942), p. 138.

Hungarian Music. *American Hungarian Observer*, issue of June 4, 1944, pp. 3 and 7.

Race Purity in Music. *Tempo*, No. 8, 1944, pp. 2–3.

[In the article 'Concert for Orchestra by Béla Bartók, analysis of this work by the author'.] *Program of the Boston Symphony Orchestra*, No. 8, 1944–1945, pp. 442 and 444.

[In the article 'Concert for Orchestra by Béla Bartók, analysis of this work by the author'.] *Concert Bulletin of the Boston Symphony Orchestra*, December 1st and 2nd, 1944, pp. 606–608.

'I salute the valiant Belgian people', *Belgium*, Vol. V, No. 12 (1945), pp. 563–564.

Some linguistic observations. *Tempo*, No. 14, 1946, pp. 5–7.

Música popular y culta en Hungría (Artículo postumo) [Folk Music and Art Music in Hungary (Posthumous article)]. *Nuestra Música* [Mexico], No. 1, 1946, pp. 14–19. Between pp. 40 and 41: the facsimile of the English draft of this article.

Béla Bartók (Önéletrajzi jegyzetek) [Béla Bartók, Autobiographical Notes]. In facsimile of the author's handwriting: Béla Bartók: Ten Easy Pieces for Piano. Liber-Southern Ltd., London [1950 or later] (without record number), p. 1.

Serbo-Croatian Folk-Songs (in collaboration with Albert B. Lord). The Introduction —pp. XV–XVIII—and also the part from p. 3 to p. 244 in this work are from Bartók. Columbia University Press, New York, 1951, No. 7 of *Columbia University Studies in Musicology* (76 tunes).

Serbo-Croatian Heroic Songs I (in collaboration with Albert B. Lord). The notation of song No. 4 (pp. 437–462) and the notes accompanying this notation (pp. 463–467) are from Bartók. Harvard University Press and the Serbian Academy of Sciences, Cambridge and Belgrade, 1954.

Slovenské L'udové Piesné — Slowakische Volkslieder Vol. I. Academia Scientiarum Slovaca. Bratislava, 1959. Vol. II, 1970. (Tunes Nos. 422–1047/b).

Romanian Folk Music I–III (Vol. I 1115 tunes for instruments, Vol. II 1440 tunes for voice, Vol. III texts). (The Romanian texts and part of the musical notes are in facsimile of Bartók's handwriting.) Martinus Nijhoff, The Hague, 1967.

WORKS PUBLISHED UNDER THE NAME OF BARTÓK AND KODÁLY, EDITED BY ZOLTÁN KODÁLY

Az új egyetemes magyar népdalgyűjtemény tervezete [A plan for the New Musical Collection of Hungarian Folk-Songs]. *Ethnographia*, 1913, pp. 313–316.

Erdélyi Magyarság. Népdalok [The Hungarians of Transylvania. Folk-Songs]. Népies Irodalmi Társaság, Budapest, n. d. [1923] (150 tunes).

Transylvanian Hungarians. Folk-Songs. Népies Irodalmi Társaság, Budapest, n. d. [1923] (150 tunes).

Les Hongrois de Transylvanie. Chansons populaires. Népies Irodalmi Társaság, Budapest, n. d. [1923] (150 tunes).

PUBLICATIONS COLLECTING SEVERAL WRITINGS OF BARTÓK

Béla Bartók, *Scrieri mărunte despre muzica populară românească* [Short Articles on Rumanian Folk Music]. Collected and translated by Constantin Brăiloiu. Bucharest, 1937.

Bartók Béla, *Önéletrajz, Írások a zenéről* [Autobiography, Writings on Music]. Collected by Lili Veszprémi-Almár, introductory study by János Demény. Egyetemi Nyomda, Budapest, 1946.

Bartók Béla válogatott zenei írásai [Selected Musical Writings]. Collected by András Szőllősy, introduction and notes by Bence Szabolcsi. Magyar Kórus, Budapest, 1948.

Béla Bartók, Scritti sulla musica popolare. (Italian translation of the above-mentioned title.) Collected by Diego Carpitella, with an introduction by Zoltán Kodály. Edizioni Scientifiche Einaudi, Torino, 1955.

Bartók Béla válogatott írásai [Selected Writings of Béla Bartók]. Collected by András Szőllősy. Művelt Nép Tudományos és Ismeretterjesztő Kiadó, Budapest, 1956.

Bartók, sa vie et son œuvre. Edited by Bence Szabolcsi. Corvina, Budapest, 1956. A new revised edition: Corvina–Boosey and Hawkes, Budapest–Paris, 1968.

Bartók Béla, Insemnări asupra cîntecului popular [Remarks on the Folk-Song]. (Partly on the basis of the volume *Selected Musical Writings*, partly of the volume *Scrieri mărunte.*) With an introduction by Zeno Vancea. Editura de stat pentru literatura si arta, Bucharest, n. d. [1956].

Béla Bartók, Weg und Werk, Schriften und Briefe. Edited by Bence Szabolcsi. Corvina, Budapest, 1957.

Bartók Breviárium (levelek, írások, dokumentumok) [Bartók Breviary (Letters, Writings, Documents)]. Collected by József Ujfalussy, Zeneműkiadó Vállalat, Budapest, 1958.

Béla Bartók: Eigene Schriften und Erinnerungen der Freunde. Edited by Willi Reich Benno Schwabe and Co., Basel–Stuttgart, 1958.

Béla Bartók: *Postrehy a názory* [Béla Bartók: Writings and Letters]. (Slovak translation of parts of the volume *Selected Writings* and of five Bartók letters. Transl. Eva Hykischová.) Statne Hudobné vydavatel'stvo, Bratislava, 1965.

Bartók Béla összegyűjtött írásai I [Collected Writings of Béla Bartók I]. Published by András Szőllősy. Zeneműkiadó Vállalat, Budapest, 1966 (on some copies 1967). Complete, critical edition of Bartók's writings.

A FACSIMILE COLLECTION OF BARTÓK'S HANDWRITINGS

Bartók Béla kézírása [The Handwriting of Béla Bartók]. Edited by Bence Szabolcsi and Benjámin Rajeczky. Zeneműkiadó Vállalat, Budapest, 1961.

DISCOGRAPHY

Compiled by László Somfai

The first part of this Discography gives a complete list of recordings made personally by Béla Bartók, and which were offered for commercial sale.

The list is supplemented by a survey of those collections transcribed for microgroove recordings which are most easily accessible to the public today (1970). It must be noted, however, that, in addition to the insufficiencies of contemporary sound technology, not all of the recordings can be regarded as faithful documents of Bartók's genius in piano technique and interpretation. Date of the recording is only given in the instance of the Washington concert on April 13, 1940, where it is undoubtedly authentic.

It has been the intention in the second part to offer at least one recording of each of Bartók's works. In the case of the works most frequently released on discs, it included those recordings that the compiler considered as deserving special attention, either for their authenticity or as extraordinary feats of interpretation, and of historic value.

Abbreviations

Ang.	= Angel
BRS	= Bartók Recording Studio (New York)
Ca.	= Columbia (USA)
Cam.	= Cambridge
Cl.	= Classic (France)
Col.	= Columbia (England)
Con. Disc	= Concert-Disc
Cont.	= Continental (USA)
DGG	= Deutsche Grammophon Gesellschaft
HMV	= His Masters Voice (AM, AN = Hungary)
Lon.	= London
Pac.	= Pacific
Per.	= Period
Pol.	= Polydor
Vic.	= RCA Victor
West.	= Westminster

I. COMPLETE LIST OF RECORDS PLAYED BY BÉLA BARTÓK

COMPOSITIONS FOR PIANO

(A) Own works

1. *Bagatelle* No. 2 (1908). [HMV AM 2622, Cont. 4006, CLP 1001, BRS 903, Remington R-199-94.]

2. *An Evening with the Székelys, Bear Dance (Ten Easy Pieces for piano*, 1908, Nos. 5 and 10). (Recording A): [HMV AN 469, BRS 903.] (Recording B): [Vox 650, Cl. C 2075, Vox PLP 6010. Turnabout Vox TV 4159.]

3. *For Children* (1908–9). [Rev. ed. 1945, Vol.1.: (a) Nos. 3, 4, 6, 10, 12; (b) 13, 15, 18, 19, 21; (c) 26, 34, 31, 30. (a–b–c:) Vox 650–651, Cl. C 2075–2076, (only a–b:) Pol. Vox PLP 6010. Turnabout Vox TV 4159.]

4. *Burlesque* No. 2 (1911). [HMV 2622, BRS 003.]

5. *Romanian Dance* No. 1 (1910). [HMV AN 469, BRS 003, BRS 903.]

6. *Allegro Barbaro* (1911). [HMV AM 2622, BRS 003, BRS 903.]

7. *Ancient Dance Tunes (15 Hungarian Peasant Songs* 1914/18, No. 7–12, 14–15). [Pat. Mr E 63, Pat. Ultravox E 172, Durium Pat. DMB 10111, Pac. 6501, BRS 903.]

8. *Three Hungarian Folk-Songs* ['Homage to Paderewski,' (publ. 1942). Cont. 4008, CLP 1001, Remington R-199-94.]

9. *Suite* op. 14 (1916). [HMV AN 486 (sequence of parts: I–III, II–IV), BRS 003, BRS 903.]

10. *Rondo* No. 1 (1916/27). [Pat. Mr 64, Durium Pat. Dac. 10242, Pac. 5010, Cont. C 1193, CLP 1001, BRS 903, Remington R-199-94.]

11. *Improvisations on Peasant Songs*. [(1920) No. 1–2, 6–8. Cont. 4007, CLP 1001, Remington R-199-94.]

12. (a) *Air; Tambourine* (recorded with 13/b); (b) *Preludio all'Ungherese (Nine Little Pieces* for piano 1926, Nos. 6, 8, 9 [(a): Pat. Mr 64, Durium Pat. Dac. 10242, Pac. 5010, Cont. C1193, BRS 903; (b): Cont. 4006, CLP 1001, Remington R-199-94.]

13. *Petite Suite* (1936) (a) complete (b) only the last movement. [(a): Cont 4005, CLP 1001, Remington R-199-94; (b): Pat. Mr. 64, Durium Pat. Dac. 10242, Pac. 5010, Cont. C 1193, BRS 903.]

14. *Mikrokosmos* (1926/39) (a) Nos. 113, 129, 131, 128; 120, 109, 138; 100, 142, 140; 133, 149, 148; 108, 150, 151; 94, 152, 153; (b) 126, 116, 130, 139, 143, 147, 144, 97, 118, 141, 136, 125, 114; (c) 124, 146. [(a): Col. Album M 455 (D 71112–71114) Odyssey 32 16 0220, (a–b): Col. ML 4419; (c): Col. DB 1790, Col. DB 1306, BRS 903.]

15. *Seven pieces from the Mikrokosmos* for two pianos and four hands, Nos. 2, 5, 6 (with Ditta Pásztory–Bartók). [Cont. 4008, CLP 1001, Remington R-199-94.]

(B) Works by other composers

16. Scarlatti, Domenico: *Four Sonatas* (Longo Nos. 286, 135, 293, 50). [BRS 903.]

17. Liszt, Franz: *Sursum corda.* [Pat. Mr E 63, Pat. Ultravox E 172, Durium Pat. DMB 10111, Pac. 6501, BRS 903.]

CHAMBER MUSIC

(A) Own works

18. *Sonata No. 2 for Violin and Piano* (1922) (with Joseph Szigeti) (date of recording April 13, 1940). [Vanguard VRS 1131.]

19. *Rhapsody No. 1 for Violin and Piano* (1928) (with Joseph Szigeti) (Recording A). [Col. LOX 519, Col. D 11410, Col. ML 2213.]

20. *Rhapsody No. 1 for Violin and Piano* (1928) (with Joseph Szigeti) (Recording B, date April 13, 1940). [Vanguard VRS 1130.]

21. *Sonata for Two Pianos and Percussion* (1937) (with Ditta Pásztory–Bartók; percussion: Harry J. Baker, Edward J. Rubsan). [Pol. Vox PLP 6010, Cl. C 2113-5, Turnabout Vox TV 4159.]

22. *Contrasts, for violin, piano and clarinet* (1938) (with Joseph Szigeti and Benny Goodman). [Col. LOX 485–486, Col. D 70666–70667, Ca. 703623, Col. ML 2213, Odyssey 32 16 0220.]

23. *Hungarian Folk Tunes for Violin and Piano,* transcription by Joseph Szigeti (with Joseph Szigeti). [Col. LX 31, Col. M 7274.]

24. *Romanian Folk Dances* for violin and piano, transcription by Zoltán Székely (with Joseph Szigeti). [Col. LB 6, Col. D 17089.]

(B) Works by other composers

25. Beethoven, Ludwig van: *Sonata in A Major* ('Kreutzer') for violin and piano, op. 47 (with Joseph Szigeti; date of recording April 13, 1940). [Vanguard VRS 1131.]

26. Debussy, Claude Achille: *Sonata for Violin and Piano* (with Joseph Szigeti, date of recording April 13, 1940). [Vanguard VRS 1131.]

TRANSCRIPTIONS OF HUNGARIAN FOLK-SONGS

(A) Own works

27. (a) 'Elindultam szép hazámbul,' 'Által mennék én a Tiszán,' 'A gyulai kert alatt'; (b) 'Nem messze van ide Kismargitta', 'Végigmentem a tárkányi sej-haj nagy utcán' (transcriptions from *Twenty Hungarian Folk-Songs,* for voice and piano, 1906) (sung by Vilma Medgyaszay). [(a): HMV AM 1676; (b) HMV AM 1678.]

28. (a) 'Fekete főd,' 'Asszonyok, asszonyok'; (b) 'Istenem, Istenem,' 'Ha kimegyek arr'a magos tetőre' (*Eight Hungarian Folk-Songs* 1907/17, Nos. 1, 2, 3, 5) (sung by Mária Basilides). [(a-b): HMV AM 1671; (b): Qualiton HLP SZK 3513.]

29. 'Töltik a nagy erdő útját,' 'Eddig való dolgom,' 'Olvad a hó' (*Eight Hungarian Folk-Songs* 1907/17, Nos. 6, 7, 8) (sung by Ferenc Székelyhidy). [HMV AN 215, Qualiton HLP SZK 3513.]

(B) From ZOLTÁN KODÁLY'S 'Hungarian Folk Music'
30. (a) Nos. 9, 7; (b) Nos. 8, 11, 10; (c) Nos. 15, 12, 16; (d) 41, 14; (e) Nos. 13, 30; (f) Nos. 6; (g) No. 1 (sung by Mária Basilides). [(a–e): HMV AM 1672–1675; (f–g): HMV AN 209–210; (c, a); Qualiton HLP SZK 3513.]
31. (a) No. 37; (b) Nos. 32, 39, 33; (c) Nos. 40, 42; (d) No. 36 (sung by Ferenc Székelyhidy). [(a): HMV AN 215, Qualiton HLP SZK 3513; (b): HMV AM 1690; (c): HMV AN 216; (only No. 40 from c): Qualiton HLP SZK 3513; (d): HMV AM 449.]
32. (a) No. 21; (b) Nos. 23, 24; (c) Nos. 19, 20; (d): No. 18 (sung by Vilma Medgyaszay). [(a–b): HMV AM 1676; (c): HMV AM 1677; (d): HMV AN 211.]

A SURVEY OF RECORDINGS WITH BÉLA BARTÓK ON LONG PLAYING RECORDS

Numbers refer to the corresponding items on the foregoing list of works played by Béla Bartók.
(A) 'Béla Bartók at the Piano'. [Bartók Records BRS 003.—Side A: 5, 1, 4, 6; Side B: 9.]
(B) 'Bartók Plays Bartók'. [Remington R-199-94.—Side A: 1, 10, 13, 12 (b); Side B: 15, 11, 8.]
(C) [Vox PLP 6010 and Turnabout Vox TV 4159.—Side A: 21^{I-II}; Side B: 21^{III}, 3(a), 3(b), 2.]
(D) 'Béla Bartók Playing His Own Works'. [Columbia Masterworks, 'Meet the Composer,' ML 4419.—Side A: 14(a); Side B: 14(b).]
(E) [Columbia ML 2213.—Side A: 22; Side B: 19.]
(F) 'Béla Bartók at the Piano'. [Bartók Records BRS 903.—Side A: 16, 17, 1, 2, 5, 4, 6; Side B: 7, 9, 10, 12(a), 13(b), 14(c), 36.]
(G) 'Hungarian Folk Songs'. [Qualiton HLP SZK 3513.—Side A: 30(c); 30(a^{I}), 28(b), 30(a^{II}); Side B: 31(a), 29, 31(c^{I}).]
(H) 'A sonata recital by Joseph Szigeti and Béla Bartók.' Recorded at the Library of Congress, Washington, D.C., April 13, 1940. [Vanguard, Library of Historic Performances, VRS 1130–1131 and Qualiton LPX 11373–74.—Disc I, Side A: 25^{I-II}; Side B: 25^{III}, 20; Disc II, Side A: 26; Side B: 18.]
(I) 'Legendary Performances.' [Odyssey 32 16 0220.—Side A: 14(a); Side B: 22.]

THE VOICE OF BARTÓK ON GRAMOPHONE RECORDS

33. (In Hungarian) Text of *Cantata Profana*, 3 min. 41 sec. [Qualiton LPX 1162.]
34. (In Hungarian) The announcements of three pieces from *For Children*, played by himself (cf. No. 3). 3 sec. each. [Vox 650–651, Cl. C 2075–2076; (only the first and second pieces) Pol. Vox PLP 6010.]

35. (In Hungarian) The announcements of two pieces from *Ten Easy Pieces for Piano, An Evening with the Székelys* and *Bear Dance*, played by himself (cf. No. 2 in this List). Two and one seconds respectively. [Vox. 650, Cl. C 2075, Pol. Vox PLP 6010.]

36. (In English) Short explanatory introduction to *Mikrokosmos, Suite* op. 14, *Rondo* No 1, and *Evening in Transylvania* [=*An Evening with the Székelys*]. 2 min. 41 sec. [BRS 903.]

II. GENERAL DISCOGRAPHY—SELECTION

Stage works

Bluebeard's Castle
37. (In Hungarian) Mihály Székely (bass version), Klára Palánkay. Budapest Philharmonic Society, cond. János Ferencsik. [Qualiton HLP MN 1001.]

38. (In Hungarian) Mihály Székely (bass version), Olga Szőnyi. London Symphony Orchestra, cond. Antal Doráti. [Mer. 50311, (stereo) 90311.]

39. (In German) Dietrich Fischer-Dieskau, Herta Töpper. The West-Berlin Radio Symphony Orchestra, cond. Ferenc Fricsay. [DGG 18565, (stereo) 138030.]

40. (In English, text by Chester Kallman) Jerome Hines, Rosalind Elias. Philadelphia Symphony Orchestra, Cond. Eugene Ormándy. [Col. ML 5825, (stereo) MS 6425.]

The Wooden Prince
41. (Complete) The New Symphony Orchestra, cond. Walter Susskind. [BRS 308.]

42. (Complete) London Symphony Orchestra, cond. Antal Doráti. [Mercury MG 50426 (Stereo) SR 90426.]

43. (Version performed by the Budapest State Opera House) Budapest Philharmonic Society, cond. János Ferencsik. [Qualiton LPX 1164.]

44. (Suite in 3 movements) Budapest Philharmonic Orchestra, cond. András Koródi. (Complete Bartók Œuvre)* [Hungaroton LPX 11314.]

The Miraculous Mandarin
45. (Complete) BBC Symphony Orchestra and Choir, cond. Antal Doráti. [Mer. 50416, (Stereo) 90416.]

46. (Complete) Budapest Radio and Television Symphony Orchestra, Cond. János Sándor. (Complete Bartók Œuvre) [Hungaroton LPX 1301.]

---

* (Complete Bartók Œuvre)—HUNGAROTON (formerly QUALITON), the Hungarian state recording company, began this undertaking in 1966, with the intention of recording all Bartók's compositions. Prominent Hungarian Bartók musicologists helped to prepare authentic score and wrote texts analysing the works, in order that the performers should be able to render a true picture of the 'Hungarian School' of Bartók interpretation.

47. (Complete, version of the Budapest State Opera House) Budapest Phil-
     harmonic Society, Cond. János Ferencsik. [Qualiton LPX 1106, (stereo) SLPX
     1106.]
48. (Suite) London Symphony Orchestra, cond. George Solti. [Lon. CM 9399,
     (stereo) SC 6399.]

Works for Choir and Orchestra
Cantata Profana
49. (In Hungarian with text read by Béla Bartók) József Réti, András Faragó,
     Budapest Radio and Television Choir and Symphony Orchestra, cond. György
     Lehel. [Qualiton LPX 1162.]
50. (In English) Richard Lewis, Marko Rothmuller. The New Symphony Orchestra
     and Choir, cond. Walter Susskind. [BRS 312.]
Three Village Scenes (Nos. 3, 4, 5 from *Five Village Scenes*)
51. (In Hungarian) Budapest Radio and Television Symphony Orchestra. Chorus
     of the Hungarian State Folk Ensemble, solo: Janka Békás, cond: György
     Lehel. [Qualiton LP 1567.]

Choral works
Twenty-Seven Choruses, for two- or three-part children's or women's chorus
52. Women's Chorus of the Győr Conservatory, cond. Miklós Szabó. (Complete
     Bartók Œuvre) [Qualiton LPX 1290.]
From Olden Times (1935), *Székely Songs* (1932)
53. (In Hungarian) State Male Choir, Budapest, cond. Lajos Vass. [Qualiton
     HLPX KK 2502.]
Four Old Hungarian Folk-Songs (1912), *Slovak-Songs* (1917)
54. (In Hungarian) State Male Choir, Budapest, cond. Lajos Vass. [Qualiton
     HLP K 2509.]
Hungarian Folk-Songs (1930)
55. (In Hungarian) Chorus of the Hungarian State Folk Ensemble, cond. Imre
     Csenki. [Qualiton LP 1567.]
Four Slovak Folk-Songs (1917)
56. (In Hungarian) Chorus of the Hungarian State Folk Ensemble, cond. Imre
     Csenki. Piano: Lajos Dévényi. [Qualiton HLP M 1551.]
     Songs
     Five Songs op. 15
57. (In Hungarian) Magda László (soprano), Leonid Hambro (piano). [BRS 927.]

Transcrtptions of Folk-Songs (cf. also Nos. 27–29)
Twenty Hungarian Folk-Songs (1929)
58. (In Hungarian No. 2, 15, 5, 7, 14, 11, 16, 17, 12) Leslie Chabay (tenor), Tibor
     Kozma (piano). [BRS 914.]

Orchestral Works

Kossuth, symphonic poem in ten tableaux (1903)
  59. Budapest Radio Symphony Orchestra, cond. György Lehel. [Qualiton LPX 1203.]

Suite No. 1, op. 3
  60. Hungarian State Symphony Orchestra, cond. János Ferencsik. [Qualiton LPX 1204.]

Suite No. 2, op. 4
  61. (Revised version, 1943) Budapest Philharmonic Society, cond. András Kórodi. [Qualiton LPX 1201.]

Two Portraits (op. 5); *Two Pictures* (op. 10); *Four Orchestal Pieces* (op. 12)
  62. Budapest Philharmonic Society, cond. Miklós Erdélyi. Violin solo by Mihály Szücs. (Complete Bartók Œuvre) [Hungaroton LPX 1302.]

Romanian Dance (Nr. 1, 1910) for orchestra
  63. Budapest Philharmonic Orchestra, cond. András Koródi. (Complete Bartók Œuvre) [Hungaroton LPX 11314. Ang. 35949, (stereo) S 35949.]

Romanian Folk Dances for small orchestra (1917)
  64. Minneapolis Symphony Orchestra, cond. Antal Doráti. [Mcr. 50132, (stereo) 90132, 50151.]

Dance Suite
  65. London Philharmonic Orchestra, cond. George Solti. [Lon. LL-709.]
  66. Berlin Radio Symphony Orchestra, cond. Ferenc Fricsay. [Decca 9747.]

Hungarian Sketches
  67. Chicago Symphony Orchestra, cond. Fritz Reiner. [Vic. LM 2374, (stereo) LSC 2374.]

Hungarian Peasant Songs
  68. Hungarian State Symphony Orchestra, cond. János Ferencsik. [Qualiton HLP MK 1516.]

Music for String Instruments, Percussion and Celesta
  69. Chicago Symphony Orchestra, cond. Fritz Reiner. [Vic. LM 2374, (stereo) LSC 2374.]
  70. Chicago Symphony Orchestra, cond. Rafael Kubelik. [Mer. 50001, 50026.]
  71. London Philharmonic Orchestra, cond. George Solti [Lon. LL-1230, (stereo) CS 6399.]
  72. Berliner Philharmoniker, cond. Herbert von Karajan.
  73. Budapest Radio Symphony Orchestra, cond. György Lehel. (Complete Bartók Œuvre) [Hungaroton LPX 1301.]

Divertimento
  74. BBC Symphony Orchestra, cond. Antal Doráti. [Mer. 50416, (stereo) 90416.]
  75. Hungarian Chamber Orchestra, concertmeister Vilmos Tátrai. [Qualiton LPX 1192.]

Concerto for Orchestra
  76. Chicago Symphony Orchestra, cond. Fritz Reiner. [Vic. 1934.]

77. Minneapolis Symphony Orchestra, cond. Antal Doráti. [Mer. 50033.]
78. Houston Symphony Orchestra, cond. Leopold Stokowski. [Everest 6069, (stereo) 3069.]

Concertos
Piano concertos
79. Nos. 1–3. Géza Anda. Berlin Radio Symphony Orchestra, cond. Ferenc Fricsay. [DGG 18708, 18611, (stereo) 138708, 138611.]
80. Nos. 1–3. Gábor Gabos. Budapest Radio Symphony Orchestra, cond. György Lehel. [Qualiton LPX 1250–1251.]
81. No. 1. Leonid Hambro. The Zimbler Sinfonietta, cond. Robert Mann. [BRS 313.]
82. No. 3. György Sándor. Philadelphia Symphony Orchestra, cond. Eugene Ormandy. [Columbia Masterworks MM 674. (78 rpm!)]
Concerto for Two Pianos (1940)
83. Ditta Pásztory–Bartók and Erzsébet Tusa. Budapest Radio and Television Orchestra. (Percussion: Ferenc Petz and József Márton.) Cond. János Sándor. (Complete Bartók Œuvre) [Hungaroton LPX 11398.]
Violin Concerto (1938)
84. Tibor Varga. Berliner Philharmoniker, cond. Ferenc Fricsay. [Decca 9545.]
85. Yehudi Menuhin. Minneapolis Symphony Orchestra, cond. Antal Doráti. [Mer. 50140, (stereo) 90003.]
86. Isaac Stern. New York Philharmonic Orchestra, cond. Leonhard Bernstein. [Col. ML 5283, (stereo) MS 6002.]
Viola Concerto (reconstructed and orchestrated by Tibor Serly)
87. Pál Lukács. Hungarian State Symphony Orchestra, cond. János Ferencsik. [Qualiton LPX 1058.]

Other Concert Pieces
Rhapsody for Piano and Orchestra op. 1
88. Andor Földes. Lamoureux Orchestra, cond. Roger Desormière. [Vox 6410.]
89. Gábor Gabos. Budapest Radio Symphony Orchestra, cond. György Lehel. [Qualiton LPX 1250.]
Scherzo for Orchestra and Piano
90. Erzsébet Tusa. Budapest Radio Symphony Orchestra, cond. György Lehel. [Qualiton LPX 1203.]
Violin Concerto (1907–1908, op. posth.)
91. André Gertler, State Symphony Orchestra, Brno, cond. János Ferencsik. [Supraphon SUA 10466.]
92. Dénes Kovács. Budapest Philharmonic Orchestra. cond. András Koródi. (Complete Bartók Œuvre) [Hungaroton LPX 11314.]
Rhapsody No. 1–2. for Violin and Orchestra (1928)
93. Nos. 1–2. André Gertler. State Symphony Orchestra, Brno, cond. János Ferencsik. [Supraphon SUA 10466.]

Chamber Music
String Quartets
94. Nos. 1–6. Hungarian String Quartet. [DGG 18650–18652; (stereo) 138650–138652.]
95. Nos. 1–6. Juilliard Quartet. [Col. D3L 317 (stereo).]
96. Nos. 1–6. Tátrai Quartet. (Complete Bartók Œuvre) [Qualiton LPX 1294–1296.]
97. Nos. 1–6. Végh Quartet. [Ang. 35240–35242.]
Sonata for Two Pianos and Percussion
98. Charlotte Zelenka, Alfred Brendel (piano); Gustav Schuster, Roland Berger, Rudolph Minarich, Heinrich Zimmermann (percussion). [Vox 9600.]
99. Aloys and Alfons Kontarsky (piano); Heinz König, Christoph Caskel (percussion). [Wergo 60007.]
100. Erzsébet Tusa, István Antal (piano); Ferenc Petz, József Márton (percussion). [Qualiton LPX 1280.]
Contrasts, for violin, clarinet and piano (cf. also No. 22)
101. Robert Mann, Stanley Drucker, Leonid Hambro. [BRS 916.]
102. Mihály Szücs, Béla Kovács, Erzsébet Tusa. [Qualiton LPX 1280.]
Sonatas for Violin and Piano (cf. also No. 18.)
103. Sonata (1903). André Gertler, Diana Andersen. [Supraphon SUA 10740.]
104. No. 1. Robert Mann, Leonid Hambro. [BRS 922.]
105. No. 2. André Gertler, Diana Andersen. [Supraphon SUA 10481.]
Rhapsodies for Violin (Violoncello) and Piano (cf. also Nos. 19–20)
106. No. 1. János Starker (violoncello), Otto Herz (piano). [Per. 602, 1093.]
Forty-Four Duos for two violins
107. Victor Ajtay, Michael Kuttner. [BRS 907.]
108. Wanda Wilkomirska, Mihály Szücs. (Complete Bartók Œuvre) [Qualiton LPX 11320.]
Sonata for Solo Violin
109. (original version) Robert Mann. [BRS 907.]
110. (version edited by Yehudi Menuhin) Yehudi Menuhin. [Elect. 80544.]
111. (version edited by Yehudi Menuhin) André Gertler. [Supraphon SUA 10481.]

Piano compositions
(A) Albums
(See also the List of Records Played by Bartók)
112. (Sándor Album) 'Bartók Piano Music (Complete).' György Sándor. Vols. 1–3 (nine discs). [Vox, 3-Vox VBX 425–427, (stereo) SVBX 5425–5427.]
113. (Földes Album) 'Andor Foldes spielt das Klavierwerk Béla Bartóks.' (four discs). [DGG LPM 18270–18273.]
(B) Complete Bartók Œuvre
Series II—Piano Music

114.   (Disc No. 1) *Four Piano Pieces; Rhapsody* op. 1. Gábor Gabos. [Hungaroton LPX 1300.]
115.   (Disc No. 2) *Ten Easy Pieces; Three Hungarian Folk-Songs from the Csík District; Fourteen Bagatelles.* Kornél Zempléni. [Hungaroton LPX 1299.]
116.   (Disc No. 3) *Two Elegies; Two Romanian Dances; Seven Sketches; Four Dirges.* Loránt Szücs. [Hungaroton LPX 11335.]
117.   (Disc No. 4–5) *For Children.* Kornél Zempléni. [Hungaroton LPX 11394–5.]
118.   (Disc No. 7) *Fifteen Hungarian Peasant Songs; Three Rondos; Eight Improvisations on Hungarian Peasant Songs; Three Studies; Dance Suite* (reduction for piano). Gábor Gabos. [Qualiton LPX 11337.]
119.   (Disc No. 8) *Sonata; Out of Doors; Nine Little Piano Pieces; Petite Suite.* Erzsébet Tusa. [Hungaroton LPX 11338.]
120.   (Disc No. 9–11) *Mikrokosmos.* Kornél Zempléni and Loránt Szücs. [Hungaroton LPX 11405–7.]

(C) Individual Recordings
Rhapsody op. 1
121.   (shorter version) Leonid Hambro. [BRS 313.]
Fourteen Bagatelles
122. Tibor Kozma. [BRS 918.]
For Children (revised version, 1945)
123.   Ditta Pásztory-Bartók. [Qualiton LPX 1153–1154.]
124.   Tibor Kozma. [BRS 919–920.]
Three Burlesques
125.   György Sebők. [Erato 3065.]
Suite Op. 14
126. Erzsébet Tusa. [Qualiton LPX 1280.]
Eight Improvisations on Hungarian Peasant Songs
127. Leonid Hambro. [BRS 902.]
Sonata (1926)
128. István Nádas. [Period SPL 736.]
Out of Doors
129.   Leonid Hambro. [BRS 902.]
130.   Gábor Gabos. [Qualiton HLPX M 1029.]
Mikrokosmos
131.   (Vols. I–VI) Ditta Pásztory-Bartók. [Qualiton HLPX M 1033–1035.]
Seven pieces from the Mikrokosmos for two pianos (see also No. 15 in this List)
132.   Aloys and Alfons Kontarsky. [Wergo 60007.]

LITERATURE

1. Letters, Photographs, Documents

Bartók Béla. Levelek, fényképek, kéziratok, kották [Béla Bartók. Letters, Photographs, Manuscripts, Scores]. Magyar Művészeti Tanács, Budapest, 1948 (Letters Vol. 1).

Bartók Béla levelei. Az utolsó két év gyűjtése [Béla Bartók's Letters. Collection of the Last Two Years]. Compiled and edited by János Demény. Preface by András Mihály. Művelt Nép, Budapest, 1951 (Letters Vol. 2).

Bartók Béla levelei [Béla Bartók's Letters]. First Part: Romanian Letters, collected by Viorel Cosma. Second Part: Czechoslovakian Letters, collected by Ladislav Burlas. Third Part: Hungarian Letters, collected by János Demény. Zeneműkiadó Vállalat, Budapest, 1955 (Letters Vol. 3).

Szabolcsi, Bence: *Bartók élete. Bartók élete képekben* [Life of Béla Bartók. Bartók's Life in Pictures]. Compiled by Ferenc Bónis. Zeneműkiadó Vállalat, Budapest, 1956.

Petzoldt, Richard: *Béla Bartók. Sein Leben in Bildern.* Enzyklopädie, Leipzig, 1958.

Béla Bartók. Ausgewählte Briefe. Collected and edited by János Demény. Corvina, Budapest, 1960.

Bartók par l'Image. Introductory study by Bence Szabolcsi. Photographs collected, and comments by Ferenc Bónis. Corvina, Budapest, 1964.

Béla Bartóks Leben in Bildern. Compiled and introduced by Ferenc Bónis. Corvina, Budapest, 1964.

Béla Bartók, His Life in Pictures. Introductory study by Bence Szabolcsi. Photographs collected and edited by Ferenc Bónis. Corvina, Budapest—Boosey & Hawkes, London, 1964.

Béla Bartók. Lettere scelte. Edited by János Demény. Translated by Paolo Ruzisca. Il Saggiatore di Alberto Mondadori Editore, Milan, 1969.

Documenta Bartókiana. Edited by Denijs Dille, Bartók Archives Budapest. B. Schott's Söhne, Mainz—Akadémiai Kiadó, Budapest, 1/1964; 2/1965; 3/1968.

2. Biographies, Biographical Studies

Bartók, Béla jr.: *Bartók Béla Békés megyei kapcsolatai* [Béla Bartók's Contacts in Békés County]. Gyula, 1961.

Citron, Pierre: *Bartok.* Editions du Seuil, Paris, 1963.

Demény, János: 'Bartók Béla tanulóévei és romantikus korszaka (1899–1903)' [Béla Bartók's Student Years and Romantic Period—1899–1903].—'Bartók Béla művészi kibontakozásának évei. Találkozás a népzenével (1906–1914)' [The Years of Béla Bartók's Artistic Development. Encounter with Folk Music—1906–1914].—'Bartók Béla művészi kibontakozásának évei. Bartók Béla megjelenése az európai zeneéletben (1914–1926)' [The Years of Béla Bartók's Artistic Development. Béla Bartók's Appearance in European Musical Culture

—1914–1926].—'Bartók Béla pályája delelőjén (1926–1940)' [Béla Bartók at the Peak of His Career—1926–1940]. *Zenetudományi Tanulmányok*, Vols. II (1954), III (1955), VII (1959), X (1962);

Bartók élete és művei [Bartók's Life and Works]. Budapesti Székesfővárosi Irodalmi és Művészeti Intézet, Budapest, 1948;

'Radegundi nyár. Emlékezés Bartók Béla édesapjára' [Radegund Summer. Reminiscences on Béla Bartók's Father]. *Sínek Között*, No. 4, December 1955;

'Bartók és a nagyvilág' [Bartók and the World]. *Magyar Zene*, I, 7–8 (II, 4–5) (August–October 1961);

Bartók Béla a zongoraművész [Béla Bartók the Pianist]. Zeneműkiadó Vállalat, Budapest, 1968.

Dille, Denijs: *Béla Bartók*. N. V. Standard Boekhandel, Antwerp, 1939.

Béla Bartók. National Instituut voor Radio-Omroep, Brussels, 1947.

'Bartók családfája' [Bartók's Family Tree]. *Új Zenei Szemle*, VI, 9 (September 1955).

'Bartók és Kodály első találkozása' [First Meeting of Bartók and Kodály]. *Magyar Zenetörténeti Tanulmányok Szabolcsi Bence 70. születésnapjára*, Zeneműkiadó Vállalat, Budapest, 1969, p. 317.

Fassett, Agatha: *Béla Bartók's American Years—The Naked Face of Genius*. Houghton Mifflin Company, Boston, 1958;

Bartók amerikai évei [Bartók's American Years]. Translated by Imre Gombos. Zeneműkiadó Vállalat, Budapest, 1960.

Geraedts, Henri en Jaap: *Béla Bartók*. J. H. Gottmer, Haarlem-Antwerp, 1/1951; 2/1961.

Haraszti, Emil: *Bartók élete és művei* [Béla Bartók, His Life and Works]. Budapest, 1930 (Studium);

Béla Bartók, His Life and Works. The Lyrebird Press. Paris, 1938.

Helm, Everett: *Béla Bartók in Selbstzeugnissen und Bilddokumenten*. Presented by—. Rowohlt, Reinbek bei Hamburg, 1965.

Kodály, Zoltán: 'Béla Bartók.' *La Revue Musicale*, II, 3 (1921); 'A folklorista Bartók' [Bartók the Folklorist]. *Új Zenei Szemle*, I, 4 (1950).

Kroó, Gy[örgy]: 'Bartók Concert in New York on July 2, 1944.' *Studia Musicologica*, XI, 1–4 (1969), p. 253.

Lesznai, Lajos: *Béla Bartók. Sein Leben—seine Werke*. Deutscher Verlag für Musik, Leipzig, 1961.

Mihály, András: *Bartók Béla*. TIT, Budapest, 1955.

Molnár, Antal: 'Adalékok Bartók Béla életrajzához' [Addenda to Béla Bartók's Biography]. *Zenei Szemle*, I, 1947.

Moreux, Serge: *Bela Bartok. Sa vie—ses œuvres—son langage*. Richard-Masse Éditeurs, Paris, 1949;

Béla Bartók. Leben — Werk — Stil. Atlantis Verlag, Zurich and Freiburg i. Br., 1/1950; 2/1952;

Béla Bartók. Preface by Arthur Honegger. Harville Press, London, 1953.

Nestiev, I.: 'Bartók a Szovjetunióban' [Bartók in the Soviet Union]. *Magyar Zene*, I, 9 (December 1961).

Pálová-Vrbová, Zuzana: *Béla Bartók 1881–1945. Zivet a dilo* [Béla Bartók 1881–1945. Life and Work]. Státni Hudebni Vydavatelstvi, Prague, 1963.

Stevens, Halsey: *The Life and Music of Béla Bartók.* New York University Press, 1/1953; 2/1964.

Szabolcsi, Bence: 'Bartók Béla élete' [The Life of Béla Bartók]. *Csillag*, IV, 9 (September 1955);

Béla Bartók, Leben und Werk. Reclam, Leipzig, 1961;

Béla Bartók. Selection of the pictures, and comments by Ferenc Bónis. Selection of Bartók's letters by János Demény. Discography compiled by László Somfai. Philipp Reclam jun., Leipzig, 1968.

Szegő, Júlia: *Bartók Béla, a népdalkutató* [Béla Bartók the Folk-Song Researcher]. Állami Irodalmi Művészeti Kiadó, Bucharest, 1956;

Bartók Béla élete [The Life of Béla Bartók]. Ifjúsági Könyvkiadó, Bucharest, 1964.

Székely, Júlia: *Elindultam szép hazámból. Bartók Béla élete* [I Left My Lovely Country. Béla Bartók's Life]. Móra Ferenc Könyvkiadó, Budapest, 1965.

Uhde, Jürgen: *Béla Bartók.* Colloquium Verlag, Berlin, 1959.

Ujfalussy, József: *Bartók Béla.* Vols. I–II. Gondolat, Budapest, 1965.

3. Recollections

Albrecht, Sándor: 'B. B.—ahogy én ismertem' [B. B.—As I Knew Him]. *Muzsika*, I, 10, 12, II, 1 (October, December 1958, January 1959).

Alte und Neue Musik. 25 Jahre Basler Kammerorchester. Zurich, 1952, pp. 70–78, 181–183, 185–187.

Balogh, Ernő: 'Milyen tanár volt Bartók?' [What Kind of Teacher Was Bartók?]. *Muzsika*, I, 10 (October 1958).

Bartók, Béla jr.: 'Apámról' [On My Father]. *Zenetudományi Tanulmányok*, III, 1955.

Fricsay, Ferenc: *Über Mozart und Bartók.* Copenhagen—Frankfurt a.M., 1962.

Harangozó, Gyula: 'Bartók Béla és A csodálatos mandarin' [Béla Bartók and *The Miraculous Mandarin*]. *Táncművészet*, V, 2 (February 1955).

Menuhin, Yehudi: 'Bartók—With My Eyes.' *The Long Player*, II, 10 (October 1953); 'Bartók — az én szememmel' [Bartók—With My Eyes]. *Új Zenei Szemle*, VI, 10 (October 1955).

Kodály, Zoltán: 'Bartók Béla, az ember' [Béla Bartók, the Man]. *Zenei Szemle*, I, 1947.

Molnár Antal: *Bartók művészete — emlékezésekkel a művész életére* [Bartók's Art— with Recollections on the Composer's Life]. Rózsavölgyi és Társa, Budapest, 1948;

'Bartók Béla, az ember' [Béla Bartók, the Man]. *Alföld*, VII, 1 (January–February 1956).

Péterfi, István: 'A Negyvenedik zsoltár' [The 40th Psalm]. *Muzsika*, II, 7 (July 1959).

Sacher, Paul: 'Béla Bartók zum Gedächtnis.' *Mitteilungen des Basler Kammerorchesters.* 1945, November.

Székely, Júlia: *Bartók tanár úr* [Professor Bartók]. Dunántúli Magvető, Pécs, 1957.

Szigeti, Joseph: 'A Tribute to Bartók.' *Tempo*, 1948–9;
With Strings Attached. Alfred A. Knopf, New York, 1/1947, 2/1967, *passim; Zwischen den Saiten.* Albert Müller, Rüschlikon–Zurich, Stuttgart, Vienna, 1962;
Beszélő húrok [Speaking Strings]. Zeneműkiadó Vállalat, Budapest, 1965.

4. Studies

Chailley, J[acques]: 'Essai d'analyse du Mandarin Merveilleux.' *Studia Musicologica*, VIII, 1–4 (1966), p. 11.

Dille, Denijs: 'Egyes Bartók-művek végleges alakjáról' [On the Final Form of Some Bartók Works]. *Muzsika*, III, 6 (June 1960);
'Le vingtième anniversaire de la mort de Bartók.' *Studia Musicologica*, VIII, 1–4 (1966), p. 3;
'Bartók, lecteur de Nietzsche et de La Rochefoucauld.' *Studia Musicologica*, X, 3–4 (1968), p. 209.

Doflein, Erich: 'Béla Bartóks Kompositionen für die Musikpädagogik.' *Musik im Unterricht*, 46/10, 12 (October, December 1955).

Dragoi, Sabin: 'Musical Folklore Research in Rumania and Béla Bartók's Contribution to It.' *Studia Memoriae Belae Bartók Sacra*, MCMLVI, p. 9.

Kárpáti, János: 'Beethoven és Bartók vonósnégyes-művészetének közös vonásai' [Common Features of Beethoven's and Bartók's String Quartet Compositions]. *Zenetudományi Tanulmányok*, X, 1962, p. 55;
'Bartók és Schönberg' [Bartók and Schoenberg]. *Magyar Zene*, IV, 6 and V, 1 (December 1963 and February 1964);
'Béla Bartók and the East.' *Studia Musicologica*, VI, 3–4 (1964), p. 179;
Bartók vonósnégyesei [Bartók's String Quartets]. Zeneműkiadó Vállalat, Budapest, 1967;
'Les gammes populaires et le système chromatique dans l'œuvre de Béla Bartók.' *Studia Musicologica*, XI, 1–4 (1969), p. 227.

Kodály, Zoltán: 'Bartók Béla első operája' [Béla Bartók's First Opera]. *Nyugat*, 1918;
'Bartók II. vonósnégyese' [Bartók's String Quartet No. 2]. *Nyugat*, 1918;
'Bartóks Kinderstücke.' *Musikblätter des Anbruch*, III, 5 (March 1921);
'Œuvres nouvelles de Béla Bartók.' *La Revue Musicale*, VI, 7 (1922);
'Les Sonates de Béla Bartók.' *La Revue Musicale*, VII, 8 (1923);
'Bartók Béla gyermekkarai' [Children's Choruses by Béla Bartók]. *Énekszó*, 1936;
'Szentirmaytól Bartókig' [From Szentirmay to Bartók]. *Új Zenei Szemle*, VI, 6 (June 1955).

Körtvélyes, Géza: *A csodálatos mandarin az Operaházban* [The Miraculous Mandarin in the Opera House]. 1960, manuscript.

Kresánek, Jozef: 'Bartóks Sammlung slowakischer Volkslieder.' *Studia Memoriae Belae Bartók Sacra*, MCMLVI.

Kroó, György: 'Három arckép. Bartók színpadi művei' [Three Portraits. Bartók's Stage Works]. *Magyar Zene*, I, 3 (December 1960); 'Duke Bluebeard's Castle.' *Studia Musicologica*, I, 3–4 (1961), p. 251; 'Monotematika és dramaturgia Bartók színpadi műveiben' [Monothematicism and Dramaturgy in Bartók's Stage Works]. *Magyar Zene*, I, 9 (December 1961); *Bartók színpadi művei* [Bartók's Stage Works]. Zeneműkiadó Vállalat, Budapest, 1962; 'Adatok "A kékszakállú herceg vára" keletkezéstörténetéhez' [Data on the History of the Origin of 'Bluebeard's Castle']. *Magyar Zenetörténeti Tanulmányok Szabolcsi Bence 70. születésnapjára*, Zeneműkiadó Vállalat, Budapest, 1969, p. 333.

László, Zsigmond: ' "A kékszakállú herceg vára" prozódiájáról' [On the Prosody of 'Bluebeard's Castle']. *Új Zenei Szemle*, VI, 9 (September 1955).

Lendvai, Ernő: 'Bevezetés a Bartók-művek elemzésébe' [Introduction to the Analysis of Bartók's Compositions]. *Zenetudományi Tanulmányok*, III, 1955; *Bartók stílusa . . .* [Bartók's Style . . .]. Zeneműkiadó Vállalat, Budapest, 1955; 'A Kékszakállú herceg vára' (Bartók operájának műhelytitkai) [Bluebeard's Castle—Workshop Secrets of Bartók's Opera]. *Magyar Zene*, I, 4 (February 1961); 'Der wunderbare Mandarin' (Werkstattgeheimnisse der Pantomime Béla Bartóks). *Studia Musicologica*, I, 3–4 (1961); 'Bartók pantomimje és táncjátéka' [Bartók's Pantomime and Ballet]. *Zenetudományi Tanulmányok*, X, 1962; *Bartók dramaturgiája* [Bartók's Dramaturgy]. Zeneműkiadó Vállalat, Budapest 1964; 'Bartók vonósnégyesei' [Bartók's String Quartets]. *Muzsika*, X, 9–12, XI, 1–2 (September–December 1967, January–February 1968); 'Bartók húros ütőhangszeres zenéjének néhány értelmezési problémájáról' [On some Analytical Problems of Bartók's Music for Strings and Percussion]. *Muzsika*, XI, 7 (July 1968); 'Über die Formkonzeption Bartóks.' *Studia Musicologica*, XI, 1–4 (1969), p. 271; 'Bartók négy zenekari darabjáról' [On Bartók's Four Orchestral Pieces]. *Muzsika*, XII, 7 (June 1969); 'Bartók Divertimentójáról' [On Bartók's Divertimento]. *Muzsika*, XII, 9 (September 1969); 'Bartók hegedűversenyéről' [On Bartók's Violin Concerto]. *Muzsika*, XII, 10–11 (October–November 1969); 'Bartók — Két kép' [Bartók—Two Pictures]. *Muzsika*, XII, 12 (December 1969);

'Bartók — Két portré' [Bartók—Two Portraits]. *Muzsika*, XIII, 2 (February 1970).

Mason, Colin: 'Bartók Through His Quartets.' *Monthly Musical Record*, 1950.

Mihály, András: 'Metrika Bartók IV. vonósnégyesének II. tételében' [Metrics in the 2nd Movement of Bartók's String Quartet No. 4]. *Muzsika*, X, 10–12 (October–December 1967).

Molnár Antal: 'Bartók kvartettje' [Bartók's Quartet]. *Zeneközlöny*, 1911;
    Bartók Béla táncdaljátéka alkalmából [On the Occasion of Béla Bartók's Ballet]. Budapest, 1917;
    'Bartók operája: A kékszakállú herceg vára' [Bartók's Opera: Bluebeard's Castle]. *Zenei Szemle*, 1918;
    Bartók két elégiájának elemzése [Analysis of Bartók's Two Elegies]. Budapest, 1921;
    Béla Bartók: Konzert für Klavier und Orchester. Analyse. Universal, Wien, [1929];
    'Bartók "Cantata Profaná"-ja a vigadói hangversenyen' [Bartók's 'Cantata Profana' at the Vigadó Concert]. *Szép Szó*, III, 3 (1936).

Nirschy, A[urél]: 'Varianten zu Bartóks Pantomime: Der wunderbare Mandarin.' *Studia Musicologica*, II, 1–4 (1962).

Nüll, Edwin von der: *Béla Bartók. Ein Beitrag zur Morphologie der neuen Musik*. Halle, 1930.

Olsvai, I[mre]: 'West Hungarian (Transdanubian) Characteristic Features in Bartók's Works.' *Studia Musicologica*, XI, 1–4 (1969), p. 333.

Somfai, László: ' "Per finire".' Ibidem, p. 391;
    'Bartók egynemű kórusainak szövegforrásairól' (On the Sources of Bartók's Male and Female Choruses). *Magyar Zenetörténeti Tanulmányok Szabolcsi Bence 70. születésnapjára*, Zeneműkiadó Vállalat, Budapest, 1969, p. 359.

Szabolcsi, Bence: 'Bartók és a népzene' [Bartók and the Folk Music]. *Új Zenei Szemle*, 1950;
    'A csodálatos mandarin' [The Miraculous Mandarin]. *Csillag*, IX, 4 (April 1955);
    'Le Mandarin Miraculeux.' *Studia Musicologica*, I, 3–4 (1961), p. 341:
    'Liszt and Bartók.' *New Hungarian Quarterly*, 1961;
    'Man and Nature in Bartók's World.' Ibidem;
    'Ember és természet Bartók világában' [Man and Nature in Bartók's World]. *Zenetudományi Tanulmányok*, X, 1962.

Tóth, Margit: 'Egy népi énekes dallamainak változása Bartók óta' [Changes in a Folk Singer's Melodies since Bartók]. *Magyar Zenetörténeti Tanulmányok Szabolcsi Bence 70. születésnapjára*, Zeneműkiadó Vállalat, Budapest, 1969, p. 377.

Traimer, Roswitha: *Béla Bartóks Kompositionstechnik dargestellt in seinen sechs Streichquartetten*. Gustav Bosse, Regensburg, 1956.

Suchoff, Benjamin: *Guide to the Mikrokosmos of Béla Bartók.* Music Services Corporation of America, Silver Spring, Md., 1956.

Uhde, Jürgen: *Bartóks Mikrokosmos. Spielanweisungen und Erläuterungen.* Gustav Bosse, Regensburg, n. d.

Ujfalussy, József: 'A híd szerkezetek néhány tartalmi kérdése Bartók művészetében' [Some Questions of the Bridge Structure in Bartók's Compositions]. *Magyar Zene*, I, 7–8 II, 4–5 (August–October 1961);
'Az Allegro Barbaro harmóniai alapgondolata és Bartók hangsorai' [Basic Harmonic Idea of the Allegro Barbaro and Bartók's Scales]. *Magyar Zenetörténeti Tanulmányok Szabolcsi Bence 70. születésnapjára*, Zeneműkiadó Vállalat, Budapest, 1969, p. 323.

Vinton, John: 'The Case of the Miraculous Mandarin.' *Musical Quarterly*, L, 1 (January 1964);
'Bartók on His Own Music.' *Journal of the American Musicological Society*, XIX, 2 (Summer 1966);
'Toward a Chronology of the Mikrokosmos.' *Studia Musicologica*, VIII, 1–4 (1966), p. 41.

In covering the enormous amount of Hungarian and foreign literature on Béla Bartók's life and works this list cannot be comprehensive. It concentrates rather on those works produced during the most recent years. János Demény's highly detailed and documented biography of Bartók (see *Zenetudományi Tanulmányok* Vols. II, III, VII and X) gives lengthy excerpts of older Bartók literature, especially from critics and reviews from contemporary daily newspapers, while Margit Prahács summarizes the bibliography of the Bartók literature written abroad up to 1948, in the Bartók issue of *Zenei Szemle*, December 1948. In addition, a detailed list of more recent foreign literature on Bartók is also included in the latest edition of Halsey Stevens's Bartók monograph (1964).

The present list does not include those studies and articles which appeared in issues of various periodicals or special publications completely dedicated to Béla Bartók. Among these, the most important are the following:

Zenei Szemle [Musical Review], December 1948.

Új Zenei Szemle [New Musical Review], September 1950, September 1955.

Musikblätter des Anbruch, March 1921.

Musik der Zeit, 1952/3.

La Revue Musicale, 1955.

Studia Musicologica, Redigit Z. Kodály. Tom. V, fasciculi 1–4, Akadémiai Kiadó, Budapest, 1963: Collection of lectures delivered during the 1961 Budapest Liszt—Bartók Conference of the Hungarian Academy of Sciences.